Personal Identity

BLACKWELL READINGS IN PHILOSOPHY

Series Editor: Steven M. Cahn

Blackwell Readings in Philosophy are concise, chronologically arranged collections of primary readings from classical and contemporary sources. They represent core positions and important developments with respect to key philosophical concepts. Edited and introduced by leading philosophers, these volumes provide valuable resources for teachers and students of philosophy, and for all those interested in gaining a solid understanding of central topics in philosophy.

Personal Identity

Edited by

Raymond Martin
and
John Barresi

Blackwell
Publishing

Editorial material © 2003 by Blackwell Publishing Ltd

350 Main Street, Malden, MA 02148-5018, USA
108 Cowley Road, Oxford OX4 1JF, UK
550 Swanston Street, Carlton South, Melbourne, Victoria 3053, Australia
Kurfürstendamm 57, 10707 Berlin, Germany

First published 2003 by Blackwell Publishing Ltd

Library of Congress Cataloging-in-Publication Data has been applied for.

ISBN 0-631-23441-1 (hardback); ISBN 0-631-23442-X (paperback)

A catalogue record for this title is available from the British Library.

Typeset in 10/12.5pt Palatino
by Kolam Information Services Pvt. Ltd, Pondicherry, India

For further information on
Blackwell Publishing, visit our website:
http://www.blackwellpublishing.com

To

David Lewis (1941–2001)

and

Robert Nozick (1938–2002)

in recognition of their contributions

to personal identity theory

Contents

Contributors

John Barresi is Professor of Psychology at Dalhousie University. He has written in the areas of personology, social cognition, philosophical psychology and the history of psychology. With Raymond Martin, he authored *Naturalization of the Soul: Self and Personal Identity in the Eighteenth Century* (2000).

Mark Johnston is Professor of Philosophy and Chair of the Philosophy Department at Princeton University. He is the author of a number of influential articles in ethics, philosophy of mind, metaphysics, philosophical logic, and personal identity theory.

Christine M. Korsgaard is the Arthur Kingsley Porter Professor of Philosophy at Harvard University. Her books include *Creating the Kingdom of Ends* (1996) and *The Sources of Normativity* (1996). She is also a co-editor of *Reclaiming the History of Ethics: Essays for John Rawls* (1997).

David Lewis, recently deceased, taught for most of his career at Princeton University. His books include *Convention* (1969), *Counterfactuals* (1973), *On the Plurality of Worlds* (1986), and *Parts of Classes* (1991). Many of his more important papers are collected in *Philosophical Papers* (1986).

Raymond Martin taught at the University of Maryland before becoming Professor of Philosophy and Chair of the department at Union College. His books include *The Past within Us* (1989) and *Self-Concern: An Experiential Approach to What Matters in Survival* (1998).

Robert Nozick, recently deceased, was Pellegrino University Professor at Harvard University. His books include *Anarchy, State, and Utopia* (1974), *Philosophical Explanations* (1981), *The Examined Life* (1989), *The Nature of*

Rationality (1993), and *Invariances: The Structure of the Objective World* (2001).

Eric T. Olson is a fellow at Churchill College, Cambridge University. He is the author of a number of influential articles in metaphysics and the philosophy of mind, and also the author of *The Human Animal: Personal Identity without Psychology* (1997).

Derek Parfit is a Senior Research Fellow of All Souls, Oxford University. He is also a Fellow of the British Academy and of the American Academy of Arts and Sciences. In addition to Oxford, he has taught at Harvard University and New York University. His *Reasons and Persons* (1984) is perhaps the most influential book of the twentieth century on personal identity theory.

Marya Schechtman is Associate Professor of Philosophy at the University of Illinois, Chicago. She is the author of a number of influential articles in personal identity theory and the philosophy of mind, and also the author of *The Constitution of Selves* (1996).

Ernest Sosa is Romeo Elton Professor of Natural Theology and Professor of Philosophy at Brown University and Distinguished Visiting Professor at Rutgers University. He is the author of numerous influential articles in the areas of epistemology, metaphysics, and moral epistemology.

Galen Strawson taught at Jesus College, Oxford University, before moving to the University of Reading, where he is Professor of Philosophy. His books include *Freedom and Belief* (1986), *The Secret Connexion: Realism, Causation, and David Hume* (1989), and *Mental Reality* (1994). Currently he is working on a book on the self.

Peter Unger is Professor of Philosophy at New York University. His books include *Ignorance: A Case for Scepticism* (1975), *Philosophical Relativity* (1984), *Identity, Consciousness and Value* (1990), and *Living High and Letting Die: Our Illusion of Innocence* (1996).

Bernard Williams is Emeritus Professor of Moral Philosophy and Fellow of All Souls, Oxford University. In 1999, he was knighted for his contributions to philosophy. His books include *Descartes: The Project of Pure Inquiry* (1979), *Moral Luck* (1981), and *Ethics and the Limits of Philosophy* (1985). Many of his most important essays on personal identity are collected in his *Problems of the Self* (1973).

Preface

Each of us assumes that we remain who we are, through various changes, from moment to moment, hour to hour, day to day, and so on. We persist until we cease, perhaps at bodily death. Each of us also assumes that one of our most fundamental egoistic desires is to persist. As we say, we want to live. But what *accounts* for the fact, if it is a fact, that we remain the same persons over time and through various changes? That question is *the philosophical problem of personal identity*. And when, in ordinary circumstances, we want to persist, what is it that we *really* want – that is, that each of us wants most fundamentally? That question is *the philosophical problem of what matters primarily in survival*. It is commonly assumed that when people want to persist, what they really want is simply to persist – that is, that their desire to persist cannot be derived from any more fundamental desire. That answer is *the thesis that identity is primarily what matters in survival*.

All of the readings in the present anthology are devoted either to answering the philosophical problem of personal identity or to testing the claim that identity is primarily what matters in survival, or both. Inserted into the introductory essay are some classic readings by Locke and Reid. Otherwise all of the readings included have been published since 1970, which is about the time that personal identity theory made a new beginning. The present anthology represents the issues that have emerged in the wake of this new beginning.

The introductory essay, "Personal Identity and What Matters in Survival: An Historical Overview," is a substantial development of material some of which has been previously published in Raymond Martin, "Personal Identity from Plato to Parfit," in D. Kolak and R. Martin, eds. *The Experience of Philosophy*, 4th edn (1999) and 5th edn. (2001), and some in Raymond Martin and John Barresi, *Naturalization of the Soul: Self and Personal Identity in the Eighteenth Century* (Routledge, 2000). We have also drawn material for our introductory essay from Raymond Martin and John Barresi, *The Rise and Fall of Soul and Self* (forthcoming).

The chapter by Eric Olson and the "Postscript" by Galen Strawson were written especially for this volume. We are very grateful for these original contributions, which are published here with the kind permission of their authors.

Acknowledgments

The editor and publisher gratefully acknowledge the permission granted to reproduce the copyright material in this book:

Chapter 1
Bernard Williams, "The Self and the Future," pp. 161–80 from *Philosophical Review* 79 (1970). Copyright © 1970 Cornell University. Reprinted by permission of the publisher.

Chapter 2
Robert Nozick, "Personal Identity through Time," reprinted by permission of the publisher from *Philosophical Explanations* by Robert Nozick, pp. 29–48, 50–1, 58–61, and 69. Cambridge, Mass.: The Belknap Press, imprint of Harvard University Press, 1981. Copyright © 1981 by Robert Nozick.

Chapter 3
Derek Parfit, "Why Our Identity Is Not What Matters," pp. 199–201, 209–10, 245–69, and 271 from *Reasons and Persons*. Oxford: Oxford University Press, 1984 (repr. 1987)

Chapter 4
David Lewis, "Survival and Identity" and "Postscript," pp. 55–70 and 73–7 from *Philosophical Papers*, vol. 1. Oxford: Oxford University Press, 1983. Copyright © by David Lewis.

Chapter 5
Christine M. Korsgaard, "Personal Identity and the Unity of Agency: A Kantian Response to Parfit," from *Philosophy and Public Affairs* 18:2 (1989), pp. 109–23, © The Johns Hopkins University Press. Reprinted by permission of the Johns Hopkins University Press.

Chapter 6
Peter Unger, "Fission and the Focus of One's Life," pp. 269–82 from *Identity, Consciousness, and Value*. Oxford: Oxford University Press, 1990. Copyright © 1990 by Peter Unger. Used by permission of Oxford University Press, Inc.

Chapter 7
Ernest Sosa, "Surviving Matters," pp. 297 and 306–30 from *Noûs* 24 (1990). © 1990 by Noûs Publications. Reprinted with permission of Blackwell Publishing.

Chapter 8
Raymond Martin, "Fission Rejuvenation," pp. 17–40 from *Philosophical Studies* 80 (1995). © 1995 Kluwer Academic Publishers. Reprinted with kind permission of Kluwer Academic Publishers.

Chapter 9
Marya Schechtman, "Empathic Access: The Missing Ingredient in Personal Identity," *Philosophical Explorations* (May 2001). Copyright © Van Gorcum Publishers. Reprinted with permission of Van Gorcum Publishers.

Chapter 10
Mark Johnston, "Human Concerns without Superlative Selves," pp. 149–79 from J. Dancy (ed.), *Reading Parfit*. Oxford: Blackwell, 1997. Reprinted with permission of Blackwell Publishing.

Chapter 11
Derek Parfit, "The Unimportance of Identity," pp. 13–45 from H. Harris (ed.), *Identity*. Oxford: Oxford University Press, 1995.

Chapter 12
Eric T. Olson, "An Argument for Animalism." © 2003 by Eric T. Olson.

Chapter 13
Galen Strawson, "The Self." First published in *Journal of Consciousness Studies* 4:5–6 (1997), pp. 405–28. Reprinted in S. Gallagher and J. Shear (eds.), *Models of the Self*. Exeter, UK: Imprint Academic, 1999. Copyright © Imprint Academic. The "Postscript" (pp. 363–70 this volume) is new material written for this publication, © 2003 by Galen Strawson.

Every effort has been made to trace copyright holders and to obtain their permission for the use of copyright material. The publisher apologizes for any errors or omissions in the above list and would be grateful if notified of any corrections that should be incorporated in future reprints or editions of this book.

Introduction: Personal Identity and What Matters in Survival: An Historical Overview

Raymond Martin and John Barresi

If you stand squarely in the middle of contemporary analytic personal identity theory and look toward the past, the evolution of Western theorizing about self and personal identity can seem to divide neatly into three phases: from Plato to John Locke, from Locke to the late 1960s, and from the late 1960s to the present.

During the first of these phases – the Platonic phase – the dominant view was that the self, or at least that part of the self that was thought to be highest and to survive bodily death, is a simple immaterial substance. During the second phase – the Lockean phase – the dominant view was that the self should be understood not as a *simple* persisting substance, whether material or immaterial, but as a constantly changing process of interrelated psychological and physical elements, later phases of which are appropriately related to earlier phases. The third, contemporary, phase features three developments.

The first of these developments is that the Lockean *intrinsic* relations view of personal identity has been superseded by an *extrinsic* relations view (which is also sometimes called the *closest-continuer* or *externalist* view). According to the older *intrinsic* relations view, what determines whether a person at one time and one at another are the same person is how the two are physically and/or psychologically related to *each other*. According to the more recent *extrinsic* relations view, what determines whether a person at one time and one at another are the same person is not just how the two are physically and/or psychologically related to *each other*, but how they are related to everything else – especially *everybody* else. For instance, in Locke's *intrinsic* relations view, you-right-now are the same person as someone who existed yesterday if *you* remember having experienced or having done things which that person of yesterday experienced or did. In an *extrinsic* version of Locke's view, one would have to take into account not only whether you remember having experienced or having done things which that person of yesterday experienced or did, but whether, besides you, *anyone else* remembers having experienced or having done things which that person of yesterday experienced or did.

The consideration of hypothetical fission examples – which at least until recently were widely thought to have been introduced for the first time into the personal identity debate in the late 1960s – is largely responsible for the recent move from *intrinsic* to *extrinsic* relations views. In the sort of fission examples that have been most discussed, a person somehow divides into two (seemingly) *numerically* different persons, each of whom, initially, is *qualitatively* identical to the other and also to the pre-fission person from whom they both descended. For example, imagine that all information in human brains were encoded redundantly so that it were possible theoretically to separate a human's brain into two parts, leaving each half-brain fully functioning and encoded with all that it needs to sustain the original person's full mental life. That is, imagine that each half-brain sustains the original person's mental life just as (except for the elimination of underlying redundancy) his whole brain would have sustained it had his whole brain never been divided. Now suppose that in some normal, healthy human we were to perform a brain-separation operation, removing the two fully functioning half-brains from his body, which is then immediately destroyed. Suppose, further, that we were to immediately implant each of these half-brains into its own, brainless body, which except for being brainless is qualitatively identical to the original person's body, so that two people simultaneously emerge. Each of these people – the fission-descendants – except for having only half a brain, would then be qualitatively identical, physically *and* psychologically, to the original person whose brain was divided and removed.

Would the fission-descendants be the same person as the brain donor? Would they be the same person as each other? On an intrinsic view of personal identity, such as Locke's, each of the fission-descendants would be the same person as the brain donor. Each would remember having experienced things and having performed actions that the original person experienced and performed. If the brain donor is indeed a person, and not merely a "person-stage," and if in deciding whether a person at one time and one at another are the same person we have to consider *only* the relations between the two of them, then it would seem that *either one* of the fission-descendants would have all that is required to be the same person as the brain donor.

The problem with supposing that in order to answer the identity question, we need consider *only* the relations between the brain donor and one of the fission-descendants at a time is that the other fission-descendant has an equal claim to be the original person, and neither of the fission-descendants are plausibly regarded as the same person as the other. Assume, as almost all contemporary philosophers do, that identity is a transitive relation – that is, that necessarily if A is the same person as B, and B the same person as C, then A is the same person as C. On that assumption, if the two fission-descendants are not the same person as each other, then both of them cannot be the same person as the brain donor. That is why many contemporary philosophers believe that in such a case the pre-fission person – the brain donor – would cease and be replaced by two qualitatively similar fission-descendants. Philosophers who believe this accept an *extrinsic relations* view of personal identity.

The second major development in personal identity theory since the late 1960s is the emergence (or reemergence) of the question of whether personal identity is primarily what matters in survival. That is, philosophers have faced the possibility that people might cease and be continued by *others* whose continuation the original people would value as much as, and in pretty much the same ways as, they would have valued their own continued existence. Variations on the fission example just presented, but in which it seems to be a better deal from an egoistic perspective for the brain donor to cease and to be replaced by his fission-descendants, have been an important source of support for this view.

The third major development since the late 1960s has been a challenge to the traditional three-dimensional view of persons according to which a person can be wholly present at a given moment – e.g., you are wholly present right now. Some philosophers have argued that we should replace the three-dimensional view with a four-dimensional view according to which only time-slices, or "stages," of persons exist at short intervals of time. On a four-dimensional view, persons are aggregates of momentary person-stages, beginning with the person-stage that came into being when the person originated, say, at his or her birth, ending with the person-stage that existed when the person ceased, say, at death, and including every person-stage between origin and end.

To see why it might matter whether a three-dimensional or a four-dimensional view of persons is correct, consider again the case of fission. It was suggested that the pre-fission person – the brain donor – is not identical with either of his or her post-fission descendants. That was a three-dimensional way of describing the situation. A four-dimensionalist would say that what we are calling "the pre-fission person" is not really a person, but a person-stage, and that what we are calling "the post-fission descendants" are also only person-stages. According to a four-dimensionalist, in a fission example what happens is that a pre-fission person-stage is shared by two persons – that is, two persons whose *post-fission* person-stages are separate from each other overlap prior to fission and thus share their pre-fission person-stages. As a consequence, in a fission example no one ceases, and hence identity is never traded for other benefits. So, some philosophers have used this four-dimensional way of conceptualizing what is going on in a fission example to argue that fission examples cannot be used to show that identity is not what matters primarily in survival.

In this brief sketch of the history of Western theorizing about self and personal identity, which we shall call *the simple view*, theoretical advances have been cumulative, seemingly with more or less continuous progress as the discussion has passed from one stage to the next. For instance, what fueled progress from the first to the second phase was the rise of modern science, and in particular the requirement that whatever unifies a person over time should be empirically accessible. What fueled progress from the second to the third phase were progressive developments in analytic philosophy, in particular better understandings of the concept of identity and the underlying metaphysics.

However, there are two ways in which the *simple view* has to be refined and developed in order to be historically accurate. First, each of the three phases of theory mentioned – from Plato to Locke, from Locke to the 1960s, and from the 1960s, to the present – was more complicated than is suggested by the simple view. For example, in the first phase, in addition to Plato's rather other-worldly view of the self and personal identity, there was, in classical Greece, Aristotle's much more this-worldly development of Plato's view, as well as several atomistic-materialist views. Second, when one acknowledges this extra complexity, it turns out that the picture of the development of theory that emerges is not nearly as rational and progressive as is suggested by the simple view. To take one example, according to the simple view, relational views of self and personal identity are supposed to be a seventeenth-century innovation. But on closer inspection it is clear that relational views were implicit in classical Greek atomistic-materialist accounts and explicit in the work of the earliest Church Fathers, all of whom were materialists. For instance, around the year 200 CE there were three great Christian contributions, those of Irenaeus, Tertullian, and Minucius Felix. Each of them was a materialist who explained personal identity along relational lines. Later in the Patristic period, when dualists, such as Origen and others, came to the fore, it had already been widely accepted that in order to make sense of the resurrection, "the body that rises," as Tertullian had put it, "must be the same as the body that falls." Since those Church Fathers who were Platonic dualists subscribed to a doctrine not just of survival, but also of bodily resurrection, even dualists had to account for the identity of the body, which they tended to do along relational lines. So, even as early as the Patristic period, relational views of personal and/or bodily identity were widely discussed. They continued to be discussed throughout the Middle Ages. Subsequently, due largely to Descartes's substance-dualism and to his relative lack of concern with the resurrection, relational views of personal and bodily identity got pushed into the background until they retook center stage in the work of Locke.

Another example of the way in which, on a more accurate history, the three-phase progressive development model of the simple view comes under strain is that in the first decade of the eighteenth century, in Britain, fission examples were introduced into the personal identity debate in what at the time was a well-known, six-part, written exchange between Samuel Clarke and Anthony Collins. Partly as a consequence of this exchange many developments in self and personal identity theory that supposedly were post-1960s innovations were introduced in the eighteenth century. These included discussion not only of fission examples, but also of the thesis that identity is not primarily what matters in survival. The fission examples discussed in the eighteenth century were not, as they have been in the twentieth century, *science*-fiction scenarios, but rather, *religious*-fiction scenarios. Theorists speculated, initially as a way of objecting to Locke's relational view, that if God at the resurrection could create one replica of a human who died, he could create two, or three, or any number. Eighteenth-century discussions of fission and its consequences for personal identity theory were subsequently forgotten. In the late 1960s, personal identity theorists invented fission examples anew.

So, one consequence of moving from the simple view to a more accurate historical account is that the development of theory no longer divides neatly into three stages. A closely related consequence is that the simple view's implicit suggestion that the history of theory has been progressive has to be put delicately. The picture that emerges is more like that of a zig-zag ascent than a steady upward climb.

This concludes our explanation of some of the ways in which *the simple view* is too simple. We want now to set the stage for the consideration of the contemporary selections that follow this introductory essay, by taking a somewhat closer look at the views of several historically important theorists.

Plato (429?–348? BCE)

When Socrates, Plato's teacher, was alive, many Greeks thought that the soul leaves the body when the person who dies expels his last breath. Probably they also thought that at the moment of bodily death the soul simply *is* that last breath. Plato, at least in the *Phaedo*, claimed that the soul is immaterial and simple – that is, without parts. That in itself is enough to distinguish the soul from breath. Yet, in Plato's writings there is no clear answer to the question of whether the soul is unextended. So, although much of what Plato said suggests that he may have believed that the soul is immaterial in a modern sense, he never quite got the whole idea out. If in fact he did intend to suggest that the vehicle for survival is not any sort of physical object, not even breath, but rather an unextended thing, then this thought was original to him (or to Socrates). Previously, when others had talked of immaterial souls, they usually meant souls consisting of invisible matter.

While Plato's arguments for immortality in the *Phaedo* are obscure, the central idea behind them seems to be his conviction that the soul is essentially alive. To him this meant that rather than perish, the soul would simply withdraw at the approach of death – being essentially alive, it could not admit its opposite, death. But it was not Plato's arguments for immortality, but rather his conception of the soul as immaterial, simple, and thereby naturally immortal that turned out to be enormously influential.

In most of the *Phaedo*, Plato seems to be thinking of survival as the persistence of naturally immortal, indivisible, individualistic souls, whether extended or not. In other dialogues, particularly the *Republic*, he proposed what today we would call an empirical psychology, in which he claimed that selves are divided into rational, spirited, and appetitive parts. It is the interaction among these parts, and in particular the question of which part dominates the other two, that explains how people behave. Elsewhere he said that only the rational part of the self is immortal, the other two parts perishing with the body. Thus, as Plato matured, he struggled to integrate his rather austere *a priori philosophy* of the self with a more complicated empirical *psychology* of human mentality. In later works, such as the *Timaeus*, the *Phaedrus*, and *Laws*, he returned to the question of how to integrate his two accounts of the soul and took bold steps in the direction of incorporating physiological theory.

However the issue of whether Plato had a settled view of the self is resolved, in the surviving literature from the West in which views of the self are expressed, nothing even remotely like Plato's intellectual sensitivity and sophistication, not to mention his imaginative daring-do, had appeared previously. He represents a new beginning. The view of the self that he expressed in the *Phaedo* was destined to become one of the most influential theories of the self ever expressed. Even so, it was not the only influential theory of the self spawned by Greek culture. Within 150 years of Socrates' death two rival theories of the self were expressed, each of which, ultimately, would become as influential as Plato's. One of these was due to Plato's student, Aristotle, the other to several related Greek thinkers, who became known as the Greek Atomists.

Aristotle (384–322 BCE)

Plato's student, Aristotle, had what we would call a more scientific turn of mind. Early in his career, he followed Plato in assuming that the rational part of the soul – *nous* – is immortal. Later, in *De Anima* and elsewhere, his statements about the persistence of *nous* are enigmatic. But, unlike Plato in the *Phaedo*, Aristotle's main theoretical concern with the soul had little to do with survival of bodily death. Neither did he follow Plato in developing a normative theory of morality based on self-interest. Rather, he was preoccupied with two other problems: the place of humans in the larger scheme of things, and the soul's relationship to the body.

In Plato's view, there was one main division in reality, that between the material and visible, on the one hand, and the "immaterial" and invisible, on the other. The former became real by "participating" in the latter; the more it "participated," the more real it was. Plato's dualism is often called a *two-worlds* view. According to Aristotle, except for "the Unmoved Mover" and possibly *nous*, there is only one world, every item in which is a union of matter and form, and hence material. Even so, in his view, not all material objects are equally real. There is a gradation of being, at the lowest end of which is inorganic matter and at the highest the Unmoved Mover. Aristotle thought of the Unmoved Mover as pure form. Later generations of Christian theologians thought of it as God.

In Aristotle's view, vegetable life is above inorganic matter; non-reasoning animals are above vegetable life; and humans are above non-reasoning animals. Except for inorganic matter, everything has a *psyche*, or soul, which is its vital principle – that is, whatever it is about it that accounts for its being alive. Most of the soul is inseparable from the body that it informs. Apparently the soul's rational part – *nous* – is separable. However, it is not clear whether, in Aristotle's view, *nous* can retain personal individuality after its separation from the body. Aristotle didn't seem to be particularly interested in the question. However, when, in the late Middle Ages and early Renaissance, Aristotle achieved among Christian scholars an authoritative status almost equal to Divine Revelation, the implications of his view of the psyche for personal survival of bodily death became an extremely contentious point, with some thinkers suggesting that Aristotle's true view must have been that no parts of the soul, not even *nous*, are separable from the body.

As for the rest of Aristotle's view of the psyche, at the bottom of the scale of souls is the nutritive or vegetative soul, which accounts for assimilation and reproduction. It is found only in plants. Next is the sensitive soul, which includes all the powers of the vegetative soul plus the additional powers of self-perception, desire, and local motion. Sensation gives rise to imagination and memory. Aristotle thought that, of the senses, touch and taste are the most important, for just as nutrition is necessary for the preservation of any sort of life, so touch and taste are necessary for the preservation of animal life. Other senses, such as sight, while not strictly necessary to the preservation of animal life, nevertheless contribute to its well-being. The sensitive soul is found only in non-human animals. Higher still is the rational soul, which possesses all the powers of the lower souls, but also possesses *nous*, or reason (or intellect). *Nous* is responsible for scientific thought, which has as its object truth for its own sake. It is also responsible for deliberation, which has as its object truth for the sake of some practical or prudential objective.

In Aristotle's view, with the possible exception of *nous* the psyche and all its parts come into being at the same time as its associated body. It is inseparable from its body and perishes along with it. Throughout most of *De Anima*, the psyche is considered to be the form of the body, the two constituting a single living substance. Aristotle defines *psyche*, or soul, as the first "perfection" of a natural organic body having the potentiality for life. This, his most general definition of soul, implies that the soul perishes at bodily death. This is how Alexander of Aphrodisias (fl. 200 CE), one of his most important early commentators, later understood Aristotle. But elsewhere Aristotle muddied this picture.

In *De Anima* 1, 1 (403a), Aristotle wrote that "if some action or passion of the soul is uniquely proper to it, it is possible that it might be separated." In 1, 4 (408b), he wrote that "the intellect seems to be a substance that comes about in a thing and is not corrupted," and in 3, 4 (429b) that "the sense faculty is not outside the body, but the intellect is separated." In 3, 5 (430a, 10–25), he wrote:

> Therefore, it is necessary that in [the soul] there be an intellect capable of becoming all things, and an intellect capable of making itself understand all things. And the intellect which is capable of understanding all things is like a condition, such as light, for light in a certain way makes potential colors be actual colors. And this intellect is separated, not mixed or passible, and, in its substance, is action. [...] Nor does it sometimes understand and sometimes not. And in its separated state, it is just what it is, and this alone is always immortal. And there is no memory, because [the agent intellect] is not passible, and the passible intellect is corruptible, and without it [i.e., the agent intellect] nothing is understood.

In *De Generatione Animalium* 2, 3 (736a), in the context of discussing conception and fetal development, Aristotle noted that the vegetative soul, having existed potentially in semen, comes into being actually when it provides the vital heat to matter supplied by the mother. He then wrote that the sensitive soul, having existed potentially in the vegetative soul, comes into being actually in a similar way. He ends by noting that the intellective or rational soul cannot have been generated internally. "It remains," he says, "that the intellect alone should come from without, and that it alone be divine." In the rational soul, he claimed, there is a power of acting and a power of being acted upon, both of which are ungenerated and incorruptible.[1]

In most interpretations of Aristotle, *nous* preexists its associated body and is immortal. Yet, even if *nous* is immortal, it is not a good vehicle for personal immortality. This is because for things of the same species, matter is what distinguishes one thing from another. Thus, although the rational part of every individual human soul may be immortal, individual humans may not thereby themselves be immortal, and not just because their bodies die, but because there is only one *nous*, which all humans share. Hence, in Aristotle's view, it may be that only what we have in common with each other, and not what distinguishes us, survives the grave. This is partly because there is only one form of the human rational soul. This one form becomes the form of many souls by joining with the matter of many human beings. In Aristotle's words, "All things which are many in number have matter; for many individuals have one and the same intelligible structure, for example, man, whereas Socrates is one."[2] Once the material human being is gone, along with his or her memories, only the form which is the same for all human beings remains.

Lucretius (95?–54 BCE?)

Lucretius, an Epicurean, lived and wrote at the beginning of the Roman era. An eloquent proponent of hedonism, materialism, and atheism, he denied both the existence of an immaterial soul and personal survival of bodily death. His major work, *De Rerum Natura*, is a philosophical poem. It is significant less for its effect on his contemporaries than on medieval and Early Modern philosophers.

Lucretius denied Plato's basic assumption that if selves were souls, people would be entitled to anticipate *having* the experiences of their post-mortem selves. In the context of Lucretius's making the point that we have nothing to fear from bodily death, he argued that "if any feeling remains in mind or spirit after it has been torn from body, that is nothing to us, who are brought into being by the wedlock of body and spirit, conjoined and coalesced."[3] In other words, in his view, regardless of what that is currently part of us persists, and regardless of whether this persisting part is capable of having experiences and of performing actions, if this part of ourselves is not attended by the very bodies we have when we die – and in order for it to be attended by these very bodies, these very bodies would have to exist continuously as integrated, functioning entities – then this part of ourselves is not us. Lucretius concluded that if this part is not us, then its experiences and actions are not something we can look forward to having and performing.

Unfortunately, Lucretius did not argue for this view, but merely asserted it. Yet, because he was so widely read during the Middle Ages and into the modern period, he introduced into the discussion of self and survival the question of what matters primarily in survival. He did this by considering the possibility that we might not persist and yet that, even from our own egoistic points of view, not much that matters would be lost – and not because our lives are awful or because we do not value ourselves, but because identity is not what matters primarily in survival. The question of whether identity or something else matters primarily in survival resurfaced again in the late eighteenth and early nineteenth centuries, and again – when it moved to center stage – in our own times.

The Patristic Period

By the middle of the second century CE the scriptural documents that would later in the century be collected together to form the New Testament were more or less complete. Attention turned increasingly to the task of interpreting what was novel and puzzling in these scriptures. This task was bequeathed to a group of classically educated pagans, known as the Apologists, who had converted to Christianity. Their response was to try to rationalize Christianity using the resources of Greek philosophy. One of their major preoccupations was the dogma of the resurrection.

According to Christian scripture, not only do people survive their bodily deaths, but they survive them in a bodily way. Many pagans found it difficult to believe that the actual bodies that people had on earth would or could be raised or, supposing that they could, that this would be a good thing. After all, many people when they die are old or injured, and all are dead! Moreover, to pagan critics, and even to many of the Apologists, it seemed prima facie that there is *no way* that the *same* body – not just a *similar* body, but the *very same* one – that dies and decomposes could later be raised from the dead. Entire treatises were devoted to responding to such difficulties. Standardly these took the form of claiming that the body which is resurrected is somehow spiritualized, glorified, or at least repaired. As a consequence, two questions in particular cried out for answers: how the body that died is reassembled to form the new body, especially if the component parts of the body that died are scattered to the winds, or perhaps even integrated into the flesh of carnivorous animals; and how the assembly of a new, improved body is compatible with its being the very same body as the old one.

In discussing how the Apologists dealt with these issues, three views about personal identity need to be distinguished: first, that personal identity depends only on the continuation of the immaterial soul; second, that it depends on the continuation of both the immaterial soul and the material body; and third, that it depends only on the continuation of the material body (which was thought to include a material soul). Some Christian thinkers who had Platonic views of survival, perhaps including Origen, adopted something like the first of these options; others, like Tertullian, adopted something like the third option. Eventually most gravitated toward the second option: that personal immortality requires the continuation of the very same immaterial soul and the very same material body.

There were three major treatments of resurrection by Church Fathers from about the year 200. These were by Irenaeus, Tertullian, and Minucius Felix, all of whom were materialists. Tertullian, who was a Stoic, wrote *A Treatise on the Soul* and *On the Resurrection of the Flesh*, in both of which he saw the resurrection in terms of the reassembly of the parts into which the body had decomposed, stressing that the very same flesh that sinned must be punished. In his view, everything, including God and the human soul, is corporeal. He pointed out that if the human soul is to suffer, it has to be corporeal. He also said that the soul of the infant is derived from the father's seed like a kind of sprout. So far as the resurrection itself is concerned, the key for Tertullian was that "the flesh is the very condition on which salvation hinges."[4] He claimed that "if God raises not men entire, he raises not the dead." But, he said, in the case of the dead, to raise a man entire *is* to repair him if he needs repair, say, by restoring him to some earlier period of his life when he was in better condition: "For what dead man is entire, although he dies entire? Who is without hurt, that is without life?" What dead body is uninjured? "Thus, for a dead man to be raised again amounts to nothing short of his being restored to his entire condition."

If you try to understand survival of bodily death on materialistic grounds, as did Irenaeus, Tertullian, and Minucius Felix, and you admit, as anyone must, that the body decomposes at death, then you have to explain how it can be recomposed in a way that sustains personal persistence. These three did that basically by proposing what would later be known as a relational view of personal identity; that is, what insures personal persistence is the way in which the body on earth that decomposes at death and the resurrected body are related to each other. Presumably also, during one's earthly life, what insures one's persistence from moment to moment, day to day, and so on is the way one's constantly changing earthly body at any given time is related to one's body at later times.

Subsequently, when Christian thinkers reverted to Platonic dualism, they were not, like Plato had been, in a position to sidestep the thorny issues that are raised by a relational account of identity. The reason that they could not do this is that they accepted the dogma of the resurrection of the body, and so had to account for how the body that falls and the one that subsequently rises are the same. In addition, because in Rome, during this period, martyred Christians were being eaten by lions, a complication that arose early for most thinkers was the so-called *chain consumption argument*, which was often considered by addressing cannibalism. As a consequence, once identity became an issue, even the dualistic theories that were introduced to account for it went considerably beyond those of the classical period. In their sophistication, these theories directly anticipated relational accounts that would come to center stage in the eighteenth century.

Origen of Alexandria (185?–254) is regarded by many as the important Christian intellectual before Augustine. So far as his view of the soul is concerned, he is perhaps best known for arguing that the souls of angels, human beings, and demons preexisted in a state of perfection before they sinned and fell. In this view, souls are rational beings created with free choice. How badly they sinned determined how far they fell. The reason why there is a world in the first place is to provide a site for the punishment and rehabilitation of souls, all of whom will be reformed eventually and then restored to an original state of perfection.

Origen also wrote about the resurrection. In *On First Principles*, he took his point of departure from scriptural sources in Matthew and Paul and claimed that after bodily death, when we are in heaven, we will have a body that is spiritual and luminous, thus composed of different stuff from any earthly body. This raised a question about identity. In defense of the idea that this spiritual body might be the very same as a previously existing material body, Origen pointed out that even prior to bodily death the material out of which our bodies are composed is constantly changing and "is perhaps not the same for even two days."[5] He said that "*river* is not a bad name for the body." So, what then accounts for the bodies of people remaining the same from day to day, month to month, and so on? In his view, what accounts for this is that "the form (*eidos*) characterizing [different temporal stages of these bodies] is the same." That is, Origen reasoned that since the material out of which bodies are composed is in constant flux, even if the bits of flesh present at the moment of death *could be* reanimated, there is no particular reason why God *would want to* reanimate those bits. He claimed that since the body changes in life, and yet retains its identity, there is no special problem about its also changing in death and retaining its identity. Moreover, he said, it is appropriate that it should change, for just as people would need to have gills if they were destined to live under water, so those who are destined to live in heaven will need spiritual bodies. Yet, in the body's transformation to this "more glorious" state, its "previous form does not disappear"; rather, "the very thing [*eidos*] which was once being characterized in the flesh will be characterized in the spiritual body."

In the light of subsequent developments in personal identity theory, two things about Origen's views are worth noting. The first has to do with how easy it would have been to object to his theory by raising the possibility of post-mortem fission. He stressed that in reconstructing the post-mortem spiritual body, God can use matter from any of the previous stages of the person who has died. Obviously, then, there is much more matter than would be needed to fashion just one spiritual person. So, one can imagine a pagan asking, "Suppose God then fashioned out of the old matter several similar spiritual bodies?" A similar question arose, first, in the eighteenth century, and then again in our own times. When this question arose in the eighteenth century, it arose specifically in the context of trying to understand the resurrection.

The second issue has to do with the question of whether assimilation time is required to preserve bodily identity. Origen stressed that the matter out of which our bodies are composed is constantly changing. But in the course of everyday life this matter is not changing all at once. Perhaps, then, the persistence of one's body is compatible only with changes in it being gradual and organic. Some Christian philosophers who were contemporaries of Origen, as well as some who came later, may have had this worry. They insisted that in order for God to resurrect someone who had died, God had to reuse not only matter out of which the person who died had been composed, but only that matter that was in use at the time of his or her death.

The kind of view for which Origen argued was destined to be revived in the eighteenth century by thinkers such as Isaac Watts (1674–1748), Charles Bonnet (1720–93), and Joseph Priestley (1733–1804), each of whom maintained, first, that for each human there is a unique "germ" embodied in the constantly changing matter out of which he or she is composed; second, that it is this germ, a formal property of at least some of the person's matter, that insures that the later stages of a person are qualitatively similar to earlier ones; and, finally, that so far as a person's bodily persistence over time and through various changes is concerned, everything about the matter of which the person is composed other than the persistence of this germ is irrelevant. Both Origen and these later writers seem to have been groping toward what today we would call the notion of genetic inheritance, to which they then gave pride of place in their accounts of bodily identity.

Plotinus (205–270)

In Plato's *philosophy* of self and personal identity, in which he put forward his view of the soul, he did not even raise the question of what accounts for the unity of the self *at any given time*. Had he raised this question, presumably he would have answered, in part, that the soul's immateriality, and hence its indivisibility, accounts for its unity. In his *psychology* of self, in the *Republic* and elsewhere, Plato suggested a more general answer. But his concern there was much more with what sort of psychology contributes to the harmony of the soul than with what sort of material or spiritual constitution is conducive to that harmony. His answer, in effect, was that when the rational part of the soul is in charge, the person lives morally, and then harmony prevails.

Six centuries after Plato, Plotinus raised more fine-grained questions about the unity of the soul and of the mind. He argued that the unity of either would be impossible if the soul were matter, because matter is inherently divisible in a way that would destroy its own and also the mind's unity. While conceding that the soul also is divisible, he argued that it is divisible in a way that does not interfere with unity. "The nature, at once divisible and indivisible, which we affirm to be soul has not the unity of an extended thing: it does not consist of separate sections; its divisibility lies in its presence at every point in the recipient, but it is indivisible as dwelling entire in any part."[6]

After making this point, Plotinus then observed that if the soul "had the nature of body, it would consist of isolated members each unaware of the conditions of each other."[7] In that case, he continued, "there would be a particular soul – say, a soul of the finger – answering as a distinct and independent entity to every local experience," and hence, "there would be a multiplicity of souls administering each individual." But the mental lives of such individuals, he pointed out, would be unlike our mental lives, so each of us cannot be administered by a multiplicity of (equal) souls. "Without a dominant unity," he concluded, our lives would be "meaningless." As we shall see, these remarks of his are similar to those in which Locke introduced to the eighteenth century what in our own times have come to be known as *fission examples* – that is, examples in which a person's consciousness divides into two parts, each of which is mentally complete in itself and neither of which is conscious, from the inside, of the other's mental states. When Locke introduced fission examples, he even used the image of a finger's retaining an independent consciousness after it has been separated from the rest of the body.

Augustine (354–430)

Augustine, one of the most influential philosophers who ever lived, made seminal contributions to an enormous number of issues that continued to be central sources of concern not only throughout the Middle Ages, but throughout the Reformation and into the modern era: Christian theology, the nature of time, Church–State relations, Rome as a historical phenomenon, and, most importantly for present purposes, the soul and human psychology. He was also among the first to become self-conscious about a problem that would persist in the tradition of Christian dualism at least until Spinoza: that of explaining the relation of the soul-substance to the body.

Plato had maintained, in effect, that the soul is related to the body like a ship's pilot to his ship. Augustine's view, by contrast, was that soul and body together form an intimate unit: "A soul in possession of a body does not constitute two persons but one man."

> A man is not a body alone, nor a soul alone, but a being composed of both. [...] [the soul is] not the whole man, but the better part of man, the body not the whole, but the inferior part of man. [...] When both are joined, they receive the name of *man*, which, however, they do not severally lose even when we speak of them singly. [...] Will they say that Scripture follows no such usage? On the contrary, it so thoroughly adopts it, that even while a man is alive, and body and soul are united, it calls each of them singly by the name, *man*, speaking of the soul as the *inward man*, and of the body as the *outward man*, as if there were two men, though both together are indeed but one.[8]

And whereas in the case of Plato, the soul at death always leaves forever the specific body with which it has been associated, and when sufficiently purified eventually leaves body itself behind forever, in Augustine's case, the dogma of bodily resurrection all but required that he work out a more intimate relationship between soul and body. Yet, in spite of his thus stressing the unity of the human person, he denied that sensation is an activity of the total psycho-physical organism, insisting instead that in sensation the soul uses the body as its instrument.

Augustine, thus, subscribes to the two-substance view that selves are composed of an immaterial soul and a material body. It is the relationship between them that must be explained. In his view, the soul, far from being immutable, can be changed either by itself or by the body. He credits Ephesians 5:29 – "No one hates his own flesh" – with helping him to realize the body's value, which is that, rather than a mere tool or, even worse, a prison, the body should be regarded as a "temple." Augustine acknowledged that the soul rules over the body, and hence that the body is subordinate, yet claimed that after death when the soul is separated from the body, it yearns to be reunited. Finally, his account of the role of memory in personal identity foreshadows Locke's view: "Great is the power of memory ... and this thing is the mind, and this am I myself."[9] Hence, Augustine resists the idea that one's identity could extend beyond what one can remember, for instance, to one's early infancy.

The Rise of Scholasticism

Aristotle's *Categories* and *De Interpretatione*, as well as Boethius's commentaries on them, were available to Latin medieval thinkers during the Middle Ages. From the mid-twelfth to the mid-thirteenth century, virtually all of the remaining works of Aristotle were translated and became readily available. The Arab philosophers Avicenna (980–1037) and Averroës (1126–98), both of whom commented extensively on Aristotle, also were translated. These new writings, which contained much hitherto unknown natural science, dazzled Latin medieval intellectuals, accustomed to the other-worldly speculations of Neoplatonists. Nevertheless, this background perfectly prepared them for the further developments of Aristotle, whose wide-ranging and systematic approach to scientific knowledge, all but complete presentation of a logical system, and confidence in human intelligence meshed nicely with the new spirit of rational naturalism that had independently begun to make its appearance in the medieval West. To a whole cadre of Christian intellectuals hungry for such developments, Aristotle became known as "the philosopher," a title he retained until the advent of modern physical science in the seventeenth century.

The new Aristotelian literature which for the next century would stimulate and confuse European intellectuals initially provoked several new questions and cast old ones in a new light. The essential problem was that, after Augustine, Western philosophers became accustomed to thinking of the soul as a simple, incorporeal substance which inhabited the body, but did not have much else in common with it. On the views inspired by Aristotle's *De Anima*, on the other hand, there was no longer just one soul, but several, and each of them had a great deal in common with the body. For the first time in European thought since Neoplatonism had gained ascendancy, the soul was undergoing a process of naturalization. It would not be the last time this would happen. In the seventeenth and eighteenth centuries, it would happen again, only more radically, until eventually the soul, except as a postulate of religious dogma, was displaced altogether by the mind/brain. The trick, for Christian thinkers struggling to assimilate Aristotle, was to explain the relationship of Aristotelian souls to each other and to the body in an account that preserved personal immortality.

In the thirteenth century, a key issue was whether the rational soul is the form of the body or a substance in its own right, or both. There were problems with each option. If the rational soul is the form of the body, then it is difficult to explain how personal immortality is possible. If it is a separate substance, then there is a problem in accounting for the unity of the person. If it is both form and substance, it is hard to explain how form can yield substance without matter.

Thirteenth-century thinkers suggested a variety of solutions to these problems. Among them were that the rational soul informs not regular matter, but spiritual matter, and that the rational soul does not inform matter of any kind. None of these "solutions" is (or was) particularly attractive. For instance, spiritual "matter" seems to be little more than just regular matter minus the matter; and form without matter of any kind is like the smile of the Cheshire cat minus the cat.

Thomas Aquinas (*c*.1224–1274)

In Aquinas's view, the human soul includes faculties or powers of acting. These exist as potentialities to act and are distinguished from each other according to their respective acts and the objects to which they are directed. These faculties or powers of acting are hierarchically arranged. The vegetative faculty, which is on the bottom, includes the powers of nutrition, growth, and reproduction and has as its object sustaining a particular human life – that is, a particular union of soul and body. Next in order of ascension is the sensitive faculty, which includes both exterior and interior senses, and after it, the rational faculty, comprising the active and passive intellects, including intellectual memory.

In Aquinas's view, some forms are capable of existing independently of matter, and some are not. The ones that are capable are called *spiritual*, or *intelligible*, substances. Some of these spiritual substances, such as angels, are complete, in that they are purely intelligible and have no functions or activities that require material bodies. What makes them substances in the first place is that they are a combination of form and existence. Other of these spiritual substances, such as human rational souls, are incomplete, in that they are not purely intelligible and have functions and activities that require material bodies. What makes even these incomplete substances nevertheless substances is that they too are a combination of form and existence. In other words, in Aquinas's view, some forms can become substances not by combining with matter but by combining with existence itself! Moreover, there is in each human just one substantial form, the rational soul, which, as a substantial form, is the same in all humans. However, the different matter out of which different humans are composed individuates humans (persons) from each other, as well as individuating their rational souls. What individuates the human rational soul after bodily death from other disembodied rational souls is partly the fact that God created it in the first place to be the soul of a particular human body which it informs and partly its historical association with that body.

An additional feature of Aquinas's view is that prior to bodily death the embodied human rational soul includes as part of its nature the power to perform the functions of the developing human embryo previously performed by the animal and vegetable souls. However, the rational soul's power to perform these lower functions does not persist after bodily death, during which time the rational soul retains only those of its powers that distinguish humans from brutes. Eventually, though, the body is reunited with the soul to form the same human person who lived on Earth. This combination of the rational human soul and that body is once again a complete substance.

Thus, in arguing for the immortality of the soul, Aquinas argued for personal immortality. Against the Averroists he argued that the intellect is not a substance distinct from the human soul and common to all men. Rather, the rational soul is a form, and the intellect is one of its faculties. When a rational soul informs matter to become a particular human being, that human has its own particular intellectual faculty as part of its soul. Aquinas thus rejected the Platonic idea that the rational soul is related to the body as a pilot to his ship in favor of the view that its connection is more intimate. An individual human begins when the rational soul is infused in the body and dies when the rational soul departs from the body. This process of uniting with a body to form a human is natural and appropriate. It is not, as Origen and then later Eriugena (810?–877?) had thought, punishment to the soul for sin in a preceding state. The soul joins a body because it is its natural destiny to do so.

There is a theme in Aquinas that bears on debates in our own time about the morality of human abortion. In his view, the human rational soul is the form of the human body, in that through it the human body lives. But this raises a thorny problem that all scholastics had to face: What is the relationship between the rational soul, created and infused into the developed body, and whatever is responsible for bringing about the growth and organization of the embryo? Surprisingly, in light of the Catholic Church's subsequent position on abortion, Aquinas did not, like Grosseteste (1168?–1253), for instance, hold that the rational soul is infused at conception but uses only its lower vegetative and sensitive powers until the body develops. Instead he claimed that since the generation of one thing necessarily entails the corruption of another, "when a more perfect form arrives, the prior form is corrupted; provided, however, that the succeeding form has everything that the first had plus something more."[10] In other words, in Aquinas's view, prior to the arrival of the rational soul, the growth and organization of the embryo is directed first by the vegetative soul, and then subsequently by the sensitive soul, upon whose arrival the vegetative soul is obliterated, since the sensitive soul takes over the functions of the vegetative soul. Both of these souls are biologically transmitted. The rational soul, by contrast, "is created by God *at the end of human generation*." This soul "is at once both sensitive and vegetative, the preexisting forms having been corrupted."

What this means is, first, that the rational soul arrives relatively late in the process of the development of the human embryo, and second, that prior to its arrival, the embryo has no human soul and no soul of any kind that is capable of surviving bodily death. In other words, in Aquinas's view, the conceptus – that is, the fertilized egg that will eventually develop into an embryo – is not, either at the moment of conception or for quite awhile afterwards, endowed with an immortal soul. In fact, technically speaking, it is not even human. All of that happens later.

The Renaissance

The main importance of the Renaissance was the contribution it made in breaking the grip of an increasingly arcane and infertile scholasticism, which by the beginning of the fourteenth century had become stultifying. By supplementing the reigning Aristotelian traditions of the High Middle Ages with humanism, Platonism, and a newly emerging spirit of empirical inquiry, the Renaissance helped to create an intellectual climate that was receptive to the great ideas of the seventeenth century. Yet, even though during the sixteenth century Aristotelianism began to be attacked in what was most central to it, its natural philosophy, throughout the Renaissance it continued to be extremely influential. Thinkers, such as

Paracelsus (1493–1541), Telesio (1509–88), Bruno (1543–1600), and others, who were themselves profoundly affected by Aristotelianism, proposed rival systems, yet failed to overthrow the Aristotelian tradition in natural philosophy. The problem was that there was no comparable alternative. The natural philosophers of the late Renaissance could bend the Aristotelian tradition, but they could not break it. The decisive attack upon Aristotelian natural philosophy would come from Galileo and other natural philosophers in the seventeenth century.

René Descartes (1596–1650)

In the early seventeenth century, Descartes freed the Platonic view of the self from its Aristotelian accretions, and in so doing inadvertently exposed its scientific theoretical irrelevance, a consequence that would not become apparent to most philosophers until the end of the eighteenth century. In Descartes's view, everything in the physical world, including the bodies of humans, is composed of matter in various configurations, which is governed by laws of motion that have remained unchanged since the origin of the universe. So far as living things are concerned, his view was that non-human animals are simply complex automata, and that humans differ only in having non-material, immortal souls. He distinguished sharply between those psychological processes that involve the thought of the non-material soul and other processes involved in sensation, perception, imagination, emotional activities, learned responses, and so on. He assumed that the latter could be brought about mechanically by the body and brain, outside the realm of human consciousness.

Descartes believed that mind was one substance, body another, and that different substances have different essential properties. The essence of mind is thinking, and of matter extension. So far as mind is concerned, what this meant for Descartes is, first, that all truly conscious thinking is done by mental (unextended) substances, and second, that mental substances are always thinking. Descartes's main argument that there are such mental substances was an epistemological one. He reasoned that each of us can be certain that he or she exists, but not (as immediately) certain that there are material objects. He thought, erroneously, that it follows from this that we cannot be material objects, an inference that had been made previously by Augustine and Avicenna.

In addition to thinking that God, angels, and human souls are mental substances and that bodies are material substances, Descartes held that each human's soul, or mind, is so intimately connected to its own body as to form with it a separate composite substance of a third sort. But how could the union of two things – mind and body – which seemingly have nothing in common be so intimate? Descartes rejected the idea, which may well have been congenial to Plato, that the soul's relation to the body was like that of a pilot to his ship:

> Nature also teaches me, by these sensations of pain, hunger, thirst and so on, that I am not merely present in my body as a sailor is present in a ship but that I am very closely joined and, as it were, intermingled with it, so that I and the body form a unit. If this were not so, I, who am nothing but a thinking thing, would not feel pain when the body was hurt, but would perceive the damage purely by the intellect, just as a sailor perceives by sight if anything in his ship is broken. Similarly, when the body needed food or drink, I should have an explicit understanding of the fact, instead of having confused sensations of hunger and thirst. For these sensations of hunger, thirst, pain and so on are nothing but confused modes of thinking which arise from the union and, as it were, intermingling of the mind with the body.[11]

In other words, in Descartes's view, self-concern for our bodies is expressed phenomenologically by a kind of identification we make with the content of our sensations. As a consequence of this identification, when we are aware that our bodies are being stimulated, we *feel* that something has happened to *us*, rather than merely *think* that it has happened to *our* bodies. The two – mind and body – form a substantial unity.

Yet, while Descartes recognized that the mind is *not* related to the body as a pilot to his ship, it seemed to some of his critics that on his view, the mind *should* be related to the body as a pilot to his ship. He tried to respond to these critics, but his response was unclear and otherwise problematic. However, what he sometimes seems to have wanted to say is that individual non-material minds and their associated bodies form one substance in virtue of their unity as a causal mechanism. In other words, they systematically affected each other, but not other things, in ways that made the two of them together function as if one thing. That was a winning idea.

Gottfried Wilhelm Leibniz (1646–1716)

Leibniz, along with Spinoza, held that dualism of mind and body is an illusion and that both are really the same thing. However, whereas Spinoza held that this thing is neither mind nor body, Leibniz held that it is mind. Refusing to take extension as primitive and unanalyzable,

Leibniz analyzed extended objects into infinite series of physical points, which, except for being real, are like mathematical points. However, in his view, "physical" points can't really be physical since they lack extension, which he accepted from Descartes to be the essence of matter. So, in Leibniz's panpsychism, these "physical" points are souls, or (spiritual) *monads*. He thus maintained that each of the infinitesimal monads of which each material thing is composed is conscious. However, the consciousness of most of these monads is vastly inferior to human consciousness and consists only in "mirroring" the rest of the universe – that is, in having various relations to other things. Leibniz's later reflections on the notion of personal identity, which were written in response to Locke's *An Essay Concerning Human Understanding* (1690), were not published until 1765, well after Leibniz's death, and so had no effect on theory until toward the end of the eighteenth century.

Leibniz's earlier work was most progressive in connection with two issues: what today we would call *the question of what matters in survival* and that of a *four-dimensional view of persons*. So far as the first of these issues is concerned, in his *Discourse on Metaphysics*, which was written in 1686 and sent to Arnauld, he distinguished between what is required for a person to persist metaphysically and what is required for him or her to persist morally: "But the intelligent soul, knowing what it is – having the ability to utter the word 'I,' a word so full of meaning – does not merely remain and subsist metaphysically, which it does to a greater degree than the others, but also remains the same morally, and constitutes the same person. For it is memory or the knowledge of this self that renders it capable of punishment or reward."[12] Leibniz then distinguished between what is required for the soul to persist metaphysically and what it would take for it to matter to the individual whose soul it is whether it persists: "Thus the immortality required in morality and religion does not consist merely in this perpetual subsistence common to all substances, for without the memory of what one has been, there would be nothing desirable about it." As we shall see, Leibniz's thoughts here are similar to Locke's later thought that "forensic" concerns involving this life, as well as any future life, do not depend on mere substance, but on memory.

Leibniz continued the remarks just quoted with thoughts that are more reminiscent of Lucretius (who may have been his source) than of ones that Locke would later employ: "Suppose that some person all of a sudden becomes the king of China, but only on the condition that he forgets what he has been, as if he were born anew; practically, or as far as the effects could be perceived, wouldn't that be the same as if he were annihilated and a king of China created at the same instant in his place?

That is something this individual would have no reason to desire."
Leibniz supposed that, without memory, even a reconstituted "self"
would not really be oneself, at least with respect to self-concern, and
that this would be so even if the reconstituted self were a continuation (or
reconstitution) of one's substance.

Leibniz's anticipations of what today we would call *a four-dimensional
view of persons* occurs against the backdrop of his distinction between the
a priori and *a posteriori* ground of the identity over time of any object,
including persons. Here he had two noteworthy ideas. One of these is
that one cannot tell from experience what individuates one person from
another: "It is not sufficient that I feel myself as a substance which thinks;
I must also distinctly conceive whatever distinguishes me from all other
spirits. But of this I have only a confused experience."[13] His second idea
is that while *a posteriori* we attempt to arrive at a true view about the
identity of things and persons by comparing their characteristics at
different times, it is a separate question, to be answered *a priori*, what
identity over time consists in. His answer to the question of what identity
over time consists in, together with his main reason for that answer, is
that "since from the very time that I began to exist it could be said of me
truly that this or that would happen to me, we must grant that these
predicates were principles involved in the subject or in my complete
concept, which constitutes the so-called me, and which is the basis of
the interconnection of all my different states," which predicates that
"God has known perfectly from all eternity."[14] In more modern language, the view that Leibniz seems to be anticipating is that the stage
(that is, time-slice) of a thing or person that exists at any given moment or
short interval is not the whole person, but only part of the person, and
that the whole person consists of an aggregate of such stages that begin
whenever the person begins, presumably at bodily birth, and ends whenever the person ends. Leibniz thought that since people are immortal they
never end.

John Locke (1632–1704)

Quick on the heels of developments in natural science in the seventeenth
century came an unprecedented confidence in human reason. Thinkers at
the forefront of progressive developments wanted to do for "moral
philosophy," which eventually they would call the *science of human
nature*, what Galileo and Newton had done for "natural philosophy,"
what today we call *physics*. Earlier in the seventeenth century it had been

primarily rationalists who had been at the forefront of this project. By the end of the century empiricism's time had arrived, and nowhere more consequentially than in the work of John Locke. So far as knowledge is concerned, Locke advanced the foundational principle of empiricism: there is nothing in the mind that was not previously in the senses. So far as the self and personal identity are concerned, he took the decisive first step away from substance accounts according to which the self is a simple immaterial thing toward relational accounts according to which it is a complex mental and/or material process the elements of which are appropriately related to each other.

Locke proposed separate accounts of the identity conditions for inanimate objects, animate objects, and persons. Setting aside, for a moment, his account of the identity conditions for artifacts, in the case of inanimate objects Locke's view was that an individual at one time and one at another are the same just if they are composed of exactly the same matter. A heap of sand remains the same heap so long as it does not either gain or lose a grain, even if the grains are rearranged. Apparently, Locke thought of composite inanimate objects, implausibly in our view, as if they were sets, rather than wholes composed of parts.

In the case of plants and animals, Locke held that an individual at one time and one at another are the same just if each has the kind of shape appropriate to that sort of plant or animal and sustains the same life. The shape of an animal, not its mentality, determines what biological kind of thing it is. Unless one recognizes this, he thought, one might be tempted to say of a rational parrot, if there were one, that it is a human. The life of a thing is simply a way in which its (perhaps exclusively) material parts are organized so as to promote its functioning in a manner appropriate to the sort of thing it is. And a plant or animal can so function even if the matter (and/or spirit) out of which it is composed at any given time is replaced by different matter (and/or spirit). In sum, still leaving the question of artifacts to one side, in Locke's view, in the case of inanimate objects, composition but not organization matters and, in the case of animate objects, shape and organization, but not composition or mentality, matter. In the case of artifacts, he acknowledged the importance of function and allowed for replacement of matter, but he did this not in his chapter on identity and not systematically, but intermittently, in different parts of the *Essay*.

In the case of the identity conditions of persons, Locke is unequivocal: consciousness and only consciousness matters. Thus, although biological kind, in virtue of its relation to shape and life, is essential to *human*hood, it is not essential to *person*hood. In Locke's view, a rational parrot could not be a human and, hence, *a fortiori*, could not be *the same* human as an individual at another time. But a rational parrot could be the same person as an individual at another time.

From An Essay Concerning Human Understanding *(2nd edn., 1694), Book II, Chapter XXVII: Of Identity and Diversity*

[1....]

2. We have the ideas but of three sorts of substances; 1. God. 2. Finite intelligences. 3. Bodies. First, God is without beginning, eternal, unalterable, and everywhere; and therefore concerning his identity, there can be no doubt. Secondly, finite spirits having had each its determinate time and place of beginning to exist, the relation to that time and place will always determine to each of them its identity, as long as it exists. Thirdly, the same will hold of every particle of matter, to which no addition or subtraction of matter being made, it is the same. For though these three sorts of substances, as we term them, do not exclude one another out of the same place; yet we cannot conceive but that they must necessarily each of them exclude any of the same kind out of the same place [...] All other things being but modes or relations ultimately terminated in substances, the identity and diversity of each particular existence of them too will be by the same way determined [...]

5. The case is not so much different in brutes, but that any one may hence see what makes an animal, and continues it the same. Some thing we have like this in machines, and may serve to illustrate it. For example, what is a watch? It is plain it is nothing but a fit organization or construction of parts to a certain end, which when a sufficient force is added to it, it is capable to attain. If we would suppose this machine one continued body, all whose organized parts were repaired, increased, or diminished by a constant addition or separation of insensible parts, with one common life, we should have some thing very much like the body of an animal; with this difference, that in an animal the fitness of the organization, and the motion wherein life consists, begin together, the motion coming from within; but in machines, the force coming sensibly from without, is often away when the organ is in order, and well fitted to receive it. [...]

6. [...] The identity of the same man consists [...] in nothing but a participation of the same continued life, by constantly fleeting particles of matter, in succession vitally united to the same organized body. He that shall place the identity of man in any thing else, but like that of other animals in one fitly organized body, taken in any one instant, and from thence continued under one organization of life in several successively fleeting particles of matter united to it, will find it hard to make an embryo, one of years, mad and sober, the same man, by any supposition, that will not make it possible for Seth, Ismael, Socrates, Pilate, St. Austin, and Caesar

Borgia, to be the same man. For if the identity of soul alone makes the same man, and there be nothing in the nature of matter why the same individual spirit may not be united to different bodies, it will be possible that those men living in distant ages, and of different tempers, may have been the same man: Which way of speaking must be, from a very strange use of the word man, applied to an idea, out of which body and shape are excluded. And that way of speaking would agree yet worse with the notions of those philosophers who allow of transmigration, and are of opinion that the souls of men may, for their miscarriages, be detruded into the bodies of beasts, as fit habitations, with organs suited to the satisfaction of their brutal inclinations. But yet I think nobody, could he be sure that the soul of Heliogabalus were in one of his hogs, would yet say that hog were a man or Heliogabalus.

7. It is not therefore unity of substance that comprehends all sorts of identity, or will determine it in every case: But to conceive and judge of it aright, we must consider what idea the word it is applied to stands for; it being one thing to be the same substance, another the same man, and a third the same person, if person, man, and substance, are three names standing for three different ideas; for such as is the idea belonging to that name, such must be the identity [. . .]

8. An animal is a living organized body; and consequently the same animal, as we have observed, is the same continued life communicated to different particles of matter, as they happen successively to be united to that organized living body. And whatever is talked of other definitions, ingenuous observation puts it past doubt, that the idea in our minds, of which the sound man in our mouths is the sign, is nothing else but of an animal of such a certain form: Since I think I may be confident, that, whoever should see a creature of his own shape and make, though it had no more reason all its life than a cat or a parrot, would call him still a man; or whoever should hear a cat or a parrot discourse, reason and philosophize, would call or think it nothing but a cat or a parrot; and say, the one was a dull, irrational man, and the other a very intelligent rational parrot. [. . .] For I presume, it is not the idea of a thinking or rational being alone that makes the idea of a man in most people's sense, but of a body, so and so shaped, joined to it: And if that be the idea of a man, the same successive body not shifted all at once, must, as well as the same immaterial spirit, go to the making of the same man.

9. This being premised, to find wherein personal identity consists, we must consider what person stands for; which, I think, is a thinking intelligent being, that has reason and reflection, and can consider itself as itself, the same thinking thing in different times and places; which it does only by that consciousness which is inseparable from thinking, and, as it seems to me, essential to it: It being impossible for any one to perceive, without perceiving that he does perceive. When we see, hear, smell, taste, feel,

meditate, or will any thing, we know that we do so. Thus it is always as to our present sensations and perceptions: And by this every one is to himself that which he calls self; it not being considered in this case whether the same self be continued in the same or divers substances. For since consciousness always accompanies thinking, and it is that which makes every one to be what he calls self, and thereby distinguishes himself from all other thinking things; in this alone consists personal identity, i.e. the sameness of a rational being: And as far as this consciousness can be extended backwards to any past action or thought, so far reaches the identity of that person; it is the same self now it was then; and it is by the same self with this present one that now reflects on it, that that action was done.

10. But it is farther enquired, whether it be the same identical substance? This few would think they had reason to doubt of, if these perceptions, with their consciousness, always remained present in the mind, whereby the same thinking thing would be always consciously present, and, as would be thought, evidently the same to itself. But that which seems to make the difficulty is this, that this consciousness being interrupted always by forgetfulness, there being no moment of our lives wherein we have the whole train of all our past actions before our eyes in one view, but even the best memories losing the sight of one part whilst they are viewing another; and we sometimes, and that the greatest part of our lives, not reflecting on our past selves, being intent on our present thoughts, and in sound sleep having no thoughts at all, or at least none with that consciousness which remarks our waking thoughts: I say, in all these cases, our consciousness being interrupted, and we losing the sight of our past selves, doubts are raised whether we are the same thinking thing, i.e. the same substance or no. Which however reasonable or unreasonable, concerns not personal identity at all: The question being, what makes the same person, and not whether it be the same identical substance, which always thinks in the same person; which in this case matters not at all: Different substances, by the same consciousness (where they do partake in it), being united into one person, as well as different bodies by the same life are united into one animal, whose identity is preserved, in that change of substances, by the unity of one continued life. For it being the same consciousness that makes a man be himself to himself, personal identity depends on that only, whether it be annexed solely to one individual substance, or can be continued in a succession of several substances. For as far as any intelligent being can repeat the idea of any past action with the same consciousness it had of it at first, and with the same consciousness it has of any present action: So far it is the same personal self. For it is by the consciousness it has of its present thoughts and actions, that it is self to itself now, and so will be the same self, as far as the same consciousness can extend to actions past or to come; and would be by distance of time, or change of substance, no more two persons, than a man be two men by wearing other clothes to-day than he did

yesterday, with a long or a short sleep between: The same consciousness uniting those distant actions into the same person, whatever substances contributed to their production.

11. That this is so, we have some kind of evidence in our very bodies, all whose particles, whilst vitally united to this same thinking conscious self, so that we feel when they are touched, and are affected by, and conscious of good or harm that happens to them, are a part of ourselves; i.e. of our thinking conscious self. Thus the limbs of his body are to every one a part of himself; he sympathizes and is concerned for them. Cut off a hand, and thereby separate it from that consciousness he had of its heat, cold, and other affections, and it is then no longer a part of that which is himself, any more than the remotest part of matter. Thus we see the substance, whereof personal self consisted at one time, may be varied at another, without the change of personal identity; there being no question about the same person, though the limbs which but now were a part of it, be cut off.

12. But the question is, "Whether if the same substance which thinks, be changed, it can be the same person; or, remaining the same, it can be different persons?" And to this I answer: First, This can be no question at all to those who place thought in a purely material animal constitution, void of an immaterial substance. For whether their supposition be true or no, it is plain they conceive personal identity preserved in some thing else than identity of substance; as animal identity is preserved in identity of life, and not of substance. And therefore those who place thinking in an immaterial substance only, before they can come to deal with these men, must shew why personal identity cannot be preserved in the change of immaterial substances, or variety of particular immaterial substances, as well as animal identity is preserved in the change of material substances, or variety of particular bodies: Unless they will say, it is one immaterial spirit that makes the same life in brutes, as it is one immaterial spirit that makes the same person in men; which the Cartesians at least will not admit, for fear of making brutes thinking things too.

13. But next, as to the first part of the question, "Whether if the same thinking substance (supposing immaterial substances only to think) be changed, it can be the same person?" I answer, that cannot be resolved, but by those who know what kind of substances they are that do think, and whether the consciousness of past actions can be transferred from one thinking substance to another. I grant, were the same consciousness the same individual action, it could not: But it being a present representation of a past action, why it may not be possible, that that may be represented to the mind to have been, which really never was, will remain to be shewn. And therefore how far the consciousness of past actions is annexed to any individual agent, so that another cannot possibly have it, will be hard for us to determine, till we know what kind of action it is that cannot be done without a reflex act of perception accompanying it, and how performed by

thinking substances, who cannot think without being conscious of it. But that which we call the same consciousness, not being the same individual act, why one intellectual substance may not have represented to it, as done by itself, what it never did, and was perhaps done by some other agent – why, I say, such a representation may not possibly be without reality of matter of fact, as well as several representations in dreams are, which yet whilst dreaming we take for true, will be difficult to conclude from the nature of things. And that it never is so, will by us, till we have clearer views of the nature of thinking substances, be best resolved into the goodness of God, who as far as the happiness or misery of any of his sensible creatures is concerned in it, will not by a fatal error of theirs transfer from one to another that consciousness which draws reward or punishment with it. How far this may be an argument against those who would place thinking in a system of fleeting animal spirits, I leave to be considered. But yet to return to the question before us, it must be allowed, that if the same consciousness (which, as has been shewn, is quite a different thing from the same numerical figure or motion in body) can be transferred from one thinking substance to another, it will be possible that two thinking substances may make but one person. For the same consciousness being preserved, whether in the same or different substances, the personal identity is preserved.

14. As to the second part of the question, "Whether the same immaterial substance remaining, there may be two distinct persons?" which question seems to me to be built on this, whether the same immaterial being, being conscious of the action of its past duration, may be wholly stripped of all the consciousness of its past existence, and lose it beyond the power of ever retrieving it again; and so as it were beginning a new account from a new period, have a consciousness that cannot reach beyond this new state. All those who hold pre-existence are evidently of this mind, since they allow the soul to have no remaining consciousness of what it did in that pre-existent state, either wholly separate from body, or informing any other body; and if they should not, it is plain, experience would be against them. So that personal identity reaching no farther than consciousness reaches, a pre-existent spirit not having continued so many ages in a state of silence, must needs make different persons. Suppose a Christian, Platonist, or Pythagorean should, upon God's having ended all his works of creation the seventh day, think his soul hath existed ever since; and should imagine it has revolved in several human bodies, as I once met with one, who was persuaded his had been the soul of Socrates; (how reasonably I will not dispute; this I know, that in the post he filled, which was no inconsiderable one, he passed for a very rational man, and the press has shewn that he wanted not parts or learning) would any one say, that he being not conscious of any of Socrates's actions or thoughts, could be the same person with Socrates? Let any one reflect upon himself, and conclude that he has in

himself an immaterial spirit, which is that which thinks in him, and in the constant change of his body keeps him the same: And is that which he calls himself: Let him also suppose it to be the same soul that was in Nestor or Thersites, at the siege of Troy (for souls being, as far as we know any thing of them in their nature, indifferent to any parcel of matter, the supposition has no apparent absurdity in it), which it may have been, as well as it is now the soul of any other man: But he now having no consciousness of any of the actions either of Nestor or Thersites, does or can he conceive himself the same person with either of them? can he be concerned in either of their actions? attribute them to himself, or think them his own more than the actions of any other men that ever existed? So that this consciousness not reaching to any of the actions of either of those men, he is no more one self with either of them, than if the soul or immaterial spirit that now informs him, had been created, and began to exist, when it began to inform his present body; though it were ever so true, that the same spirit that informed Nestor's or Thersites's body were numerically the same that now informs his. For this would no more make him the same person with Nestor, than if some of the particles of matter that were once a part of Nestor, were now a part of this man; the same immaterial substance, without the same consciousness, no more making the same person by being united to any body, than the same particle of matter, without consciousness united to any body, makes the same person. But let him once find himself conscious of any of the actions of Nestor, he then finds himself the same person with Nestor.

15. And thus we may be able, without any difficulty, to conceive the same person at the resurrection, though in a body not exactly in make or parts the same which he had here, the same consciousness going along with the soul that inhabits it. But yet the soul alone, in the change of bodies, would scarce to any one, but to him that makes the soul the man, be enough to make the same man. For should the soul of a prince, carrying with it the consciousness of the prince's past life, enter and inform the body of a cobbler, as soon as deserted by his own soul, every one sees he would be the same person with the prince, accountable only for the prince's actions: But who would say it was the same man? The body too goes to the making the man, and would, I guess, to every body determine the man in this case; wherein the soul, with all its princely thoughts about it, would not make another man: But he would be the same cobbler to every one besides himself. I know that, in the ordinary way of speaking, the same person, and the same man, stand for one and the same thing. And indeed every one will always have a liberty to speak as he pleases, and to apply what articulate sounds to what ideas he thinks fit, and change them as often as he pleases. But yet when we will enquire what makes the same spirit, man, or person, we must fix the ideas of spirit, man, or person in our minds; and having resolved with ourselves what we mean by them, it will not be hard

to determine in either of them, or the like, when it is the same, and when not.

16. But though the same immaterial substance or soul does not alone, wherever it be, and in whatsoever state, make the same man; yet it is plain consciousness, as far as ever it can be extended, should it be to ages past, unites existences and actions, very remote in time, into the same person, as well as it does the existences and actions of the immediately preceding moment; so that whatever has the consciousness of present and past actions, is the same person to whom they both belong. Had I the same consciousness that I saw the ark and Noah's flood, as that I saw an over-flowing of the Thames last winter, or as that I write now; I could no more doubt that I who write this now, that saw the Thames overflowed last winter, and that viewed the flood at the general deluge, was the same self, place that self in what substance you please, than that I who write this am the same myself now whilst I write (whether I consist of all the same substance, material or immaterial, or no) that I was yesterday. For as to this point of being the same self, it matters not whether this present self be made up of the same or other substances; I being as much concerned, and as justly accountable for any action that was done a thousand years since, appropriated to me now by this self-consciousness, as I am for what I did the last moment.

17. Self is that conscious thinking thing, whatever substance made up of (whether spiritual or material, simple or compounded, it matters not), which is sensible, or conscious of pleasure and pain, capable of happiness or misery, and so is concerned for itself, as far as that consciousness extends. Thus every one finds that, whilst comprehended under that con-sciousness, the little finger is as much a part of himself as what is most so. Upon separation of this little finger, should this consciousness go along with the little finger, and leave the rest of the body, it is evident the little finger would be the person, the same person; and self then would have nothing to do with the rest of the body. As in this case it is the consciousness that goes along with the substance, when one part is separate from another, which makes the same person, and constitutes this inseparable self; so it is in reference to substances remote in time. That with which the conscious-ness of this present thinking thing can join itself, makes the same person, and is one self with it, and with nothing else; and so attributes to itself, and owns all the actions of that thing as its own, as far as that consciousness reaches, and no farther; as every one who reflects will perceive.

18. In this personal identity, is founded all the right and justice of reward and punishment; happiness and misery being that for which every one is concerned for himself, and not mattering what becomes of any substance not joined to, or affected with that consciousness. For as it is evident in the instance I gave but now, if the consciousness went along with the little finger when it was cut off, that would be the same self which was concerned

for the whole body yesterday, as making part of itself, whose actions then it cannot but admit as its own now. Though if the same body should still live, and immediately, from the separation of the little finger, have its own peculiar consciousness, whereof the little finger knew nothing; it would not at all be concerned for it, as a part of itself, or could own any of its actions, or have any of them imputed to him.

19. This may shew us wherein personal identity consists; not in the identity of substance, but, as I have said, in the identity of consciousness; wherein, if Socrates and the present mayor of Queenborough agree, they are the same person: If the same Socrates waking and sleeping do not partake of the same consciousness, Socrates waking and sleeping is not the same person. And to punish Socrates waking for what sleeping Socrates thought, and waking Socrates was never conscious of; would be no more of right, than to punish one twin for what his brother-twin did, whereof he knew nothing, because their outsides were so like, that they could not be distinguished; for such twins have been seen.

20. But yet possibly it will still be objected, suppose I wholly lose the memory of some parts of my life beyond a possibility of retrieving them, so that perhaps I shall never be conscious of them again; yet am I not the same person that did those actions, had those thoughts that I once was conscious of, though I have now forgot them? To which I answer, that we must here take notice what the word is applied to: Which, in this case, is the man only. And the same man being presumed to be the same person, I is easily here supposed to stand also for the same person. But if it be possible for the same man to have distinct incommunicable consciousness at different times, it is past doubt the same man would at different times make different persons; which, we see, is the sense of mankind in the solemnest declaration of their opinions; human laws not punishing the mad man for the sober man's actions, nor the sober man for what the mad man did, thereby making them two persons: Which is somewhat explained by our way of speaking in English, when we say such an one is not himself, or is beside himself; in which phrases it is insinuated, as if those who now, or at least first used them, thought that self was changed, the self-same person was no longer in that man.

21. But yet it is hard to conceive that Socrates, the same individual man, should be two persons. To help us a little in this, we must consider what is meant by Socrates, or the same individual man.

First, it must be either the same individual, immaterial, thinking substance; in short, the same numerical soul, and nothing else.

Secondly, or the same animal, without any regard to an immaterial soul.

Thirdly, or the same immaterial spirit united to the same animal.

Now take which of these suppositions you please, it is impossible to make personal identity to consist in any thing but consciousness, or reach any farther than that does.

For by the first of them, it must be allowed possible that a man born of different women, and in distant times, may be the same man. A way of speaking, which whoever admits, must allow it possible for the same man to be two distinct persons, as any two that have lived in different ages, without the knowledge of one another's thoughts.

By the second and third, Socrates in this life, and after it, cannot be the same man any way, but by the same consciousness; and so making human identity to consist in the same thing wherein we place personal identity, there will be no difficulty to allow the same man to be the same person. But then they who place human identity in consciousness only, and not in some thing else, must consider how they will make the infant Socrates the same man with Socrates after the resurrection. But whatsoever to some men makes a man, and consequently the same individual man, wherein perhaps few are agreed, personal identity can by us be placed in nothing but consciousness (which is that alone which makes what we call self) without involving us in great absurdities.

22. But is not a man drunk and sober the same person? Why else is he punished for the fact he commits when drunk, though he be never afterwards conscious of it? Just as much the same person as a man, that walks, and does other things in his sleep, is the same person, and is answerable for any mischief he shall do in it. Human laws punish both, with a justice suitable to their way of knowledge; because in these cases, they cannot distinguish certainly what is real, what counterfeit: And so the ignorance in drunkenness or sleep is not admitted as a plea. For though punishment be annexed to personality, and personality to consciousness, and the drunkard perhaps be not conscious of what he did; yet human judicatures justly punish him, because the fact is proved against him, but want of consciousness cannot be proved for him. But in the great day, wherein the secrets of all hearts shall be laid open, it may be reasonable to think, no one shall be made to answer for what he knows nothing of; but shall receive his doom, his conscience accusing or excusing him.

23. Nothing but consciousness can unite remote existences into the same person, the identity of substance will not do it. For whatever substance there is, however framed, without consciousness there is no person: And a carcase may be a person, as well as any sort of substance be so without consciousness.

Could we suppose two distinct incommunicable consciousnesses acting the same body, the one constantly by day, the other by night; and, on the other side, the same consciousness acting by intervals two distinct bodies: I ask in the first case, whether the day and the night man would not be two as distinct persons, as Socrates and Plato? And whether, in the second case, there would not be one person in two distinct bodies, as much as one man is the same in two distinct clothings? Nor is it at all material to say, that this same, and this distinct consciousness, in the cases above mentioned, is owing to the same and distinct immaterial substances, bringing it with them to those bodies; which, whether true or no, alters not the case: Since it is evident the personal identity would equally be determined by the consciousness, whether that consciousness were annexed to some individual immaterial substance or no. For granting that the thinking substance in man must be necessarily supposed immaterial, it is evident that immaterial thinking thing may sometimes part with its past consciousness, and be restored to it again; as appears in the forgetfulness men often have of their past actions: And the mind many times recovers the memory of a past consciousness, which it had lost for twenty years together. Make these intervals of memory and forgetfulness, to take their turns regularly by day and night, and you have two persons with the same immaterial spirit, as much as in the former instance two persons with the same body. So that self is not determined by identity or diversity of substance, which it cannot be sure of but only by identity of consciousness.

24. Indeed it may conceive the substance, whereof it is now made up, to have existed formerly, united in the same conscious being: But consciousness removed, that substance is no more itself, or makes no more a part of it than any other substance; as is evident in the instance we have already given of a limb cut off, of whose heat, or cold, or other affections, having no longer any consciousness, it is no more of a man's self, than any other matter of the universe. In like manner it will be in reference to any immaterial substance, which is void of that consciousness whereby I am myself to myself: If there be any part of its existence, which I cannot upon recollection join with that present consciousness whereby I am now myself, it is in that part of its existence no more myself, than any other immaterial being. For whatsoever any substance has thought or done, which I cannot recollect, and by my consciousness make my own thought and action, it will no more belong to me, whether a part of me thought or did it, than if it had been thought or done by any other immaterial being anywhere existing.

25. I agree, the more probable opinion is, that this consciousness is annexed to, and the affection of one individual immaterial substance. But let men, according to their diverse hypotheses, resolve of that as they please, this every intelligent being, sensible of happiness or misery, must grant, that there is some thing that is himself that he is concerned for, and would have happy: That this self has existed in a continued duration more than one instant, and therefore it is possible may exist, as it has done, months and years to come, without any certain bounds to be set to its duration, and may be the same self, by the same consciousness continued on for the future. And thus, by this consciousness, he finds himself to be the same self which did such or such an action some years since, by which he comes to be happy or miserable now. In all which account of self, the same numerical substance is not considered as making the same self; but

the same continued consciousness, in which several substances may have been united, and again separated from it; which, whilst they continued in a vital union with that, wherein this consciousness then resided, made a part of that same self. Thus any part of our bodies vitally united to that which is conscious in us, makes a part of ourselves: But upon separation from the vital union, by which that consciousness is communicated, that which a moment since was part of ourselves, is now no more so, than a part of another man's self is a part of me: And it is not impossible, but in a little time may become a real part of another person. And so we have the same numerical substance become a part of two different persons; and the same person preserved under the change of various substances. Could we suppose any spirit wholly stripped of all its memory or consciousness of past actions, as we find our minds always are of a great part of ours, and sometimes of them all; the union or separation of such a spiritual substance would make no variation of personal identity, any more than that of any particle of matter does. Any substance vitally united to the present thinking being, is a part of that very same self which now is: Any thing united to it by a consciousness of former actions, makes also a part of the same self, which is the same both then and now.

26. Person, as I take it, is the name for this self. Wherever a man finds what he calls himself, there I think another may say is the same person. It is a forensick term appropriating actions and their merit; and so belongs only to intelligent agents capable of a law, and happiness and misery. This personality extends itself beyond present existence to what is past, only by consciousness, whereby it becomes concerned and accountable, owns and imputes to itself past actions, just upon the same ground, and for the same reason that it does the present. All which is founded in a concern for happiness, the unavoidable concomitant of consciousness; that which is conscious of pleasure and pain, desiring that that self that is conscious should be happy. And therefore whatever past actions it cannot reconcile or appropriate to that present self by consciousness, it can be no more concerned in, than if they had never been done: And to receive pleasure or pain, i.e. reward or punishment, on the account of any such action, is all one as to be made happy or miserable in its first being, without any demerit at all. For supposing a man punished now for what he had done in another life, whereof he could be made to have no consciousness at all, what difference is there between that punishment and being created miserable? And therefore conformable to this the apostle tells us, that at the great day, when every one shall "receive according to his doings, the secrets of all hearts shall be laid open." The sentence shall be justified by the consciousness all persons shall have, that they themselves, in what bodies soever they appear, or what substances soever that consciousness adheres to, are the same that committed those actions, and deserve that punishment for them. [...]

In general, when Locke used the phrase "is conscious of", in the context of talking about personal identity over time, he meant "remembers". Thus, there is a textual basis for supposing that Locke, in his capacity as a theorist of personal identity over time, was a memory theorist, and a rather simple-minded one at that; that is, there is a basis for supposing that Locke proposed to define or analyze personal identity in terms of memory. For the most part, this is how Locke has been interpreted ever since the publication of the second edition of the *Essay*, particularly by his eighteenth-century *critics*.

As far as it goes, the simple memory-interpretation of Locke's account of personal identity over time is almost, but not quite, correct. Locke made some allowances for forgetfulness. More importantly, he may not have been trying, in the first place, to present a non-circular analysis of personal identity over time. Even aside from such qualifications, however, the simple memory-interpretation of Locke is at best radically incomplete. For central to Locke's account of the self is the idea that consciousness is reflexive and that it plays a dual role in self-constitution: it is what unifies a person not only *over* time but also *at* a time. Memory-interpretations, whether simple or not, do not explain how consciousness plays this dual role.

Even so, it is clear that an important part of what Locke meant by *consciousness* has to do with memory. Most of his eighteenth-century critics seized upon this aspect of his account, while basically ignoring the rest, in order to attribute to Locke the simple memory view. According to that view, a person at one time and one at another have the same consciousness, and hence are the same person, just in case the person at the later time *remembers* having had experiences or having performed actions that were had or performed by the person at the earlier time. These critics were right in thinking that this simple memory view of personal identity is vulnerable to decisive objections. However, in the eighteenth century almost all of Locke's critics wanted to defeat the simple memory view in order to retain the (immaterial) soul view. But even the simple memory view of personal identity which they attributed to Locke is, in important respects, an advance on the soul view.

According to the soul view, personal identity depends on sameness of soul. As simple, immaterial substances, souls are not part of the natural world. Whatever exists or obtains, but not as part of the natural world, is inherently mysterious. Other peoples' souls cannot be observed either directly or indirectly. And since only the activities, and not the substance, of the soul are open to empirical investigation, there is no way to detect by observing an individual whether his soul remains the same. Hence, on the soul view, personal identity is inherently mysterious.

On the simple memory-interpretation of Locke's account, by contrast, personal identity depends on the presence of a psychological relationship – remembering – that binds together earlier and later stages of a person. Other people's rememberings, unlike their souls, can be observed indirectly. For instance, by listening to another talk, one may be able to determine that she remembers having experienced or done various things. In the case of oneself, each person may observe directly, via introspection, that he or she remembers having experienced and done various things. Only by explaining personal identity in terms of things or relations that are observable can an account of it be developed on the basis of which one can determine empirically whether a person at one time and one at another are the same.

For this reason, Locke's account of personal identity was not just another in a long tradition of such accounts that began with Plato. Rather, his account was an idea whose time had come. As Locke seems to have recognized, the *kind* of view that he was proposing was irresistible. By contrast, his critics, though right in thinking that the simple memory view that they attributed to Locke is deeply flawed, failed to notice that their own views were even more deeply flawed. So far as the verdict of history is concerned, the soul view was not just a wrong account of personal identity, it was the wrong *kind* of account. The simple memory view of personal identity, by contrast, was the right kind of account, even if it was not the right account.

For the most part, Locke used the word *self* to refer to a momentary entity, and *person* to refer to a temporally extended one. Seemingly for other reasons, he defined the two terms differently. His definition of *person* highlighted that persons are thinkers and, as such, have reason, reflection, intelligence, and whatever else may be required for transtemporal self-reference. His definition of *self* highlighted that selves are sensors and, as such, feel pleasure and pain and are capable of happiness, misery, and self-concern.

One of the most puzzling aspects of Locke's account of personal identity is his view of the ontological status of persons (or selves). There are two aspects to the puzzle: his view of the status of *humans* and his view of the status of *persons*. Commentators often assume that, in Locke's view, humans are substances, and the puzzle consists in determining whether persons are also substances. However, there is some reason to believe that in his chapter on identity Locke may have used the term *substance* in a more restricted sense than he did in the rest of the *Essay*. In this more restricted sense, only God, immaterial thinking things, and individual atoms would be particular substances. Cohesive collections of atoms – say, lumps of gold – would be collective substances. Other things that Locke elsewhere speaks of as particular substances – oak trees, horses, and persons, for example – would in this restricted sense of *substance* not be substances at all but, rather, particular mixed modes – that is, functional organizations of particular substances. If this interpretation is correct, then Locke was at least ambivalent about the substantial status of living things, including humans, and perhaps also of inanimate, macroscopic objects such as rocks and chairs. For this and other reasons Locke encouraged the view, perhaps unintentionally, that persons (or selves) are fictions, thereby laying the groundwork for others to question their substantiality, which then became a major issue.

Locke was preoccupied with the implications of *fission-like* examples, ultimately considering a case in which one's little finger is cut off and consciousness, rather than staying with the main part of the body, goes with the little finger. Locke concluded, "Though if the same Body should still live, and immediately from the separation of the little Finger have its own peculiar consciousness, whereof the little Finger knew nothing, it would not at all be concerned for it, as a part of it *self*, or could own any of its Actions, or have any of them imputed to him." In this version of his example, Locke may have been suggesting that the original consciousness went with the finger, while the rest of the body acquired a new consciousness; however, another possibility is that the original consciousness split into two parts, one part in the finger and one in the rest of the body, each part a whole consciousness qualitatively identical to the original. Although it is debatable what Locke had in mind, on the latter reading Locke's case is a genuine fission example, the first fission example to be considered explicitly in the context of personal identity theory Locke did not explore the implications of his example. But once he published his new theory, the fission example cat was out of the bag.

Samuel Clarke (1675–1729) and Anthony Collins (1676–1729)

Between 1706 and 1709 Clarke and Collins confronted each other in a six-part written debate that was well known throughout the century.[15] Their point of departure was the question of whether souls are naturally immortal, where by *soul* they agreed to mean "Substance with a Power of Thinking" or "Individual Consciousness."[16] Clarke defended the traditional Platonic idea that souls are immaterial, and hence indivisible and naturally immortal. Collins countered that the soul is material. Both agreed that individual atoms are not conscious. Their dispute turned on the question of whether it is possible for a *system* of mere matter to think, and hence to be conscious. Clarke argued that it is not possible, Collins that matter does think.

In the course of their debate, Clarke introduced a fission example to show that Collins's attribution of consciousness to material substances leads to a contradiction. The "contradiction" he had in mind arises from considering consciousness as a real property, yet admitting that it can be separated from the substance in which it inheres. Earlier Clarke had argued on general metaphysical grounds that, even though all material substances transform continously into other substances by addition or subtraction of particles, it is "absurd" to suppose that the same numerical property can be "transferred" from one substance to another. Now he argued that in attributing sameness of consciousness over time to a material substance, Collins must really be attributing it to a "flux" of substances, which contradicts the assumption of a real property's inseparability from its substance.[17]

Instead of denying Clarke's assumption directly, Collins replied by introducing *memory* as the faculty that guarantees the persistence of the same consciousness, and hence of the person.[18] He suggested that the forgetting of past but distant actions can be understood by appeal to a failure of transference in the brain, since only if the recollection of past experiences is transferred to new particles of the brain will memory for them be retained. But then, when such recollections are transferred and consciousness of past actions is maintained, consciousness – and ultimately the person – changes substances. His reply thus resulted in shifting the argument to personal identity and, accordingly, refocused Clarke's objection.

Clarke initially replied that Collins's account of transference is "an *impossible* hypothesis":

> [T]hat the *Person* may still be the same, by a continual Superaddition of the *like Consciousness*; notwithstanding the whole *Substance* be changed: Then I say, you make *individual Personality* to be a mere *external imaginary Denomination*, and nothing in reality: Just as a *Ship* is called the *same Ship*, after the whole Substance is changed by frequent Repairs; or a *River* is called the *same River*, though the Water of it be every Day new [...] But he cannot be *really and truly* the *same Person*, unless the *same individual numerical Consciousness* can be transferred from one Subject to another. For, the continued Addition or Exciting of a *like Consciousness* in the new acquired Parts, after

the Manner you suppose; is nothing but a Deception and Delusion, under the Form of Memory; a making the Man to seem himself to be conscious of having done that, which really was not done by him, but by another.[19]

In other words, Clarke's point was that if memory were able to guarantee identity of persons, then persons would be fictional.

Clarke, then, introduced the idea of fission to hammer home the point that such a sequence of like consciousnesses is not the same as a series of acts by a single consciousness:

[S]uch a Consciousness in a Man, whose Substance is wholly changed, can no more make it Just and Equitable for such a Man to be punished for an Action done by another Substance; than the Addition of the like Consciousness (by the Power of God) to two or more new created Men; or to any Number of Men now living, by giving a like Modification to the Motion of the Spirits in the Brain of each of them respectively; could make them All to be one and the same individual Person, at the same time that they remain several and distinct Persons; or make it just and reasonable for all and every one of them to be punished for one and the same individual Action, done by one only, or perhaps by none of them at all.[20]

Collins's view is thus shown to be contradictory, because it would lead in this imaginary fission scenario to saying of two or more individuals both that they are and also are not the same person.

Subsequently Clarke introduced several variations on his fission example, including the following:

If the *same Person*, after *Annihilation*, could, by restoring of the same *Consciousness*, be created again; he might as possibly be created again, by addition of the same *Consciousness* to new Matter, even before Annihilation of the first: From whence it would follow, that Two, or Two Hundred, several Persons, might All, by a Superaddition of the like *Consciousness*, be *one and the same individual Person*, at the same time that they remain *several and distinct Persons*: It being as easy for God to add *my Consciousness* to the new formed Matter of One or of One Hundred Bodies at this *present Time*, as the Dust of my present Body at the *Time of the* Resurrection. And no Reason can be given, why it would not be as just at any time, to punish for my Faults a new created Man, to whom *my Consciousness* is by the Power of God superadded: [...] This inexplicable Confusion, wherewith your Doctrine perplexes the Notion of *personal Identity*, upon which Identity the Justice of all Reward and Punishment manifestly depends; makes the *Resurrection*, in your way of arguing, to be inconceivable and impossible.[21]

Nothing in what Clarke said suggests that he may have been thinking of the fission-descendants in any of these examples as being co-conscious. Rather, his examples support the charge of contradiction only if the descendants are conceived to be, although replicas, distinct persons. Because Clarke's and Collins's debate was well known, both fission examples and the idea that they have implications for personal identity theory were brought to the attention of eighteenth-century theorists.

Joseph Butler (1692–1752)

In *The Analogy of Religion* (1736), Butler argued that people survive their bodily deaths. His argument is based on the claim that each of us is one thing and our bodies another thing. Along the way to this conclusion, he took Locke's observations about the role of appropriation in self-constitution more seriously than any other eighteenth-century critic of Locke. It is "easy to conceive," he said, "how matter, which is no part of ourselves, may be appropriated to us in the manner which our present bodies are."[22] But, he continued, where there is appropriation, there must be an appropriator. Locke had an appropriator in "man," which he distinguished from "person" and allowed might be merely a material organism. However, Butler believed that he had already shown that the appropriator must be something simple and indivisible and, hence, could not possibly be a material organism. This simple and indivisible appropriator, he assumed, is who we truly are. What this being appropriates, he went on to conclude, is not thereby part of itself, something it *is*, but rather, merely something it *owns*.

Butler astutely conceded that this appropriator might be a simple *material* entity. But, he said, since "we have *no way of determining by experience* what is the certain bulk of the living being each man calls himself, and yet, till it be determined that it is larger in bulk than the solid elementary particles of matter, which there is no ground to think any natural power can dissolve, there is no sort of reason to think death to be the dissolution of it, of the living being, even though it should not be absolutely indiscerpible." And since each of us has already "passed undestroyed through those many and great revolutions of matter, so peculiarly appropriated to us ourselves; why should we imagine death will be so fatal to us?"[23] Butler, although drawing on Plato, had learned from Locke that, for all we know, the thinking principle within us is material. Butler, in effect, adapted Plato's argument for immortality to the purposes of an age in which materialism was on the rise. For Butler, it is our simplicity, not our immateriality, that ensures our survival.

The heart of Butler's view is his claim that our bodies are not us, but things we own, our instruments. We are agents that use these instruments. It is as if our bodies were artifacts – as if, in relation to them, we are pilots in a ship. But, in Butler's view, our bodies are artifacts made not by humans but by nature, and hence, ultimately, by God: "We see with our eyes only in the same manner as we do with glasses."[24] "Upon the whole, then, our organs of sense and our limbs are certainly instruments, which the living persons, ourselves, make use of to perceive and move with: there is not any probability, that they are any more; nor consequently, that we have any other kind of relation to them, than what we may have to any other foreign matter formed into instruments of perception and motion, suppose into a microscope of a staff."[25]

When Butler turned to the topic of personal identity *per se*, the story is much the same. Here also, particularly in the uses he made not only of the notion of appropriation but also of that of concernment, he showed that he had learned his lessons from Locke: "For, personal identity has been explained so by some, as to render the inquiry concerning a future life of no consequence at all to us the persons who are making it."[26] Butler, in response to what he clearly saw as the dangers of empirical analysis, proposed that we take as primitive the idea of *personal identity*. Like the notion of *equality*, he said, it defies analysis. Just as by observing two triangles, he said, we can determine intuitively that they are equal, so also by observing ourselves in the present and remembering ourselves in the past, we can determine intuitively that we have persisted.

Butler said that we can thus determine that we have persisted not just in "a loose and popular sense" of *same*, such as we might employ in saying of a mature oak that it is the same tree as stood in its spot fifty years previously, even though it and that former tree have not one atom in common. Rather, we can determine that identity of persons obtains in "the strict and philosophical sense," which requires sameness of substance: "In a loose and popular sense, then, the life, and the organization, and the plant are justly said to be the same, not withstanding the perpetual change of the parts. But in a strict and philosophical manner of speech, no man, no being, no mode of being, no anything can be the same with that, with which it hath indeed nothing the same."[27]

In Butler's view, even though we can determine intuitively through memory that we are the same as some person who lived earlier, our current consciousness of that fact is not the same as our consciousness in the past. Each episode of consciousness is a mode of the being who is conscious. The modes come and go. The being persists. Thus, even if it were possible to provide a conceptual or empirical analysis of *personal identity*, it would not be possible to do so by appealing to sameness of consciousness, which is one more reason, he thought, if one were needed, why Locke's account of the matter will not do. On the other hand, if, *per impossible*, our being did just consist in successive acts of consciousness, then "it must follow, that it is a fallacy upon ourselves, to charge our present selves with anything we did, or to imagine our present selves interested in anything which befell us yesterday; or that our present self will be interested in what will befall us to-morrow; since our present self is not, in reality, the same with the self of yesterday, but another like self or person coming in its room, and mistaken for it: to which another self will succeed to-morrow."[28]

In other words, in Butler's view, if selfhood were as Locke has portrayed it, we would have no reason to be *concerned* either with past or future stages of ourselves, for these would be ourselves only in a *fictitious* sense; and, in an apparent allusion to fission, Butler insisted that *calling* people to whom we are only so related ourselves would not make them ourselves: "So, I think, it appears, they [Lockeans] do not, mean, that the person is *really* the same, but only that he is so in a fictitious sense: in such a sense as they assert, for this they do assert, that any number of persons whatever may be the same person." But can Butler *show* that this unwelcome conclusion – that persons are fictions – is actually false? Not really, and he knows it. True to his method, though, he did not feel that he had to show it. Why show what is obvious? "The bare unfolding this notion, and laying it thus naked and open, seems the best confutation of it."[29] Butler's death, in 1752, marks the end of an era in which religion dominated the philosophy of human nature. Henceforth, in the eighteenth century, empirical philosophy would dominate it. Later still, but gradually and in stages, psychology would become an experimental science.

David Hume (1711–1776)

When Locke, in 1690, published his *Essay*, he dreamt of the emergence of a science of human nature. When Hume, in 1739, published *A Treatise of Human Nature*, he assumed that a science of human nature had already emerged.[30] Hume's dream was not of the empirical philosophy of human nature's emerging, but of its assuming its rightful position among the sciences, as the foundation of a mighty edifice of human knowledge.

In Book I of the *Treatise* Hume argued that belief in a substantial, persisting self is an illusion. More generally, he was intent on showing that belief in the persistence of anything is an illusion. However, he also addressed the task of explaining why people are so susceptible to the illusion of self. And in Book II he explained how certain dynamic mentalistic systems in which we represent ourselves to ourselves, as well as to others, actually work, such as those systems in us that generate sympathetic responses to others. In these more psychological projects, he took for granted many things that in Book I he had subjected to withering skeptical criticism.

In Hume's view, since all ideas arise from impressions, and there is no impression of a "simple and continu'd" self, there is no idea of such a self. This critique of traditional views led him to formulate his alternative, "bundle" conception of the self, and also to compare the mind to a kind of theater in which none of the actors – the "perceptions [that] successively make their appearance" – is the traditional self, since none, strictly speaking, is either "simple" at a time or identical over time. Beyond that, he claimed, humans do not even have minds, except as fictional constructions. Thus, in his view, a crucial respect in which minds are not analogous to real theaters is that there is no site for the mental performance, at least none of which we have knowledge; rather, there "are the successive perceptions only, that constitute the mind; nor have we the most distant notion of the place, where these scenes are represented, or of the materials, of which it is compos'd."[31]

With these philosophical preliminaries out of the way, Hume turned to the psychological task of explaining how objects that are constantly changing, including the materials out of which we ourselves are constructed, nevertheless seem to persist. To begin, he distinguished "betwixt personal identity, as it regards our thought or imagination, and as it regards our passions or the concern we take in ourselves."[32] The difference that he had in mind is between, on the one hand, explaining why we regard anything that changes, including ourselves, as persisting over time (this is personal identity as it regards our thought or imagination) and, on the other, explaining the role that belief in ourselves as things that persist over time and through changes plays in the ways we represent ourselves to ourselves and to others (this is personal identity as it regards our passions or the concern we take in ourselves). The first of these occupied Hume in most of the remainder of Book I, the second in most of Book II.

In explaining personal identity as it regards our thought or imagination, the crucial psychological question for Hume was that of figuring out what causes us to forge a succession of perceptions into a persisting object. His answer, in one word, is: resemblance. When successive perceptions resemble each other, he said, it is easy to imagine that the first simply persists. In fact, "our propensity to this mistake" is so ubiquitous and strong "that we fall into it before we are aware." And even when we become aware of our error, "we cannot long sustain our philosophy, or take off this biass from the imagination."[33] Later, Hume would claim – perhaps with Locke's prince and cobbler example in mind – that "all the nice and subtle questions concerning personal identity" are merely verbal. In the present context, he insisted that "the controversy concerning identity is not merely a dispute of words."

Usually, Hume continued, when people attribute identity "to variable or interrupted objects," their "mistake" is "attended with a fiction."[34] They believe that the identity, which they have claimed obtains, is not just their (perhaps pragmatically motivated) decision to regard distinct but similar objects as the same, but that those objects really are the same, perhaps even that what makes them the same is the existence of some unifying substance, such as soul, or some unifying mode, such as life or consciousness. Thus, in his view, normally it is not just that someone, in full knowledge of the facts, innocently chooses to call distinct objects which resemble each other the same object, but rather that the person who chooses to do this is immersed in a cloud of metaphysical confusion. He concluded this part of his discussion by comparing "the soul" to "a republic or commonwealth," the seeming persistence of which is guaranteed by the relations among its parts, rather than by the persistence of any of its parts.[35]

In Locke's view, memory plays a crucial role in constituting personal identity. In Hume's view, it does so also, but for different reasons: It not only creates resemblances among successive perceptions, but also reveals to us that our perceptions are causally linked, information we then use as a basis for extending our identities to periods of our lives that we do not remember.[36] In connection with the topic of forgetfulness, Hume said that in his view, which presumably he intended to contrast with the views of Locke and perhaps also of Collins, "memory does not so much produce as discover personal identity, by shewing us the relation of cause and effect among our different perceptions." He added that it is "incumbent on those who affirm that memory produces entirely our personal identity, to give a reason why we can thus extend our identity beyond our memory."[37]

Hume extended his critique by questioning the seriousness of trying to make fine-grained distinctions, perhaps especially in the case of especially contrived, hypothetical examples, about whether personal identity obtains. He said, "Identity depends on the relations of ideas; and these relations produce identity, by means of that easy transition they occasion. But, as the relations and the easiness of the transition may diminish by insensible degrees, we have no just standard by which we can decide any dispute concerning the time when they acquire or lose a title to the name of identity." It follows, he said, that "all the disputes concerning the identity of connected objects are merely verbal, except so far as the relation of parts gives rise to some fiction or imaginary principle of union."[38] In sum, Hume's view seems to have been that disputes about identity are merely verbal if they are about which relations, were they to obtain, would constitute identity. But the disputes are based on substantive mistakes if the disputants suppose that what is merely successive is really the same. In any case, such disputes are always about fictitious imaginary constructs. In his view, that is all there is to say about identity over time and through changes. Thus Hume may have thought that a crucial difference between Locke and himself on the question of personal identity is that whereas Locke thought that there is a fact of the matter about whether a person persists, he thought that there is a fact of the matter only about the circumstances under which the illusion of persistence is nourished.

In discussing personal identity, Hume never discussed fission directly, and he had little to say, and nothing new, about how personal identity might be analyzed in a way that links it to questions of accountability and interestedness. However, in his discussion of the example of a church that burns down and then is rebuilt, it seems that he may have been aware of the special problems for judgments of identity that arise in the case of fission. In claiming that, "without breach of the propriety of language," we might regard the two churches as the same church even if the first was of brick and the second "of free-stone," he added the caveat, "but we must observe, that in these cases the first object is in manner annihilated before the second comes into existence; by which means, we are never presented in any one point of time with the idea of difference and multiplicity; and for that reason are less scrupulous in calling them the same."[39]

Thomas Reid (1710–1796)

Reid criticized Hume for supposing that there is nothing more to mind than a "succession of related ideas and impressions, of which we have an intimate memory and consciousness." He asked "to be farther instructed, whether the impressions remember and are conscious of the ideas, or the ideas remember and are conscious of the impressions, or if both remember and are conscious of both? and whether the ideas remember those that come after them, as well as those that were before them?" His point was that since ideas and impressions are passive, they cannot do anything, whereas Hume implied that the "succession of ideas and impressions not only remembers and is conscious" but also "judges, reasons, affirms, denies," even "eats and drinks, and is sometimes merry and sometimes sad." Reid concluded, "If these things can be ascribed to a succession of ideas and impressions in a consistency of common sense, I should be very glad to know what is nonsense." He concluded that in any view in which substance has no place, agency would have no place either.[40] Since Reid thought it would be absurd to deny agency, substance had to be reintroduced. But whereas he assumed that the need for substance is an argument for immaterial substance, actually, so far as his argument goes, it shows at most only the need for substance of some sort.

From Essays on the Intellectual Powers of Man (1785), Chapter 4 of "Of Memory": Of Identity

The conviction which every man has of his identity, as far back as his memory reaches, needs no aid of philosophy to strengthen it; and no philosophy can weaken it, without first producing some degree of insanity. [...]

We may observe, first of all, that this conviction is indispensably necessary to all exercise of reason. The operations of reason, whether in action or in speculation, are made up of successive parts. The antecedent are the foundation of the consequent, and, without the conviction that the antecedent have been seen or done by me, I could have no reason to proceed to the consequent, in any speculation, or in any active project whatever.

There can be no memory of what is past without the conviction that we existed at the time remembered. There may be good arguments to convince me that I existed before the earliest thing I can remember; but to suppose that my memory reaches a moment farther back than my belief and conviction of my existence, is a contradiction.

The moment a man loses this conviction, as if he had drunk the water of Lethe, past things are done away; and, in his own belief, he then begins to exist. Whatever was thought, or said, or done, or suffered before that period, may belong to some other person; but he can never impute it to himself, or take any subsequent step that supposes it to be his doing.

From this it is evident that we must have the conviction of our own continued existence and identity, as soon as we are capable of thinking or doing anything, on account of what we have thought, or done, or suffered before; that is, as soon as we are reasonable creatures.

That we may form as distinct a notion as we are able of this phenomenon of the human mind, it is proper to consider what is meant by identity in general, what by our own personal identity, and how we are led into that invincible belief and conviction which every man has of his own personal identity, as far as his memory reaches.

Identity in general I take to be a relation between a thing which is known to exist at one time, and a thing which is known to have existed at another time. If you ask whether they are one and the same, or two different things, every man of common sense understands the meaning of your question perfectly. Whence we may infer with certainty, that every man of common sense has a clear and distinct notion of identity.

If you ask a definition of identity, I confess I can give none; it is too simple a notion to admit of logical definition: I can say it is a relation, but I cannot find words to express the specific difference between this and other relations, though I am in no danger of confounding it with any other. I can say that diversity is a contrary relation, and that similitude and dissimilitude are another couple of contrary relations, which every man easily distinguishes in his conception from identity and diversity.

I see evidently that identity supposes an uninterrupted continuance of existence. That which has ceased to exist cannot be the same with that which afterwards begins to exist; for this would be to suppose a being to exist after it ceased to exist, and to have had existence before it was produced, which are manifest contradictions. Continued uninterrupted existence is therefore necessarily implied in identity.

Hence we may infer, that identity cannot, in its proper sense, be applied to our pains, our pleasures, our thought, or any operation of our minds. The pain felt this day is not the same individual pain which I felt yesterday, though they may be *similar* in kind and degree, and have the same cause. The same may be said of every feeling, and of every operation of mind. They are all successive in their nature, like time itself, no two moments of which can be the same moment. [...]

All mankind place their personality in something that cannot be divided or consist of parts. A part of a person is a manifest absurdity. When a man loses his estate, his health, his strength, he is still the same person, and has lost nothing of his personality. If he has a leg or an arm cut off, he is the same person he was before. The amputated member is no part of his person, otherwise it would have a right to a part of his estate, and be liable for a part of his engagements. It would be entitled to a share of his merit and demerit, which is manifestly absurd. A person is something indivisible, and is what Leibniz calls a *monad*.

My personal identity, therefore, implies the continued existence of that indivisible thing which I call *myself*. Whatever this self may be, it is something which thinks, and deliberates, and resolves, and acts, and suffers. I am not thought, I am not action, I am not feeling; I am something that thinks, and acts, and suffers. My thoughts, and actions, and feelings, change every moment: they have no continued, but a successive, existence; but that *self*, or *I*, to which they belong, is permanent, and has the same relation to all the succeeding thoughts, actions, and feelings which I call mine.

Such are the notions that I have of my personal identity. But perhaps it may be said, this may all be fancy without reality. How do you know – what evidence have you – that there is such a permanent self which has a claim to all the thoughts, actions, and feelings which you call yours?

To this I answer, that the proper evidence I have of all this is remembrance, I remember that twenty years ago I conversed with such a person; I remember several things that passed in that conversation: my memory testifies, not only that this was done, but that it was done by me who now remember it. If it was done by me, I must have existed at that time, and continued to exist from that time to the present: if the identical person whom I call myself had not a part in that conversation, my memory is fallacious; it gives a distinct and positive testimony of what is not true. Every man in his senses believes what he distinctly remembers, and every thing he remembers convinces him that he existed at the time remembered.

Although memory gives the most irresistible evidence of my being the identical person that did such a thing, at such a time, I may have other good evidence of things which befell me, and which I do not remember: I know who bare me, and suckled me, but I do not remember these events.

It may here be observed (though the observation would have been unnecessary, if some great philosophers had not contradicted it), that it is not my remembering any action of mine that makes me to be the person who did it. This remembrance makes me to know assuredly that I did it; but I might have done it, though I did not remember it. That relation to me, which is expressed by saying that I did it, would be the same, though I had not the least remembrance of it. To say that my remembering that I did such a thing, or, as some choose to express it, my being conscious that I did it, makes me to have done it, appears to me as great an absurdity as it would be to say, that my belief that the world was created made it to be created.

When we pass judgment on the identity of other persons than ourselves, we proceed upon other grounds, and determine from a variety of circumstances, which sometimes produce the firmest assurance, and sometimes leave room for doubt. The identity of persons has often furnished matter of serious litigation before tribunals of justice. But no man of a sound mind ever doubted of his own identity, as far as he distinctly remembered.

The identity of a person is a perfect identity: wherever it is real, it admits of no degrees; and it is impossible that a person should be in part the same, and in part different; because a person is a *monad*, and is not divisible into parts. The evidence of identity in other persons than ourselves does indeed admit of all degrees, from what we account certainty, to the least degree of probability. But still it is true, that the same person is perfectly the same, and cannot be so in part, or in some degree only. [...]

Thus it appears, that the evidence we have of our own identity, as far back as we remember, is totally of a different kind from the evidence we have of the identity of other persons, or of objects of sense. The first is grounded on memory, and gives undoubted certainty. The last is grounded on similarity, and on other circumstances, which in many cases are not so decisive as to leave no room for doubt.

It may likewise be observed, that the identity of objects of sense is never perfect. All bodies, as they consist of innumerable parts that may be disjoined from them by a great variety of causes, are subject to continual changes of their substance, increasing, diminishing, changing insensibly. When such alterations are gradual, because language could not afford a different name for every different state of such a changeable being, it retains the same name, and is considered as the same thing. Thus we say of an old regiment, that it did such a thing a century ago, though there now is not a man alive who then belonged to it. We say a tree is the same in the seed-bed and in the forest. A ship of war, which has successively changed her anchors, her tackle, her sails, her masts, her planks, and her timbers, while she keeps the same name, is the same.

The identity, therefore, which we ascribe to bodies, whether natural or artificial, is not perfect identity; it is rather something which, for the convenience of speech, we call identity. It admits of a great change of the subject, providing the change be gradual; sometimes, even of a total change. And the changes which in common language are made consistent with identity differ from those that are thought to destroy it, not in kind, but in number and degree. It has no fixed nature when applied to bodies; and questions about the identity of a body are very often questions about words. But identity, when applied to persons, has no ambiguity, and admits not of degrees, or of more and less. It is the foundation of all rights and obligations, and of all accountableness; and the notion of it is fixed and precise.

Chapter 6 of "Of Memory": Of Mr. Locke's Account of Our Personal Identity

[...] Mr. Locke tells us [...] "that personal identity, that is, the sameness of a rational being, consists in consciousness alone, and, as far as this consciousness can be extended backwards to any past action or thought, so far reaches the identity of that person. So that whatever has the consciousness of present and past actions is the same person to whom they belong."

This doctrine has some strange consequences, which the author was aware of. Such as, that if the same consciousness can be transferred from one intelligent being to another, which he thinks we cannot show to be impossible, *then two or twenty intelligent beings may be the same person.* And if the intelligent being may lose the consciousness of the actions done by him, which surely is possible, then he is not the person that did those actions; so that *one intelligent being may be two or twenty different persons,* if he shall so often lose the consciousness of this former actions.

There is another consequence of this doctrine, which follows no less necessarily, though Mr. Locke probably did not see it. It is, *that a man may be, and at the same time not be, the person that did a particular action.*

Suppose a brave officer to have been flogged when a boy at school for robbing an orchard, to have taken a standard from the enemy in his first campaign, and to have been made a general in advanced life; suppose, also, which must be admitted to be possible, that, when he took the standard, he was conscious of his having been flogged at school, and that, when made a general, he was conscious of his taking the standard, but had absolutely lost the consciousness of his flogging.

These things being supposed, it follows, from Mr. Locke's doctrine, that he who was flogged at school is the same person who took the standard, and that he who took the standard is the same person who was made a general. Whence it follows, if there be any truth in logic, that the general is the same person with him who was flogged at school. But the general's consciousness does not reach so far back as his flogging; therefore, according to Mr. Locke's doctrine, he is not the person who was flogged. Therefore the general is, and at the same time is not, the same person with him who was flogged at school.

Leaving the consequences of this doctrine to those who have leisure to trace them, we may observe, with regard to the doctrine itself,

First, that Mr. Locke attributes to consciousness the conviction we have of our past actions, as if a man may now be conscious of what he did twenty years ago. It is impossible to understand the meaning of this, unless by consciousness he meant memory, the only faculty by which we have an immediate knowledge of our past actions. [...]

When, therefore, Mr. Locke's notion of personal identity is properly expressed, it is, that personal identity consists in distinct remembrance: for, even in the popular sense, to say that I am conscious of a past action means nothing else than that I distinctly remember that I did it.

Secondly, it may be observed, that, in this doctrine, not only is consciousness confounded with memory, but, which is still more strange, personal identity is confounded with the evidence which we have of our personal identity.

It is very true, that my remembrance that I did such a thing is the evidence I have that I am the identical person who did it. And this, I am apt to think, Mr. Locke meant. But to say that my remembrance that I did such a thing, or my consciousness, makes me the person who did it, is, in my apprehension, an absurdity too gross to be entertained by any man who attends to the meaning of it; for it is to attribute to memory or consciousness a strange magical power of producing its object, though that object must have existed before the memory or consciousness which produced it. [. . .]

When a horse that was stolen is found and claimed by the owner, the only evidence he can have, or that a judge or witnesses can have, that this is the very identical horse which was his property, is similitude. But would it not be ridiculous from this to infer that the identity of a horse consists in similitude only? The only evidence I have that I am the identical person who did such actions is, that I remember distinctly I did them; or, as Mr. Locke expresses it, I am conscious I did them. To infer from this, that personal identity consists in consciousness, is an argument which, if it had any force, would prove the identity of a stolen horse to consist solely in similitude.

Thirdly, is it not strange that the sameness or identity of a person should consist in a thing which is continually changing, and is not any two minutes the same?

Our consciousness, our memory, and every operation of the mind, are still flowing like the water of a river, or like time itself. The consciousness I have this moment can no more be the same consciousness I had last moment, than this moment can be the last moment. Identity can only be affirmed of things which have a continued existence. Consciousness, and every kind of thought, are transient and momentary, and have no continued existence; and, therefore, if personal identity consisted in consciousness, it would certainly follow, that no man is the same person any two moments of his life; and as the right and justice of reward and punishment are founded on personal identity, no man could be responsible for his actions. [. . .]

Fourthly, there are many expressions used by Mr. Locke, in speaking of personal identity, which to me are altogether unintelligible, unless we suppose that he confounded that sameness or identity which we ascribed to an individual with the identity which, in common discourse, is often ascribed to many individuals of the same species. [. . .]

When Mr. Locke, therefore, speaks of "the same consciousness being continued through a succession of different substances;" when he speaks of "repeating the idea of a past action, with the same consciousness we had of it at the first," and of "the same consciousness extending to actions past and to come"; these expressions are to me unintelligible, unless he means not the same individual consciousness, but a consciousness that is similar, or of the same kind.

If our personal identity consists in consciousness, as this consciousness cannot be the same individually any two moments, but only of the same kind, it would follow, that we are not for any two moments the same individual persons, but the same kind of persons.

As our consciousness sometimes ceases to exist, as in sound sleep, our personal identity must cease with it. Mr. Locke allows, that the same thing cannot have two beginnings of existence, so that our identity would be irrecoverably gone every time we ceased to think, if it was but for a moment.

Although Reid did not specifically say so, he seemed to have supposed that, if we are rational, we automatically take ownership of the past thoughts, experiences, and actions that we remember. It seems, then, that Reid's continuing commitment to a reflexive account at least of memory, if not of all consciousness, may have prevented him from extending his new approach to a developmental account of the acquisition of self-concepts.

William Hazlitt (1778–1830)

Hazlitt's first work, *An Essay on the Principles of Human Action*, was published in 1805, when he was 27 years old.[41] It was the culmination of a kind of perspective on personal identity that had begun with Locke and been developed by Collins, Hume, and Priestley. Yet, with respect to certain questions that would become important in our own times, Hazlitt reads more like one of our contemporaries than any of his predecessors. He wrote that he was led to his central realizations by wondering "whether it could properly be said to be an act of virtue in anyone to sacrifice his own final happiness to that of any other person or number of persons, if it were possible for the one ever to be made the price of the other." Suppose that one could save 20 other persons by voluntarily consenting to suffer for them. "Why," he asked, "should I not do a generous thing, and never trouble myself about what might be the consequence to myself the Lord knows when?"

On behalf of common sense, Hazlitt answered that "however insensible" he may be now to his own interest in the future, when the time comes, he shall feel differently about it and "shall bitterly regret" his "folly and insensibility." So, he continued, still replying on behalf of common sense, "I ought, as a rational agent, to be determined now by what I shall then wish I had done, when I shall feel the consequences of my actions most deeply and sensibly." Hazlitt was dissatisfied with this commonsense answer. He claimed that he could not "have a principle of active self-interest arising out of the immediate connection" between his "present and future self," since there neither was nor could be any such connection. "I am what I am in spite of the future," he continued. "My feelings, actions, and interests must be determined by causes already existing and acting, and are absolutely independent of the future." Where there is no "intercommunity of feelings," he concluded, "there can be no identity of interests."[42]

Hazlitt conceded that because we remember only our own past experiences and are directly "conscious" only of our own present experiences, in relation to the past and the present people are naturally self-interested.[43] The reasons for this, he said, are physiological. Memories depend on physical traces of prior sensations, and these traces are not communicated among individuals. Present sensations depend on the stimulation of one's nerves, and "there is no communication between my nerves, and another's brain, by means of which he can be affected with my sensations as I am myself." In the case of the future, however, Hazlitt stressed that people are neither "mechanically" nor "exclusively" connected to themselves. They cannot be, he thought, since no one's future yet exists. Instead, people are connected both to their own futures and to the futures of others by anticipation, which, unlike memory and sensation, is a function of imagination, and thus does not respect the difference between self and other.[44] He maintained that to feel future-oriented concern for someone, one first must project oneself imaginatively into the feelings of that person, and imagination, functioning "naturally" – that is, independently of its having acquired a bias through learning – projects as easily into the feelings of others as into one's own future feelings.

It was in Hazlitt's account of the role of self-conceptions in our values and in our views of our own interests that he contrasts most sharply with the eighteenth-century tradition of which he was the culmination. According to him, people are naturally concerned about whether someone is pleased or suffers as a consequence of their actions. This is because "there is something in the very idea of good, or evil, which naturally excites desire or aversion." But, he wrote, before the acquisition of self-concepts, people are indifferent about whether those who may be pleased or suffer are themselves or others: "a child first distinctly wills or pursues his own good," he said, "not because it is his but because it is good." As a consequence, he claimed, "what is personal or selfish in our affections" is due to "time and habit," the rest to "the principle of a disinterested love of good as such, or for its own sake, without any regard to personal distinctions."[45] He claimed that such considerations provide a basis for founding morality not on self-interest, which he regarded as an "artificial" value, but on the natural concern people have to seek happiness and avoid unhappiness, regardless of whose it is.[46]

Hazlitt's adoption of this perspective prompted him to ask a question which did not arise as starkly or in the same form for any of his predecessors. The question was: If people connect to the future through imagination, which does not respect the difference between self and other, why is the force of habit almost invariably on the side of selfish feelings? In answering, he tried to account for the growth of selfish motives in humans by appeal to their acquisition of self-concepts. In his view, when very young children behave selfishly, it is not because they like themselves better than others, but because they know their own wants and pleasures better. In older children and adults, he thought, it is because they have come under the control of their self-concepts, which is something that happens in three stages. First, young children acquire an idea of themselves as beings who are capable of experiencing pleasure and pain. Second, and almost "mechanically" (since physiology insures that children remember only their own pasts), children include their own pasts in their notions of themselves. Finally, imaginatively, they include their own futures.[47] The first two of these stages may have been suggested to Hazlitt by his reading of Locke. The third, at least in the way he developed it, is original. However, even in the case of the first two, Hazlitt thought of these stages less as a philosopher and more as a psychologist might think of them, in terms of the acquisition of self-concepts, and whereas it was unclear whether Locke meant to distinguish developmental stages in the acquisition of self-concepts, Hazlitt clearly meant to do so.

Hazlitt claimed that a bias in favor of ourselves in the future could never "have gained the assent of thinking men" but for "the force" with which a future-oriented idea of self "habitually clings to the mind of every man, binding it as with a spell, deadening its discriminating powers, and spreading the confused associations which belong only to past and present impressions over the whole of our imaginary existence." However, whereas a host of previous thinkers – Descartes, Locke, Berkeley, Butler, and others – thought that people have an intuitive knowledge of their own identities, Hazlitt rejected as "wild and absurd" the idea that we have an "absolute, metaphysical identity" with ourselves in the future, and hence that people have identities that are available to be intuited. We have been misled, he claimed, by language: by "a mere play of words." In his view, both children and adults fail to look beyond the common idioms of personal identity, and as a consequence routinely mistake linguistic fictions for metaphysical realities. To say that someone has a "general interest" in whatever concerns his own future welfare "is no more," he insisted, "than affirming that [he] shall have an interest in that welfare, or that [he is] nominally and in certain other respects the same being who will hereafter have a real interest in it." No amount of mere telling "me that I have the same interest in my future sensations as if they were present, because I am the same individual," he claimed, can bridge the gulf between the "real" mechanical connections I have to myself in the past and present and the merely verbal and imaginary connections that I have to myself in the future.[48]

Since people have no mechanical connections to themselves in the future, it follows, Hazlitt thought, that so far as people's "real" interests are concerned, their "selves" in the future are essentially others. If you've injured yourself, you may in the present suffer as a consequence. But "the injury that I may do to my future interest will not certainly by any kind of reaction return to punish me for my neglect of my own happiness." Rather, he concluded, "I am always free from the consequences of my actions. The interests of the being who acts, and of the being who suffers are never one." So, it makes no difference "whether [you] pursue [your] own welfare or entirely neglect it."[49] Your suffering in the future is only nominally your suffering.

In sum, Hazlitt gave a psychological account of how people come to identify with their future selves, from which he drew a metaphysical conclusion: that people's seeming identities with their future selves are based on an illusion. He then used this metaphysical conclusion as the basis for an inference to a normative conclusion: that we have no self-interested reason to be concerned about the fate of our future selves.

Hazlitt's consideration of fission examples occurred in the context of his critique of the Lockean idea that one's identity extends as far as one's consciousness extends. What, Hazlitt asked, would a theorist committed to this idea say "if that consciousness should be transferred to some other being?" How would such a person know that he or she had not been "imposed upon by a false claim of identity"? He answered, on behalf of the Lockeans, that the idea of one's consciousness extending to someone else "is ridiculous": a person has "no other self than that which arises from this very consciousness." But, he countered, after our deaths:

> this self may be multiplied in as many different beings as the Deity may think proper to endue with the same consciousness; which if it can be so renewed at will in any one instance, may clearly be so in a hundred others. Am I to regard all these as equally myself? Am I equally interested in the fate of all? Or if I must fix upon some one of them in particular as my

representative and other self, how am I to be determined in my choice? Here, then, I saw an end put to my speculations about absolute self-interest and personal identity.[50]

Thus, Hazlitt saw that, hypothetically, psychological continuity might not continue in a single stream but instead might divide. In asking the two questions "Am I to regard all of these [fission-descendants] as equally myself?" "and Am I equally interested in the fate of all [of these fission-descendants]?," he correctly separated the question of whether identity tracks psychological continuity from that of whether self-concern tracks it. And, in direct anticipation of what would not occur again to other philosophers until the 1960s, he concluded that because of the possibility of fission neither identity nor self-concern necessarily tracks psychological continuity.

Hazlitt also used fission examples to call into question whether, in cases in which there is no fission, a person's present self-interest extends to his or her self in the future. He began by asking:

> How then can this pretended unity of consciousness which is only reflected from the past, which makes me so little acquainted with the future that I cannot even tell for a moment how long it will be continued, whether it will be entirely interrupted by or renewed in me after death, and which might be multiplied in I don't know how many different beings and prolonged by complicated sufferings without my being any the wiser for it, how I say can a principle of this sort identify my present with my future interests, and make me as much a participator in what does not at all affect me as if it were actually impressed on my senses?

Hazlitt's answer was that it cannot.

> It is plain, as this conscious being may be decompounded, entirely destroyed, renewed again, or multiplied in a great number of beings, and as, whichever of these takes place, it cannot produce the least alteration in my present being – that what I am does not depend on what I am to be, and that there is no communication between my future interests and the motives by which my present conduct must be governed.

He concluded:

> I cannot, therefore, have a principle of active self-interest arising out of the immediate connection between my present and future self, for no such connection exists, or is possible. [...] My personal interest in any thing

must refer either to the interest excited by the actual impression of the object which cannot be felt before it exists, and can last no longer than while the impression lasts, or it may refer to the particular manner in which I am mechanically affected by the idea of my own impressions in the absence of the object. I can therefore have no proper personal interest in my future impressions. [...] The only reason for my preferring my future interest to that of others, must arise from my anticipating it with greater warmth of present imagination.[51]

With the exception of F. H. Bradley, such ideas would not be taken seriously again until the 1950s.[52] They would not become a focus of discussion among philosophers until the 1970s. Hazlitt not only conceded, but embraced and celebrated, the idea that the self is a fictional construct since, in his view, this idea had the further implication that people have no special ("self-interested") reason to value their future selves. At least to his own satisfaction, and in a way that clearly anticipated the work of Derek Parfit and others in our own times, Hazlitt tried to explain how the idea that the self is a fiction, far from being destructive to theories of rationality and ethics, actually made them better. In the process, he sowed the seeds, albeit on barren ground, of a modern psychology of the acquisition of self-concepts and of a modern approach to separating the traditional philosophical problem of personal identity from the question of what matters in survival.

Hazlitt was the last progressive figure in a more or less continuous tradition of discussion of the nature of self and personal identity that began with Locke and that took place in Britain throughout the eighteenth century. Two things were mainly responsible for interrupting this tradition. One was the newly emerging separation of philosophy and psychology, which, throughout the nineteenth and increasingly into the twentieth centuries, tended to go their separate ways. Another was Kant, whose *Critique of Pure Reason* was published in Germany in 1781, but only began to be taken seriously in Britain at the beginning of the nineteenth century. However, once Kant's influence was felt, it effectively changed the focus of debate about the self.

Immanuel Kant (1724–1804)

There are four parts to Kant's views about the self: his thoughts on the soul; his theory of the noumenal self; his remarks on personal identity over time; and his thoughts on the role of self-conceptions in the unity of consciousness – what Kant, elaborating on terminology borrowed from Leibniz, called *the transcendental unity of apperception*.

In a memorable remark, Kant said that the whole point of his philosophy was to "deny knowledge in order to make room for faith." But that is only half of the truth about his philosophy. The other half is his denial of skepticism in order to make room for knowledge. In Kant's view, these two projects are intimately intertwined.

Kant's theory of the noumenal world is the key to his dual project of making a secure place both for knowledge and for faith, and has implications for his theory of the soul. The basic idea behind his theory of the noumenal world is that reality as it is itself – the noumenal world – is radically different from reality as it is in our experience – the phenomenal world. The difference between these "two worlds" is due to the fact that humans structure the objects of their experience in basic ways that don't reflect the intrinsic nature of these objects. In other words, in Kant's view, the human mind does not merely receive simple ideas of sensation, as Locke suggested, but in the process of receiving them imposes structure on what it receives. Thus, the mind in sensation is not merely passive, a *tabula rasa*, but active. A fundamental aspect of this "human" structuring of experience consists in spatial and temporal relationships. In other words, the world as it exists in itself – the noumenal world – is neither spatially nor temporally extended, whereas the world that we experience – the phenomenal world – is both. Since every real object exists both noumenally and phenomenally, so does the self, if it is real. Hence, there would be a noumenal self that is never experienced as it is in itself, and that lacks spatial and temporal extension, and a phenomenal self that is capable of being experienced and that has at least temporal extension.

In regard to personal identity, Locke had thought that the criterion of personal identity over time is sameness of consciousness. Kant disagreed. He thought that personal identity could not simply consist in sameness of consciousness, since someone's consciousness might be qualitatively similar to that of someone *else* who had existed previously. Delusions of memory, which Locke acknowledged may occur, are an obvious case in point. Kant concluded that if personal identity is going to be something that can be determined empirically, then it cannot consist simply in psychological continuity, but must consist also, or instead, in some sort of physical continuity. Thus, Kant required a more objective criterion of personal identity than did Locke.

Locke and Kant both have a relations view of personal identity over time, rather than a substance view. But whereas for Locke the relations that matter are wholly psychological, for Kant they are at least partly physical. In Kant's view, the requirement that the self be partly physical applies only to the phenomenal self, or, as he sometimes called it, *the empirical self*. It does not apply to the noumenal self, which is not temporally extended and for which no problem of personal identity over time can arise. Nevertheless, Kant held that the notion of the noumenal self is useful as a regulative idea – that is, an idea that we need for certain practical purposes, including to give us a motive to be moral and to hope for the future. We cannot know that there is any reality to this regulative idea, but neither can we act as if there were no reality to it. Hence, the immaterial substance survives in Kant's view, not as something that we can know, but as an idea that we need.

There is one final dimension of Kant's reflections on the self, which he calls *the transcendental unity of apperception*. He maintained that accompanying each experience is an "I think," which is the logical subject of the experience. In his view, there can be no experience which is not the experience of a subject. To this extent he may seem to be saying simply that thought requires a thinker, which is more or less the move that Descartes made in attempting to prove the existence of a substantial self. The difference, however, is that by *thinker* Kant doesn't mean substantial self, but something more intimately connected with experience. In one place, he tried to explain what this intimate connection consists in by saying that "in the synthetic original unity of apperception, I am conscious of myself, not as I appear to myself, nor as I am in myself, but only that I am. This *representation* is a *thought*, not an *intuition*."[53] What Kant meant by this dark doctrine is a matter of scholarly dispute. For present purposes, it would take us too far afield to even begin to explain the dynamics of this dispute, let alone to try to settle it. Instead, we shall explain one thing that Kant may have meant, with the frank acknowledgment that some will disagree that Kant actually meant this.

To set the stage, we are, first, going to explain the notion of an *intentional* object, which we will then use in our explanation of Kant's view, even though Kant in this context did not himself employ the notion. The intentional object of a thought has to do with the *aboutness* of thoughts. That is, even though every thought exists as an item in the world – a particular pattern of neural activity, perhaps – it is also *about* something. The technical name for the thing that a thought is about is its *intentional object*. So, for instance, if you were to think the thought that there is dog food in Fido's bowl, the thought itself might be a pattern of neural activity in your brain, but the intentional object of the thought would not be that neural activity, but *that* there is dog food in Fido's bowl. Unlike the pattern of neural activity, this intentional object is not a real object in the world. It would remain the intentional object of your thought whether or not there is dog food in Fido's bowl, whether or not Fido had a bowl, and for that matter even whether or not there was such a dog as Fido. In other words, you can have a thought about something even if what you think is false – indeed, even if the supposed object about which you have the thought does not exist. Yet, for your thought to even be a thought, it has to be about something – that is, it has to have an intentional object. A putative thought without an intentional object would not even be a thought.

By analogy, what it seems to us is central to what Kant is saying in his doctrine of the transcendental unity of apperception is that, in addition to each thought's having to have an intentional object, it also has to have an *intentional subject* – that is, someone whose thought it is. Yet, just as it is not necessary for the thought to exist that there be an actual object that corresponds to its intentional object, so too it is not necessary for the thought to exist that there be an actual subject that corresponds to its intentional subject. In a nutshell, what Kant seems to be saying is that thoughts, to be thoughts, have to be both unified and about something. Their intentional subject – what Kant sometimes calls *the transcendental ego* – is what unifies them. Their intentional object is what they are about. But neither what unifies them nor what they are about actually has to exist apart from the thought –, that is, neither has to exist except as a "formal property" of the thought itself.

William James (1842–1910)

The nineteenth-century philosophy of self and personal identity was dominated in the first half of the century by Kant and in the second half by Hegel. Independently of these two, there was a growing spirit of naturalized science, typified by Darwin, but represented even earlier in the century by psychological inquiry into the development of self concepts and by physiological inquiry into the brain. The American philosopher and psychologist William James integrated this naturalizing impulse with a scientific philosophy of the self. James was no friend of either Kant or Hegel: "With Kant, complication both of thought and statement was an inborn infirmity, enhanced by the musty academicism of his Königsberg existence. With Hegel, it was a raging fever."[54] James's more straightforward alternative was the philosophical movement known as *Pragmatism*, based on the principle that the criterion of an idea's merit is its usefulness.

For present purposes, the writings of James that matter most are two chapters from his *Principles of Psychology*, in the first of which – "The Stream of Thought" – he begins his "study of the mind from within."[55] In his view, this means that one does not begin with "sensations, as the simplest mental facts, and proceed synthetically, constructing each higher stage from those below it." Rather, consciousness presents itself as a much more complex phenomenon: "what we call simple sensations are results of discriminative attention, pushed often to a very high degree." Psychologists, he wrote, should begin with "the fact of thinking itself" and analyze this fact. When they do, he said, they will discover that thought tends to be part of a personal consciousness – that is, that thoughts, as they actually occur, are not separate, but belong with certain other thoughts: "My thought belongs with my other thoughts, and your thought with your other thoughts."[56] James concedes the theoretical possibility that there may be a mere thought that is not anyone's thought, but says that if there is any such thing, we cannot know that there is: "The only states of consciousness that we naturally deal with are found in personal consciousnesses, minds, selves, concrete particular I's and you's," each of which "keeps its own thoughts to itself."[57] Thoughts aren't traded, and each person has direct access only to his or her own thoughts. "Absolute insulation, irreducible pluralism, is the law." No thought of which we have knowledge is "this thought or that thought, but my thought, every thought being owned." And this ownership provides a natural barrier between thoughts, indeed, insures "the most absolute breaches in nature."

As a consequence, James claimed, the "personal self," not individual "thoughts," should be "the immediate datum in psychology." "The universal conscious fact is not 'feelings and thoughts exist,' but 'I think' and 'I feel'." It follows, he thought, that no psychology that hopes to stand "can question the existence of personal selves," and that it is not a mistake, as some psychologists have claimed, that people "personify" their thoughts. On the contrary, "it is, and must remain, true that the thoughts which psychology studies do continually tend to appear as parts of personal selves."[58]

A problem arises, though, from the fact that individual humans may have more than one personal self. As dissociative phenomena, such as automatic writing, reveal, there are "buried feelings and thoughts" that are themselves part of "secondary personal selves." These secondary selves "are for the most part very stupid and contracted, and are cut off at ordinary times from communication with the regular and normal self of the individual." Even so, "they still form conscious unities, have continuous memories, speak, write, invent distinct names for themselves, or adopt names that are suggested and, in short, are entirely worthy of that title of secondary personalities which is now commonly given them." As Janet showed, James wrote, these secondary personalities often "result from the splitting of what ought to be a single complete self into two parts, of which one lurks in the background whilst the other appears on the surface as the only self the man or woman has."[59]

In the second of James's two most relevant chapters, "The Consciousness of Self," he began by considering the widest and most empirical issues, then proceeded to the narrower and less empirical, ending with "the pure Ego." He said that "the Empirical Self" that each of us has is what each of us is most tempted to call *me*. But, he warned,

> the line between *me* and *mine* is difficult to draw. We feel and act about certain things that are ours very much as we feel and act about ourselves. Our fame, our children, the work of our hands, may be as dear to us as our bodies are, and arouse the same feelings and the same acts of reprisal if attacked. And our bodies themselves, are they simply ours, or are they us?

James thought that there are no definitive answers to such questions. However, "*in its widest possible sense,*" he continued:

> *a man's Self is the sum total of all that he CAN call his,* not only his body and his psychic powers, but his clothes and his house, his wife and children, his ancestors and friends, his reputation and works, his lands and horses, and yacht and bank-account. All these things give him the same emotions. If they wax and prosper, he feels triumphant; if they dwindle and die away, he feels cast down, – not necessarily in the same degree for each thing, but in much the same way for all.[60]

James concluded that "the constituents of the Self may be divided into two classes": the empirical self – that is, the material, social, and spiritual selves – and the pure Ego.

The material self of each of us includes our bodies, our possessions, and our families. For instance, if a family member dies, "a part of our very selves is gone. If they do anything wrong, it is our shame. If they are insulted, our anger flashes forth as readily as if we stood in their place." But each of these to different degrees. For instance, some possessions – say, our homes – may be more a part of us than others.

The social self consists of social recognition. Thus, "*a man has as many social selves*" as there are individuals and groups "*who recognize him and* carry an image of him in their mind. To wound any one of these his images is to wound him."

> The most peculiar social self which one is apt to have is in the mind of the person one is in love with. The good or bad fortunes of this self cause the most intense elation and dejection – unreasonable enough as measured by every other standard than that of the organic feeling of the individual.[61]

A person's fame, and his honor, also "are names for one of his social selves."

James said that by *the spiritual self* – that is, the empirical spiritual self – he means a person's "inner or subjective being," his or her "psychic faculties or dispositions, taken concretely," not "the bare principle of personal Unity, or 'pure' Ego, which remains still to be discussed." This inner being is a set of "psychic dispositions" that "are the most enduring and intimate part of the self." These dispositions include one's ability "to argue and discriminate," one's "moral sensibility and conscience," one's "indomitable will." It is "only when these are altered," James said, that a person is said to have been alienated from him or herself.

This spiritual self may be considered either abstractly – say, by dividing consciousness into faculties – or concretely – either as "the entire stream of our personal consciousness" or the "present 'segment' or 'section' of that stream." Either way, "our considering the spiritual self at all is a reflective process," the "result of our abandoning the outward-looking point of view" in order to "think ourselves as thinkers." James concluded this section by remarking, "This attention to thought as such, and the identification of ourselves with it rather than with any of the objects which it reveals, is a momentous and in some respects a rather mysterious operation, of which we need here only say that as a matter of fact it exists; and that in everyone, at an early age, the distinction between thought as such, and what it is 'of' or 'about,' has become familiar to the mind."[62]

Considering the spiritual self abstractly, "the stream as a whole is identified with the Self far more than any outward thing" But

> *a certain portion of the stream abstracted from the rest* is so identified in an altogether peculiar degree, and is felt by all men as a sort of innermost centre within the circle, of sanctuary within the citadel, constituted by the subjective life as a whole. Compared with this element of the stream, the other parts, even of the subjective life, seem transient external possessions, of which each in turn can be disowned, whilst that which disowns them remains. Now, what is this self of all the other selves?

James said that probably everyone would say that this "self of selves" is "the active element in all consciousness."

> It is what welcomes or rejects. It presides over the perception of sensations, and by giving or withholding its assent it influences the movements they tend to arouse. It is the home of interest, – not the pleasant or the painful, not even pleasure or pain, as such, but that within us to which pleasure and pain, the pleasant and the painful, speak. It is the source of effort and attention, and the place from which appear to emanate the fiats of the will.

A physiologist, James said, would associate the self with "the process by which ideas or incoming sensations are 'reflected' or pass over into outward acts." For it is "a sort of junction at which sensory ideas terminate and from which motor ideas proceed, and forming a kind of link between the two." Moreover, it is "more incessantly there than any other single element of the mental life, the other elements end by seeming to accrete round it and to belong to it. It becomes opposed to them as the permanent is opposed to the changing and inconstant."[63]

So much, James thought, would be a matter of common agreement. But as soon as one were to try to go further, opinions would diverge, some calling it a *simple active substance* or *soul* and others a *fiction*. Whichever, if either, is right about the nature of this self of selves, the part of the self "is felt" and not merely an object of thought. Although it is never found all by itself in consciousness, "when it is found, it is *felt*; just as the body is felt, the feeling of which is also an abstraction, because never is the body felt all alone, but always together with other things." In what does "the feeling of this central active self" consist?

> *It is difficult for me to detect in the activity any purely spiritual element at all. Whenever my introspective glance succeeds in turning round quickly enough to catch one of these manifestations of spontaneity in the act, all it can ever feel distinctly is some bodily process, for the most part taking place within the head.*
>
> In a sense, then, it may be truly said that, in one person at least, *the 'Self of selves,' when carefully examined, is found to consist mainly of the collection of these peculiar motions in the head or between the head and throat.* I do not for a moment say that this is all it consists of, for I fully realize how desperately hard is introspection in this field. But I feel quite sure that these cephalic motions are the portions of my innermost activity of which I am most distinctly aware. If the dim portions which I cannot yet define should prove to be like unto these distinct portions in me, and I like other men, *it would follow that our entire feeling of spiritual activity, or what commonly passes by that name, is really a feeling of bodily activities whose exact nature is by most men overlooked.*[64]

James then proposed that we see what the consequences would be if this hypothesis were true.

One consequence, James claimed, is that in order to have "a self that I can *care for*, nature must first present me with some *object* interesting enough to make me instinctively wish to appropriate it for its *own* sake," which I would then use as the basis for creating a material, social, and spiritual self. The origin of the entire array of self-expressions and behaviors is that "certain *things* appeal to primitive and instinctive impulses of our nature, and that we follow their destinies with an excitement that owes nothing to a reflective source." These are "the primordial constituents" of our Me's. Whatever else is subsequently "followed with the same sort of interest, form our remoter and more secondary self." Hence, James claimed, the words *me* and *self*, "*so far as they arouse feeling and connote emotional worth, are OBJECTIVE designations, meaning ALL THE THINGS which have the power to produce in a stream of consciousness excitement of a certain peculiar sort.*"[65]

James said that a human's "most palpable selfishness" is "bodily selfishness," and his "most palpable self" his body. But he does not love his body because he identifies himself with it; rather, he identifies himself with it because he loves it.[66] This self-love is part of a more general phenomenon: namely, that every creature instinctively "has a certain selective interest in certain portions of the world," where "interest in things means the attention and emotion which the thought of them will excite, and the actions which their presence will evoke." Thus, animals in every species are particularly interested in their own prey or food, enemies, sexual mates, and progeny. These things are intrinsically interesting and "are cared for for their own sakes."

In James's view, individual thoughts are in effect agents. Among the things they do is to distinguish on the basis of how the thoughts feel those which belong to the self from those which are merely conceived: "The former have a warmth and intimacy about them of which the latter are completely devoid." James said that the main question of interest is "what the consciousness may mean when it calls the present self the same with one of the past selves which it has in mind."[67] The key to his answer is "warmth and intimacy," which "in the present self, reduces itself to either of two things – something in the feeling which we have of the thought itself, as thinking, or else the feeling of the body's actual existence at the moment," or both. "We cannot realize our present self without simultaneously feeling one or other of these two things." And "which distant selves do fulfil the condition, when represented? Obviously those, and only those, which fulfilled it when they were alive."

Continuity and similarity importantly affect one's sense of self: "the distant selves appear to our thought as having for hours of time been continuous with each other, and the most recent ones of them continuous with the Self of the present moment, melting into it by slow degrees; and we get a still stronger bond of union":

> Continuity makes us unite what dissimilarity might otherwise separate; similarity makes us unite what discontinuity might hold apart. *The sense of our own personal identity, then, is exactly like any one of our other perceptions of sameness among phenomena.* And it must not be taken to mean more than these grounds warrant, or treated as a sort of metaphysical or absolute Unity in which all differences are overwhelmed. The past and present selves compared are the same just so far as they are the same, and no farther. A uniform feeling of 'warmth,' of bodily existence (or an equally uniform feeling of pure psychic energy?) pervades them all; and this is what gives them a generic unity, and makes them the same in kind. But this generic unity coexists with generic differences just as real as the unity. And if from the one point of view they are one self, from others they are as truly not one but many.[68]

James suggests that we think of the self and its unity like we might think of a herd of cattle. The owner gathers the beasts together into one herd because he finds on each of them his brand: "The 'owner' symbolized here that 'section' of consciousness, or pulse of thought, which we have all along represented as the vehicle of the judgment of identity; and the 'brand' symbolizes the characters of warmth and continuity, by reason of which the judgment is made." The brand marks the beasts as belonging together. But "no beast would be so branded unless he belonged to the owner of the herd. They are not his because they are branded; they are branded because they are his." This account, James said, knocks "the bottom out of" common sense: "For common-sense insists that the unity of all the selves is not a mere appearance of similarity or continuity, ascertained after the fact," but "involves a real belonging to a real Owner, to a pure spiritual entity of some kind." According to common sense, it is the relation of the various constituents to this entity that makes them "stick together." But in reality, the unity "is only potential, its centre ideal, like the 'centre of gravity' in physics, until the constituents are collected together." According to common sense, "there must be a real proprietor in the case of the selves, or else their actual accretion into a 'personal consciousness' would never have taken place." But what actually does the uniting is "the real, present onlooking, remembering, 'judging thought' or identifying 'section' of the stream." This is what "owns" some of what it "surveys, and disowns the rest," thus making "a unity that is actualized and anchored and does not merely float in the blue air of possibility."[69]

Yet, James recognized, his theory does not give all that common sense demands. For the unity is not present until the unifying thought creates it: "It is as if wild cattle were lassoed by a newly-created settler and then owned for the first time. But the essence of the matter to common-sense is that the past thoughts never were wild cattle, they were always owned. The Thought does not capture them, but as soon as it comes into existence it finds them already its own." How is this possible?, James asks:

> Common-sense in fact would drive us to admit what we may for the moment call an Arch-Ego, dominating the entire stream of thought and all the selves that may be represented in it, as the ever self-same and changeless principle implied in their union. The 'Soul' of Metaphysics and the 'Transcendental Ego' of the Kantian Philosophy, are, as we shall soon see, but attempts to satisfy this urgent demand of common-sense.[70]

James says that just as "we can imagine a long succession of herdsmen coming rapidly into possession of the same cattle by transmission of an original title by bequest," it is "a patent fact of consciousness" that "the 'title' of a collective self" is passed from one Thought to another in an analogous way:

> Each pulse of cognitive consciousness, each Thought, dies away and is replaced by another. The other, among the things it knows, knows its own predecessor, and finding it "warm," in the way we have described, greets it, saying: "Thou art mine, and part of the same self with me." Each later Thought, knowing and including thus the Thoughts which went before, is the final receptacle – and appropriating them is the final owner – of all that they contain and own. Each Thought is thus born an owner, and dies owned, transmitting whatever it realized as its Self to its own later proprietor. Such standing-as-representative, and such adopting, are perfectly clear phenomenal relations. The Thought which, whilst it knows another Thought and the Object of that Other, appropriates the Other and the Object which the Other appropriated, is still a perfectly distinct phenomenon from that Other; it may hardly resemble it; it may be far removed from it in space and time.[71]

James concedes that there is an obscurity in his account: "the *act of appropriation* itself." The word *appropriate*, he said, is "meaningless" unless what are appropriated are "objects in the hands of something else":

A thing cannot appropriate itself; it is itself; and still less can it disown itself. There must be an agent of the appropriating and disowning; but that agent we have already named. It is the Thought to whom the various 'constituents' are known. That Thought is a vehicle of choice as well as of cognition; and among the choices it makes are these appropriations, or repudiations, of its 'own.' But the Thought never is an object in its own hands, it never appropriates or disowns itself. It appropriates to itself, it is the actual focus of accretion, the hook from which the chain of past selves dangles, planted firmly in the Present, which alone passes for real, and thus keeping the chain from being a purely ideal thing. Anon the hook itself will drop into the past with all it carries, and then be treated as an object and appropriated by a new Thought in the new present which will serve as a living hook in turn. The present moment of consciousness is thus, as Mr. Hodgson says, the darkest in the whole series. It may feel its own immediate existence – we have all along admitted the possibility of this, hard as it is by direct introspection to ascertain the fact – but nothing can be known *about* it till it be dead and gone. Its appropriations are therefore less to *itself* than to the most intimately felt *part of its present Object, the body, and the central adjustments*, which accompany the act of thinking, in the head. *These are the real nucleus of our personal identity,* and it is their actual existence, realized as a solid present fact, which makes us say 'as sure *as I exist*, those past facts were part of myself.' They are the kernel to which the represented parts of the Self are assimilated, accreted, and knit on; and even were Thought entirely unconscious of itself in the act of thinking, these 'warm' parts of its present object would be a firm basis on which the consciousness of personal identity would rest.[72]

Such consciousness, then, James said, "can be fully described without supposing any other agent than a succession of perishing thoughts, endowed with the functions of appropriation and rejection, and of which some can know and appropriate or reject objects already known, appropriated, or rejected by the rest."

In James's view, the soul as a simple spiritual substance is *"needless for expressing the actual subjective phenomena of consciousness as they appear."* Such phenomena are "phenomenal and temporal facts exclusively, and with no need of reference to any more simple or substantial agent than the present Thought or 'section' of the stream." The immaterial soul "explains nothing," but were one to go this route, James says, rather than individual souls, "I find the notion of some sort of an anima mundi thinking in all of us to be a more promising hypothesis." In any case, the individual immaterial soul "guarantees no immortality of a sort we care for," hence, would not "seem a consummation devoutly to be wished."[73]

The core of personhood, in James's view, is "the incessant presence of two elements, an objective person, known by a passing subjective

Thought and recognized as continuing in time."[74] James resolves to use the word *me* for "the empirical person" and *I* for "the judging Thought." Since the "me" is constantly changing: "the identity found by the I in its me is only a loosely construed thing, an identity 'on the whole,' just like that which any outside observer might find in the same assemblage of facts."[75] The "I" of any given moment is a temporal slice of "a stream of thought," each part of which, as "I," can "remember those which went before, and know the things they knew" and "emphasize and care paramountly for certain ones among them as 'me,' and appropriate to these the rest." The core of what is thought to be the "me" "is always the bodily existence felt to be present at the time."[76]

Remembered past feelings that "resemble this present feeling are deemed to belong to the same me with it." And "whatever other things are perceived to be associated with this feeling are deemed to form part of that me's experience; and of them certain ones (which fluctuate more or less) are reckoned to be themselves constituents of the me in a larger sense," such as my clothes, material possessions, friends, honors, and so on. But while the "me" is "an empirical aggregate of things objectively known," the "I" which "knows them cannot itself be an aggregate." Rather, "it is a Thought, at each moment different from that of the last moment, but appropriative of the latter, together with all that the latter called its own."[77]

Notes

1   Translations of Aristotle from Richard C. Dales, *The Problem of the Rational Soul in the Thirteenth Century* (Leiden: E. J. Brill, 1995), pp. 9–10.
2   Aristotle, *Metaphysics*, trans. H. Tredennick, Loeb Classical Library (London: William Heinemann, 1936), 12.8, 1074a; see also *Metaphysics* 5.6, 1016b3; Udo Thiel, "Individuation," in *The Cambridge History of Seventeenth Century Philosophy*, vol. 1, ed. Daniel Garber and Michael Ayers (Cambridge: Cambridge University Press, 1998), ch. 9, p. 214.
3   Lucretius, *De Rerum Natura*, trans. R. E. Latham (Harmondsworth: Penguin Books, 1951), p. 121.
4   Tertullian, *On the Resurrection of the Flesh*, in *Ante-Nicene Fathers*, vol. 3: *Latin Christianity: Its founder, Tertullian*, ed. Alexander Roberts, James Donaldson, and A. Cleveland Coxe, trans. Dr. Holmes (Peabody, Mass.: Hendrickson Publishers, 1995), ch. 8, p. 551.
5   Translations by Caroline Walker Bynum, *Resurrection of the Body in Western Christianity, 200–1336* (New York: Columbia University Press, 1995), pp. 64–6.
6   Plotinus, *Ennead*, IV.2.1, trans. Stephen MacKenna and B. S. Page, in *Plotinus* (Chicago: Encyclopedia Britannica, 1952), p. 140.

7 Ibid., IV.2.2; p. 140.

8 Augustine, *City of God*, ch. 24, par. 2, in *Nicene and Post-Nicene Fathers*, 1st series, ed. Philip Schaff, trans. Rev. Marcus Dods (Peabody, Mass.: Hendrickson Publishers, 1995), p. 259, v. 2.

9 Augustine, *Confessions*, bk. 10, ch. XVII, par. 26, in *Nicene and Post-Nicene Fathers*, 1st series, ed., Philip Schaff, trans. J. G. Pilkington (Peabody, Mass.: Hendrickson Publishers, 1995), p. 149, v. 1.

10 Aquinas, *Summa Theologica*, I, q. 118, art. 2, ad 2; translations by Dales, *Problem of the Rational Soul*, p. 110.

11 Descartes, *Meditations VI*, in *The Philosophical Writings of Descartes*, vol. 2, trans. J. Cottingham, R. Stoothoff, and D. Murdoch (Cambridge: Cambridge University Press, 1984), p. 56.

12 Leibniz, *Discourse on Metaphysics*, sect. 34, in *Philosophical Essays*, trans. R. Ariew, ed. D. Garber (Indianapolis: Hackett Publishing Co., 1989), p. 65.

13 Leibniz, *Discourse on Metaphysics/ Correspondence with Arnauld/Monadology*, trans. G. R. Montgomery (La Salle, Ill.: Open Court, 1973), p. 116.

14 Ibid., p. 113.

15 *The Works of Samuel Clarke*, 4 vols (1738; repr. New York: Garland Publishing Co., (1978), vol. 3, pp. 720–913.

16 Ibid., p. 750.

17 Ibid., p. 787; see also p. 843.

18 Ibid., pp. 809, 819–20.

19 Ibid., p. 844.

20 Ibid., pp. 844–5.

21 Ibid., p. 852.

22 Joseph Butler, *The Analogy of Religion, Natural and Revealed* (London: Henry G. Bohn, 1736/1852), p. 86.

23 Ibid., pp. 87–8.

24 Ibid., p. 89.

25 Ibid., p. 90.

26 Ibid., p. 328.

27 Ibid., p. 330.

28 Ibid., pp. 331–2.

29 Ibid., p. 332.

30 David Hume, *Treatise of Human Nature* (1739), ed. L. Selby-Bigge (Oxford: Clarendon Press, 1888).

31 Ibid., p. 253.

32 Ibid.

33 In and of itself, Hume suggested, our supposing that objects persist is not so bad. But "in order to justify to ourselves this absurdity," we make up a story, often one in which the principle character is the notion of substance; that is, we invent the fictions of "soul, and self, and substance to disguise the variation" in our perceptions. When, as in the case of "plants and vegetables," we cannot fool ourselves into believing that the persistence of an

underlying substance accounts for the persistence of the organism, we invent an equally "unknown and mysterious" surrogate – presumably, "life" – to connect the successive and different perceptions (Ibid., pp. 254–5).

34 Ibid., p. 255.
35 Ibid., p. 261.
36 Ibid., pp. 261–2.
37 Ibid., p. 262.
38 Ibid., p. 262.
39 Ibid., p. 258.
40 Thomas Reid, *Essays on the Intellectual Powers of Man* (1785), in *Philosophical Works of Thomas Reid*, 1895, ed. W. Hamilton, vol. 1, pp. 213–508; reprinted Hildesheim: George Olms, p. 444.
41 William Hazlitt, *An Essay on the Principles of Human Action and some Remarks on the Systems of Hartley and Helvetius* (1805), reprinted with an introduction by J. R. Nabholtz, Gainesville, FI: Scholars' Facsimiles & Reprints, 1969.
42 Ibid., pp. 133–9.
43 Ibid., pp. 110–11.
44 "[Imagination] must carry me out of myself into the feeling of others by one and the same process by which I am thrown forward as it were into my future being and interested in it. I could not love myself, if I were not capable of loving others. Self-love, used in this sense, is in its fundamental principle the same with disinterested benevolence" (ibid., p. 3).
45 Ibid., pp. 33–4.
46 Ibid., pp. 48–9.
47 Ibid., pp. 34–5.
48 Ibid., pp. 6, 10–11, 27–9.
49 Ibid., p. 31.
50 Ibid., pp. 135–6.
51 Ibid., pp. 138–40.
52 F. H. Bradley, *Appearance and Reality: A Metaphysical Essay* (1893/1897) (Oxford: Oxford University Press, 1978); A. N. Prior, "Opposite Number," *Review of Metaphysics* 11 (1957–8), *idem*, pp. 196–201; "Time, Existence, and Identity," *Proceedings of the Aristotelian Society*, 56 (1965–6), pp. 183–92; J. Bennett, "The Simplicity of the Soul," *Journal of Philosophy*, 64 (1967), pp. 648–60; R. Chisholm and S. Shoemaker, "Identity," in *Perception and Personal Identity: Proceedings of the 1967 Oberlin Colloquium in Philosophy*, ed. Norman Care and Robert H. Grimm (Cleveland: Case Western Reserve, 1967), pp. 82–139.
53 Immanuel Kant, *Critique of Pure Reason*, [B157], trans. Norman Kemp Smith (New York: St. Martin's Press, 1929), p. 168.
54 William James, *Principles of Psychology*, vol. 1 (New York: Henry Holt & Co., 1890), pp. 365–6.
55 Ibid., p. 224.
56 Ibid., p. 225.

57 Ibid., p. 226.
58 Ibid., p. 227.
59 Ibid.
60 Ibid., pp. 291–2.
61 Ibid., p. 294.
62 Ibid., p. 297.
63 Ibid., pp. 297–8.
64 Ibid., pp. 301–2.
65 Ibid., p. 319.
66 Ibid., p. 320.
67 Ibid., p. 333.
68 Ibid., pp. 335–7.
69 Ibid., p. 338.
70 Ibid., pp. 338–9.
71 Ibid., p. 339.
72 Ibid., pp. 340–1.
73 Ibid., pp. 344–6.
74 Ibid., p. 371.
75 Ibid., p. 373.
76 Ibid., p. 400.
77 Ibid., pp. 400–1.

1

The Self and the Future

Bernard Williams

Suppose that there were some process to which two persons, *A* and *B*, could be subjected as a result of which they might be said – question-beggingly – to have *exchanged bodies*. That is to say – less question-beggingly – there is a certain human body which is such that when previously we were confronted with it, we were confronted with person *A*, certain utterances coming from it were expressive of memories of the past experiences of *A*, certain movements of it partly constituted the actions of *A* and were taken as expressive of the character of *A*, and so forth; but now, after the process is completed, utterances coming from this body are expressive of what seem to be just those memories which previously we identified as memories of the past experiences of *B*, its movements partly constitute actions expressive of the character of *B*, and so forth; and conversely with the other body.

There are certain important philosophical limitations on how such imaginary cases are to be constructed, and how they are to be taken when constructed in various ways. I shall mention two principal limitations, not in order to pursue them further here, but precisely in order to get them out of the way.

There are certain limitations, particularly with regard to character and mannerisms, to our ability to imagine such cases even in the most restricted sense of our being disposed to take the later performances of that body which was previously *A*'s as expressive of *B*'s character; if the previous *A* and *B* were extremely unlike one another both physically and psychologically, and if, say, in addition, they were of different sex, there might be grave difficulties in reading *B*'s dispositions in any possible performances of *A*'s body. Let us forget this, and for the present purpose just take *A* and *B* as being sufficiently alike (however alike that has to be) for the difficulty not to arise; after the experiment, persons familiar with *A* and *B* are just *overwhelmingly struck* by the *B*-ish character of the doings associated with what was previously *A*'s body, and conversely. Thus the feat of imagining an exchange of bodies is supposed possible in the most restricted sense. But now there is a further limitation which has to be overcome if the feat is to be not merely possible in the most restricted sense but also is to have an outcome which, on serious reflection, we are prepared to describe as *A* and *B* having changed bodies – that is, an outcome where, confronted with what was previously *A*'s body, we are prepared seriously to say that we are now confronted with *B*.

It would seem a necessary condition of so doing that the utterances coming from that body be taken as genuinely expressive of memories of *B*'s past. But memory is a causal notion; and as we actually use it, it seems a necessary condition on *x*'s present knowledge of *x*'s earlier experiences constituting memory of those experiences that the causal chain linking the experiences and the knowledge should not run outside *x*'s body. Hence if utterances coming from a given body are to be taken as expressive of memories of the experiences of *B*, there should be some suitable causal link between the appropriate state of that body and the original happening of those experiences to *B*. One radical way of securing that condition in the imagined exchange case is to suppose, with Shoemaker,[1] that the brains of *A* and of *B* are transposed. We may not need so radical a condition. Thus suppose it were possible to extract information from a man's brain and store it in a device while his brain was repaired, or even renewed, the information then being replaced: it would seem exaggerated to insist that the resultant man could not possibly have the memories he had before the operation. With regard to our knowledge of our own past, we draw distinctions between merely recalling, being reminded, and learning again, and those distinctions correspond (roughly) to distinctions between no new input, partial new input, and total new input with regard to the information in question; and it seems clear that the information-parking case just imagined would not count as new input in the sense necessary and sufficient for "learning again." Hence we can imagine the case we are concerned with in terms of information extracted into such devices from *A*'s and *B*'s brains and replaced in the other brain; this is the sort of model which, I think not unfairly for the present argument, I shall have in mind.

We imagine the following. The process considered above exists; two persons can enter some machine, let us say, and emerge changed in the appropriate ways. If *A* and *B* are the persons who enter, let us call the persons who emerge the *A-body-person* and the *B-body-person*: the *A*-body-person is that person (whoever it is) with whom I am confronted when, after the experiment, I am confronted with that body which previously was A's body – that is to say, that person who would naturally be taken for A by someone who just saw this person, was familiar with A's appearance before the experiment, and did not know about the happening of the experiment. A non-question-begging description of the experiment will leave it open which (if either) of the persons A and B the A-body-person is; the description of the experiment as "persons changing bodies" of course implies that the A-body-person is actually B.

We take two persons A and B who are going to have the process carried out on them. (We can suppose, rather hazily, that they are willing for this to happen; to investigate at all closely at this stage why they might be willing or unwilling, what they would fear, and so forth, would antici-pate some later issues.) We further announce that one of the two resultant persons, the A-body-person and the B-body-person, is going after the experiment to be given $100,000, while the other is going to be tortured. We then ask each A and B to choose which treatment should be dealt out to which of the persons who will emerge from the experiment, the choice to be made (if it can be) on selfish grounds.

Suppose that A chooses that the B-body-person should get the pleasant treatment and the A-body-person the unpleasant treatment; and B chooses conversely (this might indicate that they thought that "changing bodies" was indeed a good description of the outcome). The experi-menter cannot act in accordance with both these sets of preferences, those expressed by A and those expressed by B. Hence there is one clear sense in which A and B cannot both get what they want: namely, that if the experimenter, before the experiment, announces to A and B that he intends to carry out the alternative (for example), of treating the B-body-person unpleasantly and the A-body-person pleasantly – then A can say rightly, "That's not the outcome I chose to happen," and B can say rightly, "That's just the outcome I chose to happen." So, evidently, A and B before the experiment can each come to know either that the outcome he chose will be that which will happen, or that the one he chose will not happen, and in that sense they can get or fail to get what they wanted. But is it also true that when the experimenter proceeds *after* the experiment to act in accordance with one of the preferences and not the other, then one of A and B will have got what he wanted, and the other not?

There seems very good ground for saying so. For suppose the experi-menter, having elicited A's and B's preference, says nothing to A and B about what he will do; conducts the experiment; and then, for example, gives the unpleasant treatment to the B-body-person and the pleasant treatment to the A-body-person. Then the B-body-person will not only complain of the unpleasant treatment as such, but will complain (since he has A's memories) that that was not the outcome he chose, since he chose that the B-body-person should be well treated; and since A made his choice in selfish spirit, he may add that he precisely chose in that way because he did not want the unpleasant things to happen to *him*. The A-body-person meanwhile will express satisfaction both at the receipt of the $100,000, and also at the fact that the experimenter has chosen to act in the way that he, B, so wisely chose. These facts make a strong case for saying that the experimenter has brought it about that B did in the outcome get what he wanted and A did not. It is therefore a strong case for saying that the B-body-person really is A, and the A-body-person really is B; and therefore for saying that the process of the experiment really is that of changing bodies. For the same reasons it would seem that A and B in our example really did choose wisely, and that it was A's bad luck that the choice he correctly made was not carried out, B's good luck that the choice he correctly made was carried out. This seems to show that to care about what happens to me in the future is not necessarily to care about what happens to *this* body (the one I now have); and this in turn might be taken to show that in some sense of Descartes's obscure phrase, I and my body are "really distinct" (though, of course, nothing in these considerations could support the idea that I could exist without a body at all).

These suggestions seem to be reinforced if we consider the cases where A and B make other choices with regard to the experiment. Suppose that A chooses that the A-body-person should get the money, and the B-body-person get the pain, and B chooses conversely. Here again there can be no outcome which matches the expressed preferences of both of them: they cannot both get what they want. The experimenter announces, before the experiment, that the A-body-person will in fact get the money, and the B-body-person will get the pain. So A at this stage gets what he wants (the announced outcome matches his expressed preference). After the experiment, the distribution is carried out as announced. Both the A-body-person and the B-body-person will have to agree that what is happening is in accordance with the preference that A originally expressed. The B-body-person will naturally express this acknowledgement (since he has A's memories) by saying that this is the distribution he chose; he will recall, among other things, the experimenter announcing this outcome, his approving it as what he chose, and so forth. However, he (the B-body-person) certainly does not like what is now happening to him, and would much prefer to be receiving what the A-body-person is receiving – namely, $100,000. The A-body-person will on the other hand recall choosing an outcome other than this one, but will reckon it good luck that the experimenter did not do what he recalls choosing. It looks, then, as though the A-body-person has gotten what he wanted, but not what he chose, while the B-body-person has gotten what he chose, but not what he wanted. So once more it looks as though they are, respectively, B and A; and that in this case the original choices of both A and B were unwise.

Suppose, lastly, that in the original choice A takes the line of the first case and B of the second: that is, A chooses that the B-body-person should get the money and the A-body-person the pain, and B chooses exactly the same thing. In this case, the experimenter would seem to be in the happy situation of giving both persons what they want – or at least, like God, what they have chosen. In this case, the B-body-person likes what he is receiving, recalls choosing it, and congratulates himself on the wisdom of (as he puts it) his choice; while the A-body-person does not like what he is receiving, recalls choosing it, and is forced to acknowledge that (as he puts it) his choice was unwise. So once more we seem to get results to support the suggestions drawn from the first case.

Let us now consider the question, not of A and B choosing certain outcomes to take place after the experiment, but of their willingness to engage in the experiment at all. If they were initially inclined to accept the description of the experiment as "changing bodies" then one thing that would interest them would be the character of the other person's body. In this respect also what would happen after the experiment would seem to suggest that "changing bodies" was a good description of the experiment. If A and B agreed to the experiment, being each not displeased with the appearance, physique, and so forth of the other person's body; after the experiment the B-body-person might well be found saying such things as: "When I agreed to this experiment, I thought that B's face was quite attractive, but now I look at it in the mirror, I am not so sure"; or the A-body-person might say "When I agreed to this experiment I did not know that A had a wooden leg; but now, after it is over, I find that I have this wooden leg, and I want the experiment reversed." It is possible that he might say further that he finds the leg very uncomfortable, and that the B-body-person should say, for instance, that he recalls that he found it very uncomfortable at first, but one gets used to it: but perhaps one would need to know more than at least I do about the physiology of habituation to artificial limbs to know whether the A-body-person would find the leg uncomfortable: that body, after all, has had the leg on it for some time. But apart from this sort of detail, the general line of the outcome regarded from this point of view seems to confirm our previous conclusions about the experiment.

Now let us suppose that when the experiment is proposed (in non-question-begging terms) *A* and *B* think rather of their psychological advantages and disadvantages. *A*'s thoughts turn primarily to certain sorts of anxiety to which he is very prone, while *B* is concerned with the frightful memories he has of past experiences which still distress him. They each hope that the experiment will in some way result in their being able to get away from these things. They may even have been impressed by philosophical arguments to the effect that bodily continuity is at least a necessary condition of personal identity: *A*, for example, reasons that, granted the experiment comes off, then the person who is bodily continuous with him will not have this anxiety, while the other person will no doubt have some anxiety – perhaps in some sense his anxiety – and at least that person will not be he. The experiment is performed and the experimenter (to whom *A* and *B* previously revealed privately their several difficulties and hopes) asks the *A*-body-person whether he has gotten rid of his anxiety. This person presumably replies that he does not know what the man is talking about; he never had such anxiety, but he did have some very disagreeable memories, and recalls engaging in the experiment to get rid of them, and is disappointed to discover that he still has them. The *B*-body-person will react in a similar way to questions about his painful memories, pointing out that he still has his anxiety. These results seem to confirm still further the description of the experiment as "changing bodies." And all the results suggest that the only rational thing to do, confronted with such an experiment, would be to identity oneself with one's memories, and so forth, and not with one's body. The philosophical arguments designed to show that bodily continuity was at least a necessary condition of personal identity would seem to be just mistaken.

Let us now consider something apparently different. Someone in whose power I am tells me that I am going to be tortured tomorrow. I am frightened, and look forward to tomorrow in great apprehension. He adds that when the time comes, I shall not remember being told that this was going to happen to me, since shortly before the torture something else will be done to me which will make me forget the announcement. This certainly will not cheer me up, since I know perfectly well that I can forget things, and that there is such a thing as indeed being tortured unexpectedly because I had forgotten or been made to forget a prediction of the torture: that will still be a torture which, so long as I do know about the prediction, I look forward to in fear. He then adds that my forgetting the announcement will be only part of a larger process: when the moment of torture comes, I shall not remember any of the things I am now in a position to remember. This does not cheer me up, either, since I can readily conceive of being involved in an accident, for instance, as a result of which I wake up in a completely amnesiac state and also in great pain; that could certainly happen to me, I should not like it to happen to me, nor to know that it was going to happen to me. He now further adds that at the moment of torture I shall not only not remember the things I am now in a position to remember, but will have a different set of impressions of my past, quite different from the memories I now have. I do not think that this would cheer me up, either. For I can at least conceive the possibility, if not the concrete reality, of going completely mad, and thinking perhaps that I am George IV or somebody; and being told that something like that was going to happen to me would have no tendency to reduce the terror of being told authoritatively that I was going to be tortured, but would merely compound the horror. Nor do I see why I should be put into any better frame of mind by the person in charge adding lastly that the impressions of my past with which I shall be equipped on the eve of torture will exactly fit the past of another person now living, and that indeed I shall acquire these impressions by (for instance) information now in his brain being copied into mine. Fear, surely, would still be the proper reaction: and not because one did not know what was going to happen, but because in one vital respect at least one did know what was going to happen – torture, which one can indeed expect to happen to oneself, and to be preceded by certain mental derangements as well.

If this is right, the whole question seems now to be totally mysterious. For what we have just been through is of course merely one side, differently represented, of the transaction which we considered before; and it represents it as a perfectly hateful prospect, while the previous considerations represented it as something one should rationally, perhaps even cheerfully, choose out of the options there presented. It is differently presented, of course, and in two notable respects; but when we look at these two differences of presentation, can we really convince ourselves that the second presentation is wrong or misleading, thus leaving the road open to the first version which at the time seemed so convincing? Surely not.

The first difference is that in the second version the torture is throughout represented as going to happen to *me*: "you," the man in charge persistently says. Thus he is not very neutral. But should he have been neutral? Or, to put it another way, does his use of the second person have a merely emotional and rhetorical effect on me, making me afraid when further reflection would have shown that I had no reason to be? It is certainly not obviously so. The problem just is that through every step of his predictions I seem to be able to follow him successfully. And if I reflect on whether what he has said gives me grounds for fearing that I shall be tortured, I could consider that behind my fears lies some principle such as this: that my undergoing physical pain in the future is not excluded by any psychological state I may be in at the time, with the platitudinous exception of those psychological states which in themselves exclude experiencing pain, notably (if it is a psychological state) unconsciousness. In particular, what impressions I have about the past will not have any effect on whether I undergo the pain or not. This principle seems sound enough.

It is an important fact that not everything I would, as things are, regard as an evil would be something that I should rationally fear as an evil if it were predicted that it would happen to me in the future and also predicted that I should undergo significant psychological changes in the meantime. For the fact that I regard that happening, things being as they are, as an evil can be dependent on factors of belief or character which might themselves be modified by the psychological changes in question. Thus if I am appallingly subject to acrophobia, and am told that I shall find myself on top of a steep mountain in the near future, I shall to that extent be afraid; but if I am told that I shall be psychologically changed in the meantime in such a way as to rid me of my acrophobia (and as with the other prediction, I believe it), then I have no reason to be afraid of the predicted happening, or at least not the same reason. Again, I might look forward to meeting a certain person again with either alarm or excitement because of my memories of our past relations. In some part, these memories operate in connection with my emotion, not only on the present time, but projectively forward: for it is to a meeting itself affected by the presence of those memories that I look forward. If I am convinced that when the time comes I shall not have those memories, then I shall not have just the same reasons as before for looking forward to that meeting with the one emotion or the other. (Spiritualism, incidentally, appears to involve the belief that I have just the same reasons for a given attitude toward encountering people again after I am dead, as I did before: with the one modification that I can be sure it will all be very nice.)

Physical pain, however, the example which for simplicity (and not for any obsessional reason) I have taken, is absolutely minimally dependent on character or belief. No amount of change in my character or my beliefs would seem to affect substantially the nastiness of tortures applied to me;

correspondingly, no degree of predicted change in my character and beliefs can unseat the fear of torture which, together with those changes, is predicted for me.

I am not at all suggesting that the *only* basis, or indeed the only rational basis, for fear in the face of these various predictions is how things will be relative to my psychological state in the eventual outcome. I am merely pointing out that this is one component; it is not the only one. For certainly one will fear and otherwise reject the changes themselves, or in very many cases one would. Thus one of the old paradoxes of hedonistic utilitarianism; if one had assurances that undergoing certain operations and being attached to a machine would provide one for the rest of one's existence with an unending sequence of delicious and varied experiences, one might very well reject the option, and react with fear if someone proposed to apply it compulsorily; and that fear and horror would seem appropriate reactions in the second case may help to discredit the interpretation (if anyone has the nerve to propose it) that one's reason for rejecting the option voluntarily would be a consciousness of duties to others which one in one's hedonic state would leave undone. The prospect of contented madness or vegetableness is found by many (not perhaps by all) appalling in ways which are obviously not a function of how things would then be for them, for things would then be for them not appalling. In the case we are at present discussing, these sorts of considerations seem merely to make it clearer that the predictions of the man in charge provide a double ground of horror: at the prospect of torture, and at the prospect of the change in character and in impressions of the past that will precede it. And certainly, to repeat what has already been said, the prospect of the second certainly seems to provide no ground for rejecting or not fearing the prospect of the first.

I said that there were two notable differences between the second presentation of our situation and the first. The first difference, which we have just said something about, was that the man predicted the torture for *me*, a psychologically very changed "me." We have yet to find a reason for saying that he should not have done this, or that I really should be unable to follow him if he does; I seem to be able to follow him only too well. The second difference is that in this presentation he does not mention the other man, except in the somewhat incidental role of being the provenance of the impressions of the past I end up with. He does not mention him at all as someone who will end up with impressions of the past derived from me (and, incidentally, with $100,000 as well – a consideration which, in the frame of mind appropriate to this version, will merely make me jealous).

But why *should* he mention this man and what is going to happen to him? My selfish concern is to be told what is going to happen to me, and now I know: torture, preceded by changes of character, brain operations, changes in impressions of the past. The knowledge that one other person, or none, or many will be similarly mistreated may affect me in other ways, of sympathy, greater horror at the power of this tyrant, and so forth; but surely it cannot affect my expectations of torture? But – someone will say – this is to leave out exactly the feature which, as the first presentation of the case showed, makes all the difference: for it is to leave out the person who, as the first presentation showed, will be you. It is to leave out not merely a feature which should fundamentally affect your fears, it is to leave out the very person for whom you are fearful. So of course, the objector will say, this makes all the difference.

But can it? Consider the following series of cases. In each case we are to suppose that after what is described, A is, as before, to be tortured; we are also to suppose the person A is informed beforehand that just these things followed by the torture will happen to him:

   (i)   A is subjected to an operation which produces total amnesia;
  (ii)   amnesia is produced in A, and other interference leads to certain changes in his character;
 (iii)   changes in his character are produced, and at the same time certain illusory "memory" beliefs are induced in him; these are of a quite fictitious kind and do not fit the life of any actual person;
  (iv)   the same as (iii), except that both the character traits and the "memory" impressions are designed to be appropriate to another actual person, B;
   (v)   the same as (iv), except that the result is produced by putting the information into A from the brain of B, by a method which leaves B the same as he was before;
  (vi)   the same happens to A as in (v), but B is not left the same, since a similar operation is conducted in the reverse direction.

I take it that no one is going to dispute that A has reasons, and fairly straightforward reasons, for fear of pain when the prospect is that of situation (i); there seems no conceivable reason why this should not extend to situation (ii), and the situation (iii) can surely introduce no difference of principle – it just seems a situation which for more than one reason we should have grounds for fearing, as suggested above. Situation (iv) at least introduces the person B, who was the focus of the objection we are now discussing. But it does not seem to introduce him in any way which makes a material difference; if I can expect pain through a transformation which involves new "memory"-impressions, it would seem a purely external fact, relative to that, that the "memory"-impressions had a model. Nor, in (*iv*), do we satisfy a causal condition which I mentioned at the beginning for the "memories" actually being memories; though notice that if the job were done thoroughly, I might well be able to elicit from the *A*-body-person the kinds of remarks about his previous expectations of the experiment – remarks appropriate to the original *B* – which so impressed us in the first version of the story. I shall have a similar assurance of this being so in situation (*v*), where, moreover, a plausible application of the causal condition is available.

But two things are to be noticed about this situation. First, if we concentrate on *A* and the *A*-body-person, we do not seem to have added anything which from the point of view of his fears makes any material difference; just as, in the move from (*iii*) to (*iv*), it made no relevant difference that the new "memory"-impressions which precede the pain had, as it happened, a model, so in the move from (*iv*) to (*v*) all we have added is that they have a model which is also their cause: and it is still difficult to see why that, to him looking forward, could possibly make the difference between expecting pain and not expecting pain. To illustrate that point from the case of character: if *A* is capable of expecting pain, he is capable of expecting pain preceded by a change in his dispositions – and to that expectation it can make no difference, whether that change in his dispositions is modeled on, or indeed indirectly caused by, the dispositions of some other person. If his fears can, as it were, reach through the change, it seems a mere trimming how the change is in fact induced. The second point about situation (*v*) is that if the crucial question for *A*'s fears with regard to what befalls the *A*-body-person is whether the *A*-body-person is or is not the person *B*,[2] then that condition has not yet been satisfied in situation (*v*): for there we have an undisputed *B* in addition to the *A*-body-person, and certainly those two are not the same person.

But in situation (*vi*), we seemed to think, that is finally what he is. But if *A*'s original fears could reach through the expected changes in (*v*), as they did in (*iv*) and (*iii*), then certainly they can reach through in (*vi*). Indeed, from the point of view of *A*'s expectations and fears, there is less difference between (*vi*) and (*v*) than there is between (*v*) and (*iv*) or between (*iv*) and (*iii*). In those transitions, there were at least differences – though we could not see that they were really relevant differences – in the content and cause of what happened to him; in the present case there is absolutely no difference at all in what happens to him, the only difference being in what happens to someone else. If he can fear pain when (*v*) is predicted, why should he cease to when (*vi*) is?

I can see only one way of relevantly laying great weight on the transition from (*v*) to (*vi*); and this involves a considerable difficulty. This is to deny that, as I put it, the transition from (*v*) to (*vi*) involves merely the addition of something happening to *somebody else*; what rather it does, it will be said, is to involve the reintroduction of *A* himself, as the *B*-body-person; since he has reappeared in this form, it is for this person, and not for the unfortunate *A*-body-person, that *A* will have his expectations. This is to reassert, in effect, the viewpoint emphasized in our first presentation of the experiment. But this surely has the consequence that *A* should not have fears for the *A*-body-person who appeared in situation (*v*). For by the present argument, the *A*-body-person in (*vi*) is not *A*; the *B*-body-person is. But the *A*-body-person in (*v*) is, in character, history, everything, exactly the same as the *A*-body-person in (*vi*); so if the latter is not *A*, then neither is the former. (It is this point, no doubt, that encourages one to speak of the difference that goes with (*vi*) as being, on the present view, the *reintroduction* of *A*.) But no one else in (*v*) has any better claim to be *A*. So in (*v*), it seems, *A* just does not exist. This would certainly explain why *A* should have no fears for the state of things in (*v*) – though he might well have fears for the path to it. But it rather looked earlier as though he could well have fears for the state of things in (*v*). Let us grant, however, that that was an illusion, and that *A* really does not exist in (*v*); then does he exist in (*iv*), (*iii*), (*ii*), or (*i*)? It seems very difficult to deny it for (*i*) and (*ii*); are we perhaps to draw the line between (*iii*) and (*iv*)?

Here someone will say: you must not insist on drawing a line – borderline cases are borderline cases, and you must not push our concepts beyond their limits. But this well-known piece of advice, sensible as it is in many cases, seems in the present case to involve an extraordinary difficulty. It may intellectually comfort observers of *A*'s situation; but what is *A* supposed to make of it? To be told that a future situation is a borderline one for its being myself that is hurt, that it is conceptually undecidable whether it will be me or not, is something which, it seems, I can do nothing with; because, in particular, it seems to have no comprehensible representation in my expectations and the emotions that go with them.

If I expect that a certain situation, *S*, will come about in the future, there is of course a wide range of emotions and concerns, directed on *S*, which I may experience now in relation to my expectation. Unless I am exceptionally egoistic, it is not a condition on my being concerned in relation to this expectation, that I myself will be involved in *S* – where my being "involved" in S means that I figure in S as someone doing something at that time or having something done to me, or, again, that S will have consequences affecting me at that or some subsequent time. There are some emotions, however, which I will feel only if I will be involved in S, and fear is an obvious example.

Now the description of S under which it figures in my expectations will necessarily be, in various ways, indeterminate; and one way in which it may be indeterminate is that it leave open whether I shall be involved in S or not. Thus I may have good reason to expect that one out of us five is going to get hurt, but no reason to expect it to be me rather than one of the others. My present emotions will be correspondingly affected by this indeterminacy. Thus, sticking to the egoistic concern involved in fear, I shall presumably be somewhat more cheerful than if I knew it was going to be me, somewhat less cheerful than if I had been left out altogether. Fear will be mixed with, and qualified by, apprehension; and so forth. These emotions revolve around the thought of the eventual determination of the indeterminacy; moments of straight fear focus on its really turning out to be me, of hope on its turning out not to be me. All the emotions are related to the coming about of what I expect: and what I expect in such a case just cannot come about save by coming about in one of the ways or another.

There are other ways in which indeterminate expectations can be related to fear. Thus I may expect (perhaps neurotically) that something nasty is going to happen to me, indeed expect that when it happens it will take some determinate form, but have no range, or no closed range, of candidates for the determinate form to rehearse in my present thought. Different from this would be the fear of something radically indeterminate – the fear (one might say) of a nameless horror. If somebody had such a fear, one could even say that he had, in a sense, a perfectly determinate expectation: if what he expects indeed comes about, there will be nothing more determinate to be said about it after the event than was said in the expectation. Both these cases of course are cases of *fear* because one thing that is fixed amid the indeterminacy is the belief that it is to me to which the things will happen.

Central to the expectation of S is the thought of what it will be like when it happens – thought which may be indeterminate, range over alternatives, and so forth. When S involves me, there can be the possibility of a special form of such thought: the thought of how it will be for me, the imaginative projection of myself as participant in S.[3]

I do not have to think about S in this way, when it involves me; but I may be able to. (It might be suggested that this possibility was even mirrored in the language, in the distinction between "expecting to be hurt" and "expecting that I shall be hurt"; but I am very doubtful about this point, which is in any case of no importance.)

Suppose now that there is an *S* with regard to which it is for conceptual reasons undecidable whether it involves me or not, as is proposed for the experimental situation by the line we are discussing. It is important that the expectation of *S* is not *indeterminate* in any of the ways we have just been considering. It is not like the nameless horror, since the fixed point of that case was that it was going to happen to the subject, and that made his state unequivocally fear. Nor is it like the expectation of the man who expects one of the five to be hurt; his fear was indeed equivocal, but its focus, and that of the expectation, was that when *S* came about, it would certainly come about in one way or the other. In the present case, fear (of the torture, that is to say, not of the initial experiment) seems neither appropriate, nor inappropriate, nor appropriately equivocal. Relatedly, the subject has an incurable difficulty about how he may think about *S*. If he engages in projective imaginative thinking (about how it will be for him), he implicitly answers the necessarily unanswerable question; if he thinks that he cannot engage in such thinking, it looks very much as if he also answers it, though in the opposite direction. Perhaps he must just refrain from such thinking; but is he just refraining from it, if it is incurably undecidable whether he can or cannot engage in it?

It may be said that all that these considerations can show is that fear, at any rate, does not get its proper footing in this case; but that there could be some other, more ambivalent, form of concern which would indeed be appropriate to this particular expectation, the expectation of the conceptually undecidable situation. There are, perhaps, analogous feelings that actually occur in actual situations. Thus material objects do occasionally undergo puzzling transformations which leave a conceptual shadow over their identity. Suppose I were sentimentally attached to an object to which this sort of thing then happened; then it might be that I could neither feel about it quite as I did originally, nor be totally indifferent to it, but would have some other and rather ambivalent feeling toward it. Similarly, it may be said, toward the prospective sufferer of pain, my identity relations with whom are conceptually shadowed, I can feel neither as I would if he were certainly me, nor as I would if he were certainly not, but rather some such ambivalent concern.

But this analogy does little to remove the most baffling aspect of the present case – an aspect which has already turned up in what was said about the subject's difficulty in thinking either projectively or non-projectively about the situation. For to regard the prospective pain-sufferer *just* like the transmogrified object of sentiment, and to conceive of my ambivalent distress about his future pain as just like ambivalent distress about some future damage to such an object, is of course to leave him and me clearly distinct from one another, and thus to displace the conceptual shadow from its proper place. I have to get nearer to him than that. But is there any nearer that I can get to him without expecting his pain? If there is, the analogy has not shown us it. We can certainly not get nearer by expecting, as it were, *ambivalent* pain; there is no place at all for that. There seems to be an obstinate bafflement to mirroring in my expectations a situation in which it is conceptually undecidable whether I occur.

The bafflement seems, moreover, to turn to plain absurdity if we move from conceptual undecidability to its close friend and neighbor, conventionalist decision. This comes out if we consider another description, overtly conventionalist, of the series of cases which occasioned the present discussion. This description would reject a point I relied on in an earlier argument – namely, that if we deny that the A-body-person in (*vi*) is A (because the B-body-person is), then we must deny that the A-body-person in (*v*) is A, since they are exactly the same. "No," it may be said, "this is just to assume that we say the same in different sorts of situation. No doubt when we have the very good candidate for being A – namely, the B-body-person – we call him A; but this does not mean that we should not call the A-body-person A in that other situation when we have no better candidate around. Different situations call for different descriptions." This line of talk is the sort of thing indeed appropriate to lawyers deciding the ownership of some property which has undergone some bewildering set of transformations; they just have to decide, and in each situation, let us suppose, it has got to go to somebody, on as reasonable grounds as the facts and the law admit. But as a line to deal with a person's fears or expectations about his own future, it seems to have no sense at all. If A's fears can extend to what will happen to the A-body-person in (*v*), I do not see how they can be rationally diverted from the fate of the exactly similar person in (*vi*) by his being told that someone would have a reason in the latter situation which he would not have in the former for deciding to call another person A.

Thus, to sum up, it looks as though there are two presentations of the imagined experiment and the choice associated with it, each of which carries conviction, and which lead to contrary conclusions. The idea, moreover, that the situation after the experiment is conceptually undecidable in the relevant respect seems not to assist, but rather to increase, the puzzlement; while the idea (so often appealed to in these matters) that it is conventionally decidable is even worse. Following from all that, I am not in the least clear which option it would be wise to take if one were presented with them before the experiment. I find that rather disturbing.

Whatever the puzzlement, there is one feature of the arguments which have led to it which is worth picking out, since it runs counter to something which is, I think, often rather vaguely supposed. It is often recognized that there are "first-personal" and "third-personal" aspects of questions about persons, and that there are difficulties about the relations between them. It is also recognized that "mentalistic" considerations (as we may vaguely call them) and considerations of bodily continuity are involved in questions of personal identity (which is not to say that there are mentalistic and bodily criteria of personal identity). It is tempting to think that the two distinctions run in parallel: roughly, that a first-personal approach concentrates attention on mentalistic considerations, while a third-personal approach emphasizes considerations of bodily continuity. The present discussion is an illustration of exactly the opposite. The first argument, which led to the "mentalistic" conclusion that *A* and *B* would change bodies and that each person should identify himself with the destination of his memories and character, was an argument entirely conducted in third-personal terms. The second argument, which suggested the bodily continuity identification, concerned itself with the first-personal issue of what *A* could expect. That this is so seems to me (though I will not discuss it further here) of some significance.

I will end by suggesting one rather shaky way in which one might approach a resolution of the problem, using only the limited materials already available.

The apparently decisive arguments of the first presentation, which suggested that *A* should identify himself with the *B*-body-person, turned on the extreme neatness of the situation in satisfying, if any could, the description of "changing bodies." But this neatness is basically artificial; it is the product of the will of the experimenter to produce a situation which would naturally elicit, with minimum hesitation, that description. By the sorts of methods he employed, he could easily have left off earlier or gone on further. He could have stopped at situation (*v*), leaving *B* as he was; or he could have gone on and produced two persons each with *A*-like character and memories, as well as one or two with *B*-like characteristics. If he had done either of those, we should have been in yet greater difficulty about what to say; he just chose to make it as easy as possible for us to find something to say. Now if we had some model of ghostly persons in bodies, which were in some sense actually moved around by certain procedures, we could regard the neat experiment just as the *effective* experiment: the one method that really did result in the ghostly persons changing places without being destroyed, dispersed, or what-ever. But we cannot seriously use such a model. The experimenter has not in the sense of that model *induced* a change of bodies; he has rather produced the one situation out of a range of equally possible situations which we should be most disposed to call a change of bodies. As against this, the principle that one's fears can extend to future pain whatever psychological changes precede it seems positively straightforward. Per-haps, indeed, it is not; but we need to be shown what is wrong with it. Until we are shown what is wrong with it, we should perhaps decide that if we were the person *A* then, if we were to decide selfishly, we should pass the pain to the *B*-body-person. It would be risky: that there is room for the notion of a *risk* here is itself a major feature of the problem.

Notes

1 *Self-Knowledge and Self-Identity* (Ithaca, NY, 1963), p. 23f.
2 This of course does not have to be the crucial question, but it seems one fair way of taking up the present objection.
3 For a more detailed treatment of issues related to this, see *Imagination and the Self*, British Academy (London, 1966); reprinted in P. F. Strawson (ed.), *Studies in Thought and Action* (Oxford, 1968).

2

Personal Identity through Time

Robert Nozick

So many puzzling examples have been put forth in recent discussions of personal identity that it is difficult to formulate, much less defend, any consistent view of identity and nonidentity. One is driven to describe and judge some cases in ways apparently incompatible with how one judges and describes others. Not all of the difficulties, however, uncover something special about personal identity; some concern the general notion of identity through time, and stem, I think, from a natural but mistaken principle about identity. These issues, interesting and puzzling in their own right, raise the metaphysical question: how, given changes, *can* there be identity of something from one time to another, and in what does this identity consist?

The Closest Continuer Theory

A recent essay by Bernard Williams provides convenient entry to these issues.[1] Williams tells two stories, each individually coherent, which are designed to puzzle us together. He first presents a case, aseptically, which we are prone to describe as involving a person coming to occupy a new body, indeed as involving two people switching bodies. Two persons, A and B, enter some machine; upon leaving, the A-body person, the person (whoever that now is) now connected with that A-body, has all of (the previous person) B's memories, knowledge, values, modes of behavior, and so on. (When compatible with the constraints of the A-body, this B-material is produced exactly; otherwise, what is present in the A-body is the vector result of this previous B-material plus the limits of the A-body.) Similarly the B-body person emerges with A's memories, knowledge, modes of behavior, character traits, values, and so on. When enough details are filled in (though not details of the mechanism by which the transfer is effected), we are prone to say or conclude that the people have switched bodies. If these events were to be described beforehand, aseptically, and A was to decide solely on selfish grounds to which body something very painful was to be done afterwards, then A would designate the A-body, for he would believe that *he* would be occupying the B-body at that later time. Moreover, supposing this actually were carried out, at that later time the occupant of the B-body, with A's memories and character, would say "I'm glad I decided then that the painful thing was to be done to the A-body so that I am not feeling it now." We, readers of philosophy, are not so tied to our bodies that we find it impossible to imagine coming to inhabit another. We do not conceive of ourselves as (merely) our particular bodies, as inextricably tied to them.

We can wonder, nevertheless, what constitutes a transfer. What difference is there between your moving from one body to another, and the other body's just acquiring memories and character identical to yours, but without your moving to that body? Williams presses this question with his second story. Suppose you are told you will undergo terrible suffering. This prospect is frightening. You next receive the information that before this suffering comes, you will have changed enormously in psychological traits, perhaps so greatly as to possess exactly the character, memories, values, and knowledge of someone else who now is alive. This would frighten you even more, perhaps. You do not want to lose your character, memories, values, modes of behavior, knowledge, and loves – to lose your identity, as we might say – and afterwards to undergo enormous suffering. Yet how does this differ, asks Williams, from what happened in the first story, which we took to depict a transfer from body to body? In that story, too, the A-body loses its old memories and acquires new ones (which are those of another person); it loses its knowledge, values, and modes of behavior, acquiring new ones. When hearing the first story beforehand, why didn't the A-person have exactly the fear he would have upon learning the second story foretells his future? He reacts differently to the first story because he thinks *he* will occupy the B-body. Yet if terrible things happen to him in the second story, why do they not happen to him in the first one, also? Don't the two stories describe exactly the same events happening to the A-body? What then makes the first story one about the transfer of a person to another body, and not about something terrible happening to a person who stays where he is?

How can the difference be, asks Williams, that in one situation, the first, in addition to everything happening to the A-body, also A's memories and psychological traits end up or arise in body B? Surely, whatever

	Body A	Body B
First situation	acquires the memories and character which person B had one hour earlier.	acquires the memories and character which person A had one hour earlier.
Second situation	acquires the memories and character which person B had one hour earlier, or perhaps no previous person had.	stays with the continuation of the memories and character which it had one hour earlier.

happens elsewhere cannot affect whether or not A continues to inhabit the A-body. When it happens to just one body it is a psychological disintegration and acquisition of a new psychology. How, then, can two psychological disintegrations and acquisitions of new memories and values make or add up to an exchange of bodies?

Let us formulate the general principle that underlies Williams' discussion and leads to these perplexing questions.

> If x at time t_1 is the same individual as y at later time t_2, that can depend only upon facts about x, y, and the relationships between them. No fact about any other existing thing is relevant to (deciding) whether x at t_1 is (part of the same continuing individual as) y at t_2.

How could the existence (or nonexistence) of something else be relevant to whether x at t_1 is (part of the same continuing individual as) y at t_2? There is a related principle, also plausible:

> If y at time t_2 is (part of the same continuing individual as) x at t_1 in virtue of standing in some relationship R to x at t_1, then there *could not* be another additional thing at t_2 also standing (along with y) in R to x at t_1. If there also were this additional thing z at t_2, then neither it nor y would be identical to x. If that z could exist, even if it actually does not, then y at t_2 is not identical with x at t_1 – at least, it is not in virtue of standing in the relationship R.

Williams assumed this principle in earlier articles,[2] in order to argue that bodily continuity is a necessary condition of personal identity. We are prone, otherwise, to think that a person could enter a machine, disappear there, and appear in another machine ten feet to the left, without ever having occupied any intervening space. Williams asks us to imagine that there also had been an additional machine ten feet to the right, and at this one too had appeared simultaneously another (qualitatively) identical being. Neither of the two then would be that original person who entered the machine in the middle. Furthermore, if in that situation of double materialization, the person on the left is not the original person, then neither is he in the different situation where only one person appears on the left. The mere possibility of someone also emerging (discontinuously) on the right is enough, according to Williams, to show that anyone who emerges (discontinuously) on the left, even if all alone, is not the original person.[3]

The first principle says that identity cannot depend upon whether there is or isn't another thing of a certain sort; the second says that if there could be another thing so that then there would not be identity, then there isn't identity, even if that other thing does not actually exist. (If there were identity only when that other thing happened not to exist, the first principle would be violated; the second principle follows from the first.) Both of these principles are false.

First, consider a case that does not involve any question of a person's identity. The Vienna Circle was driven from Austria and Germany by the Nazis; one member, Hans Reichenbach, landed in Istanbul. (Later he left and went to the United States.) Suppose there were twenty members of the Circle, of whom three ended up in Istanbul. These three keep meeting through the war years, discussing philosophy. In 1943, they hear that all of the others are dead. *They* now are the Vienna Circle, meeting in Istanbul. Carrying on its discussions, they proclaim that the Vienna Circle lives on in exile. In 1945, however, they learn that nine members of the Circle had gotten to America, where they continued to meet, discuss philosophy, adhere to the same philosophical program, and so on. That group in the United States is the Vienna Circle in exile; the group in Istanbul turns out not to be the Vienna Circle but its Istanbul offshoot.

How can this be? Either the group in Istanbul is the Vienna Circle or it isn't; how can whether or not it is be affected by whether other members survived and continued to meet in another place? (Isn't it clear, though, that if these nine others had gone underground and continued to meet in Vienna, this would show that the Istanbul group was not the Vienna Circle?) It is not plausible to apply the first principle to this case; it is not plausible to say that if the group of those three persons meeting in Istanbul is the same continuing entity as the earlier Vienna Circle, then this can depend only upon relationships between the two, and not on whether anything else of a certain sort exists.

Rather, the group in Istanbul is the Vienna Circle when it is the *closest continuer* of the Vienna Circle. If no other group exists, the Istanbul group is the closest continuer; but if the group in the United States exists, *it* is the continuer (supposing no closer continuer exists) of the Vienna Circle. Whether or not a particular group constitutes the Vienna Circle depends on what other groups there actually are.[4]

To be something later is to be its closest continuer. Let us apply this view to one traditional puzzle about identity over time: the puzzle of the ship of Theseus. The planks of a ship are removed one by one over intervals of time, and as each plank is removed it is replaced by a new plank. The removal of one plank and its replacement by another does not make the ship a different ship than before; it is the same ship with one plank different. Over time, each and every plank might be removed and replaced, but if this occurs gradually, the ship still will be the same ship. It is an interesting result, but upon reflection not so very surprising, that the identity of something over time does not require it to keep all the very same parts. The story continues, however. (We can imagine this as a continuation of the previous story, or as a new one which begins like the first.) It turns out that the planks removed had not been destroyed but were stored carefully; now they are brought together again into their original shiplike configuration. Two ships float on the waters, side by side. Which one, wondered the Greeks, is the original?

The closest continuer view helps to sort out and structure the issues; it does not, by itself, answer the question. For it does not, by itself, tell which dimension or weighted sum of dimensions determines closeness; rather, it is a schema into which such details can be filled. In the case of the ships, there are two relevant properties: spatiotemporal continuity with continuity of parts, and being composed of the very same parts (in the same configuration). If these have equal weight, there is a tie in closeness of continuation. Neither, then, is the closest continuer, so neither is the original ship. However, even when the two properties receive equal weight, if there actually had been one ship existing without the other, then it, as the closest continuer, would be the original ship. Perhaps the situation is not one of a clear tie, but one of an unclear weighting. Our concepts may not be sharp enough to order all possible combinations of properties according to closeness of continuation. For complicated cases, we may feel that which is closest is a matter to decide, that we must sharpen our concept to settle which is (identical with) the original entity. It is different, though, with persons, and especially with ourselves; we are not willing to think that whether something is *us* can be a matter of (somewhat arbitrary) decision or stipulation.

Although it does not answer the question about which ship, if any, is the same as the original one, the closest continuer schema does fit and explain our response to this puzzle. When we hear the first story of the ship gradually altered, plank by plank, we are not puzzled or led to deny it really is the same ship. Only when we learn also of the reconstituted ship are we thrown into puzzlement, not only about its status but about the earlier product of gradual rebuilding, too. It is only when we learn of another candidate for closest (or equally close) continuer that we come to doubt whether that gradually altered ship is the same ship as the original one. If our notion of closeness is unsharp, we will not be able to say that either, or neither, is the original; whether one is closest will remain unclear. The nature and contours of people's responses to the puzzle of the ship fits the closest continuer schema and supports it, if not as a metaphysical truth then at least as a component of a psychological explanation of these responses.

The closest continuer view presents a necessary condition for identity; something at t_2 is not the same entity as x at t_1 if it is not x's closest continuer. And "closest" means closer than all others; if two things at t_2 tie in closeness to x at t_1, then neither is the same entity as x. However, something may be the closest continuer of x without being close enough to it to be x. How close something must be to x to be x, it appears, depends on the kind of entity x is, as do the dimensions along which closeness is measured.[5]

If the closest continuer view is correct, our judgments of identity reflect (implicit) weightings of dimensions; therefore, we might use these judgments themselves to discover those dimensions, the ordering and weighting among them. Notice that on the closest continuer view, a property may be a factor in identity without being a necessary condition for it. If persons conceivably can transfer from one body to another, still, bodily continuity can be an important component of identity, even (in some cases) its sole determinant. The dimension of bodily continuity can receive significant weight in the overall measure of closeness for persons.

To say that something is a continuer of x is not merely to say its properties are qualitatively the same as x's, or resemble them. Rather it is to say they grow out of x's properties, are causally produced by them, are to be explained by x's earlier having had its properties, and so forth. (See also our later discussion of tracking.) Indeed, even the notion of spatiotemporal continuity is not to be explained merely as something that when photographed would produce continuous film footage with no gaps; for we can imagine a substitution of one thing for another that would not break film continuity. The later temporal stages also must be causally dependent (in an appropriate way) on the earlier ones. The condition that something is a continuer incorporates such causal dependence. The closest continuer view is not committed to the thesis that identity through time depends only upon the qualitative properties of temporal stages to the exclusion of causal relations and dependencies between (aspects of) stages.

This causal dependence, however, need not involve temporal continuity. Imagine that each and every thing flickers in and out of existence every other instant, its history replete with temporal gaps. (Compare how messages are transmitted on telephone wires.) According to concepts developed later in this chapter, if every thing leads this mode of existence, then it is the best kind of continuity there actually is, so all such will count as continuing objects. However, if some have continuity without any temporal gaps, then the others that flicker, though otherwise similar, are not the best realization of continuity; so perhaps their stages do not closely enough continue each other to count as constituting objects that continue through time. How much temporal continuity is necessary for there to be a continuing object depends on how closely things continue temporally elsewhere.

If it governs our judgments about identity over time, it seems plausible that the closest continuer schema also should fit our *perception* of things continuing through time; it should fit what we see as (a later stage of) what. In parallel to Piaget's famous experiments with objects disappearing behind a screen, we should be able to devise experiments to uncover the closest continuer schema and reveal aspects of the metric of closeness. Show a film of an object x going behind a screen followed by something y coming out at a different angle (Figure 2.1); with color and shape held constant and velocity suitably maintained, a person should see this as the same object emerging, deflected by a collision with something behind the screen. Similarly, with a suitably chosen delay followed by emergence with increased velocity, it should be seen as the same object popping out after being somewhat stuck. Yet if along with y an even closer continuer z also is presented, for example, something emerging straight out at the same velocity, that thing z, rather than y, would be seen as the earlier x emerging, even though in z's absence, y would be seen so, since it then would be x's closest continuer (Figure 2.2). Following this plausible hunch that such psychological experiments could exhibit the closest continuer schema, I inquired of psychologist friends whether experiments like these had ever been done. Though the research seemed

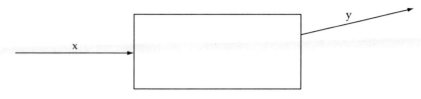

Figure 2.1

Figure 2.2

plausible, no one I spoke to knew of any, until I met an Israeli psychologist, Shimon Ullman, who had just completed his doctoral dissertation where he had done these experiments.[6] His results fit the closest continuer schema; also he included more detailed experiments in which the color, shape, and velocity of the figures were varied in order to uncover (in my terminology) the details of the metric. (Unfortunately no experiments were done that sharply focus on how people perceive the hard situations that will puzzle us below: tie cases and overlap cases.)

The closest continuer view holds that y at t_2 is the same person as x at t_1 only if, first, y's properties at t_2 stem from, grow out of, are causally dependent on x's properties at t_1 and, second, there is no other z at t_2 that stands in a closer (or as close) relationship to x at t_1 than y at t_2 does.

Closeness, here, represents not merely the degree of causal connection, but also the qualitative closeness of what is connected, as this is judged by some weighting of dimensions and features in a similarity metric. Moreover, it seems plausible that closeness is measured only among those features that are causally connected (instead of a threshold being passed when there is a causal connection, while then closeness is measured among all features of x and y, including those features of y that are causally unconnected with x, even any that pop up spontaneously and at random).

The Theory Applied

Let us now investigate how the closest continuer theory handles particular cases.

> Case 1   After precise measurements of you are taken, your body, including the brain, is precisely duplicated. In all physical properties this other body is the same as yours; it also acts as you do, has the same goals, "remembers" what you do, and so on.

Intuitively, we want to say that you (continue to) exist in this case, and also that a duplicate has been made of you, but this duplicate is not you. According to the closest continuer theory, too, that other entity is not you, since it is not your closest continuer. Although it exhibits both bodily and psychological similarity (to the earlier you), and though its psychological traits stem from yours via the intermediaries who made it, it does not show bodily continuity. That duplicated body does causally depend, in some way, on the state of your body; it is no accident that it duplicates your properties. Your own body's continuance, though, does not require a duplicator to make a choice in the causal process. The duplicate's causal connection to your earlier body is not this close, so it loses out (as being you) to the continuing you.

> Case 2   You are dying after a heart attack, and your healthy brain is transplanted into another body, perhaps one cloned from yours and so very similar though healthier. After the operation, the "old body" expires and the new body-person continues on with all your previous plans, activities, and personal relationships.

Intuitively we want to say, or at least I do, that you have continued to exist in another body. (We can imagine this becoming a standard medical technique to prolong life.) The closest continuer theory can yield this result. The new body-person certainly is your closest continuer. With psychological continuity and some bodily continuity (the brain is the same), is it a close enough continuer to still be you? I would say it is.

My intention is to show how the closest continuer schema fits my judgments. Perhaps you make different judgments; you thereby differ in judging comparative closeness, but you still are using that same schema. Then is there any content to the claim that the closest continuer schema fits our judgments? When y and z are stages occurring after x, cannot dimensions be given weights so as to yield either one as closer to x, whichever judgment a person makes? It appears that the closest continuer schema excludes nothing. However, though any judgments about one case or situation can be fit to the closest continuer schema by a suitable choice of dimensions and weights, by a suitable choice of metric, it does not follow that any and every group of judgments can be made to fit. Only some (range of) weightings can fit particular judgments J_1 and J_2; these weights, once fixed, give determinate content to the schema. Some judgments J_3 about other cases are excluded, since any weights that would yield J_3 fall outside the range of weights already fixed by judgments J_1 and J_2. The closest continuer schema is compatible with any single judgment about identity or nonidentity, but it is not compatible with each and every set of judgments. Add the assumption that the same dimensions and weights function, when applicable, in various judgments; the closest continuer schema now does exclude some (combinations of) things, and so does have determinate empirical content.

The situation is similar with utility theory. Given any one preference in a pair of alternatives, utility always can be assigned to give the preferred alternative a higher utility; however, some combinations of pairwise preferences among various alternatives cannot be fit to a utility function. To gain empirical content, the assumption must be added that the underlying preferences remain constant during the sequence of pairwise judgments, that it is one utility function which accounts for all the pairwise preferences – just as it is one metric space determining closeness, which must account for the person's various judgments of identity and nonidentity. To say that some straight line or other fits the data, has no restrictive content if there is only one data point, or two; a third point, however, might fail to fall on the straight line fixed by the other two.

Reassured that the closest continuer schema has determinate content, let us return to cases.

> Case 3 As you are dying, your brain patterns are transferred to another (blank) brain in another body, perhaps one cloned from yours. The patterns in the new brain are produced by some analogue process that simultaneously removes these patterns from the old one. (There is a greater continuity – or impression of it – with an analogue process as compared to the transmission of digitally coded data.) Upon the completion of the transfer, the old body expires.

Here, there need be no physical continuity at the time of transfer (though there may have been a previous cloning). Still, I believe, this can be you; I believe this is a way a person can continue on. When I contemplate this happening to myself, I believe this continuation would be close enough to count as me continuing.

Notice that the duplicate being in the first case may be exactly like the new you in this case. However, in that case it was not a new you, for the old you still was around – an even closer continuer existed.

> Case 4   Suppose medical technology permitted only half a brain to be transplanted in another body, but this brought along full psychological similarity.

If your old half-brain and body ceased to function during such a transplant, the new body-person would be you. This case is like case 2, except that here half a brain is transplanted instead of a full one; we are imagining the half-brain to carry with it the full psychology of the person.

> Case 5   Suppose that after an accident damages a portion of your brain, half of it is surgically removed and ceases to function apart from the body. The remaining half continues to function in the body, maintaining full psychological continuity.

Although half of your brain has been removed, you remain alive and remain you.

> Case 6   Let us now suppose the fourth and fifth cases are combined: half of a person's brain is removed, and while the remaining half-brain plus body function on with no noticeable difference, the removed half is transplanted into another body to yield full psychological continuity there. The old body plus half-brain is exactly like the continuing person of case 5, the new body plus transplanted half-brain is exactly like the continuing person of case 4. But now both are around. Are both the original person, or neither, or is one of them but not the other?

It appears that the closer continuer in case 6 is (the person of) the original body plus remaining half-brain. Both resultant persons have full psychological continuity with the original one, both also have some bodily continuity, though in one case only half a brain's worth. One appears to have closer continuity, however – not more kinds of continuity (both have psychological and physical continuity with the original) but more of one of the kinds. One has greater physical overlap with the original person.

If this one is closer, as appears, then he is the original person and the other is not. True, it feels to the other as if *he* is the original person, but so did it for the duplicate in the very first case. Still, I am hesitant about this result. Perhaps we should hold that despite appearances there is a tie for closeness, so neither is the original person; or that though one is closer to the original person, close enough to him to constitute him when there is no competitor (as shown by case 5), that closer one is not enough closer than the competitor to constitute the original person. On this last view, a continuer must be not only closest and close enough, but also enough closer than any other continuer; it must decisively beat out the competition.

> Case 7   As you die, a very improbable random event occurs elsewhere in the universe: molecules come together precisely in the configuration of your brain and a very similar (but healthier) body, exhibiting complete psychological similarity to you.

This is not you; though it resembles you, by hypothesis, it does not arise out of you. It is not any continuer of you. In the earlier cases, by *psychological continuity* I meant "stemming from" and "similar to". Of course, we can have the first without the second, as when drastic changes in psychology are brought on by physical injury or emotional trauma; case 7 shows the second without the first.

Consider the mode of long distance travel described in science fiction stories, wherein a person is "beamed" from one place to another. However, the person's body does not occupy intermediate places. Either the molecules of the decomposed body are beamed or (truer to the intent of the stories) a fully informative description of the body is beamed to another place, where the body then is reconstituted (from numerically distinct molecules) according to the received information. Yet the readers of such stories, and the many viewers of such television programs, calmly accept this as a mode of travel. They do not view it as a killing of one person with the production of another very similar person elsewhere. (We may suppose that those few who do view it that way, and refuse so to "travel", despite the fact that it is faster, cheaper, and avoids the intervening asteroid belts, are laughed at by the others.) The taking and transmission of the informative description might not involve the dematerialization of the person here, who remains also. In that case, the newly constituted person there presumably would be viewed as a similar duplicate.

Do we need to stipulate that the process of transporting by beaming, by its nature, must involve the dematerialization of the original here? In the case of people, at least, a merely accidental ending of the person here may seem inadequate for continuation there; consider the case where as the information is beamed to create what is intended to be only a duplicate, the original person is shot, so that (to speak neutrally) the life in that body ends. Yet, imagine a beamer which can work either way – dematerializing here or not – depending upon which way a switch is thrown. If the process with dematerialization is far more expensive, might not those who wished to travel there choose the less expensive method combined with an alternative ending (accidental with respect to the transporting process) of their existence here? I shall leave these issues unresolved now.

In addition to the closest continuer, we also must focus on the closest predecessor, for similar reasons. Something y may be the closest continuer of another thing x even though x is not y's closest predecessor. Though nothing at t_2 more closely continues x than y does, still, y more closely continues z at t_1 than it does x at t_1. For a later stage y to be part of the same continuing object as an earlier stage x, not only must y be the closest continuer of x, also x must be the closest predecessor of y. Let us say that two things or stages so related are mono-related. This mono-relation need not be transitive, since neither closest continuer nor closest predecessor need be transitive.

How shall a view of identity over time cope with these nontransitivities of mono-related, closest continuer, and closest predecessor? Let X refer to the entity over time that continues x at t_1. I see the following four possibilities.

1   Entity X follows the path of closest continuation. We can state this most easily if we suppose each moment of time has an immediate predecessor. The component stage at t_2 of X is just that entity, if any, which is the closest continuer of x at t_1, and which continues it closely enough to be (identical with) X at t_1. The component at t_{n+1} of X is just that entity, if any, which is the closest continuer of the component at t_n of X, and which continues it closely enough to be (identical with) the component at t_n of X. Entity X is constituted from moment to moment by the closest (and close enough) continuer of the immediately preceding component of X. When

there is no closest continuer because of a tie, or because nothing continues it at all or closely enough, then X ends.

2   Entity X follows the path of closest continuation, unless it is a short path. If a t_{n+1} is reached when there is no continuer of the component at t_n of X, then backtracking occurs to the nearest component C of X for which there exists at t_{n+1} something z which continues C closely enough to be (identical with) it. The component at t_{n+1} of X is then z, and X continues from z on the path of closest continuation. At t_{n+1}, there is a "jump" to the segment of the path that z begins.

3   This alternative is like the preceding one, except that between the time of C and t_{n+1}, the components constituting X are some continuation path of C that leads to z, without jumps. (Each succeeding step from C will be to a continuer, but not all will be to an adjacent *closest* continuer.)

4   Entity X originates with x at t_1 and each later component of X is the closest continuer existing at that time of the original x at t_1. Since everything harks back to x at t_1, there may be considerable hopping, either around or back and forth.[7]

Overlap

With these four possibilities in mind, let us consider the following most difficult case.

> Case 8   Half of an ill person's brain is removed and transplanted into another body, but the original body plus half-brain does not expire when this is being done; it lingers on for one hour, or two days, or two weeks. Had this died immediately, the original person would survive in the new body, via the transplanted half-brain which carries with it psychological similarity and continuity. However, in the intervening hour or days or weeks, the old body lives on, perhaps unconscious or perhaps in full consciousness, alongside the newly implanted body.

Does the person then die along with it (as in option 1 above)? Can its lingering on during the smallest overlapping time interval, when the lingerer is the closest continuer, mean the end of the person, while if there was no such lingerer, no temporal overlap, the person would live on? It seems so unfair for a person to be doomed by an echo of his former self. Or, does the person move to the new body upon the expiration of the old one (as in option 2 above)? But then, who was it in the new body for the hour or two days or two weeks preceding his arrival there, and what happened to that person? Perhaps during that initial time interval, it was a duplicate of the person in that new body (with old half-brain), a duplicate which becomes the person upon the expiration of the old body. It seems strange that at a certain time, without any (physical) change taking place in it, the new body could become the person when the old body expires. However, once we have become used to the idea that whether y at t_2 is (identical with) x at t_1 does not depend only upon the properties and relations of x and y, but depends also upon whether there exists a z of a certain sort (which more closely continues x), then perhaps we can swallow this consequence as well.[8] Still, there is a difficulty. If the old body plus half-brain linger on for long enough, three years say, then surely that is the person, and the person dies when that body expires – the duplicate does not suddenly become the person after three years. A one-minute period of lingering is compatible with the new body-person being the original person, a three-year period is not. But the interval can be varied gradually; it seems absurd that there should be some sharp temporal line which makes the difference to whether or not the person continues to live in the other body. ("Doctor, there's only one minute left! Hurry to end life in the old body so the person can live on in the new one." And out of which body would these words come?)[9]

Or, does the person move to the new body immediately upon the transplantation of the half-brain into it (as in option 3 above)? Are we opportunists who leave a sinking body before it is sunk? And what if, despite predictions, it has not sunk but makes it to port – where are we then? Does whether we move at one time depend upon how things turn out later, so there is identity ex post facto? If the person moves over at the time of the transplant, who is it that dies (in the old body) two days later?

None of these positions seems satisfactory. Even if our intuitions did fit one of them completely, we would have to explain why it was such an important notion. Perhaps we are willing to plunk for one of these options as compared to its close variants when the overlap involves ships, tables, countries, or universities. We do not so arbitrarily want to apply a concept or theory of identity to ourselves; we need to be shown a difference between it and its apparently close variants, deep enough to make the difference between our being there and not.

Let us examine more closely the structure of the problematic overlap situation. In Figure 2.3, the closest successor of A is B, and the closest

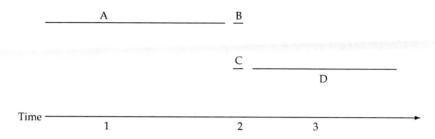

Figure 2.3

successor of A + B is D. However, the closest predecessor of D is C, and the closest predecessor of C + D is A. Neither A + B + D nor A + C + D is a mono-related entity. Taking a longer view, though, A and D are mono-related: D is the closest successor of A plus A's closest successor; also A is the closest predecessor of D plus D's closest predecessor.

When B and C are small in comparison, the mono-relation of A and D would seem to constitute them as part of the same entity. Thereby, is marked off an extensive entity. Are we mono-related entities that need not be temporally continuous? On this view, there could be a person with temporal parts A and D during times 1 and 3, yet that person does not exist during the intervening time 2. Something related does exist then, so this discontinuous person does depend upon some continuities during time 2, but these are not continuities through which he continues to exist then. (A watch repairer takes a watch completely apart and puts it together again; the customer later picks up his watch, the same one he had brought in, though there was an intervening time when it did not exist.)

This view encounters difficulties, however. C might think to himself, "Since it is unjust for someone to be punished for a crime he did not do, D may not be punished for a crime planned and executed during time 2, when D does not exist. No one will be apprehended until time 3, so it is safe for me to commit the crime without fear of punishment." Surely we may punish D for what C does. Is it B or C we punish for the acts of A? Or do we wait until time 3 and punish D? (Yet, if D certainly will escape punishment if we wait, do we punish B or C?) It would appear that D may not be punished for acts of B (unless C does not exist). However, B might assassinate a rival political candidate to bring about the election of D. If this continued a calculated plan put into effect by A, then D may be punished; but suppose B first thinks of this act during time 2, or that

A planned it thinking his life would end with B, in order to ensure that the later person D who claimed to be A – falsely on A's view – would be punished for usurping A's identity. It is clear that a morass of difficulties faces the position that one continuing entity includes A and D as parts but not the overlapping segments B and C.

The problem of temporal overlap is not unique to people, we have seen. It arises in the Greek ship case if the original planks are reconfigured into a ship one day before the ship consisting of replacement planks catches fire and burns. Is the reconfigured ship the original ship, or not?

This quandary about temporal overlap is intrinsic, I believe, to any notion of identity applicable to more than atomic-point-instants. Any such notion trades off depth to gain breadth; in order to encompass larger entities, it sacrifices some similarity among what it groups together. Maximum similarity within the groupings would limit them to atomic-point-instants. The purpose of the identity notion is wider breadth, but a grouping that included everything would not convey specific information. The closest continuer theory is the best Parmenides can do in an almost Heraclitean world.

The notion of identity itself compromises between breadth and (exact) similarity (which similarity can include being part of the same causal process). Since spatial and temporal distances involve some dissimilarity, any temporal or spatial breadth involves some sacrifice of (exact) similarity. For our cases, width and breadth are measured along spatiotemporal dimensions, closeness or similarity along other dimensions. The informativeness of a classification varies positively with the extent of its subclasses, and with the degree of similarity exhibited within each subclass; similar norms apply to the clumping of entities from the flux.[10]

Usually, the closest continuer schema – or more generally (when the temporal relation is not the most salient), the closest relation schema – serves to achieve the right measure of breadth. It extends entities X to the maximum feasible extent: further extended, something would be included that is not close enough to link with X rather than something else, or X would no longer be sharp enough to be an informative category. When there is temporal overlap, however, the immediate closest continuer view, holding that A's existence continues through B and then stops, does not give the maximum feasible extension. Yet the wider view of the entity as continuing on from A to D brings the difficulties of the overlapping segments.

For the structure of overlap in Figure 2.3, the norm of breadth would place A and D together, as would the norm of similarity. The similarity relation also would place together A and B, and C and D. Yet the disconnected spatial positions, along with the different activities occurring there simultaneously, fall under the dissimilarity relation; this relation, which places things separately in classification, separates B and C. There is no way to bring A and D, A and B, and C and D together into one entity or subclassification, while keeping B and C separate. Still, how can an entity's continuation (from A to C + D) be blocked by the merest continuing tentacle or echo (B) of its previous stage?

The quandary over the overlap situation, I have said, is intrinsic to the notion of identity over time, and stems from its uneasy compromise between the outward and the inward urges. Overlap falls at precisely the point of tension between two different modes of structuring a concept: the closest relation mode and the global mode. We are familiar with the closest continuer or closest relation mode. The global mode looks further. It holds that Y is (a later stage of the same entity as) X if Y is the closest continuer of X, and if there is no even longer extending thing Z that more closely continues X than any equally large thing of which Y is part. Since these distinct structures, local and global, are not peculiar to the one concept of identity, let us pause to notice how various philosophical concepts can each be structured in different modes.

Thereby, we will see the overlap quandary not as peculiar to the closest continuer theory but as a symptom of a wider and inescapable intellectual torque. When a writer treats an apparent refutation of his theory as a genuine antinomy, we are entitled to be very suspicious. Nevertheless, when I contemplate my entering a situation of temporal overlap, my notion of self begins to dissolve. Is temporal overlap a koan for philosophers?

Structuring Philosophical Concepts

The closest continuer theory illustrates one stage of a progression for structuring philosophical concepts. In listing the first three of the five stages, the concept of personal identity will provide a convenient example.

> I *Intrinsic abstract structural* A concept C's holding at a time is analyzed in terms of an abstract structural description involving only monadic predicates holding at that time. The personal identity of something is an intrinsic feature of it, most usefully discussed without considering any entities other than it or any of its features at any other time. (For example, the identity resides in the soul.)

II *Relational*   X falls under concept C if X stands in a certain relationship R to another, sometimes earlier, thing of a specified sort. For example, X is the same thing as the earlier Y if X is spatiotemporally continuous, or psychologically continuous, with Y.

III *Closest relative*   To the relational view is added the condition that nothing else is as closely related under R to that other (previous) thing. The closest continuer theory of personal identity is of this sort.

[...]

For some topics, a global condition and structure is a natural successor to the closest relative one. It widens horizons, holding that something satisfies concept C only if it stands closest in R to a specified y, and also is a (necessary) part of any wider thing that stands closer in R to y than do other comparably wide things. Thus, one might hold that an acceptable theory not only must fit the evidence as well as any alternative theory of the same phenomena, but also must be part of any wider theory of more inclusive phenomena that fits the evidence more closely than any other theory alternative to it. The quandary with temporal overlap stems from the tension between closest relative and global structures. The expansive purpose of an identity notion – otherwise, atomic-point-instants would be good enough – pushes toward the global view; but even more than with other notions, its being an identity notion restrains the outward move. Indeed, this inward feature of identity has led others to presume a relational view must be true, and so to ignore the possibility of even a closest relative view, though that fits their judgments better.

The global view, seen more accurately, is a form of a closest continuer view, not an alternative to it; the global view also explicitly excludes there being other equally close alternatives to what it selects. The local closest continuer structure and the global one each exhibit the same closest continuer structure but differ in the span or extent covered. The problem of temporal overlap concerns which form of closest continuer theory to adopt, local or global. [...]

Problem Cases

Temporal overlap presents an issue within a closest continuer view: should it be a local closest continuer view or a global one? Overlap exacerbates the tension between these two modes of structuring a concept, each with its own attractions and force, but the issue raises no special objection to a closest relation or closest continuer analysis.

How shall we view this issue over the appropriate mode of structuring? We might view ourselves possibly as applying different conceptual structurings to external objects, tables or ships or stars, or even to other people. Can we view our own identity through time as open to determination by this type of conceptual structuring, though; could we view it even as a matter of choice how our own identity is configured, whether locally or globally?

It is a remarkable fact that for many of the cases or examples about personal identity, we can say with reasonable confidence which if any of the resultant beings is us. We can say this without being told of the movement of a soul-pellet or any similar item. How are we able to say which will be us? Are we so familiar with the laws of motion of soul-pellets that we know where they will go? Or do we, as the soul-pellet, decide where to go; in saying which would be us, are we stating where we would choose to move? Might the soul-pellet change its decision; or end up in the wrong place by accident, because it was not paying sufficient attention? Surely, none of these possibilities holds.

We answer the question about which person, if any, we would be, by applying a general schema of identity, the closest continuer schema, to our own case. That general schema is called forth by general features of the world which press us to classify and identify, even in the face of complexities and flux.

We need to predict how something will behave or affect us, provided the world shows some patterns in that not every two properties are equally correlated. When no unchanging atoms are known to us, the closest continuer schema will serve best. This schema leaves room for specifying closeness by selecting and weighting dimensions, and so leaves room to learn from experience. Any organism whose learned appropriate responses were restricted to things exactly identical to something it already had encountered would not fare well. Sometimes, it will be useful merely to classify types of things, a job done by generalization gradients. Sometimes there will be a point to reidentifying the very same individual, distinguishing it even from others of its type; here, the closest continuer schema comes into its own. There would be no point to reidentifying some particular thing if things never behaved similarly over time, and never behaved differently from others of their kind.[11]

One philosophical approach to a tangled area of complicated relationships of varying degree, rather than trying to force these into somewhat arbitrary pigeonholes, rests content with recognizing and delineating the underlying complicated relations. Concerning personal identity, it might say that future selves will have varying degrees of closeness to us-now in virtue of diverse underlying relations and events, such as bodily continuity, psychological similarity, splitting or fusion; and that the real and whole truth to be told is of the existence and contours of these underlying phenomena.[12] Why impose any categorization – the closest continuer schema being one – over this complexity?

The underlying level itself, however, also will raise similar problems. For example, in what way is something the same body when all its cells other than neurons, as well as the particular molecules composing the neurons, are replaced over time? Should we speak again only of the complicated relations that underlie *this* level? We cannot avoid the closest continuer schema, or some other categorization, by restricting ourselves to the full complexity of the underlying relations; in the absence of changeless enduring atoms, any underlying level will present the same type of difficulties. Eventually we are pushed to a closest continuer schema or something similar at some level or other. (Even if we are able to reach unchanging particles, our subatomic theory may hold it makes no sense to reidentify particular ones of them.) The alternative to a closest continuer schema is Heraclitean flux, down through all levels. If it becomes legitimate, because necessary, to use the schema at some level, then why not simply begin with it?

Still, it is not satisfactory to say merely that we apply the same identity schema used to organize other flux to the flux underlying ourselves. About ourselves, the schema has limited predictive usefulness. True, contexts can be imagined where it has some use: am I that previous person; should I keep his promises and worry about his tendency to overeat or to behave erratically? But most of the purpose of reidentifying some particular thing, to orient our behavior toward it, is lacking when that thing is ourself. There might remain the sort of choices Bernard Williams described: in choosing which future being will suffer, we want to know which one will be us. Here, though, I do not use the schema to identify something as an aid to my goals; I use it to identify whose goals are mine. [...]

...Which particular properties, features, and dimensions constitute the measure of closeness, and with what relative weights? The closest continuer theory is merely a schema; what then are its particular contents? What precisely is the metric, why that one, and why is it precisely that which we care about? Does psychological continuity come lexically first; is there no tradeoff between the slightest loss in psychological continuity and the greatest gain in bodily continuity; is bodily continuity (to a certain degree) a necessary component of identity through time; how are psychological similarity and bodily similarity to be weighed (for non-continuers when some other continuer is present); what are the relevant subcomponents of psychological continuity or similarity (for example, plans, ambitions, hobbies, preferences in flavors of ice cream, moral principles) and what relative weights are these to be given in measuring closeness? And so forth.

I make no attempt here to fill in the details; and not merely because (though it is true that) I have nothing especially illuminating to say about these details. I do not believe that there are fixed details to be filled in; I do not believe there is some one metric space in which to measure closeness for each of our identities. The content of the measure of close-ness, and so the content of a person's identity through time, can vary (somewhat) from person to person. What is special about people, about selves, is that what constitutes their identity through time is partially determined by their own conception of themselves, a conception which may vary, perhaps appropriately does vary, from person to person. [...]

Notes

1 Williams, "The Self and the Future", reprinted in his *Problems of the Self* (Cambridge University Press, 1973) (and as ch. 1 above).
2 "Personal Identity and Individuation" and "Bodily Continuity and Personal Identity", reprinted in his *Problems of the Self*, pp. 1–25.
3 Note that this principle requires not merely some bodily continuity, but a sort that could not simultaneously be duplicated; so it excludes the result of trans-planting half of someone's brain into a new body, even supposing that there are no hemispheric asymmetries and that no other bodily parts continue.
4 Saul Kripke has pointed out to me an anticipation of the closest continuer theory in Sydney Shoemaker, "Wiggins on Identity", *Philosophical Review*, vol. 74, 1970, p. 542; see also his "Persons and Their Pasts", *American Philosophical Quarterly*, vol. 7, 1970, p. 278, note 18.
5 Is the notion of identity, "=", then elliptical for "the same K", where "K" is a term for a kind of entity? Can y be the same K_1 as x but not the same K_2 – to use the example in the literature, the same hunk of marble but not the same statue? If the kind determines the relative weights different properties have in determining identity, different kinds might give different weights to the very same properties. However, just as kinds weight properties, might not the kinds themselves also be weighted thereby to specify a nonrelativized notion of "same entity"? I do not mean the closest continuer view to be committed to any relativization of identity.

6   "The Interpretation of Visual Motion", unpublished doctoral dissertation, MIT, 1977.
7   Since as far back as we know, everything comes from something else, to find an origin is to find a relative beginning, the beginning of an entity as being of a certain kind K.
8   This instantaneous movement of a person from one place to another does not violate special relativity's constraint on the transmission of energy or a causal signal faster than light.
9   Compare the case of abortion, where also no sharp line or threshold (between the times of conception and birth) seems appropriate. However, we can imagine a presumption against abortion that increases in moral weight as the fetus develops, so that only reasons of increasing significance could justify (later) abortion. Unlike the abortion case, there is nothing in our present concern, the lingering overlap, that can vary continuously like the moral weight of a presumption. One might be tempted to consider the (continuously varying) probability of the healthier one's being the same (earlier) person, but what additional fact would there be to fix how that probability comes out?
10 Amos Tversky, "Features of Similarity", *Psychological Review*, vol. 84, 1977, pp. 327–52, especially pp. 347–9, proposes a general formula for the formation of categories. Tversky, surprisingly but convincingly, explains how two things can be the most similar entities within a group and also the most dissimilar, and he provides data to show that people do make such judgments. Hence, a formula for category formation cannot speak only of degrees of similarity within a category; it also must speak, nonredundantly, of (minimizing) degrees of dissimilarity within categories.
11 I leave aside the purpose in identifying some particular things, behaving exactly like others of the kind, as yours.
12 See Derek Parfit, "Personal Identity", *Philosophical Review*, vol. 80, 1971, pp. 3–28.

3

Why Our Identity Is Not What Matters

Derek Parfit

I enter the Teletransporter. I have been to Mars before, but only by the old method, a space-ship journey taking several weeks. This machine will send me at the speed of light. I merely have to press the green button. Like others, I am nervous. Will it work? I remind myself what I have been told to expect. When I press the button, I shall lose consciousness, and then wake up at what seems a moment later. In fact I shall have been unconscious for about an hour. The Scanner here on Earth will destroy my brain and body, while recording the exact states of all of my cells. It will then transmit this information by radio. Travelling at the speed of light, the message will take three minutes to reach the Replicator on Mars. This will then create, out of new matter, a brain and body exactly like mine. It will be in this body that I shall wake up.

Though I believe that this is what will happen, I still hesitate. But then I remember seeing my wife grin when, at breakfast today, I revealed my nervousness. As she reminded me, she has been often teletransported, and there is nothing wrong with *her*. I press the button. As predicted, I lose and seem at once to regain consciousness, but in a different cubicle. Examining my new body, I find no change at all. Even the cut on my upper lip, from this morning's shave, is still there.

Several years pass, during which I am often Teletransported. I am now back in the cubicle, ready for another trip to Mars. But this time, when I press the green button, I do not lose consciousness. There is a whirring sound, then silence. I leave the cubicle, and say to the attendant: 'It's not working. What did I do wrong?'

'It's working', he replies, handing me a printed card. This reads: 'The New Scanner records your blueprint without destroying your brain and body. We hope that you will welcome the opportunities which this technical advance offers.'

The attendant tells me that I am one of the first people to use the New Scanner. He adds that, if I stay for an hour, I can use the Intercom to see and talk to myself on Mars.

'Wait a minute', I reply, 'If I'm here I can't *also* be on Mars'.

Someone politely coughs, a white-coated man who asks to speak to me in private. We go to his office, where he tells me to sit down, and pauses. Then he says: 'I'm afraid that we're having problems with the New Scanner. It records your blueprint just as accurately, as you will see when you talk to yourself on Mars. But it seems to be damaging the cardiac systems which it scans. Judging from the results so far, though you will be quite healthy on Mars, here on Earth you must expect cardiac failure within the next few days.'

The attendant later calls me to the Intercom. On the screen I see myself just as I do in the mirror every morning. But there are two differences. On the screen I am not left-right reversed. And, while I stand here speechless, I can see and hear myself, in the studio on Mars, starting to speak.

What can we learn from this imaginary story? Some believe that we can learn little. This would have been Wittgenstein's view.[1] And Quine writes: 'The method of science fiction has its uses in philosophy, but...I wonder whether the limits of the method are properly heeded. To seek what is "logically required" for sameness of person under unprecedented circumstances is to suggest that words have some logical force beyond what our past needs have invested them with.'[2]

This criticism might be justified if, when considering such imagined cases, we had no reactions. But these cases arouse in most of us strong beliefs. And these are beliefs, not about our words, but about ourselves. By considering these cases, we discover what we believe to be involved in our own continued existence, or what it is that makes us now and ourselves next year the same people. We discover our beliefs about the nature of personal identity over time. Though our beliefs are revealed most clearly when we consider imaginary cases, these beliefs also cover actual cases, and our own lives. [...] I shall argue that some of these beliefs are false, then suggest how and why this matters.

75   Simple Teletransportation and the Branch-Line Case

At the beginning of my story, the Scanner destroys my brain and body. My blueprint is beamed to Mars, where another machine makes an organic *Replica* of me. My Replica thinks that he is me, and he seems to remember living my life up to the moment when I pressed the green button. In every other way, both physically and psychologically, we are exactly similar. If he returned to Earth, everyone would think that he was me.

Simple Teletransportation, as just described, is a common feature in science fiction. And it is believed, by some readers of this fiction, merely to be the fastest way of travelling. They believe that my Replica *would* be *me*. Other science fiction readers, and some of the characters in this fiction, take a different view. They believe that, when I press the green button, I die. My Replica is *someone else*, who has been made to be exactly like me.

This second view seems to be supported by the end of my story. The New Scanner does not destroy my brain and body. Besides gathering the information, it merely damages my heart. While I am in the cubicle, with the green button pressed, nothing seems to happen. I walk out, and learn that in a few days I shall die. I later talk, by two-way television, to my Replica on Mars. Let us continue the story. Since my Replica knows that I am about to die, he tries to console me with the same thoughts with which I recently tried to console a dying friend. It is sad to learn, on the receiving end, how unconsoling these thoughts are. My Replica then assures me that he will take up my life where I leave off. He loves my wife, and together they will care for my children. And he will finish the book that I am writing. Besides having all of my drafts, he has all of my intentions. I must admit that he can finish my book as well as I could. All these facts console me a little. Dying when I know that I shall have a Replica is not quite as bad as, simply, dying. Even so, I shall soon lose consciousness, forever.

In Simple Teletransportation, I am destroyed before I am Replicated. This makes it easier to believe that this *is* a way of travelling – that my Replica *is* me. At the end of my story, my life and that of my Replica overlap. Call this the *Branch-Line Case*. In this case, I cannot hope to travel on the *Main Line*, waking up on Mars with forty years of life ahead. I shall stay on the Branch-Line, here on Earth, which ends a few days later. Since I can talk to my Replica, it seems clear that he is *not* me. Though he is exactly like me, he is one person, and I am another. When I pinch myself, he feels nothing. When I have my heart attack, he will again feel nothing. And when I am dead he will live for another forty years.

If we believe that my Replica is not me, it is natural to assume that my prospect, on the Branch-Line, is almost as bad as ordinary death. I shall deny this assumption. As I shall argue later, being destroyed and Replicated is about as good as ordinary survival. [...]

79   The Other Views

I am asking what is the criterion of personal identity over time – what this identity involves, or consists in. I first described the spatio-temporal physical continuity that, on the standard view, is the criterion of identity of physical objects. I then described two views about personal identity, the Physical and Psychological Criteria [Parfit's descriptions not included here].

There is a natural but false assumption about these views. Many people believe in what is called *Materialism*, or *Physicalism*. This is the view that that there are no purely mental objects, states, or events. On one version of Physicalism, every mental event is just a physical event in some particular brain and nervous system. There are other versions. Those who are not Physicalists are either *Dualists* or *Idealists*. Dualists believe that mental events are *not* physical events. This can be so even if all mental events are causally dependent on physical events in a brain. Idealists believe that all states and events are, when understood correctly, purely mental. Given these distinctions, we may assume that Physicalists must accept the Physical Criterion of personal identity.

This is not so. Physicalists could accept the Psychological Criterion. And they could accept the version that allows any reliable cause, or any cause. They could thus believe that, in Simple Teletransportation, my Replica would be me. They would here be rejecting the Physical Criterion.[3]

These criteria are not the only views about personal identity. I shall now describe some of the other views that are either sufficiently plausible, or have enough supporters, to be worth considering. This description may be hard to follow; but it will give a rough idea of what lies ahead. If much of this summary seems either obscure or trivial, do not worry.

I start with a new distinction. On the Physical Criterion, personal identity over time just involves the physically continuous existence of enough of a brain so that it remains the brain of a living person. On the Psychological Criterion, personal identity over time just involves the various kinds of psychological continuity, with the right kind of cause. These views are both *Reductionist*. They are Reductionist because they claim

(1)   that the fact of a person's identity over time just consists in the holding of certain more particular facts.

They may also claim

(2)   that these facts can be described without either presupposing the identity of this person, or explicitly claiming that the experiences in this person's life are had by this person, or even explicitly claiming that this person exists. These facts can be described in an *impersonal* way.

It may seem that (2) could not be true. When we describe the psychological continuity that unifies some person's mental life, we must mention this person, and many other people, in describing the *content* of many thoughts, desires, intentions, and other mental states. But mentioning this person in this way does not involve either asserting that these mental states are had by this person, or asserting that this person exists. These claims need further arguments, which I shall later give.

Our view is *Non-Reductionist* if we reject both of the two Reductionist claims.

Many Non-Reductionists believe that *we are separately existing entities.* On this view, personal identity over time does not just consist in physical and/or psychological continuity. It involves a further fact. A person is a separately existing entity, distinct from his brain and body, and his experiences. On the best-known version of this view, a person is a *purely mental* entity: a Cartesian Pure Ego, or spiritual substance. But we might believe that a person is a separately existing *physical* entity, of a kind that is not yet recognised in the theories of contemporary physics.

There is another Non-Reductionist View. This view denies that we are separately existing entities, distinct from our brains and bodies, and our experiences. But this view claims that, though we are not separately existing entities, personal identity *is* a further fact, which does not just consist in physical and/or psychological continuity. I call this the *Further Fact View.* [...]

87   Divided Minds

Some recent medical cases provide striking evidence in favour of the Reductionist View. Human beings have a lower brain and two upper hemispheres, which are connected by a bundle of fibres. In treating a few people with severe epilepsy, surgeons have cut these fibres. The aim was to reduce the severity of epileptic fits, by confining their causes to a single hemisphere. This aim was achieved. But the operations had another unintended consequence. The effect, in the words of one surgeon, was the creation of 'two separate spheres of consciousness'.[4]

This effect was revealed by various psychological tests. These made use of two facts. We control our right arms with our left hemispheres, and vice versa. And what is in the right halves of our visual fields we see with our left hemispheres, and vice versa. When someone's hemispheres have been disconnected, psychologists can thus present to this person two different written questions in the two halves of his visual field, and can receive two different answers written by this person's two hands.

Here is a simplified version of the kind of evidence that such tests provide. One of these people is shown a wide screen, whose left half is red and right half is blue. On each half in a darker shade are the words, 'How many colours can you see?' With both hands the person writes, 'Only one'. The words are now changed to read, 'Which is the only colour that you can see?' With one of his hands the person writes 'Red', with the other he writes 'Blue'.

If this is how this person responds, there seems no reason to doubt that he is having visual sensations – that he does, as he claims, see both red and blue. But in seeing red he is not aware of seeing blue, and vice versa. This is why the surgeon writes of 'two separate spheres of consciousness'. In each of his centres of consciousness the person can see only a single colour. In one centre, he sees red, in the other, blue.

The many actual tests, though differing in details from the imagined test that I have just described, show the same two essential features. In seeing what is in the left half of his visual field, such a person is quite unaware of what he is now seeing in the right half of his visual field, and vice versa. And in the centre of consciousness in which he sees the left half of his visual field, and is aware of what he is doing with his left hand, this person is quite unaware of what he is doing with his right hand, and vice versa.

One of the complications in the actual cases is that for most people, in at least the first few weeks after the operation, speech is entirely con-trolled by the right-handed hemisphere. As a result, 'if the word "hat" is flashed on the left, the left hand will retrieve a hat from a group of concealed objects if the person is told to pick out what he has seen. At the same time he will insist verbally that he saw nothing.'[5] Another complication is that, after a certain time, each hemisphere can sometimes control both hands. Nagel quotes an example of the kind of conflict which can follow:

A pipe is placed out of sight in the patient's left hand, and he is then asked to write with his left hand what he was holding. Very laboriously and heavily, the left hand writes the letters P and I. Then suddenly the writing speeds up and becomes lighter, the I is converted to an E, and the word is completed as PENCIL. Evidently the left hemisphere has made a guess based on the appearance of the first two letters, and has interfered...But then the right hemisphere takes over control of the hand again, heavily crosses out the letters ENCIL, and draws a crude picture of a pipe.[6]

Such conflict may take more sinister forms. One of the patients complained that sometimes, when he embraced his wife, his left hand pushed her away.

Much has been made of another complication in the actual cases, hinted at in Nagel's example. The left hemisphere typically supports or 'has' the linguistic and mathematical abilities of an adult, while the right hemisphere 'has' these abilities at the level of a young child. But the right hemisphere, though less advanced in these respects, has greater abilities of other kinds, such as those involved in pattern recognition, or musicality. It is assumed that, after the age of three or four, the two hemispheres follow a 'division of labour', with each developing certain abilities. The lesser linguistic abilities of the right hemisphere are not intrinsic, or permanent. People who have had strokes in their left hemispheres often regress to the linguistic ability of a young child, but with their remaining right hemispheres many can re-learn adult speech. It is also believed that, in a minority of people, there may be no difference between the abilities of the two hemispheres.

Suppose that I am one of this minority, with two exactly similar hemispheres. And suppose that I have been equipped with some device that can block communication between my hemispheres. Since this device is connected to my eyebrows, it is under my control. By raising an eyebrow I can divide my mind. In each half of my divided mind I can then, by lowering an eyebrow, reunite my mind.

This ability would have many uses. Consider

My Physics Exam   I am taking an exam, and have only fifteen minutes left in which to answer the last question. It occurs to me that there are two ways of tackling this question. I am unsure which is more likely to succeed. I therefore decide to divide my mind for ten minutes, to work in each half of my mind on one of the two calculations, and then to reunite my mind to write a fair copy of the best result. What shall I experience?

When I disconnect my hemispheres, my stream of consciousness divides. But this division is not something that I experience. Each of my two streams of consciousness seems to have been straightforwardly continuous with my one stream of consciousness up to the moment of division. The only changes in each stream are the disappearance of half my visual field and the loss of sensation in, and control over, one of my arms.

Consider my experiences in my 'right-handed' stream. I remember deciding that I would use my right hand to do the longer calculation. This I now begin. In working at this calculation I can see, from the movements of my left hand, that I am also working at the other. But I am not aware of working at the other. I might, in my right-handed stream, wonder how, in my left-handed stream, I am getting on. I could look and see. This would be just like looking to see how well my neighbour is doing, at the next desk. In my right-handed stream I would be equally unaware both of what my neighbour is now thinking and of what I am now thinking in my left-handed stream. Similar remarks apply to my experiences in my left-handed stream.

My work is now over. I am about to reunite my mind. What should I, in each stream, expect? Simply that I shall suddenly seem to remember just having worked at two calculations, in working at each of which I was not aware of working at the other. This, I suggest, we can imagine. And, if my mind had been divided, my apparent memories would be correct.

In describing this case, I assumed that there were two separate series of thoughts and sensations. If my two hands visibly wrote out two calculations, and I also claimed later to remember two corresponding series of thoughts, this is what we ought to assume. It would be most implausible to assume that either or both calculations had been done unconsciously.

It might be objected that my description ignores 'the necessary unity of consciousness'. But I have not ignored this alleged necessity. I have denied it. What is a fact must be possible. And it is a fact that people with disconnected hemispheres have two separate streams of consciousness – two series of thoughts and experiences, in having each of which they are unaware of having the other. Each of these two streams separately displays unity of consciousness. This may be a surprising fact. But we can understand it. We can come to believe that a person's mental history need not be like a canal, with only one channel, but could be like a river, occasionally having separate streams. I suggest that we can also imagine what it would be like to divide and reunite our minds. My description of my experiences in my Physics Exam seems both to be coherent and to describe something that we can imagine.

It might next be claimed that, in my imagined case, I do not have a divided mind. Rather, I have two minds. This objection does not raise a real question. These are two ways of describing one and the same outcome.

A similar objection claims that, in these actual and imagined cases, the result is not a single person with either a divided mind or two minds. The result is two different people, sharing control of most of one body, but each in sole control of one arm. Here too, I believe that this objection does not raise a real question. These are again two ways of describing the same outcome. This is what we believe if we are Reductionists.

If we are not yet Reductionists, as I shall assume, we believe that it is a real question whether such cases involve more than a single person. Perhaps we can believe this in the actual cases, where the division is permanent. But this belief is hard to accept when we consider my imagined Physics Exam. In this case there are two streams of consciousness for only ten minutes. And I later seem to remember doing both of the calculations that, during these ten minutes, my two hands could be seen to be writing out. Given the brief and modest nature of this disunity, it is not plausible to claim that this case involves more than a single person. Are we to suppose that, during these ten minutes, I cease to exist, and two new people come into existence, each of whom then works out one of the calculations? On this interpretation, the whole episode involves three people, two of whom have lives that last for only ten minutes. Moreover, each of these two people mistakenly believes that he is me, and has apparent memories that accurately fit my past. And after these ten minutes I have accurate apparent memories of the brief lives of each of these two people, except that I mistakenly believe that I myself had all of the thoughts and sensations that these people had. It is hard to believe that I am mistaken here, and that the episode does involve three quite different people.

It is equally hard to believe that it involves two different people, with me doing one of the calculations, and some other person doing the other. I admit that, when I first divide my mind, I might in doing one of the calculations believe that the other calculation must be being done by someone else. But in doing the other calculation I might have the same belief. When my mind has been reunited, I would then seem to remember believing, while doing each of the calculations, that the other calculation must be being done by someone else. When I seem to remember both these beliefs, I would have no reason to think that one was true and the other false. And after several divisions and reunions I would cease to have such beliefs. In each of my two streams of consciousness I would believe that I was now, in my other stream, having thoughts and sensations of which, in this stream, I was now unaware.

88   What Explains the Unity of Consciousness?

Suppose that, because we are not yet Reductionists, we believe that there must be a true answer to the question, 'Who has each stream of consciousness?' And suppose that, for the reasons just given, we believe that this case involves only a single person: me. We believe that for ten minutes I have a divided mind.

Remember next the view that psychological unity is explained by ownership. On this view, we should explain the unity of a person's consciousness, at any time, by ascribing different experiences to this person, or 'subject of experiences'. What unites these different experiences is that they are being had by the same person. This view is held both by those who believe that a person is a separately existing entity, and by some of those who reject this belief. And this view also applies to the unity of each life.

When we consider my imagined Physics Exam, can we continue to accept this view? We believe that, while my mind is divided, I have two separate series of experiences, in having each of which I am unaware of having the other. At any time in one of my streams of consciousness I am having several different thoughts and sensations. I might be aware of thinking out some part of the calculation, feeling writer's cramp in one hand, and hearing the squeaking of my neighbour's old-fashioned pen. What unites these different experiences?

On the view described above, the answer is that these are the experiences being had by me at this time. This answer is incorrect. I am not just having these experiences at this time. I am also having, in my other stream of consciousness, several other experiences. We need to explain the unity of consciousness within each of my two streams of consciousness, or in each half of my divided mind. We cannot explain these two unities by claiming that all of these experiences are being had by me at this time. This makes the two unities one. It ignores the fact that, in having each of these two sets of experiences, I am unaware of having the other.

Suppose that we continue to believe that unity should be explained by ascribing different experiences to a single subject. We must then believe that this case involves at least two different subjects of experiences. What unites the experiences in my left-handed stream is that they are all being had by one subject of experiences. What unites the experiences in my right-handed stream is that they are all being had by another subject of experiences. We must now abandon the claim that 'the subject of experiences' is the person. On our view, I am a subject of experiences. While my mind is divided there are two different subjects of experiences. These are not the same subject of experiences, so they cannot both be me. Since it is unlikely that I am one of the two, given the similarity of my two streams of consciousness, we should probably conclude that I am neither of these two subjects of experiences. The whole episode therefore involves three such entities. And two of these entities cannot be claimed to be the kind of entity with which we are all familiar, a person. I am the only person involved, and two of these subjects of experiences are *not* me. Even if we assume that I *am* one of these two subjects of experiences, *the other* cannot be me, and is therefore not a person.

We may now be sceptical. While the 'subject of experiences' was the person, it seemed plausible to claim that what unites a set of experiences is that they are all had by a single subject. If we have to believe in subjects of experiences that are not persons, we may doubt whether there really are such things. There are of course, in the animal world, many subjects of experiences that are not persons. My cat is one example. But other animals are irrelevant to this imagined case. On the view described above, we have to believe that the life of a *person* could involve subjects of experiences that are not persons.

Reconsider my experiences in my right-handed stream of consciousness. In this stream at a certain time I am aware of thinking about part of a calculation, feeling writer's cramp, and hearing the sounds made by my neighbour's pen. Do we explain the unity of these experiences by claiming that they are all being had by the same subject of experiences, this being an entity which is *not* me? This explanation does not seem plausible. If this subject of experiences is *not* a person, what kind of thing is it? It cannot be claimed to be a Cartesian Ego, if I am claimed to be such an Ego. This subject of experiences cannot be claimed to be such an Ego, since it is not me, and this case involves only one person. Can this subject of experiences be a Cartesian Sub-Ego, a persisting purely mental entity which is merely part of a person? We may decide that we have insufficient grounds for believing that there are such things.

I turn next to the other view mentioned above. Some people believe that unity is explained by ownership, even though they deny that we are separately existing entities. These people believe that what unites a person's experiences at any time is the fact that these experiences are being had by this person. As we have seen, in this imagined case this belief is false. While I am having one set of experiences in my right-handed stream, I am also having another set in my left-handed stream. We cannot explain the unity of either set of experiences by claiming that these are the experiences that I am having at this time, since this would conflate these two sets.

A Reductionist may now intervene. On his view, what unites my experiences in my right-handed stream is that there is, at any time, a single state of awareness of these various experiences. There is a state of awareness of having certain thoughts, feeling writer's cramp, and hearing the sound of a squeaking pen. At the same time, there is another state of awareness of the various experiences in my left-handed stream. My mind is divided because there is no single state of awareness of both of these sets of experiences.

It may be objected that these claims do not explain but only redescribe the unity of consciousness in each stream. In one sense, this is true. This unity does not need a deep explanation. It is simply a fact that several experiences can be *co-conscious*, or be the objects of a single state of awareness. It may help to compare this fact with the fact that there is short-term memory of experiences within the last few moments: short-term memory of what is called 'the specious present'. Just as there can be a single memory of just having had several experiences, such as hearing a bell strike three times, there can be a single state of awareness both of hearing the fourth striking of this bell, and of seeing ravens fly past the bell-tower. Reductionists claim that nothing more is involved in the unity of consciousness at a single time. Since there can be one state of awareness of several experiences, we need not explain this unity by ascribing these experiences to the same person, or subject of experiences.

It is worth restating other parts of the Reductionist View. I claim:

> Because we ascribe thoughts to thinkers, it is true that thinkers exist. But thinkers are not separately existing entities. The existence of a thinker just involves the existence of his brain and body, the doing of his deeds, the thinking of his thoughts, and the occurrence of certain other physical and mental events. We could therefore redescribe any person's life in impersonal terms. In explaining the unity of this life, we need not claim that it is the life of a particular person. We could describe what, at different times, was thought and felt and observed and done, and how these various events were inter-related. Persons would be mentioned here only in the descriptions

of the content of many thoughts, desires, memories, and so on. Persons need not be claimed to be the thinkers of any of these thoughts.

These claims are supported by the case where I divide my mind. It is not merely true here that the unity of different experiences does not *need* to be explained by ascribing all of these experiences to me. The unity of my experiences, in each stream, *cannot* be explained in this way. There are only two alternatives. We might ascribe the experiences in each stream to a subject of experiences which is *not* me, and, therefore, not a person. Or, if we doubt the existence of such entities, we can accept the Reductionist explanation. At least in this case, this may now seem the best explanation.

This is one of the points at which it matters whether my imagined case is possible. If we could briefly divide our minds, this casts doubt on the view that psychological unity is explained by ownership. As I argued, if we are not Reductionists, we ought to regard my imagined case as involving only a single person. It then becomes impossible to claim that the unity of consciousness should be explained by ascribing different experiences to a single subject, the person. We could maintain this view only by believing in subjects of experiences that are not persons. Other animals are irrelevant here. Our belief is about what is involved in the lives of persons. If we have to admit that in these lives there could be two kinds of subjects of experiences, those that are and those that are not persons, our view will have lost much of its plausibility. It would help our view if we could claim that, because persons are indivisible, my imagined case could never happen.

My case is imagined. But the essential feature of the case, the division of consciousness into separate streams, *has* happened several times. This undermines the reply just given. My imagined case may well become possible, and could at most be merely technically impossible. And in this case the unity of consciousness in each stream cannot be explained by ascribing my experiences to me. Because this explanation fails, this case refutes the view that psychological unity can be explained by ascribing different experiences to a single person. [...]

89 What Happens When I Divide?

I shall now describe another natural extension of the actual cases of divided minds. Suppose first that I am one of a pair of identical twins, and that both my body and my twin's brain have been fatally injured. Because of advances in neuro-surgery, it is not inevitable that these injuries will cause us both to die. We have between us one healthy brain and one healthy body. Surgeons can put these together.

This could be done even with existing techniques. Just as my brain could be extracted, and kept alive by a connection with an artifical heart-lung machine, it could be kept alive by a connection with the heart and lungs in my twin's body. The drawback, today, is that the nerves from my brain could not be connected with the nerves in my twin's body. My brain could survive if transplanted into his body, but the resulting person would be paralysed.

Even if he is paralysed, the resulting person could be enabled to communicate with others. One crude method would be some device, attached to the nerve that would have controlled this person's right thumb, enabling him to send messages in Morse Code. Another device, attached to some sensory nerve, could enable him to receive messages. Many people would welcome surviving, even totally paralysed, if they could still communicate with others. The stock example is that of a great scientist whose main aim in life is to continue thinking about certain abstract problems.

Let us suppose, however, that surgeons are able to connect my brain to the nerves in my twin's body. The resulting person would have no paralysis, and would be completely healthy. Who would this person be?

This is not a difficult question. It may seem that there is a disagreement here between the Physical and Psychological Criteria. Though the resulting person will be psychologically continuous with me, he will not have the whole of my body. But, as I have claimed, the Physical Criterion ought not to require the continued existence of my whole body.

If all of my brain continues both to exist and to be the brain of one living person, who is psychologically continuous with me, I continue to exist. This is true whatever happens to the rest of my body. When I am given someone else's heart, I am the surviving recipient, not the dead donor. When my brain is transplanted into someone else's body, it may seem that I am here the dead donor. But I am really still the recipient, and the survivor. Receiving a new skull and a new body is just the limiting case of receiving a new heart, new lungs, new arms, and so on.[7]

It will of course be important what my new body is like. If my new body was quite unlike my old body, this would affect what I could do, and might thus indirectly lead to changes in my character. But there is no reason to suppose that being transplanted into a very different body would disrupt my psychological continuity.

It has been objected that 'the possession of some sorts of character trait requires the possession of an appropriate sort of body'. Quinton answers this objection. He writes, of an unlikely case,

> It would be odd for a six-year old girl to display the character of Winston Churchill, odd indeed to the point of outrageousness, but it is not utterly inconceivable. At first, no doubt, the girl's display of dogged endurance, a world-historical comprehensiveness of outlook, and so forth, would strike one as distasteful and pretentious in so young a child. But if she kept it up the impression would wear off.[8]

More importantly, as Quinton argues, this objection could show only that it might matter whether my brain is housed in a certain *kind* of body. It could not show that it would matter whether it was housed in any *particular* body. And in my imagined case my brain will be housed in a body which, though not numerically identical to my old body, is – because it is my twin's body – very similar.

On all versions of the Psychological Criterion, the resulting person would be me. And most believers in the Physical Criterion could be persuaded that, in this case, this is true. As I have claimed, the Physical Criterion should require only the continued existence of *enough* of my brain to be the brain of a living person, provided that no one else has enough of this brain. This would make it me who would wake up, after the operation. And if my twin's body was just like mine, I might even fail to notice that I had a new body.

It is in fact true that one hemisphere is enough. There are many people who have survived, when a stroke or injury puts out of action one of their hemispheres. With his remaining hemisphere, such a person may need to re-learn certain things, such as adult speech, or how to control both hands. But this is possible. In my example I am assuming that, as may be true of certain actual people, both of my hemispheres have the full range of abilities. I could thus survive with either hemisphere, without any need for re-learning.

I shall now combine these last two claims. I would survive if my brain was successfully transplanted into my twin's body. And I could survive with only half my brain, the other half having been destroyed. Given these two facts, it seems clear that I would survive if half my brain was success-fully transplanted into my twin's body, and the other half was destroyed.

What if the other half was *not* destroyed? This is the case that Wiggins described: that in which a person, like an amoeba, divides.[9] To simplify the case, I assume that I am one of three identical triplets. Consider

My Division   My body is fatally injured, as are the brains of my two brothers. My brain is divided, and each half is successfully transplanted into the body of one of my brothers. Each of the resulting people believes that he is me, seems to remember living my life, has my character, and is in every other way psychologically continuous with me. And he has a body that is very like mine.

This case is likely to remain impossible. Though it is claimed that, in certain people, the two hemispheres may have the same full range of abilities, this claim might be false. I am here assuming that this claim is true when applied to me. I am also assuming that it would be possible to connect a transplanted half-brain with the nerves in its new body. And I am assuming that we could divide, not just the upper hemispheres, but also the lower brain. My first two assumptions may be able to be made true if there is enough progress in neurophysiology. But it seems likely that it would never be possible to divide the lower brain, in a way that did not impair its functioning.

Does it matter if, for this reason, this imagined case of complete division will always remain impossible? Given the aims of my discussion, this does not matter. This impossibility is merely technical. The one feature of the case that might be held to be *deeply* impossible – the division of a person's consciousness into two separate streams – is the feature that has actually happened. It would have been important if this had been impossible, since this might have supported some claim about what we really are. It might have supported the claim that we are indivisible Cartesian Egos. It therefore matters that the division of a person's consciousness is in fact possible. There seems to be no similar connection between a particular view about what we really are and the impossibility of dividing and successfully transplanting the two halves of the lower brain. This impossibility thus provides no ground for refusing to consider the imagined case in which we suppose that this can be done. And considering this case may help us to decide both what we believe ourselves to be, and what in fact we are. As Einstein's example showed, it can be useful to consider impossible thought-experiments.

It may help to state, in advance, what I believe this case to show. It provides a further argument against the view that we are separately existing entities. But the main conclusion to be drawn is that *personal identity is not what matters*.

It is natural to believe that our identity is what matters. Reconsider the Branch-Line Case, where I have talked to my Replica on Mars, and am about to die. Suppose we believe that I and my Replica are different people. It is then natural to assume that my prospect is almost as bad as ordinary death. In a few days, there will be no one living who will be me. It is natural to assume that *this* is what matters. In discussing My Division, I shall start by making this assumption.

In this case, each half of my brain will be successfully transplanted into the very similar body of one of my two brothers. Both of the resulting people will be fully psychologically continuous with me, as I am now. What happens to me?

There are only four possibilities: (1) I do not survive; (2) I survive as one of the two people; (3) I survive as the other; (4) I survive as both.

The objection to (1) is this. I would survive if my brain was successfully transplanted. And people have in fact survived with half their brains destroyed. Given these facts, it seems clear that I would survive if half my brain was successfully transplanted, and the other half was destroyed. So how could I fail to survive if the other half was also successfully transplanted? How could a double success be a failure?

Consider the next two possibilities. Perhaps one success is the maximum score. Perhaps I shall be one of the two resulting people. The objection here is that, in this case, each half of my brain is exactly similar, and so, to start with, is each resulting person. Given these facts, how can I survive as only one of the two people? What can make me one of them rather than the other?

These three possibilities cannot be dismissed as incoherent. We can understand them. But, while we assume that identity is what matters, (1) is not plausible. My Division would not be as bad as death. Nor are (2) and (3) plausible. There remains the fourth possibility: that I survive as both of the resulting people.

This possibility might be described in several ways. I might first claim: 'What we have called "the two resulting people" are not two people. They are one person. I do survive this operation. Its effect is to give me two bodies, and a divided mind.'

This claim cannot be dismissed outright. As I argued, we ought to admit as possible that a person could have a divided mind. If this is possible, each half of my divided mind might control its own body. But though this description of the case cannot be rejected as inconceivable, it involves a great distortion in our concept of a person. In my imagined Physics Exam I claimed that this case involved only one person. There were two features of the case that made this plausible. The divided mind was soon reunited, and there was only one body. If a mind was permanently divided, and its halves developed in different ways, it would become less plausible to claim that the case involves only one person.

(Remember the actual patient who complained that, when he embraced his wife, his left hand pushed her away.)

The case of complete division, where there are also two bodies, seems to be a long way over the borderline. After I have had this operation, the two 'products' each have all of the features of a person. They could live at opposite ends of the Earth. Suppose that they have poor memories, and that their appearance changes in different ways. After many years, they might meet again, and fail even to recognise each other. We might have to claim of such a pair, innocently playing tennis: 'What you see out there is a single person, playing tennis with himself. In each half of his mind he mistakenly believes that he is playing tennis with someone else.' If we are not yet Reductionists, we believe that there is one true answer to the question whether these two tennis-players are a single person. Given what we mean by 'person', the answer must be No. It cannot be true that what I believe to be a stranger, standing there behind the net, is in fact another part of myself.

Suppose we admit that the two 'products' are, as they seem to be, two different people. Could we still claim that I survive as both? There is another way in which we could. I might say: 'I survive the operation as two different people. They can be different people, and yet be me, in the way in which the Pope's three crowns together form one crown.'[10]

This claim is also coherent. But it again greatly distorts the concept of a person. We are happy to agree that the Pope's three crowns, when put together, are a fourth crown. But it is hard to think of two people as, together, being a third person. Suppose the resulting people fight a duel. Are there three people fighting, one on each side, and one on both? And suppose one of the bullets kills. Are there two acts, one murder and one suicide? How many people are left alive? One or two? The composite third person has no separate mental life. It is hard to believe that there really would be such a third person. Instead of saying that the resulting people together constitute me – so that the pair is a trio – it is better to treat them as a pair, and describe their relation to me in a simpler way.

Other claims might be made. It might be suggested that the two resulting people are *now* different people, but that, before My Division, they *were* the same person. Before My Division, they were me. This suggestion is ambiguous. The claim may be that, before My Division, they *together* were me. On this account, there were three different people even before My Division. This is even less plausible than the claim I have just rejected. (It might be thought that I have misunderstood this sugges-tion. The claim may be that the resulting people did not exist, as separate people, before My Division. But if they did not then exist, it cannot have been true that they together were me.)

It may instead be suggested that, before My Division, *each* of the resulting people *was* me. After My Division, neither is me, since I do not now exist. But, if each of these people *was* me, whatever happened to me must have happened to each of these people. If I did not survive My Division, neither of these people survived. Since there *are* two resulting people, the case involves *five* people. This conclusion is absurd. Can we deny the assumption that implies this conclusion? Can we claim that, though each of the resulting people *was* me, what happened to me did not happen to these people? Assume that I have not yet divided. On this suggestion, it is now true that each of the resulting people *is* me. If what happens to me does not happen to X, X cannot be me.

There are far-fetched ways to deny this last claim. These appeal to claims about tensed identity. Call one of the resulting people *Lefty*. I might ask, 'Are *Lefty* and *Derek Parfit* names of one and the same person?' For believers in tensed identity, this is not a proper question. As this shows, claims about tensed identity are radically different from the way in which we now think. I shall merely state here what I believe others to have shown: these claims do not solve our problem.

David Lewis makes a different proposal. On his view, there are two people who share my body even before My Division. In its details, this proposal is both elegant and ingenious. I shall not repeat here why, as I have claimed elsewhere, this proposal does not solve our problem.[11]

I have discussed several unusual views about what happens when I divide. On these views, the case involves a single person, a duo, a trio two of whom compose the third, and a quintet. We could doubtless conjure up the missing quartet. But it would be tedious to consider more of these views. All involve too great distortions of the concept of a person. We should therefore reject the fourth suggested possibility: the claim that, in some sense, I survive as both of the two resulting people.

There are three other possibilities: that I shall be *one*, or *the other*, or *neither* of these people. These three claims seemed implausible. Note next that, as before, we could not *find out* what happens even if we could actually perform this operation. Suppose, for example, that I do survive as one of the resulting people. I would believe that I have survived. But I would know that the other resulting person falsely believes that he is me, and that he survived. Since I would know this, I could not trust my own belief. I might be the resulting person with the false belief. And, since we would both claim to be me, other people would have no reason to believe one of us rather than the other. Even if we performed this operation, we would therefore learn nothing.

Whatever happened to me, we could not discover what happened. This suggests a more radical answer to our question. It suggests that the Reductionist View is true. Perhaps there are not here different possibilities, each of which might be what happens, though we could never know which actually happens. Perhaps, when we know that each resulting person would have one half of my brain, and would be psychologically continuous with me, we know everything. What are we supposing when we suggest, for instance, that one of the resulting people might be me? What would make this the true answer?

I believe that there cannot be different possibilities, each of which might be the truth, unless we are separately existing entities, such as Cartesian Egos. If what I really am is one particular Ego, this explains how it could be true that one of the resulting people would be me. It could be true that it is in this person's brain and body that this particular Ego regained consciousness.

If we believe in Cartesian Egos, we might be reminded of Buridan's ass, which starved to death between two equally nourishing bales of hay. This ass had no reason to eat one of these bales of hay before eating the other. Being an overly-rational beast it refused to make a choice for which there was no reason. In my example, there would be no reason why the particular Ego that I am should wake up as one of the two resulting people. But this might just happen, in a random way, as is claimed for fundamental particles.

The more difficult question, for believers in Cartesian Egos, is whether I would survive at all. Since each of the resulting people would be psychologically continuous with me, there would be no evidence supporting either answer to this question. This argument retains its force, even if I am a Cartesian Ego.

As before, a Cartesian might object that I have misdescribed what would happen. He might claim that, if we carried out this operation, it would not in fact be true that *both* of the resulting people would be psychologically continuous with me. It might be true that one or other of these people was psychologically continuous with me. In either of these cases, this person would be me. It might instead be true that neither person was psychologically continuous with me. In this case, I would not survive. In each of these three cases, we would learn the truth.

Whether this is a good objection depends on what the relation is between our psychological features and the states of our brains. As I have said, we have conclusive evidence that the carrier of psychological continuity is *not* indivisible. In the actual cases in which hemispheres have been disconnected, this produced two series of thoughts and sensations. These two streams of consciousness were both psychologically continuous with the original stream. Psychological continuity has thus, in several actual cases, taken a dividing form. This fact refutes the objection just given. It justifies my claim that, in the imagined case of My Division, both of the resulting people would be psychologically continuous with me. Since this is so, the Cartesian View can be advanced here only in the more dubious version that does not connect the Ego with any observable or introspectible facts. Even if I am such an Ego, I could never know whether or not I had survived. For Cartesians, this case is a problem with no possible solution.

Suppose that, for the reasons given earlier, we reject the claim that each of us is really a Cartesian Ego. And we reject the claim that a person is any other kind of separately existing entity, apart from his brain and body, and various mental and physical events. How then should we answer the question about what happens when I divide? I distinguished four possibilities. When I discussed each possibility, there seemed to be strong objections to the claim that it would be what happens. If we believe that these are different possibilities, any of which might be what happens, the case is a problem for us too.

On the Reductionist View, the problem disappears. On this view, the claims that I have discussed do not describe different possibilities, any of which might be true, and one of which must be true. These claims are merely different descriptions of the same outcome. We know what this outcome is. There will be two future people, each of whom will have the body of one of my brothers, and will be fully psychologically continuous with me, because he has half of my brain. Knowing this, we know everything. I may ask, 'But shall I be one of these two people, or the other, or neither?' But I should regard this as an empty question. Here is a similar question. In 1881 the French Socialist Party split. What happened? Did the French Socialist Party cease to exist, or did it continue to exist as one or other of the two new Parties? Given certain further details, this would be an empty question. Even if we have no answer to this question, we could know just what happened.

I must now distinguish two ways in which a question may be empty. About some questions we should claim both that they are empty, and that they have no answers. We could decide to *give* these questions answers. But it might be true that any possible answer would be arbitrary. If this is so, it would be pointless and might be misleading to give such an answer. [. . .]

There is another kind of case in which a question may be empty. In such a case this question has, in a sense, an answer. The question is empty because it does not describe different possibilities, any of which might be true, and one of which must be true. The question merely gives us different descriptions of the same outcome. We could know the full truth about this outcome without choosing one of these descriptions. But, if we do decide to give an answer to this empty question, one of these descriptions is better than the others. Since this is so, we can claim that this description is the answer to this question. And I claim that there is a best description of the case where I divide. The best description is that neither of the resulting people will be me.

Since this case does not involve different possibilities, the important question is not, 'Which is the best description?' The important question is: 'What ought to matter to me? How ought I to regard the prospect of division? Should I regard it as like death, or as like survival?' When we have answered this question, we can decide whether I have given the best description. [...]

90 What Matters When I Divide?

Some people would regard division as being as bad, or nearly as bad, as ordinary death. This reaction is irrational. We ought to regard division as being about as good as ordinary survival. As I have argued, the two 'products' of this operation would be two different people. Consider my relation to each of these people. Does this relation fail to contain some vital element that is contained in ordinary survival? It seems clear that it does not. I would survive if I stood in this very same relation to only one of the resulting people. It is a fact that someone can survive even if half his brain is destroyed. And on reflection it was clear that I would survive if my whole brain was successfully transplanted into my brother's body. It was therefore clear that I would survive if half my brain was destroyed, and the other half was successfully transplanted into my brother's body. In the case that we are now considering, my relation to each of the resulting people thus contains everything that would be needed for me to survive as that person. It cannot be the *nature* of my relation to each of the resulting people that, in this case, causes it to fail to be survival. Nothing is *missing*. What is wrong can only be the duplication.

Suppose that I accept this, but still regard division as being nearly as bad as death. My reaction is now indefensible. I am like someone who, when told of a drug that could double his years of life, regards the taking of this drug as death. The only difference in the case of division is that the extra years are to run concurrently. This is an interesting difference; but it cannot mean that there are *no* years to run. We might say: 'You will lose your identity. But there are different ways of doing this. Dying is one, dividing is another. To regard these as the same is to confuse two with zero. Double survival is not the same as ordinary survival. But this does not make it death. It is even less like death.' [...]

If it was put forward on its own, it would be difficult to accept the view that personal identity is not what matters. But I believe that, when we consider the case of division, this difficulty disappears. When we see *why* neither resulting person will be me. I believe that, on reflection, we can also see that this does not matter, or matters only a little. [...]

[...] I might regard my division as being somewhat better than ordinary survival, or as being somewhat worse.

Why might I think it somewhat worse? I might claim that the relation between me and each of the resulting people is not quite the relation that matters in ordinary survival. This is not because something is missing, but because division brings *too much*. I may think that each of the resulting people will, in one respect, have a life that is worse than mine. Each will have to live in a world where there is someone else who, at least to start with, is exactly like himself. This may be unpleasantly uncanny. And it will raise practical problems. Suppose that what I most want is to write a certain book. This would be what each of the resulting people would most want to do. But it would be pointless for both to write this book. It would be pointless for both to do what they most want to do.

Consider next the relations between the resulting people and the woman I love. I can assume that, since she loves me, she will love them both. But she could not give to both the undivided attention that we now give to each other.

In these and other ways the lives of the resulting people may not be quite as good as mine. This might justify my regarding division as being not quite as good as ordinary survival. But it could not justify regarding division as being much less good, or as being as bad as death. And we should note that this reasoning ignores the fact that these two lives, taken together, would be twice as long as the rest of mine.

Instead of regarding division as being somewhat worse than ordinary survival, I might regard it as being better. The simplest reason would be the one just given: the doubling of the years to be lived. I might have more particular reasons. Thus there might be two life-long careers both of which I strongly want to pursue. I might strongly want both to be a novelist and to be a philosopher. If I divide, each of the resulting people could pursue one of these careers. And each would be glad if the other succeeds. Just as we can take pride and joy in the achievements of our children, each of the resulting people would take pride and joy in the other's achievements.

If I have two strong but incompatible ambitions, division provides a way of fulfilling both, in a way that would gladden each resulting person. This is one way in which division could be better than ordinary survival. But there are other problems that division could not wholly solve. Suppose that I am torn between an unpleasant duty and a seductive desire. I could not wholly solve this problem by quasi-intending one of the resulting people to do my duty, and quasi-intending the other to do what I desire. The resulting person whom I quasi-intend to do my duty would himself be torn between duty and desire. Why should *he* be the one to do my unpleasant duty? We can foresee trouble here. My duty might get done if the seductive desire could not be fulfilled by more than one person. It might be the desire to elope with someone who wants only one companion. The two resulting people must then compete to be this one companion. The one who fails in this competition might then, grudgingly, do my duty. My problem would be solved, though in a less attractive way.

These remarks will seem absurd to those who have not yet been convinced that the Reductionist View is true, or that identity is not what matters. Such a person might say: 'If I shall not *be* either of the resulting people, division could not fulfil my ambitions. Even if one of the resulting people is a successful novelist, and the other a successful philosopher, this fulfils neither of my ambitions. If one of my ambitions is to be a successful novelist, my ambition is that *I* be a successful novelist. This ambition will not be fulfilled if I cease to exist and *someone else* is a successful novelist. And this is what would happen if I shall be neither of the resulting people.'

This objection assumes that there is a real question whether I shall be one of the resulting people, or the other, or neither. It is natural to assume that these are three different possibilities, any of which might be what happens. But as I have argued, unless I am a separately existing entity, such as a Cartesian Ego, these cannot be three different possibilities. There is nothing that could make it true that any of the three might be what really happens. (This is compatible with my claim that there is a best description of this case: that I shall be neither resulting person. This does not commit me to the view that there are different possibilities. This would be so only if one of the other descriptions *might* have been the truth – which I deny.)

We *could* give a different description. We could say that I shall be the resulting person who becomes a successful novelist. But it would be a mistake to think that my ambition would be fulfilled if and only if we *called* this resulting person me. How we choose to describe this case has no rational or moral significance. [...]

91 Why There is No Criterion of Identity that can Meet Two Plausible Requirements

[...] Williams claims that the criterion of personal identity must meet two requirements. I shall claim that *no* plausible criterion of identity can meet both requirements. In contrast, on the Reductionist View, the analogous requirements can be met. The argument therefore gives us further grounds for accepting this view. But Williams's argument does not assume the Reductionist View. In discussing the argument, I shall therefore briefly set aside this view. It can wait in the wings, to reappear when the action demands it.

Williams's argument develops a remark of Reid's, against Locke's claim that whoever 'has the consciousness of present and past actions is the same person to whom they belong'. This implies, as Reid writes, 'that if the same consciousness can be transferred from one intelligent being to another...then two or twenty intelligent beings may be the same person'.[12]

Williams argues as follows. Identity is logically a one-one relation. It is logically impossible for one person to be identical to more than one person. I cannot be one and the same person as two different people. As we have seen, psychological continuity is not logically a one-one relation. Two different future people could both be psychologically continuous with me. Since these different people cannot both be me, psychological continuity cannot be the criterion of identity. Williams then claims that, to be acceptable, a criterion of identity must itself be logically a one-one relation. It must be a relation which could not *possibly* hold between one person and two future people. He therefore claims that the criterion of identity cannot be psychological continuity.[13]

Some reply that this criterion might appeal to *non-branching* psychological continuity. This is the version of this criterion that I have discussed. On what I call the Psychological Criterion, a future person will be me if he will be R-related to me, and there is no other person who will be R-related to me. Since this version of this criterion is logically a one-one relation, it has been claimed that it answers Williams's objection.[14]

Williams rejects this answer. He claims

Requirement (1): Whether a future person will be me must depend only on the *intrinsic* features of the relation between us. It cannot depend on what happens to *other* people.

Requirement (2): Since personal identity has great significance, whether identity holds cannot depend on a trivial fact.[15]

These requirements are both plausible. And neither requirement is met by non-branching psychological continuity. Williams therefore rejects this version of the Psychological Criterion.

This objection may seem too abstract to be convincing. Its force can be shown if I vary the imagined story with which I began. Consider Simple Teletransportation, where the Scanner destroys my brain and body. After my blueprint is beamed to Mars, the Replicator makes a perfect organic copy. My Replica on Mars will think that he is me, and he will be in every way psychologically continuous with me.

Suppose that we accept the Psychological Criterion which appeals to relation R when it holds in a one-one form. And suppose that we accept the Wide version, which allows R to have any reliable cause. This criterion implies that my Replica on Mars will be me. But we might learn that my blueprint is also being beamed to Io, one of the satellites of Jupiter. We must then claim that it will be me who wakes up on Mars, and that I shall continue to exist if my blueprint is ignored by the scientists on Io. But if the scientists on Io later make another Replica of me, when that Replica wakes up I shall cease to exist. Though the people around me on Mars will not notice any change, at that moment a new person will come into existence in my brain and body. Williams would object that, if I *do* wake up on Mars, whether I continue to exist there cannot depend, as we claim, on what happens to someone else millions of miles away near Jupiter. Our claim violates Requirement (1).

As I have argued, what fundamentally matters is whether I shall be R-related to at least one future person. It is relatively trivial whether I shall also be R-related to some other person. On this version of the Psychological Criterion, whether I shall be identical to some future person depends upon this relatively trivial fact. This violates Requirement (2).

Williams would add these remarks. Once we see that Teletransportation could produce many Replicas of me, who would be different people from each other, we should deny that I would in fact wake up on Mars even if they make only a single Replica. If they made two Replicas, these could not both be me. If they could not both be me, but they are produced in just the same way, we ought to conclude that neither would be me. But my relation to one of the Replicas is intrinsically the same whether or not they make the other. Since identity must depend on the intrinsic features of a relation, I would be neither Replica even if they did not make the other.[16] [...]

[...] Suppose that My Division proceeds as follows. I have two fatally brain-damaged brothers, Jack and Bill. A surgeon first removes and divides my brain. The halves are then taken to different wings of the hospital, where they will be transplanted into the bodies of my two brothers. If we appeal to the Physical Criterion, we must claim the following. Suppose that one half of my brain is successfully transplanted into Jack's body. Before the other half can be transplanted, it is dropped onto a concrete floor. If this is what happens, I shall wake up in Jack's body. But if the other half was successfully transplanted, I would wake up in neither body. [...]

[...] What is my relation to the person waking up in Jack's body? This relation is psychological continuity, with its normal cause, the continued existence of enough of my brain. There is also very close physical similarity. As a Reductionist, I claim that my relation to the person in Jack's body contains what fundamentally matters. This claim stands whatever happens to other people elsewhere. With one revision, my view meets Williams's first requirement. He claims that whether I shall be some future person ought to depend only on my relation to this future person. I make a similar claim. Instead of asking whether I shall be some future person, I ask whether my relation to this person contains what matters. Like Williams, I can claim that the answer must depend only on the *intrinsic* features of my relation to this future person.

The Reductionist View can meet this revised version of Requirement (1). Suppose that the other operation succeeds. Someone wakes up in Bill's body. On my view, this does not change the relation between me and the person in Jack's body. And it makes at most a little difference to the importance of this relation. This relation still contains what fundamentally matters. Since this relation now holds in a branching form, we are forced to change its *name*. We cannot call each branch of this relation personal identity. But this change in the relation's name has no significance.

This Reductionist View also meets the analogue of Requirement (2). Judgements of personal identity have great importance. Williams therefore claims that we should not make one such judgement and deny another without an important difference in our grounds. On this Reductionist

View, we should take the importance that we give to a judgement of identity, and we should give this importance to a different relation. On this view, what is important is relation R: psychological connectedness and/or continuity, with the right kind of cause. Unlike identity, this relation cannot fail to hold because of a trivial difference in the facts. If this relation fails to hold, there is a deep difference in the facts. This meets Requirement (2).

In the case where I divide, though my relation to each of the resulting people cannot be called identity, it contains what fundamentally matters. When we deny identity here, we need not be denying an important judgement. Since my relation to each of the resulting people is about as good as if it were identity, it may carry most of the ordinary implications of identity. Thus it might be claimed that, even when the person in Jack's body cannot be called me, because the other transplant succeeds, he can just as much deserve punishment or reward for what I have done. So can the person in Bill's body. [...]

Notes

[The notes for this chapter have been reformatted for this volume.]

1   See, for example, [L. Wittgenstein,] *Zettel*, edited by G. Anscombe and B. von Wright and translated by G. Anscombe (Oxford: Blackwell, 1967), proposition 350: 'It is as if our concepts involve a scaffolding of facts.... If you imagine certain facts otherwise ... then you can no longer imagine the application of certain concepts.'
2   W. V. Quine, review of *Identity and Individuation*, ed. Milton K. Munitz, *Journal of Philosophy* (1972), p. 490.
3   Quinton ('The Soul', *Journal of Philosophy* 59, no. 15 (July 1962); reprinted in J. Perry, ed., *Personal Identity* (Berkeley: University of California Press, 1975)) defends this view.
4   R. W. Sperry, in J. C. Eccles, ed., *Brain and Conscious Experience* (Berlin: Springer Verlag, 1966), p. 299.
5   T. Nagel, 'Brain Bisection and the Unity of Consciousness', *Synthese* 22 (1971); reprinted in T. Nagel, *Mortal Questions* (Cambridge: Cambridge University Press, 1979), p. 152.
6   Ibid., p. 153.
7   I follow S. Shoemaker, *Self-Knowledge and Self-Identity* (Ithaca, NY: Cornell University Press, 1963), p. 22.
8   Quinton, 'The Soul', p. 60.
9   D. Wiggins, *Identity and Spatio-Temporal Continuity* (Oxford: Blackwell, 1967), p. 50. I decided to study philosophy almost entirely because I was enthralled by Wiggins's imagined case.

10 Cf. ibid., p. 40. I owe this suggested way of talking, and one of the objections to it, to Michael Woods.

11 See Lewis's 'Survival and Identity' [ch. 4 below] and my 'Lewis, Perry, and What Matters', both in A. Rorty, ed., *The Identities of Persons* (Berkeley: University of California Press, 1976).

12 T. Reid, *Essays on the Intellectual Powers of Man*, first published in 1785, 'Of Memory', ch. 4; reprinted in Perry, ed., *Personal Identity*, p. 114.

13 In B. Williams, 'Bodily Continuity and Personal Identity', *Analysis* 20, no. 5; reprinted in B. Williams, *Problems of the Self* (Cambridge: Cambridge University Press, 1973), pp. 19–25.

14 J. M. Shorter, 'More About Bodily Continuity and Personal Identity', *Analysis* 22 (1961–2); and J. M. R. Jack (unpublished), who requires that this criterion be embedded in a causal theory.

15 Williams, *Problems of the Self*, p. 20.

16 Wiggins, *Identity and Spatio-Temporal Continuity; idem*, 'Essentialism, Continuity, and Identity', *Synthese* 23 (1974); and *idem, Sameness and Substance* (Oxford: Blackwell, 1980) advance similar arguments. Some of the issues raised, which I do not discuss here, are crisply discussed in R. Nozick, *Philosophical Explanations* (Cambridge, Mass.: Harvard University Press, 1981), pp. 656–9.

4

Survival and Identity

David Lewis

What is it that matters in survival? Suppose I wonder whether I will survive the coming battle, brainwashing, brain transplant, journey by matter-transmitter, purported reincarnation or resurrection, fission into twins, fusion with someone else, or what not. What do I really care about? If it can happen that some features of ordinary, everyday survival are present but others are missing, then what would it take to make the difference between something practically as good as commonplace survival and something practically as bad as commonplace death?

I answer, along with many others: *what matters in survival is mental continuity and connectedness*. When I consider various cases in between commonplace survival and commonplace death, I find that what I mostly want in wanting survival is that my mental life should flow on. My present experiences, thoughts, beliefs, desires, and traits of character should have appropriate future successors. My total present mental state should be but one momentary stage in a continuing succession of mental states. These successive states should be interconnected in two ways. First, by bonds of similarity. Change should be gradual rather than sudden, and (at least in some respects) there should not be too much change overall. Second, by bonds of lawful causal dependence. Such change as there is should conform, for the most part, to lawful regularities concerning the succession of mental states – regularities, moreover, that are exemplified in everyday cases of survival. And this should be so not by accident (and also not, for instance, because some demon has set out to create a succession of mental states patterned to counterfeit our ordinary mental life) but rather because each succeeding mental state causally depends for its character on the states immediately before it.

I refrain from settling certain questions of detail. Perhaps my emphasis should be on *connectedness*: direct relations of similarity and causal dependence between my present mental state and each of its successors; or perhaps I should rather emphasize *continuity*: the existence of step-by-step paths from here to there, with extremely strong local connectedness from each step to the next. Perhaps a special place should be given to the special kind of continuity and connectedness that constitute memory;[1] or perhaps not. Perhaps the "mental" should be construed narrowly, perhaps broadly. Perhaps nonmental continuity and connectedness – in my appearance and voice, for instance – also should have at least some weight. It does not matter, for the present, just which version I would prefer of the thesis that what matters is mental continuity and connectedness. I am sure that I would endorse some version, and in this paper I want to deal with a seeming problem for any version.

The problem begins with a well-deserved complaint that all this about mental connectedness and continuity is too clever by half. I have forgotten to say what should have been said first of all. What matters in survival is survival. If I wonder whether I will survive, what I mostly care about is quite simple. When it's all over, will I myself – the very same person now thinking these thoughts and writing these words – still exist? Will any one of those who do exist afterward be me? In other words, *what matters in survival is identity* – identity between the I who exists now and the surviving I who will, I hope, still exist then.

One question, two answers! An interesting answer, plausible to me on reflection but far from obvious: that what matters is mental connectedness and continuity between my present mental state and other mental states that will succeed it in the future. And a compelling commonsense answer, an unhelpful platitude that cannot credibly be denied: what matters is identity between myself, existing now, and myself, still existing in the future.

If the two answers disagreed and we had to choose one, I suppose we would have to prefer the platitude of common sense to the interesting philosophical thesis. Else it would be difficult to believe one's own philosophy! The only hope for the first answer, then, is to show that we need not choose: the answers are compatible, and both are right. That is the claim I wish to defend. I say that it cannot happen that what matters in survival according to one answer is present while what matters in survival according to the other answer is lacking.

I   Parfit's Argument

Derek Parfit has argued that the two answers cannot both be right, and we must therefore choose.[2] (He chooses the first.) His argument is as follows:

(a)   Identity is a relation with a certain formal character. It is one-one and it does not admit of degree.

(b)   A relation of mental continuity and connectedness need not have that formal character. We can imagine problem cases in which any such relation is one-many or many-one, or in which it is present to a degree so slight that survival is questionable.

Therefore, since Parfit believes as I do that what matters in survival is some sort of mental continuity or connectedness,

(c)   What matters in survival is not identity. At most, what matters is a relation that coincides with identity to the extent that the problem cases do not actually arise.

Parfit thinks that if the problem cases did arise, or if we wished to solve them hypothetically, questions of personal identity would have no compelling answers. They would have to be answered arbitrarily, and in view of the discrepancy stated in (a) and (b), there is no answer that could make personal identity coincide perfectly with the relation of mental continuity and connectedness that matters in survival.

Someone else could just as well run the argument in reverse. Of course what matters in survival is personal identity. Therefore what matters cannot be mental continuity or connectedness, in view of the discrepancy stated in premises (a) and (b). It must be some better-behaved relation.

My task is to disarm both directions of the argument and show that the opposition between what matters and identity is false. We can agree with Parfit (and I think we should) that what matters in questions of personal identity is mental continuity or connectedness, and that this might be one-many or many-one, and admits of degree. At the same time we can consistently agree with common sense (and I think we should) that what matters in questions of personal identity – even in the problem cases – is identity.

I do not attack premises (a) and (b). We could, of course, say "identity" and just mean mental continuity and connectedness. Then we would deny that "identity" must have the formal character stated in (a). But this verbal maneuver would not meet the needs of those who think, as I do, that what matters in survival is literally *identity*: that relation that everything bears to itself and to no other thing. As for (b), the problem cases clearly are possible under Parfit's conception of the sort of mental continuity or connectedness that matters in survival: or under any conception I might wish to adopt. The questions about continuity and connectedness which I left open are not relevant, since no way of settling them will produce a relation with the formal character of identity. So we do indeed have a discrepancy of formal character between identity and any suitable relation of mental continuity and connectedness.

But what does that show? Only that the two relations are different. And we should have known that from the start, since they have different relata. He who says that what matters in survival is a relation of mental continuity and connectedness is speaking of a relation among more or less momentary person-stages, or time-slices of continuant persons, or persons-at-times. He who says that what matters in survival is identity, on the other hand, must be speaking of identity among temporally extended continuant persons with stages at various times. What matters is that one and the same continuant person should have stages both now and later. Identity among stages has nothing to do with it, since stages are momentary. Even if you survive, your present stage is not identical to any future stage.[3] You know that your present stage will not survive the battle – that is not disconcerting – but will *you* survive?

II   The R-relation and the I-relation

Pretend that the open questions have been settled, so that we have some definite relation of mental continuity and connectedness among person-stages in mind as the relation that matters in survival. Call it the *R-relation*, for short. If you wonder whether you will survive the coming battle or what-not, you are wondering whether any of the stages that will exist afterward is R-related to you-now, the stage that is doing the wondering. Similarly for other "questions of personal identity." If you wonder whether this is your long-lost son, you mostly wonder whether the stage before you now is R-related to certain past stages. If you also wonder whether he is a reincarnation of Nero, you wonder whether this stage is R-related to other stages farther in the past. If you wonder whether it is in your self-interest to save for your old age, you wonder whether the stages of that tiresome old gaffer you will become are

R-related to you-now to a significantly greater degree than are all the other person-stages at this time or other times. If you wonder as you step into the duplicator whether you will leave by the left door, the right door, both, or neither, you are again wondering which future stages, if any, are R-related to you-now.

Or so say I. Common sense says something that sounds different: in wondering whether you will survive the battle, you wonder whether you – a continuant person consisting of your present stage along with many other stages – will continue beyond the battle. Will you be identical with anyone alive then? Likewise for other questions of personal identity.

Put this way, the two answers seem incomparable. It is pointless to compare the formal character of identity itself with the formal character of the relation R that matters in survival. Of course the R-relation among stages is not the same as identity either among stages or among continuants. But identity among continuant persons induces a relation among stages: the relation that holds between the several stages of a single continuant person. Call this the *I-relation*. It is the I-relation, not identity itself, that we must compare with the R-relation. In wondering whether you will survive the battle, we said, you wonder whether the continuant person that includes your present stage is identical with any of the continuant persons that continue beyond the battle. In other words: whether it is identical with any of the continuant persons that include stages after the battle. In other words: you wonder whether any of the stages that will exist afterward is I-related to – belongs to the same person as – your present stage. If questions of survival, or personal identity generally, are questions of identity among continuant persons, then they are also questions of I-relatedness among person-stages; and conversely. More precisely: *if common sense is right that what matters in survival is identity among continuant persons, then you have what matters in survival if and only if your present stage is I-related to future stages.* I shall not distinguish henceforth between the thesis that what matters in survival is identity and the thesis that what matters in survival is the I-relation. Either way, it is a compelling platitude of common sense.

If ever a stage is R-related to some future stage but I-related to none, or if ever a stage is I-related to some future stage but R-related to none, then the platitude that what matters is the I-relation will disagree with the interesting thesis that what matters is the R-relation. But no such thing can happen, I claim; so there can be no such disagreement. In fact, I claim that *any stage is I-related and R-related to exactly the same stages*. And I claim this not only for the cases that arise in real life, but for all possible problem cases as well. Let us individuate relations, as is usual, by necessary coextensiveness. Then I claim that *the I-relation is the R-relation*.

A continuant person is an aggregate[4] of person-stages, each one I-related to all the rest (and to itself). For short: a person is an I-*inter*related aggregate. Moreover, a person is not part of any larger I-interrelated aggregate; for if we left out any stages that were I-related to one another and to all the stages we included, then what we would have would not be a whole continuant person but only part of one. For short: a person is a maximal I-interrelated aggregate. And conversely, any maximal I-interrelated aggregate of person-stages is a continuant person. At least, I cannot think of any that clearly is not.[5] So far we have only a small circle, from personhood to I-interrelatedness and back again. That is unhelpful; but if the I-relation is the R-relation, we have something more interesting: a noncircular definition of personhood. I claim that *something is a continuant person if and only if it is a maximal R-interrelated aggregate of person-stages*. That is: if and only if it is an aggregate of person-stages, each of which is R-related to all the rest (and to itself), and it is a proper part of no other such aggregate.

I cannot tolerate any discrepancy in formal character between the I-relation and the R-relation, for I have claimed that these relations are one and the same. Now although the admitted discrepancy between identity and the R-relation is harmless in itself, and although the I-relation is not identity, still it may seem that the I-relation inherits enough of the formal character of identity to lead to trouble. For suppose that S_1, S_2, ... are person-stages; and suppose that C_1 is the continuant person of whom S_1 is a stage, C_2 is the continuant person of whom S_2 is a stage, and so on. Then any two of these stages S_i and S_j are I-related if and only if the corresponding continuant persons C_i and C_j are identical. The I-relations among the stages mirror the structure of the identity relations among the continuants.

I reply that the foregoing argument wrongly takes it for granted that every person-stage is a stage of one and only one continuant person. That is so ordinarily; and when that is so, the I-relation does inherit much of the formal character of identity. But ordinarily the R-relation also is well behaved. In the problem cases, however, it may happen that a single stage S is a stage of two or more different continuant persons. Worse, some or all of these may be persons to a diminished degree, so that it is questionable which of them should count as persons at all. If so, there would not be any such thing (in any straightforward way) as *the* person of whom S is a stage. So the supposition of the argument would not apply. It has not been shown that the I-relation inherits the formal character of identity in the problem cases. Rather it might be just as ill behaved as the R-relation. We shall examine the problem cases and see how that can happen.[6]

It would be wrong to read my definition of the I-relation as saying that person-stages S_1 and S_2 are I-related if and only if the continuant person of whom S_1 is a stage and the continuant person of whom S_2 is a stage are identical. The definite articles require the presupposition that I have just questioned. We should substitute the indefinite article: S_1 and S_2 are I-related if and only if a continuant person of whom S_1 is a stage and a continuant person of whom S_2 is a stage are identical. More simply: if and only if there is some one continuant person of whom both S_1 and S_2 are stages.

One seeming discrepancy between the I-relation and the R-relation need not disturb us. The I-relation must be symmetrical, whereas the R-relation has a direction. If a stage S_2 is mentally connected to a previous stage S_1, S_1 is available in memory to S_2 and S_2 is under the intentional control of S_1 to some extent – not the other way around.[7] We can say that S_1 is R-related *forward* to S_2, whereas S_2 is R-related *backward* to S_1. The forward and backward R-relations are converses of one another. Both are (normally) antisymmetrical. But although we can distinguish the forward and backward R-relations, we can also merge them into a symmetrical relation. That is the R-relation I have in mind: S_1 and S_2 are R-related simpliciter if and only if S_1 is R-related either forward or backward to S_2.

While we are at it, let us also stipulate that every stage is R-related – forward, backward, and simpliciter – to itself. The R-relation, like the I-relation, is reflexive.

Parfit mentions two ways for a discrepancy to arise in the problem cases. First, the R-relation might be one-many or many-one. Second, the R-relation admits in principle of degree, and might be present to a degree that is markedly subnormal and yet not negligible. Both possibilities arise in connection with fission and fusion of continuant persons, and also in connection with immortality or longevity.

III   Fission and Fusion

Identity is one-one, in the sense that nothing is ever identical to two different things. Obviously neither the I-relation nor the R-relation is one-one in that sense. You-now are a stage of the same continuant as many other stages, and are R-related to them all. Many other stages are stages of the same continuant as you-now, and are R-related to you-now.

But when Parfit says that the R-relation might be one-many or many-one, he does not just mean that. Rather, he means that one stage might be R-related to many stages that are not R-related to one another, and that many stages that are not R-related to one another might all be R-related to one single stage. (These possibilities do not differ once we specify that the R-relation is to be taken as symmetrical.) In short, the R-relation might fail to be transitive.

In a case of fission, for instance, we have a prefission stage that is R-related forward to two different, simultaneous postfission stages that are not R-related either forward or backward to each other. The forward R-relation is one-many, the backward R-relation is many-one, and the R-relation simpliciter is intransitive.

In a case of fusion we have two prefusion stages, not R-related either forward or backward to each other, that are R-related forward to a single postfusion stage. The forward R-relation is many-one, the backward R-relation is one-many, and the R-relation simpliciter is again intransitive.

Identity must be transitive, but the I-relation is not identity. The I-relation will fail to be transitive if and only if there is partial overlap among continuant persons. More precisely: if and only if two continuant persons C_1 and C_2 have at least one common stage, but each one also has stages that are not included in the other. If S is a stage of both, S_1 is a stage of C_1 but not C_2, and S_2 is a stage of C_2 but not C_1, then transitivity of the I-relation fails. Although S_1 is I-related to S, which in turn is I-related to S_2, yet S_1 is not I-related to S_2. In order to argue that the I-relation, unlike the R-relation, must be transitive, it is not enough to appeal to the uncontroversial transitivity of identity. The further premise is needed that partial overlap of continuant persons is impossible.

Figure 4.1 shows how to represent fission and fusion as cases of partial overlap. The continuant persons involved, C_1 and C_2, are the two maximal R-interrelated aggregates of stages marked by the two sorts of cross-hatching. In the case of fission, the prefission stages are shared by both continuants. In the case of fusion, the postfusion stages are likewise shared. In each case, we have a shared stage S that is I-related to two stages S_1 and S_2 that are not I-related to each other. Also S is R-related to S_1 and S_2 (forward in the case of fission, backward in the case of fusion) but S_1 and S_2 are not R-related to each other. More generally, the I-relation and the R-relation coincide for all stages involved in the affair.

There is, however, a strong reason for denying that continuant persons can overlap in this way. From this denial it would indeed follow (as it does not follow from the transitivity of identity alone) that the I-relation cannot share the possible intransitivities of the R-relation.

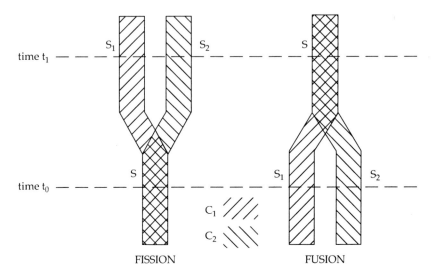

Figure 4.1

The trouble with overlap is that it leads to overpopulation. To count the population at a given time, we can count the continuant persons who have stages at that time; or we can count the stages. If there is overlap, there will be more continuants than stages. (I disregard the possibility that one of the continuants is a time traveler with distinct simultaneous stages.) The count of stages is the count we accept; yet we think we are counting persons, and we think of persons as continuants rather than stages. How, then, can we tolerate overlap?

For instance, we say that in a case of fission *one* person becomes *two*. By describing fission as initial stage-sharing we provide for the two, but not for the one. There are two all along. It is all very well to say from an eternal or postfission standpoint that two persons (with a common initial segment) are involved, but we also demand to say that on the day before the fission only *one* person entered the duplication center; that his mother did not bear twins; that until he fissions he should only have one vote; and so on. Counting at a time, we insist on counting a person who will fission as one. We insist on a method of counting persons that agrees with the result of counting stages, though we do not think that counting persons just *is* counting (simultaneous) stages.

It is not so clear that we insist on counting a product of fusion as one (or a time traveler meeting himself as two). We are not sure what to say. But suppose we were fully devoted to the doctrine that the number of different persons in existence at a time is the number of different person-stages at that time. Even so, we would not be forced to deny that continuant persons could overlap. We would therefore not be driven to conclude that the I-relation cannot share the possible intransitivities of the R-relation.

The way out is to deny that we must invariably count two nonidentical continuants as two. We might count not by identity but by a weaker relation. Let us say that continuants C_1 and C_2 are *identical-at-time-t* if and only if they both exist at t and their stages at t are identical. (More precisely: C_1 and C_2 both have stages at t, and all and only stages of C_1 at t are stages of C_2 at t.) I shall speak of such relations of identity-at-a-time as relations of *tensed identity*. Tensed identity is not a kind of identity. It is not identity among stages, but rather a derivative relation among continuants which is induced by identity among stages. It is not identity among continuants, but rather a relation that is weaker than identity whenever different continuants have stages in common. If we count continuants by tensed identity rather than by identity, we will get the right answer – the answer that agrees with the answer we get by counting stages – even if there is overlap. How many persons entered the duplication center yesterday? We may reply: C_1 entered and C_2 entered, and no one else; although C_1 and C_2 are not identical today, and are not identical simpliciter, they were identical yesterday. So counting by identity-yesterday, there was only one. Counting by identity-today, there were two; but it is inappropriate to count by identity-today when we are talking solely about the events of yesterday. Counting by identity simpliciter there were two; but in talking about the events of yesterday it is as unnatural to count by identity as it is to count by identity-today. There is a way of counting on which there are two all along; but there is another way on which there are first one and then two. The latter has obvious practical advantages. It should be no surprise if it is the way we prefer.

It may seem far-fetched to claim that we ever count persons otherwise than by identity simpliciter. But we sometimes *do* count otherwise. If an infirm man wishes to know how many roads he must cross to reach his destination, I will count by identity-along-his-path rather than by identity. By crossing the Chester A. Arthur Parkway and Route 137 at the brief stretch where they have merged, he can cross both by crossing only one road. Yet these two roads are certainly not identical.

You may feel certain that you count persons by identity, not by tensed identity. But how can you be sure? Normal cases provide no evidence. When no stages are shared, both ways of counting agree. They differ only in the problem cases: fission, fusion, and another that we shall soon consider. The problem cases provide no very solid evidence either. They are problem cases just because we cannot consistently say quite all the things we feel inclined to. We must strike the best compromise among our conflicting initial opinions. Something must give way; and why not the opinion that of course we count by identity, if that is what can be sacrificed with least total damage?

A relation to count by does not have to be identity, as the example of the roads shows. But perhaps it should share the key properties of identity. It should at least be an *equivalence* relation: reflexive, symmetrical, and transitive. Relations of tensed identity are equivalence relations. Further, it should be an *indiscernibility* relation; not for all properties whatever, as identity is, but at least for some significant class of properties. That is, it ought to be that two related things have exactly the same properties in that class. Identity-at-time-t is an indiscernibility relation for a significant class of properties of continuant persons: those properties of a person which are logically determined by the properties of his stage at t. The class includes the properties of walking, being tall, being in a certain room, being thirsty, and believing in God at time t; but not the properties of being forty-three years old, gaining weight, being an ex-Communist, or remembering one's childhood at t. The class is sizable enough, at any rate, to make clear that a relation of tensed identity is more of an indiscernibility relation than is identity-along-a-path among roads.

If we are prepared to count a product of fusion as two, while still demanding to count a person who will fission as one, we can count at t by the relation of identity-at-all-times-up-to-t. This is the relation that holds between continuants C_1 and C_2 if and only if (1) they both exist at some time no later than t, (2) at any time no later than t, either both exist or neither does, and (3) at any time no later than t when both exist, they have exactly the same stages. Again, this is a relation among continuants that is weaker than identity to the extent that continuants share stages. Although derived from identity (among stages) it is of course not itself identity. It is even more of an indiscernibility relation than identity-at-t, since it confers indiscernibility with respect to such properties as being forty-three years old, gaining weight (in one sense), being an ex-Communist, and remembering one's childhood at t; though still not with respect to such properties as being, at t, the next winner of the State Lottery.

It may be disconcerting that we can have a single name for one person (counting by tensed identity) who is really two nonidentical persons because he will later fission. Isn't the name ambiguous? Yes; but so long as its two bearers are indiscernible in the respects we want to talk about, the ambiguity is harmless. If C_1 and C_2 are identical-at-all-times-up-to-now and share the name "Ned" it is idle to disambiguate such remarks as "Ned is tall," "Ned is waiting to be duplicated," "Ned is frightened," "Ned only decided yesterday to do it," and the like. These will be true on both disambiguations of "Ned," or false on both. Before the fission, only predictions need disambiguating. After the fission, on the other hand, the ambiguity of "Ned" will be much more bother. It can be expected that the ambiguous name "Ned" will then fall into disuse, except when we wish to speak of the shared life of C_1 and C_2 before the fission.

But what if we don't know whether Ned will fission? In that case, we don't know whether the one person Ned (counting by identity-now) is one person, or two, or many (counting by identity). Then we don't know whether "Ned" is ambiguous or not. But if the ambiguity is not a practical nuisance, we don't need to know. We can wait and see whether or not we have been living with a harmless ambiguity.

This completes my discussion of fission and fusion. To summarize: if the R-relation is the I-relation, and in particular if continuant persons are maximal R-interrelated aggregates of person-stages, then cases of fission and fusion must be treated as cases of stage-sharing between different, partially overlapping continuant persons. If so, the R-relation and the I-relation are alike intransitive, so there is no discrepancy on that score. If it is granted that we may count continuant persons by tensed identity, then this treatment does not conflict with our opinion that in fission one person becomes two; nor with our opinion (if it really is our opinion) that in fusion two persons become one.

IV Longevity

I turn now to a different problem case. Parfit has noted that mental connectedness will fade away eventually. If the R-relation is a matter of direct connectedness as well as continuity, then intransitivities of the R-relation will appear in the case of a person (if it is a person!) who lives too long.

Consider Methuselah. At the age of 100 he still remembers his childhood. But new memories crowd out the old. At the age of 150 he has hardly any memories that go back before his twentieth year. At the age of 200 he has hardly any memories that go back before his seventieth year; and so on. When he dies at the age of 969, he has hardly any memories that go beyond his 839th year. As he grows older he grows wiser; his callow opinions and character at age 90 have vanished almost without a trace by age 220, but his opinions and character at age 220 also have vanished almost without a trace by age 350. He soon learns that it is futile to set goals for himself too far ahead. At age 120, he is still somewhat interested in fulfilling the ambitions he held at age 40; but at age 170 he cares nothing for those ambitions, and it is beginning to take an effort of will to summon up an interest in fulfilling his aspirations at age 80. And so it goes.

We sometimes say: in later life I will be a different person. For us short-lived creatures, such remarks are an extravagance. A philosophical study of personal identity can ignore them. For Methuselah, however, the fading-out of personal identity looms large as a fact of life. It is incumbent on us to make it literally true that he will be a different person after one and one-half centuries or so.

I should imagine that this is so just in virtue of normal aging over 969 years. If you disagree, imagine that Methuselah lives much longer than a bare millennium (Parfit imagines the case of immortals who change mentally at the same rate as we do). Or imagine that his life is punctuated by frequent amnesias, brain-washings, psychoanalyses, conversions, and what not, each one of which is almost (but not quite) enough to turn him into a different person.

Suppose, for simplicity, that any two stages of Methuselah that are separated by no more than 137 years are R-related; and any two of his stages that are separated by more than 137 years are not R-related. (For the time being, we may pretend that R-relatedness is all-or-nothing, with a sharp cut-off.)

If the R-relation and the I-relation are the same, this means that two of Methuselah's stages belong to a single continuant person if and only if they are no more than 137 years apart. (Therefore the whole of Methuselah is not a single person.) That is the case, in particular, if continuant persons are maximal R-interrelated aggregates. For if so, then segments of Methuselah are R-interrelated if and only if they are no more than 137 years long; whence it follows that all and only the segments that are exactly 137 years long are maximal R-interrelated aggregates; so all and only the 137-year segments are continuant persons.

If so, we have intransitivity both of the R-relation and of the I-relation. Let S_1 be a stage of Methuselah at the age of 400; let S_2 be a stage of Methuselah at the age of 500; let S_3 be a stage of Methuselah at the age of 600. By hypothesis S_1 is R-related to S_2 and S_2 is R-related to S_3, but S_1 and S_3 are not R-related. Being separated by 200 years, they have no direct mental connections. Since S_1 and S_2 are linked by a 137-year segment (in fact, by infinitely many) they are I-related; likewise S_2 and S_3 are I-related. But S_1 and S_3 are not linked by any 137-year segment, so they are not I-related. The R-relation and the I-relation are alike intransitive.

The problem of overpopulation is infinitely worse in the case of Methuselah than in the cases of fission or fusion considered hitherto. Methuselah spends his 300th birthday alone in his room. How many persons are in that room? There are infinitely many different 137-year segments that include all of Methuselah's stages on his 300th birthday. One begins at the end of Methuselah's 163rd birthday and ends at the end of his 300th birthday; another begins at the beginning of his 300th and ends at the beginning of his 437th. Between these two are a continuum of other 137-year segments. No two of them are identical. Every one of them puts in an appearance (has a stage) in Methuselah's room on Methuselah's 300th birthday. Every one of them is a continuant person, given our supposition that Methuselah's stages are R-related if and only if they are not more than 137 years apart, and given that continuant persons are all and only maximal R-interrelated aggregates of person-stages. It begins to seem crowded in Methuselah's room!

Tensed identity to the rescue once more. True, there are continuum many nonidentical continuant persons in the room. But, counting by the appropriate relation of tensed identity, there is only one. All the continuum many nonidentical continuant persons are identical-at-the-time-in-question, since they all share the single stage at that time. Granted that we may count by tensed identity, there is no over crowding.

V   Degree

We turn now to the question of degree. Identity certainly cannot be a matter of degree. But the I-relation is not defined in terms of identity alone. It derives also from personhood: the property of being a continuant person. Thus personal identity may be a matter of degree because personhood is a matter of degree, even though identity is not. Suppose two person-stages S_1 and S_2 are stages of some one continuant that is a person to a low, but not negligible, degree. Suppose further that they are not stages of anything else that is a person to any higher degree. Then they are I-related to a low degree. So if personhood admits of degree, we have no discrepancy in formal character between the I-relation and the R-relation.

Parfit suggests, for instance, that if you fuse with someone very different, yielding a fusion product mentally halfway between you and your partner, then it is questionable whether you have survived. Not that there is a definite, unknown answer. Rather, what matters in survival – the R-relation – is present in reduced degree. There is less of it than in clear cases of survival, more than in clear cases of nonsurvival.[8] If we want the I-relation and the R-relation to coincide, we may take it that C_1 and C_2 (see Fig. 4.1 for cases of fusion) are persons to reduced degree because they are broken by abrupt mental discontinuities. If persons are maximal R-interrelated aggregates, as I claim, that is what we should expect; the R-relations across the fusion point are reduced in degree, hence the R-interrelatedness of C_1 and C_2 is reduced in degree, and hence the personhood of C_1 and C_2 is reduced in degree. C_1 and C_2 have less personhood than clear cases of persons, more personhood than continuant aggregates of stages that are clearly not persons. Then S and S_1, or S and S_2, are I-related to reduced degree just as they are R-related to reduced degree.

Personal identity to reduced degrees is found also in the case of Methuselah. We supposed before that stages no more than 137 years apart are R-related while states more than 137 years apart were not. But if the R-relation fades away at all – if it is a relation partly of connectedness as well as continuity – it would be more realistic to suppose that it fades away gradually. We can suppose that stages within 100 years of each other are R-related to a high enough degree so that survival is not in doubt; and that stages 200 or more years apart are R-related to such a low degree that what matters in survival is clearly absent. There is no significant connectedness over long spans of time, only continuity. Then if we want the R-relation and the I-relation to coincide, we could say roughly this: 100-year segments of Methuselah are persons to a high degree, whereas 200-year segments are persons only to a low degree. Then two stages that are strongly R-related also are strongly I-related, whereas stages that are weakly R-related are also weakly I-related. Likewise for all the intermediate degrees of R-relatedness of stages, of personhood of segments of Methuselah, and hence of I-relatedness of stages.

It is a familiar idea that personhood might admit of degrees. Most of the usual examples, however, are not quite what I have in mind. They concern continuants that are said to be persons to a reduced degree because their stages are thought to be person-stages to a reduced degree. If anyone thinks that the wolf-child, the "dehumanized" proletarian, or the human vegetable is not fully a person, that is more because he regards the stages themselves as deficient than because the stages are not strongly enough R-interrelated. If anyone thinks that personhood is partly a matter of species membership, so that a creature of sorcery or a freak offspring of hippopotami could not be fully a person no matter how much he resembled the rest of us, that also would be a case in which the stages themselves are thought to be deficient. In this case the stages are thought to be deficient not in their intrinsic character but in their causal ancestry; there is, however, nothing wrong with their R-interrelatedness. A severe case of split personality, on the other hand, does consist of perfectly good person-stages that are not very well R-related. If he is said not to be fully a person, that *is* an example of the kind of reduced personhood that permits us to claim that the R-relation and the I-relation alike admit of degrees.

Let us ignore the complications introduced by deficient person-stages. Let us assume that all the stages under consideration are person-stages to more or less the highest possible degree. (More generally, we could perhaps say that the degree of I-relatedness of two stages depends not on the absolute degree of personhood of the continuant, if any, that links them; but rather on the relative degree of personhood of that continuant compared to the greatest degree of personhood that the degree of person-stage-hood of the stages could permit. If two wolf-child-stages are person-stages only to degree 0.8, but they are stages of a continuant that is a person to degree 0.8, we can say that the stages are thereby I-related to degree 1.)

If we say that a continuant person is an aggregate of R-interrelated person-stages, it is clear that personhood admits of degree to the extent that the R-relation does. We can say something like this: the degree of R-interrelatedness of an aggregate is the minimum degree of R-relatedness between any two stages in the aggregate. (Better: the greatest lower bound on the degrees of R-relatedness between any two stages.) But when we recall that a person should be a maximal such aggregate, confusion sets in. Suppose we have an aggregate that is R-interrelated to degree 0.9, and it is not included in any larger aggregate that is R-interrelated to degree 0.9 or greater. Suppose, however, that it *is* included in a much larger aggregate that is R-interrelated to degree 0.88. We know the degree to which it qualifies as an R-interrelated aggregate, but to what degree does it qualify as a maximal one? That is, to what degree does it qualify as a person, if persons are maximal R-interrelated aggregates? I am inclined to say: it passes the R-interrelatedness test for personhood to degree 0.9, but at the same time it flunks the maximality test to degree 0.88. Therefore it is a person only to degree 0.02!

This conclusion leads to trouble. Take the case of Methuselah. Assuming that R-relatedness fades out gradually, every segment that passes the

R-interrelatedness test to a significant degree also flunks the maximality test to almost the same degree. (If the fadeout is continuous, delete "almost.") So *no* segment of Methuselah passes both tests for personhood to any significant degree. No two stages, no matter how close, are stages of some *one* continuant that is a person to high degree. Rather, nearby stages are strongly I-related by being common to many continuants, each one of which is strongly R-interrelated, is almost as strongly nonmaximal, and therefore is a person only to a low degree.

We might sum the degrees of personhood of all the continuants that link two stages, taking the sum to be the degree of I-relatedness of the stages.

But there is a better way. Assume that R-relatedness can come in all degrees ranging from 0 to 1 on some scale. Then every number in the interval from 0 to 1 is a possible location for an arbitrary boundary between pairs of stages that are R-related and pairs that are not. Call every such number a *delineation* of this boundary. Every delineation yields a decision as to which stages are R-related. It thereby yields a decision as to which continuants are R-interrelated; a decision as to which continuants are included in larger R-interrelated aggregates; a decision as to which continuants are persons, given that persons are maximal R-interrelated aggregates; and thence a decision as to which stages are I-related. We can say that a certain continuant is a person, or that a certain pair of stages are I-related, *relative* to a given delineation. We can also say whether something is the case relative to a set of delineations, provided that all the delineations in the set agree on whether it is the case. Then we can take the degree to which it is the case as the size (more precisely: Lebesgue measure) of that set. Suppose, for instance, that two stages count as I-related when we set the cut-off for R-relatedness anywhere from 0 to 0.9, but not when we set the cut-off more stringently between 0.9 and 1. Then those two stages are I-related relative to delineations from 0 to 0.9, but not relative to delineations from 0.9 to 1. They are I-related to degree 0.9 – the size of the delineation interval on which they are I-related. Yet there may not be any continuant linking those stages that is a person to degree more than 0. It may be that any continuant that links those stages is both R-interrelated and maximal only at a single delineation. At any more stringent delineation, it is no longer R-interrelated; while at any less stringent delineation it is still R-interrelated but not maximal.

The strategy followed here combines two ideas. (1) When something is a matter of degree, we can introduce a cut-off point. However, the choice of this cut-off point is more or less arbitrary. (2) When confronted with an arbitrary choice, the thing to do is not to make the choice. Rather, we should see what is common to all or most ways (or all or most reasonable ways) of making the choice, caring little what happens on any particular way of making it. The second idea is van Fraassen's method of super-valuations.[9]

On this proposal the I-relation admits of degree; and further, we get perfect agreement between degrees of I-relatedness and degrees of R-relatedness, regardless of the degrees of personhood of continuants. For at any one delineation, two stages are R-related if and only if they belong to some one maximal R-interrelated aggregate; hence if and only if they belong to some one continuant person; hence if and only if they are I-related. Any two stages are R-related and I-related relative to exactly the same set of delineations. Now if two stages are R-related to a degree x, it follows (given our choice of scale and measure) that they are R-related at all and only the delineations in a certain set of size x. Therefore they are I-related at all and only the delineations in a certain set of size x; which means that they are I-related to degree x. The degree of I-relatedness equals the degree of R-relatedness. In this way personal identity can be just as much a matter of degree as the mental continuity or connectedness that matters in survival. [...]

Postscript

A   Two Minds with but a Single Thought

Derek Parfit rejects my attempt to square his views (which are mine as well) with common sense.[10] He objects that before I bring off the recon-ciliation, I must first misrepresent our commonsensical desire to survive. Consider a fission case as shown. I say there are two continuant persons all along, sharing their initial segments. One of them, C_1, dies soon after the fission. The other, C_2, lives on for many years. Let S be a shared stage at time t_0, before the fission but after it is known that fission will occur. The thought to be found in S is a desire for survival, of the most com-monsensical and unphilosophical kind possible. Since S is a shared stage, this desire is a shared desire. Certainly C_2 has the survival he desired, and likewise has what we think matters: mental continuity and connect-edness (the R-relation) between S and much later stages such as S_2. But how about C_1?

I wrote that "if common sense is right that what matters in survival is identity..., then you have what matters in survival if and only if your present stage is I-related to future stages" where stages are I-related iff

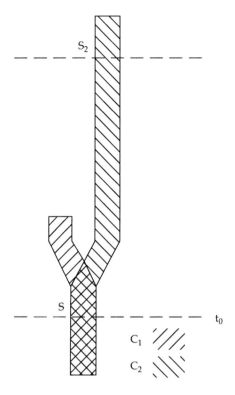

Figure 4.2

they belong to some single continuant person (p. 148 above). If that is right, then C_1 has what he commonsensically desired. For C_1's stage S at time t_0 is indeed I-related to stages far in the future such as S_2. These stages are I-related via the person C_2 – "But isn't this the *wrong* person?" says Parfit. C_1 himself survives only a short time. The one who lives longer is another person, one with whom C_1 once shared stages. If his desire is satisfied by this vicarious survival, it cannot really have been a commonsensical desire to survive.

If C_1 really had the commonsensical desire that he himself – the continuant person C_1 – survive well into the future, then I grant that his desire is not satisfied. But I don't think he could have had exactly that desire. I said that the desire found in S was to be *of the most commonsensical and unphilosophical kind possible*. And there is a limit to how commonsensical one's desires can possibly be under the peculiar circumstance of stage-sharing.

The shared stage S does the thinking for both of the continuants to which it belongs. Any thought it has must be shared. It cannot desire one thing on behalf of C_1 and another thing on behalf of C_2. If it has an urgent, self-interested desire for survival on the part of C_1, that very thought must also be an urgent, self-interested (and not merely benevolent) desire for survival on the part of C_2. It is not possible that one thought should be both. So it is not possible for S to have such a desire on behalf of C_1. So it is not possible for C_1 at t_0 to have the straightforward commonsensical desire that he himself survive.

If C_1 and C_2 share the most commonsensical kind of desire to survive that is available to them under the circumstances, it must be a plural desire: let *us* survive. Now we must distinguish two different plural desires: existential and universal, weak and strong.

> (weak)   Let at least one of us survive.
> (strong) Let all of us survive.

Because these desires are plural instead of singular, they are not perfectly commonsensical. Because they are put in terms of survival of continuants rather than relations of stages, they are more commonsensical than the "philosophical" desire for R-relatedness of one's present stage to future stages.

If C_1's (imperfectly) commonsensical desire for survival is predominantly the weak desire, then my reconciliation goes through. For C_1's weak desire is satisfied even though it is his stage-sharer rather than himself who survives. The weak desire is indeed equivalent to a desire for I-relatedness to future stages. Then if I am right that the I-relation is the R-relation, it is equivalent also to the desire for R-relatedness to future stages.

If C_1's desire is predominantly the strong desire, on the other hand, it is not satisfied. Then his desire for survival is not equivalent to the "philosophical" desire for R-relatedness to future stages, and my reconciliation fails. (However, the strong desire is equivalent to a more complicated desire concerning R-relatedness of stages.) But should we say that C_1 has the strong desire, and that since it is not satisfied, he does not have what commonsensically matters in survival? I think not. For if we say that of C_1, we must say it also of C_2. If one has the strong desire, both do. The strong desire is no more satisfied for C_2 than it is for C_1. But it seems clear that C_2, at least, *does* have what commonsensically matters in survival.

It is instructive to consider a system of survival insurance described by Justin Leiber, in *Beyond Rejection*.[11] (But let us imagine it without the risks and unpleasantness that Leiber supposes.) From time to time your mind is recorded: should a fatal accident befall you, the latest recording is played back into the blank brain of a fresh body. This system satisfies the weak desire for survival, but not the strong desire. Let S at t_0 be the stage that desires survival and therefore decides to have a recording made; the fission occurs at the time of recording; C_1 dies in an accident not long after; C_2 survives. The only extra peculiarities, compared with a simple case of fission, are that C_2 is interrupted in time and undergoes a body transplant. If this system would fairly well satisfy your desire for survival – or if your misgivings about it concern the body transplant rather than the fission – then your desire is predominantly the weak desire.

So far, I have supposed that C_1 and C_2 at t_0 already anticipate their fission. Now suppose not. Now, cannot they share the perfectly common-sensical singular desire: let *me* survive? After all, the desire to be found in the stage S in this case is no different from the desire that would be there if S were what it takes itself to be: a stage of a single person with no fission in his future. I agree that C_1 and C_2 have the singular desire. But it is not a desire that can be satisfied, for it rests on the false presupposition that they are a single person. The "me" in their shared thought (unless it refers to the thinking stage) has the status of an improper description. It cannot refer to C_1 in C_1's thought and to C_2 in C_2's thought, for these thoughts are one and the same. But their desire to survive *is* satisfied; at least C_2's is, and C_1's is no different. Therefore their desire for survival cannot consist only of their unsatisfiable singular desire. They must have the weak plural desire as well, despite the fact that they don't anticipate fission. And so must we. Doubtless we seldom have it as an occurrent desire. But many of our urgent desires are not occurrent, for instance your present desire not to suffer a certain torture too fiendish for you to imagine.

(At this point the reader of "Attitudes *De Dicto* and *De Se*" (in this volume [David Lewis, *Philosophical Papers*, vol. 1 (New York: Oxford University Press, 1986)]) may wonder how well I have learned my own lesson. There I taught that desire is a relation of wanting-to-have – take this as indivisible – that the subject bears to a property. Why can't C_1 and C_2 bear the very same wanting-to-have relation to the very same property of surviving, so that they think the very same thought, and yet each thereby desire his own survival? But recall that the subject that wants-to-have properties was taken to be a stage, not a continuant. [...] Under this analysis, my point is that S's wanting-to-have the property being such that the unique continuant of which it is a stage survives

is an unsatisfiable desire. That is so whether we think of it as a desire of S's or, more naturally, as a desire of C_1 and C_2. S had better want survival on behalf of C_1 and C_2 by wanting to have a different property:

being such that some continuant of which it is a stage survives.

This is the satisfied desire for survival that C_1 and C_2 share.)

B   In Defense of Stages[12]

Some would protest that they do not know what I mean by "more or less momentary person-stages, or time-slices of continuant persons, or persons-at-times." Others do know what I mean, but don't believe there are any such things.

The first objection is easy to answer, especially in the case where the stages are less momentary rather than more. Let me consider that case only; though I think that instantaneous stages also are unproblematic, I do not really need them. A person-stage is a physical object, just as a person is. (If persons had a ghostly part as well, so would person-stages.) It does many of the same things that a person does: it talks and walks and thinks, it has beliefs and desires, it has a size and shape and location. It even has a temporal duration. But only a brief one, for it does not last long. (We can pass over the question how long it can last before it is a segment rather than a stage, for that question raises no objection of principle.) It begins to exist abruptly, and it abruptly ceases to exist soon after. Hence a stage cannot do everything that a person can do, for it cannot do those things that a person does over a longish interval.

That is what I mean by a person-stage. Now to argue for my claim that they exist, and that they are related to persons as part to whole. I do not suppose the doubters will accept my premises, but it will be instructive to find out which they choose to deny.

First: it is possible that a person-stage might exist. Suppose it to appear out of thin air, then vanish again. Never mind whether it is a stage *of* any person (though in fact I think it is). My point is that it is the right sort of thing.

Second: it is possible that two person-stages might exist in succession, one right after the other but without overlap. Further, the qualities and location of the second at its appearance might exactly match those of the first at its disappearance. Here I rely on a *patchwork principle* for possibility: if it is possible that X happen intrinsically in a spatiotemporal region, and if it is likewise possible that Y happen in a region, then also it is possible that both X and Y happen in two distinct but adjacent regions. There are no necessary incompatibilities between distinct existences. Anything can follow anything.

Third: extending the previous point, it is possible that there might be a world of stages that is exactly like our own world in its point-by-point distribution of intrinsic local qualities over space and time.

Fourth: further, such a world of stages might also be exactly like our own in its causal relations between local matters of particular fact. For nothing but the distribution of local qualities constrains the pattern of causal relations. (It would be simpler to say that the causal relations supervene on the distribution of local qualities, but I am not as confident of that as I am of the weaker premise.)

Fifth: then such a world of stages would be exactly like our own simpliciter. There are no features of our world except those that supervene on the distribution of local qualities and their causal relations.

Sixth: then our own world is a world of stages. In particular, person-stages exist.

Seventh: but persons exist too, and persons (in most cases) are not person-stages. They last too long. Yet persons and person-stages, like tables and table-legs, do not occupy spatiotemporal regions twice over. That can only be because they are not distinct. They are part-identical; in other words, the person-stages are parts of the persons.

Let me try to forestall two misunderstandings. (1) When I say that persons are maximal R-interrelated aggregates of person-stages, I do *not* claim to be reducing "constructs" to "more basic entities." (Since I do not intend a reduction to the basic, I am free to say without circularity that person-stages are R-interrelated aggregates of shorter person-stages.) Similarly, I think it is an informative necessary truth that trains are maximal aggregates of cars interrelated by the ancestral of the relation of being coupled together (count the locomotive as a special kind of car). But I do not think of this as a reduction to the basic. Whatever "more basic" is supposed to mean, I don't think it means "smaller." (2) By a part, I just mean a subdivision. I do not mean a well-demarcated subdivision that figures as a unit in causal explanation. Those who give "part" a rich meaning along these lines[13] should take me to mean less by it than they do.

Notes

1 Better, *quasi-memory*: that process which is memory when it occurs within one single person, but might not be properly so-called if it occurred in a succession of mental states that did not all belong to a single person.

2 Derek Parfit, "Personal Identity," *Philosophical Review* 80 (1971): 3–27.

3 Unless time is circular, so that it is in its own future in the same way that places are to the west of themselves. But that possibility also has nothing to do with survival.

4 It does not matter what sort of "aggregate." I prefer a mereological sum, so that the stages are literally parts of the continuant. But a class of stages would do as well, or a sequence or ordering of stages, or a suitable function from moments or stretches of time to stages.

5 The least clear-cut cases are those in which the stages cannot be given any "personal time" ordering with respect to which they vary in the way that the stages of an ordinary person vary with respect to time. But it is so indeterminate what we want to say about such bizarre cases that they cannot serve as counter-examples to any of my claims.

6 The argument also takes it for granted that every person-stage is a stage of at least one person. I do not object to that. If there is no way to unite a stage in a continuant with other stages, let it be a very short-lived continuant person all by itself.

7 As before, it would be better to speak here of quasi-memory; and likewise of quasi-intentional control.

8 No similar problem arises in cases of fission. We imagine the immediate postfission stages to be pretty much alike, wherefore they can all be strongly R-related to the immediate prefission stages.

9 See Bas van Fraassen, "Singular Terms, Truth-Value Gaps, and Free Logic," *Journal of Philosophy* 63 (1966): 481–95. See also the discussion of vagueness in my "General Semantics," in this volume [David Lewis, *Philosophical Papers*, vol.1 (New York: Oxford University Press, 1986)].

10 "Lewis, Perry and What Matters," in Amélie Rorty [ed.], *The Identities of Persons* (Berkeley: University of California Press, 1976), pp. 91–6.

11 (New York: Ballantine, 1980).

12 On this topic I am much indebted to discussions with Saul Kripke and with Denis Robinson. Kripke's views on related matters were presented in his lectures on "Identity through Time," given at Princeton in 1978 (and elsewhere); Robinson's in "Re-Identifying Matter," *Philosophical Review* 91(1982): 317–41.

13 Such as D. H. Mellor, in his *Real Time* (Cambridge: Cambridge University Press. 1981), chapter 8.

5

Personal Identity and the Unity of Agency: A Kantian Response to Parfit

Christine M. Korsgaard

[...]

II The Unity of Agency

Suppose Parfit has established that there is no deep sense in which I am identical to the subject of experiences who will occupy my body in the future.[1] In this section I will argue that I nevertheless have reasons for regarding myself as the same rational agent as the one who will occupy my body in the future. These reasons are not metaphysical, but practical.

To see this, first set aside the problem of identity over time, and think about the problem of identity at any given time. Why do you think of yourself as one person now? This problem should seem especially pressing if Parfit has convinced you that you are not unified by a Cartesian Ego which provides a common subject for all your experiences. Just now you are reading this article. You may also be sitting in a chair, tapping your foot, and feeling hot or tired or thirsty. But what makes it one person who is doing and experiencing all this? We can add to this a set of characteristics which you attribute to yourself, but which have only an indirect bearing on your conscious experiences at any given time. You have loves, interests, ambitions, virtues, vices, and plans. You are a conglomerate of parts, dispositions, activities, and experiences. As Hume says, you are a bundle.[2] What makes you one person even at one time?

In *On the Soul*, Aristotle says that the practical faculty of the soul must be one thing.[3] We think of it as having parts, of course, because we sometimes have appetites that are contrary to practical reason, or experience conflict among our various desires. Still, the faculty that originates motion must be regarded as a single thing, because we do act. Somehow, the conflicts are resolved, and no matter how many different things you want to do, you in fact do one rather than another.

Your conception of yourself as a unified agent is not based on a metaphysical theory, nor on a unity of which you are conscious. Its grounds are practical, and it has two elements. First, there is the raw necessity of eliminating conflict among your various motives. In making his argument for Reductionism, Parfit appeals to a real-life example which has fascinated contemporary philosophers: persons with split brains (245–46).[4] When the corpus callosum, the network of nerves between the two hemispheres of the brain, is cut, the two hemispheres can function separately.[5] In certain experimental situations, they do not work together and appear to be wholly unconscious of each other's activities. These cases suggest that the two hemispheres of the brain are not related in any metaphysically deeper way than, say, two people who are married. They share the same quarters and, with luck, they communicate. Even their characteristic division of labor turns out to be largely conventional, and both can perform most functions. So imagine that the right and left halves of your brain disagree about what to do. Suppose that they do not try to resolve their differences, but each merely sends motor orders, by way of the nervous system, to your limbs. Since the orders are contradictory, the two halves of your body try to do different things.[6] Unless they can come to an agreement, both hemispheres of your brain are ineffectual. Like parties in Rawls's original position, they must come to a unanimous decision somehow. You are a unified person at any given time because you must act, and you have only one body with which to act.

The second element of this pragmatic unity is the unity implicit in the *standpoint* from which you deliberate and choose. It may be that what actually happens when you make a choice is that the strongest of your conflicting desires wins. But that is not the way you think of it when you deliberate. When you deliberate, it is as if there were something over and above all your desires, something that is *you*, and that *chooses* which one to act on. The idea that you choose among your conflicting desires, rather than just waiting to see which one wins, suggests that you have reasons for or against acting on them.[7] And it is these reasons, rather than the desires themselves, which are expressive of your will. The strength of a desire may be counted *by you* as a reason for acting on it; but this is different from *its* simply winning. This means that there is some principle or way of choosing that you regard as expressive of *yourself*, and that provides reasons that regulate your choices among your desires. To identify with such a principle or way of choosing is to be "a law to yourself,'' and to be unified as such. This does not require that your agency be located in a separately existing entity or involve a deep metaphysical fact. Instead, it is a practical necessity imposed upon you by the nature of the deliberative standpoint.[8]

It is of course important to notice that the particular way you choose which desires to act on *may* be guided by your beliefs about certain metaphysical facts. Parfit evidently thinks that it should. When he argues about the rationality of concern about the future, Parfit assumes that my attitude about the desires of the future inhabitant of my body should be based on the metaphysics of personal identity. That is, I should treat a future person's desires as *mine* and so as normative for me if I have some metaphysical reason for supposing that she is *me*.[9] But this argument from the metaphysical facts to normative reasons involves a move from ''is'' to ''ought'' which requires justification. I will argue shortly that there may be other, more distinctively normative grounds for determining which of my motives are ''my own''; metaphysical facts are not the only possible ground for this decision. For now, the important points are these: First, the *need* for identification with some unifying principle or way of choosing is imposed on us by the necessity of making deliberative choices, not by the metaphysical facts. Second, the metaphysical facts do not obviously settle the question: I must still decide whether the consideration that some future person is ''me'' has some special normative force for me. It is practical reason that requires me to construct an identity for myself; whether metaphysics is to guide me in this or not is an open question.

The considerations I have adduced so far apply to unification at any given moment, or in the context of any given decision. Now let us see whether we can extend them to unity over time. We might start by pointing out that the body which makes you one agent now persists over time, but that is insufficient by itself. The body could still be a series of agents, each unified pragmatically at any given moment. More telling considerations come from the character of the things that human agents actually choose. First of all, as Parfit's critics often point out, most of the things we do that matter to us take up time. Some of the things we do are intelligible only in the context of projects that extend over long periods. This is especially true of the pursuit of our ultimate ends. In choosing our careers, and pursuing our friendships and family lives, we both presuppose and construct a continuity of identity and of agency.[10] On a more mundane level, the habitual actions we perform for the sake of our health presuppose ongoing identity. It is also true that we think of our activities and pursuits as interconnected in various ways: we think that we are carrying out plans of life. In order to carry out a rational plan of life, you need to be one continuing person. You normally think you lead one continuing life because you are one person, but according to this argument the truth is the reverse. You are one continuing person because you have one life to lead.

You may think of it this way: suppose that a succession of rational agents *do* occupy my body. I, the one who exists now, need the cooperation of the others, and they need mine, if together we are going to have any kind of a *life*. The unity of our life is forced upon us, although not deeply, by our shared embodiment, together with our desire to carry on long-term plans and relationships. But actually this is somewhat misleading. To ask why the present self should cooperate with the future ones is to assume that the present self has reasons with which it already identifies, and which are independent of those of later selves. Perhaps it is natural to think of the present self as necessarily concerned with present satisfaction. But it is mistaken. In order to make deliberative choices, your present self must identify with something from which you will derive your reasons, but not necessarily with something present. The sort of thing you identify yourself with may carry you automatically into the future; and I have been suggesting that this will very likely be the case. Indeed, the choice of any action, no matter how trivial, takes you some way into the future. And to the extent that you regulate your choices by identifying yourself as the one who is implementing something like a particular plan of life, you need to identify with your future in order to be *what you are even now*.[11] When the person is viewed as an agent, no clear content can be given to the idea of a merely present self.[12]

Still, Parfit might reply that all this concedes his point about the insignificance of personal identity. The idea that persons are unified as agents shares with Reductionism the implication that personal identity is not very deep. If personal identity is just a prerequisite for coordinating action and carrying out plans, individual human beings do not have to be its possessors. We could, for instance, always act in groups. The answer to this is surely that for many purposes we do; there *are* agents of different sizes in the world. Whenever some group wants or needs to act as a unit, it must form itself into a sort of person – a legal person, say, or a corporation. Parfit himself likes to compare the unity of persons to the unity of nations. A nation, like a person, exists, but it does not amount to anything more than "the existence of its citizens, living together in certain ways, on its territory" (211–12). In a similar way, he suggests, a person just amounts to "the existence of a brain and body, and the occurrence of a series of interrelated physical and mental events" (211). On the view I am advancing, a better comparison would be the state. I am using "nation" here, as Parfit does, for a historical or ethnic entity, naturalistically defined by shared history and traditions; a state, by contrast, is a moral or formal entity, defined by its constitution and deliberative procedures. A state is not merely a group of citizens living on a shared territory. We have a state only where these citizens have constituted themselves into a single agent. They have, that is, adopted a way of resolving conflicts, making decisions, interacting with other states, and planning together for an ongoing future. For a group of citizens to view themselves as a state, or for us to view them as one, we do not need to posit the state as a separately existing entity. All we need is to grant an authoritative status to certain choices and decisions made by certain citizens or bodies, as its legislative voice. Obviously, a state is not a deep metaphysical entity underlying a nation, but rather something a nation can make of itself. Yet the identity of states, for practical reasons, must be regarded and treated as more determinate than the identity of nations.

But the pragmatic character of the reasons for agent unification does not show that the resulting agencies are not *really* necessary. Pragmatic necessity can be overwhelming. When a group of human beings occupy the same territory, for instance, they have an imperative need to form a unified state. And when a group of psychological functions occupy the same human body, they have an even more imperative need to become a unified person. This is why the human body must be conceived as a unified agent. As things stand, it is the basic kind of agent.

Of course if our technology were different, individual human bodies might not be the basic kind of agent. My argument supports a physical criterion of identity, but only a conditional one. *Given the technology we have now*, the unit of action is a human body. But consider Thomas Nagel's concept of a "series-person." Nagel imagines a society in which persons are replicated in new matter once every year after they reach the age of thirty. This prevents them from aging, and barring accidents and incurable diseases, may even make them immortal (289–90). On my concept, a series-person, who would be able to carry out unified plans and projects, and have ongoing relations with other persons, would be a person.[13] But the fact that the basic unit of action might be different if technology were different is neither here nor there. The relevant necessity is the necessity of acting and living, and it is untouched by mere technological possibilities. The main point of the argument is this: a focus on agency makes more sense of the notion of personal identity than a focus on experience. There is a necessary connection between agency and unity which requires no metaphysical support.

III   The Unity of Consciousness

Many will feel that my defense of personal unity simply bypasses what is most unsettling in Parfit's arguments. Parfit's arguments depend on what we may broadly call an "Aristotelian" rather than a "Cartesian" metaphysics of the person. That is, matter is essentially particular; form is essentially copiable; and form is what makes the person what she is, and so is what is important about her. The "Cartesian" metaphysics, by contrast, holds that the important element of a person is something essentially particular and uncopiable, like a Cartesian Ego. What tempts people to believe this is an entrenched intuition that something like a Cartesian Ego serves as the locus of the particular consciousness that is mine and no one else's. And my argument about the unity of agency in no way responds to this intuition.

Parfit writes: "When I believed that my existence was a further fact, I seemed imprisoned in myself. My life seemed like a glass tunnel, through which I was moving faster every year, and at the end of which there was darkness. When I changed my view, the walls of my glass tunnel disappeared. I now live in the open air" (281). Parfit's glass tunnel is a good image of the way people think of the unity of consciousness. The sphere of consciousness presents itself as something like a room, a place, a lit-up area, within which we do our thinking, imagining, remembering, and planning, and from out of which we observe the world, the passing scene. It is envisioned as a tunnel or a stream, because we think that one moment of consciousness is somehow directly continuous with others, even when interrupted by deep sleep or anesthesia. We are inclined to think that memory is a deeper thing than it is, that it is *direct* access to an earlier stage of a continuing self, and not merely one way of knowing what happened. And so we may think of amnesia, not merely as the loss of knowledge, but as a door that blocks an existing place.

The sense that consciousness is in these ways unified supports the idea that consciousness requires a persisting psychological subject. The unity of consciousness is supposed to be explained by attributing all one's experiences to a single psychological entity. Of course, we may argue that the hypothesis of a unified psychological subject does nothing to *explain* the unity of consciousness. It is simply a figure for or restatement of that unity. Yet the idea of such a subject seems to have explanatory force. It is to challenge this intuition that Parfit brings up the facts about persons with divided brains. People are often upset by these facts because they think that they cannot imagine what it is like to be such a person. When the hemispheres function separately, the person seems to have two streams of consciousness. If consciousness is envisioned as a sort of place, then this is a person who seems to be in two places at the same time. If consciousness requires a subject, then this person's body seems, mysteriously, to have become occupied by two subjects. Here, the hypothesis of a psychological subject brings confusion rather than clarity.

Parfit's own suggestion is that the unity of consciousness "does not need a deep explanation. It is simply a fact that several experiences can be co-conscious, or be the objects of a single state of awareness" (250). Split-brain people simply have experiences which are not co-conscious, and nothing more needs to be said. This seems to me close to the truth but not quite right. Privileging the language of "having experiences" and "states of awareness" gives the misleading impression that we can count the experiences we are now having, or the number of objects of which we are aware, and then ask what unifies them. The language of activities and dispositions enables us to characterize both consciousness and its unity more accurately.[14]

Consciousness, then, is a feature of certain activities which percipient animals can perform. These activities include perceiving; various forms of attending such as looking, listening, and noticing; more intellectual activities like thinking, reflecting, recalling, remembering, and reading; and moving voluntarily. Consciousness is not a state that makes these activities possible, or a qualification of the subject who can perform them. It is a feature of *the activities themselves*. It is misleading to say that you must be conscious in order to perform them, because your being able to perform them is all that your being conscious amounts to.

Voluntary motion is an important example because of a distinction that is especially clear in its case. When we move voluntarily, we move consciously. But this is not to say we are conscious that we are moving. Much of the time when we move nothing is further from our minds than *the fact* that we are moving. But of course this does not mean that we move unconsciously, like sleepwalkers. It is crucial, in thinking about these matters, not to confuse *being engaged in a conscious activity* with *being conscious of an activity*. Perhaps such a confusion lies behind Descartes' bizarre idea that nonhuman animals are unconscious. In the direct, practical sense, an adult hunting animal which is, say, stalking her prey, knows exactly what she is doing. But it would be odd to say that she is aware *of* what she is doing or that she knows anything *about* it. What she is aware of is her environment, the smell of her prey, the grass bending quietly under her feet. The consciousness that is inherent in psychic activities should not be understood as an inner *observing* of those activities, a theoretic state. An animal's consciousness can be entirely practical.

The unity of consciousness consists in one's ability to coordinate and integrate conscious activities. People with split brains cannot integrate these activities in the same way they could before. This would be disconcerting, because the integration itself is not something we are ordinarily aware of. But it would not make you feel like two people. In fact, such persons learn new ways to integrate their psychic functions, and appear normal and normally unified in everyday life. It is only in experimental situations that the possibility of unintegrated functioning is even brought to light.[15]

What makes it possible to integrate psychic functions? If this is a causal question, it is a question for neurologists rather than philosophers. But perhaps some will still think there is a conceptual necessity here – that such integration requires a common psychological subject. But think again of persons with split brains. Presumably, in ordinary persons the corpus callosum provides means of communication between the two hemispheres; it transmits signals. When split-brain persons are not in experimental situations, and they function normally, the reason appears to be simply that the two hemispheres are able to communicate by other means than the corpus callosum. For example, if the left hemisphere turns the neck to look at something, the right hemisphere necessarily feels the tug and looks too.[16] Activities, then, may be coordinated when some form of communication takes place between the performers of those activities. But communication certainly does not require a common psychological subject. After all, when they can communicate, two different people can integrate their functions, and, for purposes of a given activity, become a single agent.

Communication and functional integration do not require a common subject of conscious experiences. What they do require, however, is the unity of agency. Again, there are two aspects of this unity. First, there is the raw practical necessity. Sharing a common body, the two hemispheres of my brain, or my various psychic functions, must work together. The "phenomenon" of the unity of consciousness is nothing more than the *lack* of any perceived difficulty in the coordination of psychic functions. To be sure, when I engage in psychic activities *deliberately*, I regard myself as the subject of these activities. *I* think, *I* look, *I* try to remember. But this is just the second element of the unity of agency, the unity inherent in the deliberative standpoint. I regard myself as the employer of my psychic capacities in much the same way that I regard myself as the arbiter among my conflicting desires.

If these reflections are correct, then the unity of consciousness is simply another instance of the unity of agency, which is forced upon us by our embodied nature.

IV   Agency and Identity

At this point it will be useful to say something about why I take the view I am advancing to be a Kantian one. Kant believed that as rational beings we may view ourselves from two different standpoints.[17] We may regard ourselves as objects of theoretical understanding, natural phenomena whose behavior may be causally explained and predicted like any other. Or we may regard ourselves as agents, as the thinkers of our thoughts and the originators of our actions. These two standpoints cannot be completely assimilated to each other, and the way we view ourselves when we occupy one can appear incongruous with the way we view ourselves when we occupy the other. As objects of theoretical study, we see ourselves as wholly determined by natural forces, the mere undergoers of our experiences. Yet as agents, we view ourselves as free and responsible, as the authors of our actions and the *leaders* of our lives. The incongruity need not become contradiction, so long as we keep in mind that the two views of ourselves spring from two different relations in which we stand to our actions. When we look at our actions from the theoretical standpoint our concern is with their explanation and prediction. When we view them from the practical standpoint our concern is with their justification and choice. These two relations to our actions are equally legitimate, inescapable, and governed by reason, but they are separate. Kant does not assert that it is a matter of theoretical fact that we are agents, that we are free, and that we are responsible. Rather, we must view ourselves in these ways when we occupy the standpoint of practical reason – that is, when we are deciding what to do. This follows from the fact that we must regard ourselves as the causes – the first causes – of the things that we will. And this fundamental attitude is forced upon us by the necessity of making choices, regardless of the theoretical or metaphysical facts.[18]

From the theoretical standpoint, an action may be viewed as just another experience, and the assertion that it has a subject may be, as Parfit says, "because of the way we talk." But from the practical point of view, actions and choices must be viewed as having agents and choosers. This is what *makes* them, in our eyes, our own actions and choices rather than events that befall us. In fact, it is only from the practical point of view that actions and choices can be distinguished from mere "behavior" determined by biological and psychological laws. This does not mean that our existence as agents is asserted as a further fact, or requires a separately existing entity that should be discernible from the theoretical point of view.[19] It is rather that from the practical point of view our relationship to our actions and choices is essentially *authorial*: from it, we view them as *our own*. I believe that when we think about the way in which our own lives matter to us personally, we think of ourselves in this way. We think of living our lives, and even of having our experiences, as something that we *do*. And it is this important feature of our sense of our identity that Parfit's account leaves out.[20]

What sort of difference does this make? To put it in Parfit's terms, it privileges certain kinds of psychological connection – roughly speaking, authorial ones – over others. In discussing the events that according to Reductionism comprise a person's life, Parfit introduces the idea of a *boring* event – for instance, the continued existence of a belief or a desire (211). His point in including these, of course, is to cover the fact that one of the things that makes you the same person at time$_2$ that you were at time$_1$ is that certain things about you have remained the same. But we can distinguish beliefs and desires that continue merely because, having been acquired in childhood, they remain unexamined from beliefs and desires that continue because you have arrived at, been convinced of, decided on, or endorsed them. In an account of personal identity which emphasizes agency or authorship, the latter kind of connection will be regarded as much less boring than the former. This is because beliefs and desires you have actively arrived at are more truly your own than those which have simply arisen in you (or happen to inhere in a metaphysical entity that is you).[21] Recall Mill's complaint:

> Not only in what concerns others, but in what only concerns themselves, the individual or the family do not ask themselves, what do I prefer? or, what would suit my character and disposition? or, what would allow the best and highest in me to have fair play and enable it to grow and thrive? ...I do not mean that they choose what is customary in preference to what suits their own inclination. It does not occur to them to have any inclination except for what is customary. Thus the mind itself is bowed to the yoke: even in what people do for pleasure, conformity is the first thing thought of; they like in crowds..., and are generally without either opinions or feelings of home growth, or *properly their own*.[22]

It is, I think, significant that writers on personal identity often tell stories about mad surgeons who make changes in our memories or characters.[23] These writers usually emphasize the fact that after the surgical intervention we are altered, we have changed. But surely part of what creates the sense of lost identity is that the person is changed by *intervention*, from outside. The stories might affect us differently if we imagined the changes initiated by the person herself, as a result of her own choice. You are not a different person *just* because you are very different.[24] Authorial psychological connectedness is consistent with drastic changes, provided those changes are the result of actions by the person herself or reactions for which she is responsible.[25]

It is important to see how these claims do and do not violate Parfit's thesis that we should not care what the causal mechanism of connection is (286). Given a suitable understanding of the idea of a causal mechanism, the Kantian can agree. If I can overcome my cowardice by surgery or medication rather than habituation I might prefer to take this less arduous route. So long as an authentic good will is behind my desire for greater courage, and authentic courage is the result, the mechanism should not matter. But for the Kantian it does matter who is initiating the use of the mechanism. Where I change myself, the sort of continuity needed for identity may be preserved, even if I become very different. Where I am changed by wholly external forces, it is not. This is because the sort of continuity needed for what matters to me in my own personal identity essentially involves my agency. [...]

Notes

1   This formulation is not, I believe, quite right. Parfit's arguments show that there is not a one-to-one correspondence between persons and human animals, but of course there is no implication that a person ever exists apart from a human animal. So perhaps we should say that what his arguments show is that the subject of *present* experiences is not the person, but the animal on whom the person supervenes. There are several difficulties with this way of talking, for there are pressures to attribute experiences to the person, not to the animal. It is the person to whom we attribute memory of the experience, and what the person remembers is "such and such happened to me," not "such and such happened to the animal who I was then." And, to the extent that the character of your experiences is conditioned by memories and character, we should say that the character of your experiences is more determined by which person you are than by which animal you are (see note 14 below). In fact, however, none of this blocks the conclusion that the animal is the subject of experiences in the sense that it is immediately conscious of them when they are present. And I will suggest that we attribute experiences to the person in a

different sense: the person is the agent in whose activities these experiences figure, the one who is engaged in having them. It is only if we insist on saying that the person and not the animal is the conscious subject of present experiences that we can get the conclusion in the text.

2   [David] Hume, [A] *Treatise of Human Nature*, [ed. L. A. Selby-Bigge and P. H. Nidditch (Oxford: Clarendon Press, 1978),] p. 252. Hume, however, would not accept the description of the problem I have just given, for two reasons. First, he thinks that we do not experience more than one thing at a time, but rather that our perceptions "succeed each other with an inconceivable rapidity" (ibid.). Second, he is talking only about the persistence of a subject of "perceptions," or as he puts it, "personal identity, as it regards our thought or imagination," which he separates from personal identity "as it regards our passions or the concern we take in ourselves" (ibid., p. 253). Taken together, these two points leave Hume with only the diachronic problem of what links a perception to those that succeed and follow it.

3   Aristotle, *On the Soul*, III. 9–10.

4   Page numbers in parentheses are to Derek Parfit, *Reasons and Persons* (Oxford: Clarendon Press, 1984).]

5   In my account of these persons. I rely on Thomas Nagel's "Brain Bisection and the Unity of Consciousness," *Synthese* 20 (1971), repr. in *Moral Questions* (Cambridge: Cambridge University Press, 1979), pp. 147–64.

6   This is not an entirely fantastic idea. In one case, a man with a split brain attempted to push his wife away with one hand while reaching out to embrace her with the other. See Parfit, *Reasons and Persons*, p. 246, and Nagel, "Brain Bisection and the Unity of Consciousness," in *Moral Questions*, p. 154.

7   See Stephen Darwall, "Unified Agency," in *Impartial Reason* (Ithaca: Cornell University Press, 1983), pp. 101–13.

8   The problem of personal identity often gets compared to the problem of free will, as both are metaphysical issues that bear on ethics. I hope it is clear from the above discussion that there is another similarity between them. The conception of myself as one and the conception of myself as free (at least free to choose among my desires) are both features of the deliberative standpoint. And from this standpoint both conceptions find expression in my identification with some principle or way of choosing.

9   This view is also found in Sidgwick. When Sidgwick attempts to adjudicate between egoistic and utilitarian conceptions of practical reason, the consideration that favors egoism is this: "It would be contrary to Common Sense to deny that the distinction between any one individual and any other is real and fundamental, and that consequently, 'I' am concerned with the quality of my existence as an individual in a sense, fundamentally important, in which I am not concerned with the quality of the existence of other individuals: and this being so, I do not see how it can be proved that this distinction is not to be taken as fundamental in determining the ultimate end of rational action" (*The Methods of Ethics* (Indianapolis: Hackett, 1981), p. 498). But the utilitarian,

appealing to metaphysics rather than common sense, replies, "Grant that the Ego is merely a system of coherent phenomena, that the permanent identical 'I' is not a fact but a fiction, as Hume and his followers maintain: why, then, should one part of the series of feelings into which the Ego is resolved be concerned with another part of the same series, any more than with any other series?" (ibid., p. 419). Parfit endorses the basic form of Sidgwick's argument explicitly in *Reasons and Persons*, p. 139. Neither Sidgwick nor Parfit shows why these metaphysical views are supposed to have the normative force suggested.

10   As Susan Wolf points out. "Love and moral character require more than a few minutes. More to the point, love and moral character as they occur in the actual world occur in persons, or at any rate in psychophysical entities of some substantial duration" ("Self-Interest and Interest in Selves," *Ethics* 96 (1986): 709).

11   This way of looking at things places a constraint on how we formulate the reasons we have for desiring to carry on long-term projects and relationships. We cannot say that we want them because we expect to survive for a long time; instead, these things give us reasons for surviving. So the reasons for them must be independent of expected survival. See Bernard Williams. "Persons, Character, and Morality," in *Moral Luck* (Cambridge: Cambridge University Press, 1981). pp. 1–19, especially the discussion of Parfit on pp. 8–12.

12   I would like to thank the Editors of *Philosophy & Public Affairs* for prompting me to be clearer on this point.

13   On the other hand. Williams's person-types, of whom a number of copies (tokens) exist simultaneously, are not persons, since the tokens would not necessarily lead a common life. See Parfit, *Reasons and Persons*, pp. 293–7, and Bernard Williams, "Are Persons Bodies?," in *The Philosophy of the Body*, ed. Stuart F. Spicker (Chicago: Quadrant Books, 1970). repr. in Bernard Williams. *Problems of the Self* (Cambridge: Cambridge University Press, 1973), pp. 64–81.

14   I have argued that the idea of a momentary agent is unintelligible: I would also like to suggest, perhaps more surprisingly, that even the idea of a momentary experience is suspect. Consider, for instance, what seems to be one of the clearest cases of a temporally localized experience: physical pain. There is a clear sense in which pain is worse if you have been in pain for a long while. If pain is a momentary experience, we must suppose that this particular form of badness can be explicated in terms of the quality of the experience you are having now – so that, I suppose, a clever brain surgeon by stimulating the right set of nerves could make you have exactly the experience of a person who has been in pain for a long while even if you have not. The idea that the intrinsic goodness or badness of an experience can always be explicated in terms of the felt quality of the experience at the time of having it is defended in Sidgwick's *Methods of Ethics*, bk. II, chaps. II–III. and bk. III, chap. XIV. I do not think Sidgwick's arguments are successful, but at

least he sees that the point needs defending. A more complex challenge to Sidgwick's thesis comes from the fact that there is a sense in which a pain (I feel like saying: the *same* pain) can be worse if in the face of it you panic, or lose your sense of humor, or give way to it completely. And this will be determined not just by how bad the pain is, but by your character. There is a kind of courage that has to do with how one handles pain, and this suggests that even "experiencing pain" is something that can be *done* in various ways. Privileging the language of conscious states or experiences can cause us to overlook these complications.

15 Nagel, in "Brain Bisection and the Unity of Consciousness," also arrives at the conclusion that the unity of consciousness is a matter of functional integration, but he believes that there is something unintuitive or unsatisfactory about thinking of ourselves in this way.

16 Ibid., in *Mortal Questions*, p. 154.

17 No single reference is adequate, for this conception unfolds throughout Kant's writings. But for the most explicit account of the "two standpoints" view see [Immanuel Kant], *Foundations of the Metaphysics of Morals*, [ed. and trans. R. P. Wolff (Indianapolis: Bobbs-Merrill, 1969)] pt. III.

18 Some people suppose that this means that freedom and agency are an *illusion* produced by the practical standpoint. But this presupposes the primacy of the theoretical standpoint, which is in fact the point at issue. Free agency and, according to my argument, unified personal identity are what Kant calls "Postulates of Practical Reason" (see *The Critique of Practical Reason*, trans. Lewis White Beck (Indianapolis: Bobbs-Merrill, 1956), pp. 137ff; Prussian Academy ed., pp. 132ff).

19 Contrary to the view of Gruzalski in "Parfit's Impact on Utilitarianism," [*Ethics* 96 (1986): 721–45]. Gruzalski claims that a deep further fact is required to support any conception of agency more libertarian than Hume's (ibid., p. 767).

20 That it is lives and not merely experiences that matter, and that lives cannot be understood merely as sequences of experiences, is a point that several of Parfit's commentators have made. Thus Wolf urges that "the value of these experiences depends on their relation to the lives of the persons whose experiences these are" ("Self-Interest and Interest in Selves," p. 709). And Darwall, commenting on Scheffler's response to Parfit, emphasizes "a conception of the kind of life one would like oneself and others to lead as opposed to the kind of things that befall people" ("Scheffler on Morality and Ideals of the Person." [*Canadian Journal of Philosophy* 12 (1982): 229–64] pp. 249–50).

21 Other critics of Parfit have stressed the importance of what I am calling the authorial connection. Darwall, in "Scheffler on Morality and Ideals of the Person," reminds us that "the capacity to choose our ends, and rationally to criticize and assess even many of our desires, means that our future intentions and desires do not simply befall us; rather, they are to some degree in

our own hands" (p. 254). And in "Self-Interest and Interest in Selves" Wolf writes. "Being a rational agent involves recognizing one's ability to make one's own decisions, form one's own intentions, and plan for one's own future" (p. 719). Alternatively, a desire or a belief that has simply arisen in you may be reflectively endorsed, and this makes it, in the present sense, more authentically your own. See Harry Frankfurt, "Freedom of the Will and the Concept of a Person," *Journal of Philosophy* 68 (1971): 5–20; "Identification and Externality," in *The Identities of Persons*, ed. Amélie Rorty (Berkeley and Los Angeles: University of California Press, 1976). pp. 239–51; and "Identification and Wholeheartedness," in *Responsibility, Character, and the Emotions: New Essays in Moral Psychology*, ed. Ferdinand Schoeman (Cambridge: Cambridge University Press, 1988), pp. 27–45. Parfit himself suggests that Reductionism "gives more importance to how we choose to live" (*Reasons and Persons*, p. 446).

22   Mill, *On Liberty* (Indianapolis: Hackett, 1978), pp. 58–9 (emphasis added).

23   Some of Parfit's own stories involve surgical intervention, and in this he follows Bernard Williams in "The Self and the Future," *Philosophical Review* 79 (1970), repr. in *Problems of the Self*, pp. 46–63 [and as ch. 1 above]. It is also significant, in a related way, that these writers focus on the question of future physical pains. Although it is true that there is an important way in which my physical pains seem to happen to *me* and no one else, it is also true that they seem to have less to do with who I am (which *person* I am) than almost any other psychic events. (But see note 14 above for an important qualification of this remark.) The *impersonal* character of pain is part of what makes it seem so intrusive. Williams uses pain examples to show how strongly we identify with our bodies. One might say, more properly, that they show how strongly we identify with the animals who we (also) are. It is important to remember that each of us has an animal identity as well as our more specifically human identity and that some of the most important problems of personal integration come from this fact (see note 1 above). One might say, a little extravagantly, that the growing human animal is disciplined, frustrated, beaten, and shaped until it becomes a person – and then the person is faced with the task of reintegrating the animal and its needs back into a human life. That we are not much good at this is suggested by psychoanalytic theory and the long human history of ambivalence (to say the least) about our bodily nature. Pain examples serve to show us how vulnerable our animal identity can make our human identity.

24   One of the few things I take issue with in Wolf's "Self-Interest and Interest in Selves" is a suggestion that persons who regarded themselves as R-related to rather than identical with their future selves would be less likely to risk projects that might involve great psychological change. Wolf reasons that great changes would be viewed as akin to death (ibid., p. 712). It should be clear from the above that I think this depends on how one envisages the changes arising.

25   Parfit does notice the difference between deliberate changes and those brought about by "abnormal interference, such as direct tampering with the brain" (*Reasons and Persons*, p. 207), but he seems to take it for granted that those who feel that identity is threatened by the latter kind of changes are concerned about the fact that they are *abnormal*, not the fact that they are *interference*. Of course the sorts of considerations that feed worries about free will and determinism make it hard to distinguish cases in which a person has been changed by external forces from cases in which she has changed herself. Surgical intervention seems like a clear case of external interference because the person's prior character plays no role in producing the result. But what of someone who changes drastically in response to tragedy or trauma? I do not take up these problems here, but only note that from our own perspective we do distinguish cases in which we change our minds, desires, or characters from those in which the changes are imposed from without.

6

Fission and the Focus of One's Life

Peter Unger

1 The Standard Fission Case and the Standard One-sided Case

[...] When I fission into two people, each of these people may, at the same time, go on to have a different sort of demanding career that, according to my values, is both personally attractive and deeply worthwhile. But, even so, given our actual values, there may not be much value for me, who fissioned before that, in this whole situation. At first, this may not be very obvious. But it might become clearer when we consider the century fission case: When I fission into a hundred people, each of these hundred may, at the same time, have a different sort of demanding career, all of these careers also being highly worthwhile. When the person who fissions beforehand has values much like ours, then, no matter how pleasant and worthwhile are the hundred lives led after the fission, there will be a loss for the person who leads his life before. Most of this loss, or perhaps even all of it, will be the loss in the focus of the original person's life.

As I see it, most of the focus of my life may be lost even in the standard two-sided fission case. Between two branches and a hundred, the main difference concerns *not how much* of my life's focus is lost, but, rather, it concerns *how clear it is* that I have indeed lost much of the focus of my life. In other words, when the number of my descendants is just two, it may be easier for us to overlook the loss; but, when the number is a hundred, it is hard not to notice that there is a loss.

Although there are huge differences between the examples, there is a similarity worth noting between these present fission cases and [...] examples of purely informational taping processes. [...] In informational taping, there is no survival when the number of people emerging is only one. But when the number is one, it may be easy to overlook the fact that, in these purely informational processes, there is missing something that is crucial to our surviving. When the number of people simultaneously emerging is notably larger, say, two, or a hundred, then it is hard not to notice that something is missing. And, once the case with the larger number is before us, it is hard not to notice that this factor is missing even in the case where only one person emerges. [...] [W]e have the second-order intuition that, as regards survival, those cases are very much alike.

Somewhat similarly, when we think about the century fission case, it is hard not to notice that, even in the standard fission case, with only its two people emerging, there is missing something that is important to our values. As we now note, we have the second-order intuition that, as regards this important something, those cases are very much alike. It is this shared factor, common to both of those cases, that we are calling the focus of the original person's life.

In the actual world, different people have different numbers of children. A certain man may have only two children. Another man, perhaps a polygamous sultan, may have a hundred children. Perhaps the first man may take a much more intense interest in each of his two children than the second can take in each of his hundred, and the former can keep better track of what children he has. For reasons like this, it might be that the ordinary man may be more elated by the joy of one of his children than the sultan will be elated by the joy of one of his offspring. And the sadness caused by one child's sadness might also be greater in the more ordinary case. None of this, however, has much to do with, or is even closely analogous with, the focus of a person's life.

For those who want a sign that this is so, perhaps these following considerations will be helpful: Regarding one's concerned attention for one's children, there is a rather gradual fading out, starting with a small loss with the move from one child to two. When going from one to a hundred, almost all of the loss occurs between two and a hundred; indeed, most occurs between four and a hundred. By contrast, regarding the focus of one's own life, almost all of the loss already occurs with the jump from one, the person himself, to two, his smallest number of fission descendants. As recently noted, the further loss between two and a hundred really is not a great loss at all.

[...] [I]t can be misleading to speak of the focus of our lives as something that we value. [...] [I]t is more accurate to say that the focus of my life is a *precondition for certain things that I value*: Roughly, if other things will go well, either for me or for my fission descendants, then a highly focused life in the future will be, for me now, much better than a much less highly focused life. In particular, it will be best of all for me to survive. But, if those other things will go horribly badly, for me or for my fission descendants, then a future with much focus may be, for me now, worse than a future with little focus.

Suppose that, for anyone emerging from the considered processes, there will be a long future life filled with naught but great pain. Then, for me, it will be worse to survive than it will be to fission. And, for me, it will be worse to fission only two ways than to fission in a hundred directions. When things are going to be terrible, anyway, then, like a loss of survival itself, a loss of my life's focus will allow them to be less terrible for me. And, other things equal, the greater the loss of this focus, the less terrible for me will be that terrible future.

Thinking about horribly negative futures clarifies the idea that the focus of a person's life is a precondition of certain of our values. Once we appreciate the potential dangers in saying that the focus of our lives is itself one of the things we much value, then we may often speak, safely enough, about the value that we place on the focus of our lives. Just as it is convenient for us to say that our survival is something that we value, and that consciousness is something that we value, so we may conveniently say, too, that we value the focus of our lives. It is pedantic to insist that, instead, we always employ the wordy talk of preconditions.

The focus of my life is always forward-looking, or directed toward the future. Whenever I fission, there will be at least some loss in the focus of my life. But if my fission descendants themselves never become involved in any other branching processes, then there will never be any loss in the focus of any of their lives. Accordingly, when there is to be only great pain, then, as a way of making that future pain a less terrible thing from the perspective of my own ego-centric concerns, I may welcome fission shortly before the pain begins: The more branches to the fission, the more welcome it will be. But, from the perspectives of my fission descendants, the fission that already will have happened cannot make any pain that is yet to occur any less terrible. Having already fissioned, and lost much of my life's focus, I have already benefited, somewhat, as regards the awfulness of this pain that will soon occur. But, as each of their lives is fully focused, and will remain so, there is nothing here to reduce, for them, the awfulness of the protracted pain that soon will begin to occur.

A further source of clarification may come from certain temporal considerations: At the end of the standard fission operation, just one of my two fission products may be super frozen and may be kept in that state for fifty years. During those fifty years, the other person may lead a rather normal active life, enjoying his demanding career as a philosopher.

Right after this philosopher dies, the super frozen man may be super thawed. Then he may go on to live, quite normally, for another fifty years, enjoying his rather different demanding career as an experimental psychologist.[1]

As compared with a case where there is no branching at all, even this "no overlap of life case" will mean some loss of the focus of my life. But, because there is no temporal overlap in these people's lives, that is, in their activities and experiences, this strange sequential situation will not yield as great a loss of focus as did the fission cases previously considered. So, in this no overlap of life case, there will be less loss of focus than in the standard fission case where a philosopher lives for fifty years on one branch and, at the same time, a psychologist lives on the other. Along the same general lines, we may compare both of these cases with yet another. In this third case, things are just as in the no overlap case except for this difference: The impending psychologist is super thawed a day before the old philosopher's conscious life ends. In this day of overlap case, there is more loss of focus than in the no overlap case; but there is less loss than in the case where, quite completely, the two descendant lives run concurrently.

[...] Some brief remarks about two quite modest cases may [...] help clarify what I mean by the focus of my life: After my standard fission, each of my two descendants may, for just five minutes, live very painfully before he is shot to death. On each branch, the man will be allowed no activity whatsoever, but will have his painful experience be provided wholly by an experience inducer. Now, in one case, the two experience inducers will provide my fission descendants with precisely the same sort of painful experience: As each seems to perceive, he is being horribly mauled, for five excruciating minutes, by a ferocious tiger. In a second case, just one of my two descendants will get experience of that sort. The other will get experience that, while just as terribly painful, is of a very different character: As he seems to perceive, by way of wires attached to his hands and to his feet, a mad scientist is giving him excruciating electric shocks. In the first case, the short horrible lives of my two descendants run in parallel. In the second, their equally short and equally horrible lives significantly diverge. When their lives run in parallel, there is less of a loss of focus of my life. In these two cases, the futures are quite horrible short futures. So, with a choice between just these two cases, it is somewhat better for me that the second example, with significant divergence and a greater loss of focus, be the case that obtains.

As I believe, the focus of one's life is a precondition of certain things that we pretty strongly value. Moreover, like my survival itself, the focus of my life is a basic precondition, not a derived one. Although basic for us, I do not claim that this is a precondition for any rational beings that there may be. In other galaxies, there may be people for whom this focus means nothing. And, there may be other distant people for whom this focus is a precondition only of what they very weakly value.

2   The Focus of Life and Heavily Discounted Branches

The number of fission descendants is a significant factor in the loss of focus of my life. But, as suggested, it is not an enormously important factor. A more important factor is the extent to which various branches may be *heavily discounted*. When *all but one* branch may be *very* heavily discounted, then, even when I have many fission descendants, there may be little loss in the focus of my life. That is because, in such an event, most of the focus of my life may resolve on the single branch that has not been so discounted. But, then, when can a branch be heavily discounted? [...]

There are several reasons why a branch might be heavily discounted. All of them, I think, can be understood as sharing fundamental features with the simplest reason for such discounting. The simplest reason is simply this: On that branch, the person may exist only for a very short time, after which he completely ceases, or expires. So, after I fission into a hundred people, all but one may expire after a minute, while that one lives normally for another fifty years. Especially if there is no pain for any of the short-lived people when that happens, then all but one of the branches may be heavily discounted. For the focus of my life, and so for me, this situation may be *almost* as good as when I do not fission at all. If all but *two* of the hundred should expire after a minute, however, and those two each live normally for fifty more years, then neither of those two branches may be heavily discounted. In such a case, the situation may not be enormously bad for me, but it will not be very good, either. To be sure, in such a case, the situation may be nearly as good for me as one where I fission into just two people. But even when I fission into just two people, there is much that is lost as concerns the focus of my life. So, unless all but *one* branch may be heavily discounted, typically a fission will be significantly worse for the focus of my life, and so for me, than when I do not fission at all.

In addition to the cases with very short branches, when else may branches be heavily discounted? Let us say that when a life is desirable for a person, or when that life is undesirable for the person, the life is, for that person, *personally significant*. Of course, this may be a matter of degree. Even so, the answer to our questions may be put like this: A branch may be discounted insofar as, and only insofar as, the branch does *not* contain the *preconditions* for the person on that branch to have a life that, from the relevant perspective, is personally significant for that person. If the life will never be at all significant, then it may be completely discounted; if the life will be only very mildly significant, then the branch may be discounted, not completely, but very heavily.

But what determines which perspective is the relevant one? This is determined by certain of the attitudes, before the fission occurs, of the person who enters the fission process. Roughly, these are the person's attitudes toward the *content* or the *character* of a life that he may lead, in contrast to the consequences, for people and things distinct from himself and his life, of his leading such a life. In jargon and also roughly, we want to consider the lives that, according to the person's own values, are *intrinsically*, rather than instrumentally, desirable or undesirable for him.

Given my relevant attitudes, a life with no conscious experience and no purposeful activity is never personally significant for me. Such a life is merely something that I will just live through. When there is a long branch that always contains just a person in a deep coma, having no experience and no activity, then this branch does not contain the preconditions for a personally significant life for me. Accordingly, I may heavily discount this branch. If I fission into a hundred people, and all but one are always in a deep coma, then, for me, there is little loss in the focus of my life. In such an event, the situation may be nearly as good, in these respects, as one in which I actually survive and never fission at all.

Given my attitudes, even if a life has purposeful activity, it will not be personally significant should it entirely lack conscious experience. So, if I am always on a Trancelife drug, I will be leading a life that, for me, is not personally significant at all. If this is right, then, in assessing my prospective fission, I should heavily discount branches with wholly non-conscious intentional activity: If all but one of my fission descendants are moving around in a creative trance, while only the one leads a normal conscious life, I will discount all of those other branches. When this is the fission situation, there will be only a small loss in the focus of my life.

According to slightly different attitudes, a life with much successful intentional activity, but with no conscious experience, may be mildly, but only mildly, desirable. And a non-conscious life with much frustrated intentional activity may be mildly undesirable. A person with these slightly different attitudes will not discount Trancelife branches quite so heavily as will I, but he will still discount them fairly heavily.

What do we think of a branch where there is much conscious experience but no intentional activity? This may occur when, from right after the fission until my eventual demise, my descendants are inactively under the influence of an experience inducer. Given my values, each of them may have a life that is mildly desirable. But, given these same values, each may have a life that is *highly undesirable*. For, if suitably stimulated by an inducer, each person may always be in very great pain. Because each person may have a highly undesirable life, each branch contains the preconditions of a life that is, for me, *highly personally significant*. Because this is so, this time *no* branch of my prospective fission will be heavily discounted.

That seems quite right. Suppose that I fission in two and, while the person on one branch always lives a normal life, the person on the other branch is always conscious in an inducer. This situation is certainly worse for me than ordinary survival, or than fission with one very short branch. Even if the man in the inducer never does feel any pain, the fact of his having experience means a substantial loss in the focus of my life. This loss is just as great, or is quite nearly as great, as the loss when the people on both branches lead normal, conscious, active lives. Consequently, if, by making a sacrifice before, I can avoid this fission with one person in the inducer, I will make a substantial sacrifice.

What is important is that, in every case but one, I avoid branches that contain the preconditions for lives that, from the perspective of my attitudes, are personally significant for the people on those branches. For when there are personally significant lives on more than one branch, there is a significant loss of the focus of my life. And when there is a significant loss of this focus, there is a loss that, for me, is a significant loss.

3   A Person's Singular Goods

In addition to loss of focus, there is another undesirable feature that typically attends cases of fission. For example, there is a single person who is my wife. That person is Susan. For me to have a most desirable life, I must spend a lot of my life with Susan engaged in certain sorts of activities. Moreover, it is also important to me that no other man, but only this one, spend much time with her and engage in all of those favored activities. When I fission, however, there will be at least two people who may compete for Susan's time, attention and affections. At the most, only one of my fission descendants can enjoy the importantly exclusive arrangement with that very woman. An undesirable feature of my fission, then, is that only one of my intimate descendants can have this *singular good of mine.*

[...] Suppose that, by a statistical miracle, by taping with temporal overlap, or whatever, there comes to be a precise duplicate of Susan, right down to the last molecule. I may be offered two options: Option One is the continuance of my life with Susan herself and the deportation to a near duplicate of earth, a planet just like ours except for its lacking a person just like Susan or, in other words, just like the duplicate of Susan. That is the end of what happens on Option One. Option Two is the continuance of my life with the duplicate instead of my wife, and the deportation of Susan to that near duplicate planet, with its slot for a person just like her. But that is not the end of what happens on Option Two. Rather, unlike One, on Two I get some "external" advantages. One of these advantages may be, for example, a hundred million dollars.

As would many in similar circumstances, I choose Option One. Evidently, I do not just care about the very many highly specific qualities my wife has, or just about there being only one woman on earth with just those qualities, or just about my spending much time, in exclusive arrangements, with the only woman on earth with just those specific qualities. Quite beyond any of that, I care about the one particular person who is my wife: I care about Susan and, as well, I care about the continuance of my particular relationship with her. Now, unlike myself and these many people, there are, I suppose, many others who do not care very much about their mates or their lovers. But many of them will, at the least, care about each of the individual children that he or she might have. At all events, notwithstanding wild and superficial beliefs to the contrary, almost all of us have *some* singular goods about which we care a great deal.

In any standard fission scenario, at most one of my fission descendants can have all, or even most, of my main singular goods. To have a life nearly as desirable as mine, he must have nearly all of them. Suppose that one of them does have all. Perhaps all of the others are placed in experience inducers; or perhaps they may be confined to many foreign countries, which they may then explore. Then all of the others will have lives that, from the relevant perspective, are less desirable than the life of the one descendant who gets to be with my wife and my son. A significant factor in the badness of my fission may be, then, the absence of my singular goods in the lives of my fission descendants.

The *focus means nothing view* is a position that is at odds with my view concerning the importance of the focus of a particular life: When fission occurs, the *only significant loss* is a loss concerning singular goods. When one descendant gets to be with Susan, the others must do without her. Because they must do without, these others will have less desirable lives than that one will have and, perforce, than the life I led before the fission.

On the most plausible view of fission, for people with values like ours, fission will generally be a pretty bad thing. And when all the futures are positive even while several branches, or all, cannot be heavily discounted, then fission will almost always be a bad thing. As he should, the proponent of the focus means nothing view may grant all of this. Even so, he is still unimpressed with our view. But then how will he explain the badness, for us, that generally attends our fissioning?

That proponent might say this: In assessing how bad my fission is for me, we should average, in a most suitable fashion, the desirability and the undesirability of the lives of my fission descendants. When we average them appropriately, then the lives after the fission score lower, on average, than my life before the fission. It is because there is this low average of the lives afterwards that, for me, fission is a bad thing.

How will this focus means nothing view deal with the discounting of branches? On the face of it, that may be a problem for the view. After all, it would seem that a life in a deep coma, being pretty worthless, should get a score near zero. Then, if I fission in twenty ways, with nineteen descendants always in deep coma, the average of the later lives may be pretty near zero. On any usual averaging, then, such a fission will be very bad for me indeed. But, because the nineteen coma branches may be so heavily discounted, this fission is not so awful as that.

By giving it a suitable dressing, perhaps the focus means nothing view can be made to look pretty good: When a branch is very short, or otherwise lacks the preconditions for a personally significant life for me, perhaps we may give the score for that branch a *very low weighting* in our computation of the average. More than that, perhaps, in computing the average, we may give *all such branches together* a very low weighting. Here is a possible rationale for this maneuver: When branches lack the relevant preconditions, then it may not matter very much, to me, that the people on them miss out on my singular goods. After all, people in a deep coma, for example, cannot really appreciate those goods anyway. If this rationale is solid, and the special weighting it recommends is allowed, then we get a new perspective on why certain fissions are not very bad for me: On the sophisticated way of most appropriately averaging for those fission cases where all branches but one are heavily discounted as a group, the average of the lives of my fission descendants will be nearly as high as the score for my life before the fission.

Although it may now look pretty good, the focus means nothing view cannot be correct. For one thing, there are people who live quite apart from others and who, in general, have little attachment to any particulars. These "reclusive" people may have many goods, but they will have little in the way of important singular goods. They may, for example, like their plants and their televisions. But given their attitudes – and for the example to be relevant, their attitudes must be relevantly similar to yours and mine – the replacement of their plants with precise duplicates will mean only a minor loss. And the precise replacement of their televisions will mean scarcely any loss at all. Nonetheless, even for these people, it will be pretty bad to fission with many branches that cannot be discounted. For, just as with you and me, when such a fission happens to these people, they lose much of the focus of their lives.

A less central difficulty is also worth our consideration: In situation A, I fission in two. In situation B, I fission in twenty. In both situations, all but one of my descendants spend the many years of their entire lives pleasantly, but also inactively and deceptively, in experience inducers. The branches of these people cannot, of course, be discounted. In A, one of my two descendants is always in an inducer; in B, nineteen of my twenty descendants are always, in that way, without my main singular goods. In both situations, my single remaining descendant is positioned so that he may lead a life that is a most natural continuation of my present life. And, indeed, for many years, he alone does enjoy my main singular goods.

Intuitively, situation B is somewhat worse for me, but not very much worse, than situation A. This is the result given by a most plausible version of the view that, in assessing these matters, the focus of life is the dominant factor. On such a view, when I fission in two, I lose most of what there is to lose as regards the focus of my life. If loss of this focus is the dominant factor, and most of my loss is a loss of this focus, then, when I fission in two, I already lose most of what there ever is to lose simply as a direct result of my fissioning. Thus, for me, fissioning in twenty is not terribly much worse.

On a most plausible version of the focus means nothing view, by contrast, quite an opposite result is obtained. When I fission in twenty, the average of the later lives will be very little higher than the score given for a life in an experience inducer. For, even as none of the branches may be discounted, nineteen of twenty get this low score. So, on this sort of view, B is a whole lot worse for me than A. But, intuitively, although B is worse than A, it is not really all that much worse for me.

4   Three Ways for Singular Goods to Go Two Ways

Apart from what matters in my survival, in the prudential use of the term, when I fission, generally there will be two main sorts of loss. One will be a loss concerning the focus of my life and the other will be a loss concerning my singular goods. This being so, the following question takes on some considerable interest: How do these two factors interact, or compare, in situations where no branches can be heavily discounted? We already have some idea about the answer. For, when they standardly fission in two, things will be pretty bad even for very reclusive people with hardly any singular goods. Nonetheless, to understand these factors at all well, we must place them in a wider perspective. In that way, we do not confine our thinking to how we may compare with recluses. Rather, even in our own case, we may notice the differential operation of the two factors. Three complex cases may help us to gain a properly wide per-spective on these matters.

Before introducing these three examples, I shall make some brief remarks about what are, for almost all of us, our main singular goods: Many of us place at least some slight special value, quite beyond mere financial considerations, on certain unique inanimate objects: a particular painting or sculpture, a wedding ring, a letter written by Abraham Lincoln, whatever. For us, no duplicate of the original, not even one that is exact down to the last molecule, will quite fill the bill. For a few of us, indeed, in some few of these cases, the replacement of the des-troyed original by the precise duplicate is a disaster. But, for most of us, this difference does not really matter a very great deal. Unlike some exclusive aesthetes, for example, most of us are mainly concerned about people themselves, not about what they have made. And, for the most part, each of us is mainly concerned about those comparatively few people whom he actually knows quite well. For the most part, then, our main singular goods are certain particular people and, in addition, the enduring relationships that we have with them.

This being so, there will be some interest for us in the following *case of standard fission with one new solar system*: Suppose that, along with your own fissioning in two, all of the people you most care about also stand-ardly fission in two, say, there is this fission all the way down to all of your uncles, and your cousins, and your hundredth best friend. In each case, half of the person's brain goes one way, into one new duplicate body, while the other half goes the other way, into another dupli-cate body. The original bodies are, of course, destroyed. Right after that, each of the two descendants is fully reconstructed, getting a duplicate of the missing half-brain. Minus duplicates of just yourself and your chosen people, far away a new solar system may be created that is qualitatively just like our own solar system. One of each fission descendant goes into its slot, into the vacancy awaiting it, in the newly created solar system. The other stays here. Partly because the newly created solar system is so very far away from this old one, there will be no communication, nor any other interesting causation, between the people in the two solar systems. At all events, all of the relevant people go on to lead rather normal lives for quite a few years. What shall we say about this grandiose example?

First, while it is true that, in certain ways, this case is quite unrealistic, it appears that the example is not disconcertingly unrealistic. Let us say that it is "moderately" realistic: True enough, unless we put everything on hold for a very long time, perhaps by way of some vast super freeze, the example includes travel, by half-brains at least, at speeds far greater than the speed of light. And that is hardly the only departure from realism that we are making. But, for purposes of confident relevant response to the case, and as will become clearer as we proceed, these departures do not seem to matter very much. Second, this present case is obviously asymmetric. One of my two fission descendants gets to stay in the old solar system while the other must get involved with all of those new individuals out there. Third, and finally, this example is not very disastrous; nobody is made to cease in anything like the ordinary, quite awful way. (In just a few moments, we will complement this example with two others: One will also be moderately realistic, but it will be both symmetric and disastrous. The other also will not be disastrous, but it will be symmetric and highly unrealistic. Yet I have some mercy: I will not bother to sketch a case that is, at once, symmetric and moderately realistic, but not very disastrous.)

How do you feel about this case of standard fission with one new solar system? First, you must feel bad about the loss in the focus of the lives of yourself and the other people who also fission. But, for the moment, let us place this undesirable feature to the side. Bracketing that loss of focus, how important a loss is there, for you, in the way of singular goods. First let us consider the loss in way of singular goods that are not personal.

When I think of myself as being the central character, it appears that, for me, there is some loss of this sort, but the loss is a pretty small one. Only one of my descendants, it is true, will have the advantage of being in contact with the familiar streets and buildings of New York itself, while the other will have to make do with perfect duplicates. Although this other descendant does not have it *quite* as good as the homebody descendant, the difference does not seem worth enduring any very significant pain. So, excepting such singular goods as are involved with people – and perhaps certain fissioned pets – there does not seem much of a loss here.

How much is lost in the way of personal singular goods? Only the homebody descendant gets to be with the people he never cared very much about anyway. The other makes do with duplicates of them. That is only a small loss on the side of the traveler descendant. But what about the chosen few, who are destined to fission? Before the fission I have a certain relationship with Susan, who is a particular person. After the fission, each of my two intimate descendants has a very highly similar relationship with just one of the two precisely similar intimate descendants of Susan. As regards my singular goods, there is a significant loss here. But although it is significant, the loss is not a truly terrible loss. In that very area, it is much less of a loss than others I might suffer. In particular, it is much less of a loss than will occur with the ordinary death of my wife and her replacement by a duplicate.

In this post-fission situation, there will be, of course, a certain complex of losses of focus of lives: There will be a loss of focus of my own life, a loss of focus of Susan's life, a loss of focus of Andrew's life, and so on. This raises an interesting question: As regards the loss of my main singular goods, is there, beyond the loss of focus to the lives of those dearest to me, any further loss? I suspect that there is. But, if there is, this further loss is quite hard to articulate in any helpfully illuminating way. Perhaps partly because it is hard to articulate, but only partly for that reason, this further loss may be a rather small one.

Second, we turn to look at the moderately realistic, but symmetric and disastrous, *case of standard fission with two new solar systems*: As in the case just before, you and yours fission in the standard way. But now much more than your old bodies are destroyed. Disastrously, everyone who is not among the chosen few is destroyed completely, along with the rest of our familiar solar system. On the other hand, minus the chosen few, two new solar systems are created, far away from each other, each being a precise duplicate of our present solar system minus the chosen few. Each fission descendant of a chosen person goes into an appropriate slot in one of the two duplicate solar systems. How do we feel about this related example?

We may take a broad ego-centric view toward this vast situation. True enough, the sudden death of the billions is a terribly bad thing and, in a way, it is even a terrible loss. But how great a loss is it for me, that is, for the one who chooses the few who are allowed to fission instead of die? From my broader self-interested concerns, the loss does not appear to be a terribly great one. We shall briefly examine this appearance.

For the moment, let us forget the peculiarities of fission. Now, assume that I must choose between the destruction of my original solar system, minus my chosen few, and, on the other side, the destruction of a precisely similar solar system, also already in existence for a very long time, minus duplicates of the chosen few. As we are supposing, either way, all of my chosen few will get to live for many years in a solar system that, at the very least, is just like my original so recently was. While I have a preference for saving my original system, the preference is not very great. I will not endure great pain to get the preferred alternative. Nor will I choose death, or great pain, for those dearest to me in order to get the preferred astronomical option.

Because we like our old bodies, our old artworks, our old acquaintances and other familiar points of contact, in the case of fission with two new solar systems there is *some* distinctive loss of singular goods. And, of course, in this present case, the loss of these goods occurs with respect to both branches equally. But, because a person's most important singular goods may, along with that person himself, fission quite effectively, the distinctive loss in way of singular goods may not be a terribly great loss for the person.

For some, a very wild example to the same general effect may prove useful. Our third and last case, the *case of the fission of our solar system itself*, is symmetric and not so very disastrous; but, of these three, it is perhaps the most unrealistic example. Still, it serves to provide a nice completion to the present group of examples: As we may imagine, an amoeba might divide symmetrically in two. Much more fantastically, everything in our solar system might symmetrically divide in two in such a way that there come to be two descendants each precisely similar to their mutual original just before its division. Very rapidly, both descendant solar systems may then be moved very far away from the locus of their mutual origin. After their relocation, there will be no interesting causation between them. How do we feel about this rather wild example? For what it is worth, my response to this case is quite in line with those elicited by the two previous examples.

Noting the consistent pattern of responses to these three cases, I offer this following vague, but perhaps distinctive, position: In cases of fission, when futures are positive and cannot be discounted, the loss in the focus of lives is a more "dominant" loss, or is a more "distinctive" loss, than is the loss in singular goods.

Note

1 See Parfit's *Reasons and Persons* (Oxford: Clarendon Press, 1984), p. 264.

7

Surviving Matters

Ernest Sosa

I The Paradox

Life may turn sour and, *in extremis*, not worth living. On occasion it may be best, moreover, to lay down one's life for a greater cause. None of this is any news, debatable though it may remain, in general or case by case. Now comes the news that life does not matter in the way we had thought. No resurgence of existentialism, nor tidings from some ancient religion or some new cult, the news derives from the most sober and probing philosophical argument (the extraordinary Parfit, 1984, Part III), and takes more precisely the following form:

> *The Paradox*   Even though life L is optimal (in all dimensions), and even though if it were extended L would continue to be optimal, it does not follow that it is best to extend it, *even for the subject whose life L is.*

What is the argument? [. . .]

[. . .]

III Does Survival Matter?

Part II [not included here] has defended the view that stage S at t is a later stage of a life with earlier history L iff there is some minimum combination of psychological connectedness and/or physical continuity between S and L, and S meets the relevant criteria (for successor of L) better than any competitor at t. It may now be argued very plausibly that if our survival amounts to the foregoing, then it cannot have the importance we normally give it. More specifically, we are led to *The Paradox*.

If one cares about the person whose brain is to be split and wants that person to survive the operation, then one has a weighty reason to prevent branching. And this seems plausible even in the special case where one is oneself the person at risk. One hence has a weighty reason to prevent that *both* hemispheres be transplanted, each into a healthy body of its own. And one may even have a weighty reason to ensure an early end to one or the other of the two branching lives – for again one may thus act in defense of someone close, maybe even oneself.

And yet from an egoist standpoint, if one is constituted by a certain body with its functioning brain at a certain time, how reasonable would it be to care whether one's life continues through a *single* hemisphere transplant or branches through a *double* transplant? It seems incredible that it should matter very much, even if one would survive in one case but not in the other. It can be made to seem that what matters is at most having successors (causally related in appropriate ways to one's present stage), but not how many. If one's own body is cancerous, including a brain hemisphere, the other hemisphere may be transplanted to a healthy body, with the plan of destroying all cancerous tissue left behind. Would there be any good reason for one to fear that one's abandoned hemisphere should turn out healthy and should hence be implanted in a third, healthy body? There seems little merit in such fear.

A   *What matters in survival?*

Derek Parfit has argued that ordinary (nonbranching) survival matters little in itself, but that we may retain something important of such survival once the nonbranching requirement is put aside. (Parfit, 1984, Part III.) What we can retain, which remains intrinsically important for Parfit, is the appropriate causal relation that links together the stages of a life so long as it does not branch. Take the effluent branches of a life that does branch. The appropriate causal relation links each of them with the main stream whence they branch. Since it should not matter to us whether or not our life branches, what remains important of the ordinary idea of personal survival is just this notion of appropriate stages appropriately linked by causation. But consider the ideas now before us: (a) what should matter even to the egoist is to retain such causal influence on the future; (b) the future stages which should matter even to the radical egoist are simply future stages with the pertinent causal relations to his present stage(s); and (c) one also bears important causal relations to other people. These ideas, (a)–(c), broaden our self-regarding concerns. If there is nothing ontologically special that unifies the stages of a life (as would the persistence of a soul), if what unifies one's own life is essentially certain causal relations, and if finally we are also tied to others by important causal ties, we thus reach a rational rapprochement of the egoist with his neighbors. Caring strongly about ordinary survival, whether as an egoist or not, may thus bring one closer to neighbors, for how stages of a single life are related is very similar to how stages from neighboring lives may be related. (Thus Parfit writes: "we may compare the weakening of the connections between the child and his adult self to the absence of connections between different people." Parfit, 1984, p. 333.)

Let us stop this train of reasoning at its first station, however, before it reaches the ingenious and remote conclusions of later stations. We are told that what matters is *not* to extend causally without branching, but only to extend causally *with or without* branching. But why exactly is branching thus negligible?

Suppose one is much taken by the form of a cube and longs for something with that shape, while indifferent to the number of its edges. Eight edges would do as well as twelve, and so would sixteen. The difference between eight, twelve, and sixteen edges is to one a matter of little or no consequence. What is more, one cares little about the number of sides, and if asked for a preference between a six-sided object and one that is four-sided or eight-sided, would sincerely avow total indifference. What then if it so happens that being a cube consists in having six square sides and twelve equal straight edges. Can it still remain a matter of indifference how many sides or edges one's gift will have? One now sees that necessarily the gift will be a cube if and only if it has six sides and twelve edges, and indeed that the cubicity of one's cube would consist in its being a regular solid with six square sides and twelve straight edges. It no longer seems coherent to long for a cube without caring whether it has six sides or twelve edges. How is rational coherence to be restored? In either of two ways: either by valuing cubicity less, or by valuing six-sidedness and twelve-edgedness more. But logic alone will not decide our choice.

Compare now cubicity with survival (see table 7.1). In each case a desideratum in bold is necessarily equivalent (at least with some plausibility, and to a first approximation) to a possibility or fact in italics. And, in each case, before grasping the equivalence one cares little about the possibility in italics. In the first case once having grasped the equivalence it is most natural and appropriate for one to start caring

Table 7.1: Supervenience, Constitution, Analysis, or the Like

In each case the fact or possibility in bold type supervenes on, consists in, or is approximately constituted or analyzed by the one in italics.

My receiving a cube.
My receiving a regular solid with six square sides and twelve straight edges.

My surviving.
My life's extending without branching, by means of appropriate causal relations linking present and past stages to future stages.

---

about the possibility in italics. Yet we are warned against responding thus in the second case. It is supposed that we neither do nor should react to the discovered equivalence by extending the reach of our caring to cover the italics as well as the bold. In this case it is supposed that the direction of influence is normally reversed and in any case *should* be reversed. Thus we should now *remove* our caring from the possibility in bold, extending our antecedent indifference about the possibility in italics so that it covers also the equivalent possibility in bold. We shall return to this whole question below, but for now let's go along for the sake of argument. It is proposed that we extend the table, as shown in (table 7.2).

Though true survival may be best described as on the table, at least to a first approximation, yet it is not true survival that really does or should matter to us: on reflection we really do and should care only about "survival" as defined.

Why however should it be *this* that merits our concern? Does such "survival" have merit independently of being contained or not in ordinary survival? Is our causal influence on the future always something with

Table 7.2: Supervenience, Constitution, Analysis, or the Like

In each case the fact or possibility in bold type supervenes on, consists in, or is approximately constituted or analyzed by the one in italics.

My receiving a cube.
My receiving a regular solid with six square sides and twelve straight edges.

My surviving.
My life's extending without branching, by means of appropriate causal relations linking present and past stages to future stages.

My "surviving."
That my influence extend by means of appropriate causal relations linking present and past stages of my life to future psychological states, with or without branching.

---

its own proper and intrinsic importance to us? The proposal of "survival" depends on the intrinsic merit to be found in such a notion of extending one's causal influence into the future. For suppose that this "survival" is not properly a desideratum in itself, that it has no merit at all intrinsically and separately from its inclusion in true survival. Then by parity of reasoning we would need to conclude that "survival" should meet the same fate as nonbranching.

Let us consider accordingly whether it is really "survival" that should matter, whether we ought to care that our present psychological stages appropriately influence the future, the appropriateness of this influence not depending at all on avoidance of branching. Can there be intrinsically obvious merit in such causal influence? Suppose a "replicator" machine which produces as many replicas as may be desired with the right causal relation to one's psychology. Would there be a great demand for that machine? Suppose the practical problems could all be solved: e.g., all replicas might be sent immediately to distant galaxies. Even so, is such mere multiplication of one's own causal influence an obvious desideratum?

Have we misinterpreted the proposal that "survival" replace survival as the proper object of our concern? Perhaps the proposal is *not* that *any* instance of the extension of one's causal influence must have its own measure of value, value which might then accumulate through multiple replications. Perhaps the proposal is rather this: that at the core of our egoistic concern lies rather the value of extending the causal influence of our psychology into the future *at least once*. That is what we really do or should seek for its own intrinsic worth. And this goal is *compatible* with branching, while it does not follow that more and more branchings will give us more and more of what we want. This goal therefore seems *not* to commit us to repeated uses of the replicator, not even prima facie and defeasibly. For nothing follows about the desirability of multiple effluents from the desirability of having at least one.

The foregoing response seems to me quite coherent in strict logic. What is logically coherent is not necessarily reasonable or even sane, however, and it remains to be seen whether we can accept that response. Suppose that (a) it is desirable to have at least one of a certain sort of thing or at least one unit of a certain sort of stuff without (b) the sort of thing or the sort of stuff having *any* measure of value for one just for being that sort of thing or that sort of stuff. If so, then (a) would *not* entail that more and more of the sort of thing or that sort of stuff would be better and better. One can of course have "too much of a good thing," for a variety of reasons. In general, overpopulation and oversupply can have effects or can form wider patterns that defeat the good contained in the sort of thing or stuff involved. So it could be reasonable to desire that there be at least one without any commitment to "the more the better." The "over-supply" mode of defeating the good contained in a kind of thing or stuff, in a commodity, seems unavailable, however, where the commodity is the causal influence of one's life stream into the future. At least, it would seem possible to construct examples in which there is no apparent defeating factor that would set in with increasing lines of such causal influence, with more and more effluents flowing out of one's mainstream life; no such factor whose presence might then defeat the good contained in such causal extension *per se*.

The preceding reasoning assumes that appeal to the presence or ab-sence of true survival is not allowed. Of course, with more than one effluent flowing from one's mainstream life one would lose one's own true survival, and *that*, I believe, *is* an important defeating factor. How-ever, we are now considering the simple extension of the causal influence of one's psychology into the future, with or without branching, as what truly matters at the core of our egoistic concerns. And this is proposed precisely by those who wish to downplay the importance of true survival. So it would seem incoherent for them now to appeal to the importance of true survival as a factor that can defeat the good contained in the causal extension of our psychology *per se*, thus explaining how we can reason-ably desire that our psychology be extended at least once without desir-ing more and more extensions of it as opportunities arise.

Take another example. In a polygamous society someone may desire to have at least one spouse while reasonably stopping short of a desire for more and more spouses. And this is easy to understand since for one thing closeness may be threatened by multiplicity. So we can understand how there can be values that defeat the worth of spousehood to one, leading one to desire at least one spouse but no more than one, or perhaps at most some limited number.

What about the proposal that what truly matters to us at the core of our egoistic concerns is "survival," i.e., extending our psychology causally into the future; that what we truly care about, or should reasonably care about, from the perspective of our mainstream life, is simply that this life have at least one effluent at forthcoming junctures? Compare this with the fact that one might care to have at least one spouse but no more than one. Comparing the two, there appears an important difference: we can see the sorts of values that would be threatened by having too many spouses; but I for one have no inkling of what important values would be endangered by the existence of more than one effluent, in cases such as that of our "replicator" machine, to take only one example; it is not easy to see what values would be endangered in such cases *except* only for the true survival of the mainstream protagonist. And *this* is obviously useless to the advocate of "survival" in *preference* to survival.

Ordinary self-regarding motivation contains no germ of explanation for the supposed value intrinsic to such causal influence. Accordingly, it seems doubtful that influencing the future is for us in itself an important desideratum. Suppose on the contrary that whatever value of a self-regarding sort might be found in such causal influence derives from the fact that it is contained in our ordinary personal survival, in such a way that our true survival necessarily requires it. If it is *thus* we defend the value of causal influence, then the same strategy will serve to defend nonbranching.

If on the other hand we put aside causal influence as a relation for bringing together a sequence of states into a single desirable life, what then might possibly unify a sequence of states as the stages of a single desirable life? Earlier we demoted full survival, without branching, in favor of a weak relation of appropriate causal influence, allowing branching. There the strategy was to discount the importance of true survival, and to replace it in our self-regarding concern with a partial component of ordinary survival: namely causal interlocking of an appropriate sort among psychological stages; even though this does not necessarily unify the interlocked stages into stages of a single life. As we know, it fails to do so, for example, in any case of branching, that is, in any case of true, equipoised branching; which is why it can no longer serve as an object of true *self*-regarding concern. Yet it was proposed as the worthiest substitute.

Now the strategy is to emphasize once again that according to the reasoning under review we must discount the importance of the unity of a life as the life of a single perduring person. Being the very same person in the future is stripped of importance, and even causal influence seems diminished. What might retain some importance? Perhaps only some *part* of the concept of appropriate causal influence: "similarity" along with spatiotemporal continuity; even though this relation fails to unify psychological states as stages of a single life (a failure found already in the relation of appropriate causal influence).

Putting aside both the nonbranching and the causal influence requirements, we add a fourth pair to our table (see table 7.3). "Quasi-surviving" might be proposed as what truly matters, in light of our doubts on causal influence.

Yet why should even "quasi-survival" be desired in itself? Because it is what remains of survival once we pare off the requirements of

Table 7.3: Supervenience, Constitution, Analysis, or the Like

In each case the fact or possibility in bold type supervenes on, consists in, or is approximately constituted or analyzed by the one in italics.

My receiving a cube.
My receiving a regular solid with six square sides and twelve straight edges.

My surviving.
My life's extending without branching, by means of appropriate causal relations linking present and past stages to future stages.

My "surviving."
That my influence extend by means of appropriate causal relations linking present and past stages of my life to future psychological states, with or without branching.

My "quasi-surviving"
That the sequence of psychological states constitutive of my past and present life be followed by further psychological states with a certain "similarity," whether accompanied or not by either causal influence or nonbranching.

nonbranching and of causal influence? As we have seen already, this response won't buttress *any* such proposal as to what truly matters in self-regarding motivations. It won't help that it is what *remains* of our notion of true survival – the ordinary survival nearly all prize so highly. For that would never suffice to save any proposal from the fate allegedly suffered by the concept of nonbranching and by the very concept of true, ordinary survival – the fate of being diminished in our concern when it is found to contain a logical component with no discernible intrinsic merit. If "quasi-survival" is to matter in the present context, therefore, it must matter by its own intrinsic merit, and not by having been contained in the prized ordinary survival. So we must consider the value of "quasi-survival" in its own terms. Is it really "quasi-survival" that matters by its own intrinsic merit? Let us imagine a machine that produces in one's closest spatiotemporal proximity other human beings with properties randomly related to one's own. Should one want a double of oneself as the next random creation? I confess to having no desire for any such thing, nor, I think, would most people. Are we simply missing something important? If so, that needs to be shown. The relation of "similarity" along with spatiotemporal continuity seems unimportant, at least intrinsically or for its own sake. If one's life is unhappy, then the similarity of future stages cannot be a proper object of desire – such similarity cannot on its own serve as a source of value for one's life. If one's life has contained intense suffering and little else, one will want rather difference than similarity for future stages. What one wants for such future stages relative to one's present stages would seem to be primarily high quality of life and not necessarily either (a) causal derivation, or (b) similarity.

By this train of reasoning a station is eventually reached at which only the utility contained in psychological states or stages matters fundamentally, any stage of any life, or at least any future stage of any life with such a stage. What is more, thus may we reach a more radical station yet, where it may not even matter whether those future states constitute stages of any lives at all; it mattering only that they be states with content of high quality.

Finally, we have found no train of reasoning for the return to more plausible desiderata except such as would carry us all the way to the original departure station, where what matters is one's full personal survival. And if this requires nonbranching, perhaps there is after all no plausible way to avoid this requirement. So far as we have been able to determine, no intermediate station offers coherent and stable refuge.

There remains however a nagging question: What can be said in favor of the thesis that what matters fundamentally is not true survival but some weaker ersatz? Why has this thesis proved so influential? What reasons have actually been offered against the importance of survival?

B Main arguments against survival

Two interesting lines of argument have led to the conclusion that survival is a misvalued commodity. By the first line of argument the worth of personal survival can only be "derivative," and must derive from the concern that we invest in our "nonprivate" projects. (Perry, 1976. pp. 67–91.) By the second line of argument what matters in the personal survival of a continuing life (a) cannot depend on features "extrinsic" to the pertinent relation among its stages, and (b) cannot depend on any "trivial" fact. (Parfit, 1984, Part III, *passim*, e.g., pp. 267ff; which acknowledges a debt to writings of Bernard Williams; see, e.g., Williams, 1973, p. 20. Parfit suggests that requirements (a) and (b) are plausible, though strictly his argument is offered to those who accept Williams's view, and Parfit does not himself endorse (a) and (b) explicitly and categorically. Of course, if it is not *thus* one shows survival misvalued, then *how*? This question gains urgency from section A above, and anyone endorsing neither argument of section B owes us some alternative argument.) We take a closer look at both lines of argument.

1   First line of argument

Premise 1   The worth of personal survival must be "derivative," and must derive from the concern that we invest in our "nonprivate" projects.

Premise 2   But one's "nonprivate" projects would sometimes be advanced even better by a team of duplicate "survivors" than by a solitary one.

Conclusion   Sometimes it would be better for one's life to branch (yielding two or more duplicate "survivors") than for it *not* to branch (yielding only a solitary survivor).

That survival does not matter fundamentally is supported by assuming that the desiderata which matter fundamentally must be "nonprivate" – in the way in which "that a paper be written" (N) is now a nonprivate project of mine, while "that I write a paper" (P) is rather a private project. The importance to me of project P and the like is derivative from the more fundamental importance to me of projects like N. The importance of one's own survival to oneself would then normally derive from the fact that one's surviving self is normally in the best position to further one's present nonprivate projects. But there might be little or nothing to choose between on one hand true personal survival (requiring, on the most plausible accounts, nonbranching), and, on the other, "surviving" through two or more equipoised effluent branches. For in either case one's present nonprivate projects might be furthered equally well, at least, by several "surviving" successors as by a lone one.

Why should it be thought that private projects must have their actual and proper importance derivatively from that of nonprivate projects? This might be inferred from a constraint on fundamental value such as the following.

CFV   Fundamental principles of value must make no essential reference to any particular individuals or actual events: they must be purely general.

Thus the Principle of Utility would qualify, whereas no Principle of Egoism such as "I matter most" could count as fundamental.

CFV would support the reasoning whereby one's own survival cannot be postulated rationally as fundamentally valuable. The importance of one's own survival must derive instead from its contributions to other desiderata, which are hence more fundamental. And it does follow that, conceivably, there may be little to choose between one's true survival and one's "survival" through two or more effluent branches. Indeed, the latter might conceivably be a *more* desirable outcome. That depends on the character of one's rational nonprivate projects. Suppose they include the desideratum (D) that people's favorings (pro-attitudes, positive valuings) be satisfied within their ken. The desire for food when hungry, the desire for drink when thirsty, the desire to flee when afraid – such desires now have a derivative claim to rational satisfaction. Defeasible though it is, this claim is none the less real and pressing for that, and rationally so. Some such desires might well be reduced or eliminated for the sake of a more coherent life. Certain fears may be silly, for example, and cause much unnecessary suffering. One would be better off without them and should try to remove them. But other desires are firmly inherent to human physiology or psychology, and the absurdity would lie not in their presence but in the attempt to remove them. So it can be absurd to argue against hunger or thirst, when these are strong and physiologically based.

Of course someone might care more for "survival" than survival, and this could be like hunger or thirst in its primitiveness and resistance to rational persuasion. However, it seems to me that what most of us humans *in fact* care about in that primitive way is survival rather than "survival." And I do not see that this has been shown to be irrational, especially for those who have not even thought about the recent philosophical reasoning on this topic. Take now those who *have* been through such reasoning, and emerge with the intuition that in the science fiction cases, they would care more about "survival" than about survival. Suppose they go further and find themselves right now caring more about "survival" than about survival. I have absolutely no objection to this reaction. It is simply not my own. What I still find unclear, however, is the claim that even for such philosophers it is "survival" that really matters (or should matter) *in survival*. Compare the following way of describing the matter, which begins by comparing "survival" with succession. Having offspring is in some ways more similar to having "survivors" than is the latter to surviving. Why not say that for the philosophers in question it turns out that having offspring or successors of a certain sort is preferable to surviving? I suppose one might even compare this with cases in which one has to choose between surviving and having two sons who will be very much the way one is, where either one oneself ceases to exist or the two sons cease to exist (or do not come into existence – different cases are possible here for comparison). I would guess that those who do not care so much about surviving as about "surviving" would also opt for the sons, at least in some of the cases that one might construct here, even at the cost of their own survival. But I would describe this as their being more succession-oriented than survival-oriented, and not by saying that what they *really* care about *in their own survival* is just their "survival" – at least not if in saying this one is saying that one cares about survival only derivatively, only because it contains the truly prized "survival."

Not that I reject the idea that "survival" is in some sense *in* survival (as somehow part of its logical content). Nor of course do I deny that such philosophers care about "survival." And so, in that sense, in caring about "survival" they do care about something *in survival*. But even so it is not clear that "survival" is *all* they care about in survival. Don't they care also about *survival* itself? If so, I do not think that such philosophers do or need to replace survival with "survival," and to care about survival only because it contains the prized "survival." After all, why could they not continue to care *primitively and nonderivatively* about survival itself in most circumstances, even if they would prefer "survival" to survival in certain science fiction cases where a choice must be made? Their continuing to care primitively about survival is no more threatened by such a response to the science fiction cases, than it would be by the response of those who would opt in favor of the sons' rather than their own survival in cases where a choice was forced. And that seems so to me even if there is a relation between their own pre-reproduction life and the lives of the sons which is analogous to if not identical with a relation between their own pre-reproduction life and their own post-reproduction life, and even if we find this relation to be the one involved in their concern for their offspring.

Might one's instinct of self-preservation constitute a desire relatively resistant to persuasion or argument, rather like hunger and thirst? If so, it may be more rationally furthered than undermined. And this yields a sufficient response to the first line of argument against the importance of personal survival. Yes, the importance of personal survival may be in a sense derivative (*may* be), but it is then derivative from its own stubborn existence and not just from its being a means to the satisfaction of some *other* "antecedent" desire – in the way the importance of an airplane ticket may be derivative from its enabling us to fly somewhere, which must itself be a desideratum if the ticket is to be one. So long as the desire for survival stubbornly remains, so long does it remain stubbornly important, and rationally so, normally anyhow: at least as rationally as does, often, the desire to slake one's thirst. Granted, this defense is no proof, since as it stands it would also serve to defend stubborn pathological desires. But we have yet to be shown that the desire for survival is more like a pathological desire than like a healthy desire for food or drink. True, if survival requires nonbranching it will demand a sort of population control, but not even radical utilitarians would all favor the unlimited growth of population.

In any case, it is important to draw out more fully the consequences of CFV, which include not only the rejection of egoism as a fundamental value or norm but also a parallel rejection of loyalty, on the same basis. Perhaps CFV leaves room for reinstating loyalty as a virtue with some sort of derivative justification, maybe through its utilitarian value in any well ordered group. But then it remains to be seen how well or ill "loyalty" to oneself would fare, what place there would be for self-preservation and the desire for true survival within such a framework.

2 SECOND LINE OF ARGUMENT

Premise 1   What matters in the personal survival of a continuing life (a) cannot depend on features "extrinsic" to the pertinent relation among its stages, and (b) cannot depend on any "trivial" fact.

Premise 2   (Suppose the main stream M of a life arrives at a certain juncture J. And consider how that main stream may be related to an effluent E flowing from main stream M at juncture J. Are there *other* effluents, "equipoised" to E, which also flow from M at J?) Whether or not there are such effluents is a matter that must be "extrinsic" to the relation between M and E in virtue of which E might constitute the continuation of M; moreover, it is a matter that must be "trivial" to the protagonist of that mainstream M.

Conclusion   What matters in the survival of life M through an effluent E beyond that juncture J (or, equivalently, what matters in the survival of the protagonist of M through E) cannot involve or depend upon whether or not there are other effluents flowing out of M at J, and equipoised to E.

Accounts of personal survival tend to require continuity either physical or psychological or both. If the life of a person is to lengthen, it might be said, enough of that person's psychology must be preserved causally; or enough of its physical *seat* must be preserved; or both. As we have seen, however, "enough" of such psychological or physical continuity can relate a main stream of a life to more than one effluent branch. Since the several branches cannot be one and the same, and since no significant difference may justify privileging any one as the continuing main stream, the mainstream life is said to end at such a point of branching, where two new lives, the effluents, both begin.

Take again a case of branching, where two effluent branches B1 and B2 originate in one main stream M. If either of the two branches had been the sole effluent it would have been the continuing main stream. Whether a branch B is the continuation of the very same life as a main stream M depends therefore on whether another branch B' is present as well. But such a further branch would seem something extrinsic to the relation between B and M, and also something relatively trivial from a self-regarding point of view, or let us so grant for argument's sake. Thus, returning to the brain transplant above, grant it to be of little self-regarding importance whether or not one's other hemisphere turns out not to be cancerous after all, and is accordingly transplanted into a healthy body of its own. If so, there seems little merit in fearing such an outcome.

There is moreover a second way in which personal survival can be seen to depend on something trivial, given a continuity account of survival. For continuity between stages L and L' of a life requires that there be intermediate stages L1, ..., Ln, each strongly enough "connected" to its neighbors, where the difference between strong enough connection and what falls barely short of that would seem trivial, at least sometimes.

We have seen the conclusion drawn from such reasoning that ordinary survival should not truly and fundamentally matter. And we have seen it argued further that what truly and fundamentally matters in our personal survival is only "survival," namely continuity with or without equipoised branching. (This deals with extrinsicness and with the triviality inherent in whether or not there are further equipoised branches. But it does not deal with the triviality inherent in the cutoff constitutive of minimum connectedness. Nor is this problem obviously removed by allowing *any* strength of connectedness, no matter how weak. For when differences of a penny are generally trivial, it is not obvious that the difference between zero pennies and one penny can avoid triviality.)

Such reasoning is questionable because of a crucial ambiguity. When it is said to be "...of little self-regarding importance whether or not one's other hemisphere turns out not be be cancerous after all, and is accordingly transplanted into a healthy body of its own," who is the subject in question, and what is the target time? Is it the protagonist of M preoperatively, prior to juncture J, or is it rather the protagonist of E postoperatively, at a time after juncture J? If the latter, then the subject in question should be self-regardingly glad that things are as they are, *however they may be*, with respect to the presence or absence of equipoised branches, since if they had been different in that respect, then *that* subject would not have existed. It does not follow from this that the protagonist of M should *prior to juncture J* be equally glad that things will turn out as they will turn out, irrespective of how they will in fact turn out. Nor does it even follow that the protagonist of E should, *after* juncture J, harbor the attitude: "Regardless of whether my current life is equipoised to other branches, it would have been to me of no self-regarding importance if things had turned out the opposite." Granted, this last might seem surprising. Who *else* may be alive at any given moment, with whatever origins, might seem of little or no essential *self*-regarding importance to anyone at that moment. Yet compare the fact that if one's parents had never existed, then one would not have existed either. Besides, logical and analytical consequences can be unexpected even to the quickest and most astute of us.

Most seriously questionable in the present argument is anyhow the assumption that the important cannot "depend" on the "trivial" or "extrinsic," i.e., on what is *in itself* "trivial" or "extrinsic." This question was raised above and is re-emphasized now by appeal to concrete examples, as follows.

Exclusive ownership of a piece of property normally entails one's right to dispose of it in various ways *while no-one else enjoys a similar right*. What of the pertinent relation that one bears to a thing when one is its exclusive owner? Consider the fact that no-one else is similarly related to the thing. Is that fact "intrinsic" or "extrinsic" to the pertinent relation which one bears to the thing? If we say "intrinsic," then it is a mystery why the nonexistence of a competing effluent branch cannot be thus "intrinsic" to one's *pertinent* relation to the one effluent through which one will survive. If on the other hand the fact that no-one else owns the piece of property (which one exclusively owns) is regarded as "extrinsic" to one's pertinent relation to the piece of property, which matters greatly to one, then an important relation can after all depend on a feature "extrinsic" to it while retaining its own importance. And one is left to wonder why true survival cannot be another such. (A similar example is provided by the relation of *unanticipated* authorship, so dear to creative people in many walks of life; see James Watson's *The Double Helix* for a detailed account.

But the basic pattern is ubiquitous: consider marriage, and all sorts of competitions and prizes.)

Recall secondly the case of cubicity, a shape which might be invested with powerful meaning and attraction. (Compare the Greek fascination with circularity.) Yet twelve-edgedness may be in itself of no importance to one, and the difference between twelve and sixteen edges may matter not at all. One wants a cube, yet cares not a bit whether it comes with twelve or with sixteen edges. One is inclined to account cubes sixteen-edged, but one never has studied the matter, and if they turn out twelve-edged, that's just fine. Either way, it's a cube one wants. And the same goes for the number of sides. One is inclined to think cubes six-sided, but is far from certain and would not mind if they turned out eight-sided. And similarly again for the number of corners. (Perhaps one could not possibly be wrong about *all* of these things at once, while retaining one's grip on the very concept of a cube. I tend to doubt it myself, and incline to think that a good recognitional capacity would suffice, but grant the point for argument's sake. Still, there seems little doubt that one can be wrong on any one of edges, corners, or sides, so long as one is right on the others.)

Yet a cube may be defined as a regular solid with twelve equal straight edges, or with six equal square sides. Take your pick as analysis, and still one might desire the analysandum without desiring the analysans. Small differences on the number of sides or edges may be trivial matters of no concern even though having a cube is a most cherished desire. In light of this example it seems clear that something important may depend on something in itself trivial. Let it not be answered that through the dependence of the important on it, the "trivial" is invested with importance. For this would just invite the rejoinder that nonbranching *is* after all important since it is crucial for our very survival. If the appeal to the triviality of nonbranching is not to beg the question, then that triviality must reflect importance "in itself," and independently of unnoticed and unknown connections with what one already regards as important (perhaps rightly and rationally so). But then, again, the lover of cubes might long for a cube without caring how many edges it brings, which is therefore "in itself" for him a trivial matter. And we have the result that the important can after all depend on the trivial.

It may be objected, finally, that since personal survival or identity consists in or supervenes upon or is to be analyzed by reference to the holding of certain other relations, therefore survival must either not matter or must matter in a way that requires explanation by reference to the other relations. (Cf. Perry, 1976, top of p. 68: "That I will be run over by a truck means, says Locke, that the person who is run over by a truck will remember thinking and doing what I am thinking and doing now. But why would I care especially about that? Why should a person who is having such memories be of any more concern to me than anyone else? One is inclined to respond, "because to have such memories is just to be you"; but now the explanation goes wrong way round...." Compare also Parfit, 1984, Part III, *passim*; e.g., p. 478: "Since personal identity over time just consists in the holding of certain other relations, what matters is not identity but some of these other relations.") *Response*: "Matters" can mean either "matters actually" or "ought to matter," or the like. Either way, it is just not clear why or in what sense the analysandum must always matter derivatively from the analysans. Recall the example of cubicity above. Our discussion of that example and our comparison of it with personal survival raises a question about our concern: Does it or should if flow from analysans to analysandum, and never in the opposite direction? We need to be shown why in the case of personal survival our concern cannot properly flow from analysandum to analysans, and extend from survival to nonbranching.

References

Parfit, Derek. 1984: *Reasons and Persons* (Oxford: Oxford University Press).
Perry, John. 1976: "The Importance of Being Identical," in Amelie Rorty (ed.), *The Identities of Persons* (Berkeley: University of California Press), pp. 67–91.
Williams, Bernard. 1973: *Problems of the Self* (Cambridge: Cambridge University Press).

8

Fission Rejuvenation

Raymond Martin

From Plato until John Locke, personal identity was explained in the West primarily by appeal to the notion of a spiritual substance, or soul. From Locke until the late 1960s, it was explained primarily by appeal to physical and/or psychological relations between a person at one time and one at another (and theorists assumed that how earlier and later persons are related to each other, and to intervening persons, *by itself* determines whether the two are the same person).

Since the late 1960s there have been three major developments. First, *intrinsic* relational views have been largely superseded by *extrinsic* relational (or closest-continuer, or externalist) views, according to which what determines whether a person at one time and one at another are identical is not just how the two are physically and/or psychologically related to *each other*, and to intervening persons, but also how they are related to *every other* person. Second, the traditional, *metaphysical* debate over personal identity has spawned a closely related but seemingly novel debate over egoistic survival *values*, that is, over whether identity or other relations that do not suffice for identity do, or should, matter primarily in survival. And, third, some theorists have replaced the traditional "three-dimensional" view of persons with a "four-dimensional" view, according to which the relata of the identity relation are not persons at short intervals of time but, rather, appropriately unified aggregates of person-stages that collectively span a lifetime.

Two of these recent developments seem to be here to stay. Extrinsic relational views, while somewhat controversial, have largely replaced the older intrinsic relational views. And four-dimensional views, while they haven't replaced the three-dimensional view, are widely accepted, even by those who still prefer a three-dimensional view, as an alternative way to understand persons. However, the fate of the remaining third-phase development, the revolutionary idea that identity is not what matters primarily in survival, still hangs in the balance.

Although this revolutionary idea was endorsed by Shoemaker (1970) and Parfit (1971, 1984) (and then later by Nozick (1981)), subsequently several other influential philosophers, including Lewis (1976, 1983), Sosa (1990) and Unger (1991), have argued persuasively for the traditional idea that identity *is* what matters primarily in survival, or at least that it is a precondition of what matters (henceforth, the phrase, "what matters in survival," should be understood to include the qualification, "or is a precondition of what matters"). Still other philosophers (e.g., Wilkes (1988), Donagan (1990)) have questioned the philosophical significance of hypothetical examples of (possibly) impossible situations, on which the whole debate over what matters in survival depends.

In this paper I want to introduce an example – "fission rejuvenation" – which, I claim, is invulnerable to neo-conservative attempts to show that identity really is what matters in survival. I shall argue that this example provides a sound basis for claiming that for many people (whose beliefs and values are rationally permissible) identity is *not* what matters primarily in survival. To save space I am going to assume, what I think the neo-conservatives whose views I shall consider would grant, that the question of what matters in survival is best approached from a thoroughly naturalistic perspective. So, among other things, I shall assume that personal identity is not best explained by appeal to spiritual substances, to immaterial souls, or to any other sort of essentially indivisible entity.

Fission rejuvenation

20 years old, John is athletic, handsome, healthy and vital. He knows that even without undergoing fission rejuvenation his prospects are good for a long and happy life. He also knows that he will never be in better physical condition – never better positioned – to undergo fission rejuvenation. He worries that he may already have waited too long.

In the morning he will go to the hospital where he will be put under a general anesthetic and then have his brain divided into functionally equivalent halves, each capable of sustaining his full psychology. Each half of his brain will then be put into a body of its own that is qualitatively identical to his own body, which will then be destroyed. Hours later, one of his fission-descendants, A, will wake up in the recovery room and begin a painless, two-week-long recovery after which he will leave the hospital in excellent health, looking and feeling like John looked and felt just prior to his undergoing the procedure. A's subsequent physical and psychological development (and ultimate decay) will be like John's would have been had John not undergone the procedure, except for such differences as are occasioned by A's knowing that the procedure took place and that B also exists.

B will have a different fate. Before he awakens from the anesthetic he will be administered a drug that will put him into a deep, dreamless coma. The drug will preserve B's body in its initial state until he is awakened. As it happens that will not be for another fifty-five years. Throughout these years B will be kept safely in the hospital.

During the operation a small device hooked up to a tiny microcomputer will be implanted into A's brain. This device will continuously scan all of A's brain activity and immediately transmit complete information about what it finds to a similarly small device, designed to receive its signals, which will be implanted into B's brain. This latter device will immediately encode onto B's brain the information received from the transmitter, just as it would have been encoded had it been acquired as the normal product of changes originating in B. As a consequence, every psychological change encoded in A's brain (which will function normally throughout) is encoded almost instantly in B's brain and in virtually the same way as it was encoded in A's brain. Thus, throughout the time B is in a dreamless coma he will have a *dispositional* psychology exactly like A's of a few seconds in the past, but he will be completely unconscious and he will not age *physically*. Except for the encoding in his (B's) brain, B will remain as John was just prior to his undergoing fission rejuvenation.

Fifty-five years after the procedure is performed A will die from an independently caused heart attack. As he draws his last breath the device implanted in his brain will send a signal to the device in B's brain that will cause B to wake up and begin a two-week-long recovery period similar to the one A underwent. After B's recovery B will leave the hospital, a *psychological* replica of *A* when A died and a *physical* replica of *John* when John was 20 years old. Once awake, B will age normally.

I claim that it would be relatively easy to develop this example so that John's undergoing the *fission rejuvenation* procedure described in it is unquestionably a good deal for John.

What it *means* to say that fission rejuvenation is a good deal for John is that were he faced with the option of either undergoing fission rejuvenation or of continuing normally, his better selfish choice (even though his prospects, without fission rejuvenation, are bright) would be to undergo fission rejuvenation. What *makes* fission rejuvenation such a good deal for John is that by undergoing it he will secure a benefit as good (or, almost as good) as potentially doubling what would have been his remaining adult lifespan plus a benefit as good (or, almost as good) as recovering physical youth in what otherwise would have been his old age.

A natural, but somewhat controversial, way to characterize John's benefits is to say that by undergoing fission rejuvenation he (John) will survive *as* A in pretty much the same ways and for the same length of time that he would have survived *as* John and then, instead of dying when he would have died, he will continue to survive *as* B, thereby recovering his physically youthful body and his youthful life expectancy but without sacrificing A's psychological development or memories. Nothing in the present paper will hinge on whether one accepts this latter way of characterizing John's benefits.

A crucial part of what makes it possible for John to secure such benefits is that by undergoing fission rejuvenation he creates two fission-descendants of himself with each of whom he can fully and rationally identify. This implies that John can anticipate (or quasi-anticipate) having the conscious experiences (and performing the actions) of each of his fission-descendants pretty much as he would otherwise have anticipated having his own future conscious experiences (and performing his own future actions). (See Parfit, 1984, pp. 220, 260–1; Martin, 1993a.)

What, in this example, facilitates John's fully identifying with each of his fission-descendants is that prior to his undergoing fission rejuvenation he knows, first, that only one of his fission-descendants will be conscious at any given time; second, that the fission-descendant who is conscious initially will cease to be conscious before the other becomes conscious; third, that the causal mechanisms underlying the conscious experiences of whichever of his fission-descendants is conscious at any given time are (initially) a proper subset of the same ones that redundantly underlie his pre-fission experiences; and, fourth, that as long as John's fission-descendants are both alive, their dispositional psychologies will develop in tandem. I call these four features of fission rejuvenation *the strategies of identification*. I will explain below why they matter.

So-called extrinsic considerations, such as whether John thinks his fission-descendants will be able to maintain his significant personal relationships and, more generally, whether he thinks they will be able to play the social roles he now plays might also influence John's ability to identify with his fission-descendants. But since, in this example, there is little reason to think that A, at least, would have to have any trouble slipping neatly into all of John's social roles (John and A could keep it a secret that the procedure is performed) I shall not have much to say about these extrinsic considerations. (For more about their importance, see, especially, White, 1989, but also Rovane, 1990.) For now it is enough to note that were fission rejuvenation inexpensive, reliable, and painless, it would be a good deal not only for John but for virtually any young person with normal, Western values who is in good physical and psychological shape. Personally, I would give a lot to have been in John's position when I was twenty. Had I been in it (and had my current attitudes), I would have undergone fission rejuvenation gladly, without hesitation or reservations.

Parfit and others have appealed to fission examples to argue that there may be ways of continuing that are *almost as good* as ordinary survival. And, as noted, even this relatively modest claim has been hotly contested. Fission rejuvenation, assuming it describes a procedure in which identity is lost, portrays an option that most people, I think, would prefer to persisting, even if their normal prospects, like John's in the example, were bright. That is one of the ways in which fission rejuvenation is superior to previous fission examples. Another way is that it is less vulnerable to neo-conservative attempts to show that identity really is what matters primarily in survival.

One might doubt whether fission rejuvenation does describe a procedure in which identity is lost. I shall deal with the main metaphysical motivation for this worry when I consider Lewis's views. I want now to consider the possibility that even though A and B, in the example, are physically separate and there is only one-way causal influence between them, fission rejuvenation may not be a genuine case of fission. The source of this worry is that A's brain and B's brain do not develop independently of each other until after A's death. So, someone may think, A and B may simply be one person with two bodies and two brains.

To dispose of this worry I shall briefly sketch two variations on fission rejuvenation that clearly are genuine cases of fission. In one of these, B is awakened once a year for a few continuous hours and allowed to walk around the hospital grounds, thereby accumulating sensory input different from A's. On these occasions B is asked whether he (still) thinks the procedure was a good idea (and is thereby treated by others as a separate person). Each year, after a few hours of being awake B is put back to sleep. Everything else is as in the original example. In another variation, B remains unconscious until A dies, just as in the original example, but B processes the input he receives from A differently – in a slightly psycho-logically healthier way – than A processes it. So, for instance, bad mem-ories of a variety of sorts (say, of personal rejection) which, in spite of A's best efforts to counter their influence nevertheless detract from his hap-piness, detract less from B's happiness. It is not that B forgets the un-pleasant incidents. He remembers everything that A remembers. But his memories of these incidents affect him differently – say, whereas they embitter A somewhat, they don't embitter him.

In these variations on the original example, the two brains that emerge from the procedure are allowed to go out of synch just enough to quiet any doubts one might have about whether there has been genuine fission. While the details would have to be specified more fully to avoid problems of a variety of sorts, I don't see any difficulty in principle in so specifying them. I shall assume, then, that were someone to object to the uses to which I am going to put the original example on the grounds that the procedure described in it does not induce genuine fission, I could make much the same points by appealing instead to one of these variations on it.

Real Values

Thought-experiments of (possibly) impossible situations have been a mainstay of the personal identity literature since John Locke's *Essay* and of philosophy generally since Plato's *Republic* (Gyges' ring). Recently, however, their use in connection with the discussion of identity and survival values has been challenged. In an influential and perhaps the most radical version of his challenge, Wilkes claims that:

> ...we can rule out *absolutely* the fission of fusion of humans; this is not theoretically possible.... The thought-experimenter can play with that notion for as long as he likes, but he has crossed the tenuous and amorph-ous line between philosophy and fairy story, and *his play is not philosophy*; for the original, and originally worrying, question was what we would say if *we* divided or fused. (1988, p. 37, emphasis added; Donagan, 1990, endorses this claim.)

In other words, Wilkes claims that if *we* can't divide, what we should say about people who can divide is irrelevant to what we should say about *our own* identities or about what matters *to us* in survival.

Whatever the merits of this criticism in connection with the debate over identity, it has little application to that over what matters in survival. To see why, first separate the basis for Wilkes's prohibition against the use of fission examples from other more local worries that philosophers have expressed. For instance, one of these, as we have seen, is whether fission would indeed undermine personal identity, something that may be doubted either from the standpoint of a four-dimensional view of persons (Lewis, 1976, 1983 [ch. 4 above]) or from that of questioning the transitivity of identity (Perry, 1972). Another worry is whether a person's narrowly self-interested choice to fission could be rational (discussed in Martin, 1992). These (and other) more local worries are not based on fission examples being of (possibly) impossible situations, but on other aspects of them. In Wilkes's view, by contrast, even if fission were to undermine identity and even if many people, for narrowly self-interested reasons, could and would rationally choose to undergo fission, the choices of these people would still be irrelevant to how we should assess the importance of personal identity among their egoistic survival values.

Why, though, does it matter so much to Wilkes that fission examples may be of impossible situations? The reason, it seems, is that fission examples depend for their evidential value on our being able to project ourselves into the positions of the choosers in them. Wilkes thinks that an obstacle to so projecting ourselves is that we would have to suppose that we are different than we actually are. But if this complaint is to have any force, her point must be that we would have to suppose not only that we are different than we are, but also that we are different in ways that block inferences back to our current values. And there is the rub. The fact that a choice-situation is impossible does not imply that we cannot use it in a way that provides evidence about our values.

A fission example, such as fission rejuvenation, can expose what people would choose who were just like us except for differences that do not affect their values but simply afford them options we do not now have. So long as the psychologies of the choosers in these examples, including their desires, motives, beliefs, intentions, and so on, are just like ours and so long as how the choosers process whatever affects their psychologies, except possibly for processing it redundantly, is just like we would process it, then how they would choose can be revealing. For on these assumptions, how *they* would choose, on their values, is how *we* would choose (if we had their options), on ours. Hence, how *they* would choose is evidentially relevant to determining what *our* values actually are.

One might think that people in a society in which fission rejuvenation were a genuine option would *have to be* radically different from us since the science and/or technology of such a society would be so much more advanced than our own (Wilkes, 1988, p. 11; Baillie, 1993, pp. 82ff). But even if it were true that people in such a society *generally* would be different from people now it would not *follow* that *everybody* in such a society would have to have a psychology and/or background informa- tion different from people now. All we have to imagine is that there is one person, John, whose psychology and background information are rela- tively similar to our own. Surely it's *possible* that even in such an ad- vanced society there is one such person.

In sum, if we assume, for the sake of argument, that our brains cannot, even in principle, be split into functionally identical halves each capable of sustaining our full psychologies, we can still imagine people who are just like us except that their brains can be so split, and split in ways that never cause *them* to decide differently than *we* would decide if we were faced with their options. We can imagine that we *are* such people. And what *we* would choose if we were in the positions that such imaginary choosers are in is obviously relevant to determining what *we* value. For the assumption that we are such people does not require us to suppose that our values and/or how we process and express them are any different, except for redundancy, than they actually are. And redundancy is not a kind of difference that would block inferences from the choices such people make back to our values.

Wilkes's criticism, then, provides no basis whatsoever for doubting whether examples of (possibly) impossible situations, and fission examples in particular, can shed light on what matters to us in survival. There are more local worries about the uses to which fission examples have been put, but these do not motivate a *general* prohibition against the consideration of fission examples. (For additional responses to Wilkes *et al.*, see Martin, 1993b; Unger, 1991; Sorensen, 1992; and Kolak, 1993.) I shall deal with these more local worries as they arise.

Peter Unger's View

Unger's subtle and complicated account of what matters in survival cul- minates in the following central claim on which almost all of his important conclusions depend: "[N]o case that lacks strict survival will be as good as *any* case in which the original person himself really does survive" (Unger, 1991, pp. 211–12, my emphasis). Unger is committed to accepting fission rejuvenation as a genuine case of fission and to accepting that a person does not persist through fission. He is, thus, committed to the idea that since John, in the example, has the option of continuing to lead a normally desirable life it would be better for him to take that option and forego fission rejuvenation than to undergo it. But, as we have seen, fission rejuvenation seems to be John's better selfish choice. So, the example of fission rejuvenation directly challenges Unger's central claim.

Unger distinguishes different senses of "what matters in survival" and intends that his central claim about the priority of identity should be understood only in what he calls his "prudential sense," which he says should be understood "in some such rough way as this":

> From the perspective of a person's concern for herself, or from a slight and rational extension of that perspective, what future being there is or, possibly which future beings there are, for whom the person *rationally should be* "intrinsically" concerned. Saying that this rational concern is "intrinsic" means, roughly, that, even apart from questions of whether or not he [sic] might advance the present person's projects, there is this rational concern for the welfare of the future being. So, in particular, this prudential use is to connect directly with our favorite sacrifice for future well-being test, namely, the avoidance of future great pain test. (1991, p. 94, my emphasis)

Unger defines this prudential sense of what matters in terms of what a person rationally *ought to be* concerned about, not in terms of what a person rationally *may be* concerned about or in terms of what people *actually are* or *may become* concerned about. Thus, his central claim about the priority of identity, in its application to the fission rejuvenation example, is not directly about what people *do* or *may* prefer when faced with fission rejuvenation but, rather, about what they *rationally ought* to prefer, ultimately, as we shall see, about whether they rationally ought to be willing to sacrifice as much now to protect their fission-descendants from future torture as to protect themselves from future torture.

In the "avoidance of future great pain test" you are asked to imagine that it is you who is about to undergo whatever process, say, fission rejuvenation, is under discussion and that you have the following choice: You can experience a lesser, but still considerable, pain now so as to ensure that the conscious being (or beings) who emerges from the process will experience no pain later; or, alternatively, you can experience no pain now and thereby ensure that the conscious being (or beings) who emerges later will "undergo really excruciating tortures for quite a long time" (Unger, 1991, p. 29).

To illustrate the pain test, Unger imagines that tomorrow he becomes a complete amnesiac with regard to all of his past life. Without personal memories, he concedes, "there will be quite a lot less" of what otherwise would have made his continued survival a desirable thing for him. Still, he insists, "even in this sad amnesia case there may be all of what [prudentially] matters" in his survival. He knows this since "to spare myself from great electric shocks in two days time, I will rationally undergo just as many slight shocks now on the confident belief that I will become highly amnesiac, or at least very nearly as many, as I would on the equally confident belief that I will not become amnesiac" (1991, p. 93).

In the fission rejuvenation example, John knows that without the procedure his prospects are good for a long and happy life. Yet, even on the assumption that John would not persist through the procedure, his opting for it could result in prospects *for him* that are even brighter. This is puzzling if identity is as important a prudential value as Unger says that it is. Unger does not even try to explain how such a puzzle might be resolved. On the assumption that identity is lost in fission rejuvenation, the most reasonable resolution, as we shall see, is that identity is not as important a prudential value as Unger says that it is.

For instance, suppose that John confidently and rationally believed, first, that were he to opt *not to undergo* fission rejuvenation he would continue normally for many years and, second, that X is the highest number of *slight* shocks that it would be rational for him to experience now in order *to spare himself* the same number of *really serious* shocks a month hence. Suppose also that John confidently and rationally believed that were he to opt *to undergo* fission rejuvenation, then for quite some time after undergoing it, A would be his only conscious fission-descendant. On these suppositions, would it be rationally *permissible*, were John *to undergo* fission rejuvenation, for him to opt for experiencing X number of slight shocks now *to spare A* the same number of really serious shocks a month hence? Unger if I understand him, would answer, "No, it would not be rationally permissible for John to undergo just as many slight shocks now to spare A as to spare himself the subsequent torture." Unger even suggests that it would not be rationally permissible for John to undergo just as many slight shocks now to spare *both* A that subsequent torture *and also* B a similar torture a month after B becomes conscious (1991, p. 263). But *why* wouldn't it be rationally permissible?

Unger would almost surely want to answer this question by appealing to his idea that fission inevitably involves a serious enough "loss of focus" in the life of the person who fissions that fission is never prudentially preferable to persistence. Unfortunately, though, instead of explaining what he means by "loss of focus" Unger instead takes the notion as primitive and merely illustrates it in a variety of examples. And the illustrations are unclear. For instance, in one of them Unger claims that it should be easy for us to appreciate that fission into a hundred descendants would seriously diminish "the focus" of our lives and that once we have appreciated this, it should then be easy for us to see that most of this loss of focus occurs even when we would fission into just two descendants (1991, p. 269 [and pp. 184–5 above]).

I agree with Unger that there is *something* to the "loss of focus" idea. Since he doesn't explain what *he* means by "loss of focus" it's hard to know whether what I have in mind is what was worrying him. I shall explain my idea below (in the section on Sosa's view). Relying for now just on unexplained intuitions, it seems to me that whether or not any sort of loss of focus that has negative value is a problem either in old-fashioned fission examples or in the newer variations on them that Unger considers, none is a problem in the case of fission rejuvenation.

Unger briefly considers a few examples that raise problems for his view similar to those raised by fission rejuvenation. In the most relevant of these, his "no overlap case," he imagines that at the end of a standard fission operation one of his two fission-descendants is super frozen (and thereby rendered completely unconscious). This descendant is kept frozen for fifty years while the other fission-descendant enjoys his normal, active life as a philosopher. Unger further imagines that as soon as the philosopher dies, the super frozen man is instantly super thawed, after which he lives quite normally for another fifty years, enjoying his different career as an experimental psychologist (1991, p. 271 [and p. 187 above]; cp. Parfit, 1984, p. 264). Unger says that in this case there would be *more* loss of focus than in normal persistence but *less* than in a standard fission scenario. He also says there would be *less* loss of focus than in a "day of overlap" case in which the "impending psychologist is super thawed a day before the old philosopher's conscious life ends" (1991, p. 272 [and p. 187 above]). What, though, explains these comparative judgments?

The only explanation Unger offers is that under certain circumstances fission-branches may be "heavily discounted" and that when all but one is so discounted then, even when a person has many fission-descendants, there may be little loss in the focus of that person's life. He says that for someone with his own (Unger's) attitudes, a life with no conscious experience would *not* be "personally significant" and, hence, may be heavily discounted (1991, pp. 273–4 [and p. 188 above]). This suggests that, in his view, the main reason there is so little loss of focus in his no overlap case is that there is never a time when *both* fission-descendants are *conscious*. However, he never *explains* why there is *any* loss of focus in his no overlap case, or why however much loss of focus he thinks there is *necessarily affects* how many slight shocks a person would be willing to endure to save his or her fission-descendants from torture. Rather, he simply draws out for these examples the implications required by his central claim.

Fission rejuvenation differs from Unger's no-overlap case in that when the second fission-descendant becomes conscious he takes up psychologically not where the donor left off but where the first fission-descendant left off. Whether such a difference affects how much loss of focus there might be in such a case depends on what one means by "loss of focus." On Unger's account, it's impossible to say. On the account I will provide, it probably would affect it. It is clear, though, that whether or not Unger thinks this feature of fission rejuvenation would affect how much loss of focus there might be in fission rejuvenation, he would still think that a rational person *ought* to be willing to undergo more shocks now to spare him or herself from torture than to spare either one or both of his or her fission-descendants from similar torture. But to back up this claim Unger has only unexplained intuitions.

How many slight shocks a selfishly motivated person *may* rationally be willing to endure to spare a continuer torture surely ought to be heavily influenced by whether the selfish person can rationally anticipate (or quasi-anticipate) *having* that continuer's future painful experiences in pretty much the same ways he or she could anticipate having his or her own future painful experiences (see Martin, 1993a). If the person can so rationally anticipate *having* the future torture, then it's hard to see why it should matter all that much whether he or she is the same person as the continuer who will later experience the torture. In the fission rejuvenation example, the strategies of identification ensure that John should be able to so rationally anticipate having A's torture, at least if John's extrinsic relations to A also support his identifying with A. For instance, John knows that the physical mechanisms that would underlie A's experiencing torture are, except for the elimination of redundancy, the same ones that would underlie his own future experiences were he to forego fission rejuvenation and continue normally. There is no reason why the elimination of redundant mechanisms rationally has to prevent John's conscious anticipation of having A's torture. After all, if John were to survive normally except for losing redundancy in his brain this loss of redundancy would not have to diminish his ability to consciously anticipate having his own subsequent experiences. Thus, it is surely rationally *permissible* for John to be willing to endure as many slight shocks now to prevent A's torture as to prevent his own future torture. This is all that's required to show that Unger's central claim is false and to rebut his attack on the revolutionary idea.

Ernest Sosa's View

Sosa agrees with Unger that identity is lost in fission and that identity is at least a precondition of what matters primarily in survival. However, Sosa couches his defense of the traditional idea in terms of a distinction between what he calls, *surviving*, that is, persisting or continuing in a way that preserves one's identity, and what he calls, *"surviving,"* that is *"*extending causally into the future *with or without* branching." Sosa challenges those who think that it is not *surviving* but only *"surviving"* that matters to explain why branching does not diminish the value of continuing. He claims that they will not be able to do this.

Sosa assumes that most of us, even if it were easy to massively fission-replicate ourselves, would not desire (or at least would not strongly desire) to produce as many replicas of ourselves as possible. He suggests, then, that the revolutionary proposal that identity is not what matters primarily in survival is probably just that "at the core of our egoistic concern lies rather the value of extending the causal influence of our psychology into the future *at least once.*" He asks, in effect, "Why not the more the better?" (Sosa, 1990, p. 309, [and p. 203 above]).

Sosa concedes that "one can have too much of a good thing." For instance, one can, even in a polygamous society, have too many spouses. But he claims that in cases of multiple fission-replication in which over-supply is not a problem most of us still would not strongly desire to replicate as many times as possible. He, thus, claims that while we can see the sorts of values that would be threatened, say, by having too many spouses, there seem to be no important values that would be threatened by having multiple fission-descendants, *except* for the value of securing the (true) survival of the mainstream protagonist (1990, p. 311 [and p. 205 above]). Sosa's point, then, is that while there must be a "defeating factor" to having multiple fission-descendants, oversupply is not that factor and the only other plausible defeating factor is loss of one's (true) survival. He concludes that loss of one's (true) survival is probably what explains why most of us would have so little interest in having multiple fission-descendants.

Sosa claims, in addition, that the attempt to show that it is "survival" – that is, continuing with or without branching – that matters primarily puts one on a slippery slope: any reason one could give why it is only "survival" that matters would apply as well to the claim that it is only "quasi-survival" ("survival" minus causal relatedness) that matters, Hence:

> we have found no train of reasoning for the return to more plausible desiderata except such as would carry us all the way to the original departure station, where what matters is one's full personal survival. And if this requires nonbranching, perhaps there is after all no plausible way to avoid this requirement. As far as we have been able to determine, no intermediate station offers coherent and stable refuge (p. 313 [and p. 207 above]).

He concludes that identity *is* what matters primarily in survival.

In reply, I want to begin by conceding that for most of us the core of our egoistic survival values probably does consist, as Sosa puts it, "in extending the causal influence of our psychology into the future *at least once*" or, as I would put it, in having at least one continuer with whom we can fully and rationally identify. It seems to me that in comparison with that benefit, the benefits, if any, of having two or more fission-descendants are typically minor. Of course, there are cases – fission rejuvenation is one – in which the benefits of having multiple fission-descendants are major. But in all such cases of which I am aware, "extending into the future" more than once is desirable primarily as a means of ensuring that farther down the line one extends into the future at least once.

Why, then, would most of us have so little interest in fission-replicating as many times as possible? What is the defeating factor? Oversupply might *often* be the problem. We might fear that fission-descendants would compete with each other for our jobs or for the affection of loved ones. Could oversupply *always* be the problem? In a passage reminiscent of Unger's concern about "loss of focus" Stephen White has suggested that the core problem with multiple fission-replication is that it would interfere with many of "the external sources of access" one normally has to a single future extension of oneself (White, 1989, p. 300). It would interfere, White thinks, because our knowing about our future behavior depends importantly on our knowing about "our future environment – the people to whom we have significant relations, the roles we play, the problems they present, and the opportunities they offer" – and, in a multiple-fission case, our environment "could never absorb the number of replicas in question." In such a case, White thinks, it would be hard for us to predict what the lives of our descendants would be like with anything like the same degree of assurance that most of us can predict our own future lives. So, he concludes, we could not "maintain the pattern of concern that characterizes our relations to our future selves for this many future extensions." He admits that if one were to fission into only two descendants the loss in one's ability to predict and control them might not be significant. (So, he and Unger have somewhat different worries about the losses involved in fission.) But, he insists, in extreme cases of multiple-fission the loss would be overwhelming.

While White has a point, it doesn't answer Sosa's challenge (nor, it should be noted, did he propose it to answer Sosa's challenge). Most of us, it seems, would have little interest in massive fission-replication even if fission erased any memory of our having fissioned and even if each of our fission-descendants were put into separate replica environments similar enough to our pre-fission environments that our normal external sources of access to future extensions of ourselves were kept intact. We would have little interest even though, in such cases of massive replication, life for each of our fission-descendants would be just as predictable and controllable as our own future lives. Of course, unbeknownst to our fission-descendants the loved ones they would interact with would not be our current loved ones but, rather, fission-descendants of them. But to say that this is what would make such a future unattractive, or even radically diminish its interest, is in effect to say that loss of identity, that is, loss of (true) survival (at least in the cases of the identities of our loved ones), is the problem, not lack of external sources of access to our future behavior.

Why, then, would most of us not have more interest in massive fission-replication? In my view, the basic reason is that to feel the sort of special concern for one's fission-descendants that normally one would feel only for oneself one has to be able to anticipate *having* the experiences (and performing the actions) that these fission-descendants will subsequently have (and perform). And to do that one has to be able to project oneself into the psychologies of these fission-descendants in pretty much the same ways most of us currently project ourselves into our own future psychologies. As a matter of contingent fact, few of us can easily project ourselves into the psychologies of more than one simultaneously conscious fission-descendant. The often unpleasant and disorienting difficulty in trying to so project ourselves is immediately apparent in the case, say, of our trying to project ourselves into the psychologies of a hundred such fission-descendants. But for most of us it will also be present even in a case in which we would have only two simultaneously conscious fission-descendants (cp. Williams, 1970, pp. 177–8). Thus, this difficulty helps to explain why fission rejuvenation is such an attractive option even though fission, say, into a hundred simultaneously conscious fission-descendants may hold so little appeal.

In fission rejuvenation the strategies of identification remove all likely intrinsic obstacles to one's identifying fully and rationally with his or her fission-descendants. That is why it may not be any more difficult for John to project himself fully into the one conscious psychology at a time that his fission-descendants will have than it would be, were he to forego the procedure, to project himself into his own psychology in the future. And even if it were a *little* more difficult for John to project himself into B's *conscious* psychology because the transition from A to B would require adjustment to a youthful body, there is no reason why such a welcome adjustment "problem" should affect whether John is as rationally motivated to spare B subsequent torture as he would be to spare himself subsequent torture. After all, the prospect of a similar adjustment "problem" didn't keep people from pursuing the fountain of youth.

When we anticipate *having* our own experience in the future we do not *merely* expect that these experiences will occur to an appropriately causally related non-branching continuer of ourselves. We also think of this continuer's experiences as *ours*, that is, we *appropriate* the experiences (for more detail see Martin, 1993a). Yet the best *explanatory* justification we can give for this act of appropriation is not that the continuer's future experiences are *ours* (that "explanation" is vacuous) but, rather, that the causal mechanisms that underlie our currently having experiences will persist continuously into the future and underlie our continuer's (and, hence, our own) future experiences. If this is a good reason to appropriate *our own* future experiences, that is, to anticipate not only *that* these experiences will occur but also to anticipate *having* them, then anyone who satisfies this causal condition is a rationally *permissible* focus of our special egoistic concern, even if the person is one of many simultaneously conscious fission-descendants. So, we may have *as much reason* to anticipate *having* the experiences of more than one simultaneously conscious fission-descendant as we have to anticipate having our own future experiences.

Still, most of us, I think, would have trouble *actually anticipating* having the experiences of more than one simultaneously conscious fission-descendant. In other words, in a fission example in which the causal mechanisms that underlie our currently having experiences persist continuously into the future and also underlie the future experiences of our fission-descendants, whatever difficulties most of us may feel in trying to project ourselves into the psychologies of more than one simultaneously conscious fission-descendant typically will not be based on there being *rational obstacles* to our doing so but, rather, simply on there being *practical limitations* on our imaginative abilities. And that, I claim, is largely why the prospect of having more than one simultaneously conscious fission-descendant holds so little appeal.

In sum, what I am suggesting is that the answer to Sosa's challenge is that in cases of massive fission-replication most of us experience a failure of anticipatory imagination. This failure is not a "defeater" in the same sense in which "oversupply," as in Sosa's spousal example, is a defeater; that is, this imaginative inability does not imply that there is any value we have that is threatened by fission. Rather, this inability merely prevents us from appreciating the positive value that is potentially in a case of fission. But even though it is not a defeater, this inability is all that's required to make us indifferent to the prospect of fission into simultaneously conscious descendants. Hence, it's all that's required to answer Sosa's challenge.

What, then, of Sosa's slippery slope argument? The first problem with it is that it cuts both ways. That is, it's doubtful that Sosa – or anyone – could give a non question-begging justification for why survival – that is, persisting normally – matters that did not apply equally to the value of "survival" – that is, continuing with or without branching – since it would seem that the only sort of non question-begging justification one could give for why survival matters would rely importantly on the idea that survival sustains the rational anticipation of having experiences and/or of performing actions in the future, and the same could be said of "survival." In any case, Sosa does not try to give such a justification. So, until someone does give one the same sort of slippery slope objection Sosa says defeats the suggestion that it is "survival" that matters applies equally to Sosa's own view that it is survival that matters.

The second problem with Sosa's argument is that his projected slide from "survival" all the way to "quasi-survival" (that is, "survival" without causal relatedness) can perhaps be stopped. In the cases both of survival and "survival" the people whose future experiences (and actions) one anticipates having (and performing) are one's causal descendants. Thus, whether or not identity has been preserved the causal mechanisms that underlie one's own experiences may, except for the elimination of redundancy, be the same ones that underlie the future experiences of such descendants. In the case of "quasi-survival" *this* justification for rationally anticipating having the experiences that this person in the future will have and/or of performing the actions he or she will perform *cannot be given. And there may be no alternative justification.*

In any case, even if, contrary to what I'm suggesting now, the slide to "quasi-survival" cannot be stopped, Sosa's slippery slope argument has been answered. In sum, my suggestion is that at the core of our egoistic survival values is a desire to have (even if only through our fission-descendants) a continuing opportunity to have experiences and to act. Initially, of course, we think this requires survival, and that is why survival seems so important. However, once we discover that whenever there is survival there is also "survival" and that having such an opportunity requires only "survival," many of us may come to feel that survival *per se* is not so important.

David Lewis's View

Lewis's view is that both identity and also psychological connectedness and continuity are what matter primarily in survival (Lewis, 1976, 1983). In challenging the revolutionary idea that identity is not what matters he relies on what I have called a four-dimensional view of persons. Although this is a profound change from a three-dimensional view, surprisingly its main relevance to the question of what matters in survival is simply that one may not be able to appeal to fission examples in the same way, if at all, to challenge the traditional idea that identity is what matters primarily in survival. That leaves open the possibility that there are *non-fission* examples that challenge the traditional idea. I have suggested elsewhere that there are such examples (Martin, 1991; for criticism, see Hanley, 1994).

The main question I want to consider now is whether Lewis's "postscript" argument for his view disposes of the challenge to the traditional idea posed even by *fission* examples. Although there is not space here to do justice to Lewis's view, I want to briefly indicate two reasons for being doubtful that it does dispose of the challenge. The reasons are, first, that Lewis's argument rests on a dubious assumption and, second, that even if this assumption is granted the most that Lewis can show by his argument is that in fission examples the preservation of identity *coincides* with outcomes that also realize what matters in survival, not that identity itself *is* what matters in survival.

Lewis bases his postscript argument on the assumption that since a pre-fission person-stage is a shared stage any thought it has must also be shared. He understands this assumption to imply that if a pre-fission person-stage desires one thing on behalf of one of its fission-descendants, then that very thought would also be a desire for the same thing on behalf of the other fission-descendant. Lewis does not argue for this shared-desire assumption, which, as we shall see, is questionable. I concede, though, that if Lewis's shared-desire assumption is granted, then for the (postscript) fission example he considers, in which it is assumed that one of the people involved, C2, gets what he or she wants in survival, then Lewis can show that the other person, C1, who dies soon after the fission, also gets what he or she wants in survival. Lewis can show this since he can show that C1 could not want that he or she individually survive or that *both* fission-descendants survive but at most that at least one of the fission-descendants survive; and, of course, one of the fission-descendants, C2, does survive.

Yet even if this argument of Lewis's works for the fission example he considers, it is an open question whether it would work for certain other fission examples. For instance, if C2 were a person like we have imagined John to be and C2 were faced not with the scenario Lewis sketches but, rather, with the prospect of undergoing fission rejuvenation, then C2 would have had "the strong plural desire" that both fission-descendants survive. For in a failed attempt at fission rejuvenation, in which only one fission-descendant that lasts is produced, it would be curious, at best, to say that every survival desire the person (or, shared person-stage) had who underwent the procedure was satisfied. After all, the reason most people would undergo fission rejuvenation in the first place is to satisfy the strong plural desire. And not only would C2 have had such a desire but C2 would see the satisfaction of his or her own survival values as depending on the *different but coordinated* fates of each of the fission-descendants (thus, apparently violating Lewis's shared-desire assumption).

Lewis might reply that in a case like fission rejuvenation, wanting to satisfy the strong plural desire is not part of what matters *in survival* to the person-stage contemplating fission. It's unclear, though, how he could establish this claim and also how important it would be even if he could establish it. For whatever we *call* the wants of someone who chooses to undergo fission rejuvenation it seems clear that he or she might be acting only for strongly self-interested reasons and yet still be acting primarily to fulfill the strong plural desire. It's hard, on Lewis's view, to even characterize what a person who chooses to undergo fission rejuvenation would be trying to accomplish.

Finally, even if Lewis can successfully dismiss all such reservations about his argument, it still seems that he hasn't shown that identity matters primarily in survival. For instance, imagine that you are twenty years old (but with your current attitudes) and in good physical and psychological shape. You are deliberating about whether to undergo fission rejuvenation and you are uncertain as to whether a three-dimensional or a four-dimensional view of persons is correct. How important would it be to you, *in deciding whether to undergo fission rejuvenation*, to determine which view of persons is correct? If you are like me, it would not be important at all. You would opt for fission rejuvenation *whether or not* in doing so you sacrificed your identity. That strongly suggests that for such people – which, I think, would include most of us – persisting (identity), is *not* what *actually* matters primarily in survival. And I can think of no plausible reason for claiming that it *should be* what matters primarily.

The Bottom Line

Most of us do not want to die, at least not soon. Rather, we want a continuing opportunity, under at least minimally acceptable circumstances, to have experiences and to perform actions. Given available technology, we believe we cannot have such an opportunity unless we persist. So, we value persistence, probably not in and of itself but because we think it is a pre-condition of other things we value (Unger, 1991, pp. 212–7). And we are right to think this. *Under the circumstances*, identity (persistence) *is* a pre-condition of other things we value. That's why, *under the circumstances*, it is so important and also why it *seems* to be so important not only under the circumstances but also more generally.

But the supposition that there are ways of our continuing – fission, say, or other exotic possibilities – that might not preserve our identities but would (without too many unwanted side effects) allow us to fully and rationally anticipate having our continuers' experiences and performing their actions reveals that for many of us identity is *not* nearly as important as it may have seemed that it was. I have suggested in the present paper that many of us, if we had the chance, would opt for fission rejuvenation *whether or not* it meant that we sacrificed our identities. If I am right about this, then *the most* that many of us want primarily in survival is just to have continuers who have lives that are as advantaged as possible, whose experiences we can fully and rationally anticipate having, and whose actions we can fully and rationally anticipate performing. (For more detail, see Martin, 1991, 1993a.) And, in spite of the protestations of the neo-conservatives, there seems to be no reason to doubt that our wanting this is rationally permissible. Thus, the bottom line is that the revolutionary idea that, for many of us at least, identity is *not* what matters primarily in survival is secure.[1]

Note

1   I am very grateful to Peter Unger, Ernest Sosa, Ingmar Persson, Kadri Vihvelin, John Barresi, James Baillie, Stiv Fleishman and Xiao-Guang Wang, each of whom commented copiously and very helpfully on earlier written versions of this paper. I am grateful also for the many perceptive comments I received when I read an earlier version of this paper at Dalhousie University. Some amendments to the original have been made in this reprinting.

References

Baillie, James (1993) *Problems in Personal Identity*. New York: Paragon House.
Donagan, Alan (1990) Real Human Persons. *Logos* 11, 1–16.
Hanley, Richard (1994) On Valuing Radical Transformation. *Pacific Philosophical Quarterly*, 74, 209–220.
Kolak, Daniel (1993) The Metaphysics and Metapsychology of Personal Identity: Why Thought Experiments Matter in Deciding Who We Are. *American Philosophical Quarterly* 30, 39–53.
Kolak, Daniel and Raymond Martin (eds.) (1991) *Self and Identity*. New York: Macmillan.
Lewis, David (1976) Survival and Identity. In Rorty, 1976, 17–40 [also ch. 4 above].
Lewis, David (1983) Postscripts to 'Survival and Identity'. *Philosophical Papers*, vol. 1, New York: Oxford University Press, 55–77 [also repr. in part at end of ch. 4 above].
Martin, Raymond (1991) Identity, Transformation, and What Matters in Survival. In Kolak and Martin, 1991, 289–301.
Martin, Raymond (1992) Self-Interest and Survival. *American Philosophical Quarterly* 29, 165–84.
Martin, Raymond (1993a) Having the Experience: The Next Best Thing to Being There. *Philosophical Studies* 68, 63–79.
Martin, Raymond (1993b) Real Values. *Metaphilosophy* 24, 400–6.
Nozick, Robert (1981) *Philosophical Explanations*. Cambridge, MA: Harvard University Press.
Parfit, Derek (1971) Personal Identity. *Philosophical Review* 80, 3–27.
Parfit, Derek (1984) *Reasons and Persons*. Oxford: Clarendon Press.
Perry, John (1972) Can the Self Divide? *Journal of Philosophy* 69, 463–88.
Rorty, Amelie (ed.) (1976) *The Identities of Persons*. Berkeley: University of California Press.
Rovane, Carol (1990) Branching Self-Consciousness. *Philosophical Review* 99, 355–95.
Shoemaker, Sydney (1970) Persons and Their Pasts. *American Philosophical Quarterly* 7, 269–85.

Sorensen, Roy (1992) *Thought Experiments*. New York: Oxford University Press.

Sosa, Ernest (1990) Surviving Matters. *Nous* 24, 305–30 [also ch. 7 above].

Unger, Peter (1991) *Identity, Consciousness, and Value*. New York: Oxford University Press. [Repr. in part in ch. 6 above.]

White, Stephen (1989) Metapsychological Relativism and the Self. *Journal of Philosophy* 86, 298–323.

Wilkes, Kathleen (1988) *Real People*. Oxford: Clarendon Press.

Williams, Bernard (1970) The Self and the Future. *Philosophical Review* 79, 161–80 [also ch. 1 above].

9

Empathic Access: The Missing Ingredient in Personal Identity

Marya Schechtman

Although substance-based views of personal identity still have adherents, psychologically-based accounts have achieved an undeniable prominence in contemporary analytic philosophy. Support for these views comes chiefly from thought experiments and puzzle cases. These cases are limited only by the imaginations of the philosophers who have offered them, and take a dazzling variety of forms. One important distinction to be drawn is between those cases which imagine a wholesale movement of a psychological life from one body to another and those which depict partial psychological change taking place within the scope of a single human life. The former category includes John Locke's prince who "enters and informs" the body of a cobbler, as well as the teleportation, brain rejuvenation, and brain transplant cases found in more modern authors. The latter includes cases based on real-life situations (e.g. conversion, amnesia, brainwashing, dementia) as well as science fiction scenarios (e.g. involving evil neurosurgeons who can manipulate the brain to change traits or psychological states at will).

These two types of cases play somewhat different roles within the discussion of personal identity. The first is used essentially to show that personal identity should be defined in terms of psychological rather than physical features. The second supports this case (by showing that the right kind or degree of psychological change within a human life threatens identity), but it also speaks to the more complicated question of what psychological continuation involves. Cases in which a person's psychological life moves intact to a new venue make a good case for the claim that between body and mental life it is the continuation of mental life which is required for personal continuation, but fall short of telling us exactly what this entails. It is too much to require the exact preservation of psychological makeup for personal identity, since this is something we virtually never encounter. People do change in their beliefs, desires, character traits and values, and this does not usually imply a change of identity.[1]

A theorist who wishes to define personal identity in terms of psychological continuation thus needs to tell us what "psychological continuation" means, and this requires, among other things, specifying the degree and kind of psychological change that is permissible. A psychological account of identity must, that is, define the difference between ordinary personal development and identity-destroying psychological discontinuity. There have been two main attempts to offer such a definition in the literature: psychological continuity theories and narrative accounts. In what follows I will argue that neither is adequate to capturing this crucial distinction, at least with respect to one important class of thought experiments. With respect to the intuitions generated by these thought experiments, I claim, both psychological continuity theories and narrative views leave out a necessary ingredient which I call "empathic access."[2]

I begin with a description of the class of thought experiments on which I will focus, offering two as representatives for further discussion, and briefly describing their importance in the discussion of personal identity and personal survival. I then show how the standard psychological accounts fail to capture the intuitions generated by these examples, and diagnose their failure by introducing the concept of empathic access. After further definition of empathic access and a sketch of some of work which will be needed to develop the concept further, I conclude by discussing the broader goal of providing a viable psychological account of personal survival.

I

Puzzle cases raising the question of identity preservation through psychological change are very common in the literature on personal identity. David Lewis, for instance, imagines Methuselah living "much longer than a bare millennium" or having his life "punctuated by frequent amnesias, brainwashings, psychoanalyses, conversions, and what not," and suggests that this will help us "make it literally true that he will be a different person after one and one-half centuries or so" (Lewis, 1983, p. 66 [and p. 156 above]). Perhaps the largest store of such cases, however, is to be found in Derek Parfit's *Reasons and Persons*. He gives us the "psychological spectrum" (a range of psychological surgeries in which a surgeon is able to replace anywhere from one to all of a person's psychological features with those of Napoleon) (Parfit, 1984, p. 231); fusion (in which two or more people fuse into a single person who mixes and matches psychological states of the original people) (Parfit, 1984, pp. 302–3); and, like Lewis, cases of longevity with gradual psychological change (Parfit, 1984, pp. 303–5). These cases are used for a variety of purposes.[3] In the course of such arguments, however, it is always assumed that there is some point at which psychological alteration will lead to a change in identity, and so a central purpose is to serve as a testing ground which can unearth our views about the conditions under which psychological change undermines identity.

Among the many creative science fiction scenarios described in the literature there are also many which draw upon more homey and ordinary cases of psychological change. These include cases like religious (or political) conversion, partial amnesia, dementia or just straightforward character change. Parfit offers examples of this sort as well. One such case is his story of a nineteenth-century Russian couple. It revolves around a young Socialist who knows that he will inherit vast estates and fears that this change of fortune will alter his values. To protect his current ideals he tries to insure that the land he inherits will be given to the peasants even if he is corrupted by his new wealth. He signs a legal document which transfers the land – a document that can be revoked only with his wife's consent – and tells her not to revoke it even if he later asks her to. He says "I regard my ideals as essential to me. If I lose these ideals, I want you to think that I cease to exist. I want you to regard your husband then, not as me, the man who asks you for this promise . . ." (Parfit, 1984, p. 327). Although this may sound a bit melodramatic, we understand what he is saying, and Parfit suggests that we take his claim of changed identity seriously when considering the commitments on which his wife should act.

A similar, more contemporary example can also serve as a supplement to Parfit's. Imagine a carefree and wild young woman who eventually settles down into a solid career, a marriage and motherhood. Growing into the responsibilities these life changes require, she may well change drastically. Her concerns about juggling her time, sorting out child care arrangements, getting the mortgage check in the mail, and framing her report in a way that will reflect well on the company will be a far cry from the old concerns about juggling dates, finding the most exciting parties, and initiating adventures. The responsible matron is going to think, feel and act quite differently from the party girl, and when her old friends try to drag her out for a night of revelry she might reply that the wild friend they knew is no more. The present woman does not care about the same things as the party girl, she does not have the capacity for witty bar chatter, nor the uncanny ability to locate parties. Her sleep patterns are different as are her thought patterns. She is, in many respects, a different subject in the same body.

These cases are more complicated than the science fiction examples, and in many ways more controversial. While both kinds of cases involve only partial psychological change, the extremes of the science fiction cases make it somehow more convincing that the radical changes in psychology they describe bring about a change of identity. In the ordinary cases, however, it may seem at best metaphorical to say that the psychological change described threatens personal survival. When a vicious criminal somehow finds religion and becomes a great and sincere spiritual leader, or when a carefree, outgoing person turns depressed and angry as the result of a setback, we might *say* that she has become a different person, but there is some sense in which we clearly do not mean it. The change is only remarkable *because* she also remains the same person. The same is true, of course, for our young Russian and party girl.

While there is something to this observation, the assumption that this makes such examples irrelevant or tangential to a philosophical investigation of personal identity is too hasty. This conclusion rests on the assumption that only the sense in which characters like the young Russian and party girl *do* survive (call this "basic" or "primitive" survival) is *genuine* survival, and that the sense in which they fail to survive (call this "subtle" survival) is only metaphorical. There is, however, no sound basis for this assumption. Note first that this more subtle sense of survival is clearly at issue in mainstream analytical discussions of personal identity. For one thing, while the lack of wild technologies may make cases like that of the young Russian sound less radical than fusions and combined spectrums, they raise essentially the same issues. In each case what we see is partial psychological change. More to the point, the case of the young Russian comes from Parfit; and we have already seen that Lewis's Methuselah case rests on the psychological changes brought about by conversion, psychoanalysis and brainwashing. These kinds of examples are totally standard in the literature. At the very least, then, this more subtle form of survival is very much at stake in philosophical discussions of personal identity as they have been conducted.

There is, moreover, a reason for this. Although the kind of survival at issue in cases like these may not be the absolutely most basic sense, it is nonetheless one which is deeply important in our lives. It is this more subtle form of survival which is most deeply intermeshed with the many significant practical implications of personal continuation such as morality, self-interested concern, autonomy and authenticity. It is, moreover, this sense of survival which is woven into the many discussions in moral psychology which view the very existence of the person as dependent on his capacity to identify with some features of a human life, and which place the limits of the person at the limits of such identification.[4] While this sense of survival may not be the only one which interests us, then, it is certainly not peripheral or unimportant, nor has it fallen outside of the realm of mainstream philosophical discussion of personal identity.

One strand of our thinking about personal identity – a strand that some of the foremost theorists of identity have been trying to capture – rests on the idea that radical enough psychological change literally brings about a loss of identity. Psychologically oriented identity theorists have set themselves the task of capturing the distinction between psychological changes which are survival-threatening in this way and those which are benign. Analytic philosophy offers two major proposals for making this distinction. The first is found in psychological continuity theories, the second in narrative accounts. Each has an initial intuitive appeal, and each captures some important features of identity-preserving psychological continuation, but in the end neither succeeds.

II

The psychological continuity theory begins with the intuition that what distinguishes cases of identity-undermining change from those of identity-preserving change is the abruptness with which the alterations take place. Here they take their inspiration from famous examples concerning the persistence of complex physical objects. The Ship of Theseus, for instance, is thought to survive a complete change in physical composition provided that this comes about by replacing one plank of the ship at a time over the course of many years. This is contrasted with the simultaneous replacement of *all* of the planks, which would count as building a replica. What is important, then, is that from each moment to the next there is a ship that differs only very slightly from the one before. This, it is often thought, provides the continuity that yields persistence. Similarly, psychological continuity theorists suggest, a person can survive a change in psychological make-up, provided that this change happens gradually, one belief, value, desire or trait at a time.

There is a great deal of initial plausibility to this understanding of psychological continuity. Changes which are violent and radical seem to disrupt identity, while changes which occur gradually, in small increments, are far more likely to constitute acceptable personal development. It does not take much reflection, however, to see that it is not the fact that the change is gradual which does the work here. While slow change is undoubtedly more likely than rapid change to represent psychological continuation, it is not inevitably so. Even quite gradual change can lead to a loss of identity of the sort we discussed earlier. To see this, we need only revisit our two examples. The young Marxist will likely have available the theoretical tools to describe something very like a brainwashing that happens gradually rather than all at once, and his transition to greedy landowner will not be any the more palatable to him for its slowness. Similarly, there seems no obvious reason why the serious matron should feel any more connected to the party girl because she was domesticated slowly rather than all at once. It is true that sudden, radical changes in psychological make-up are particularly jarring, and it is especially difficult to see how identity can be preserved in such cases. A person can, however, be robbed of her identity slowly as well as quickly, and a slow rate of psychological change is not enough to guarantee personal persistence.

The narrative view seems, initially, to make good the deficits of the psychological continuity theory, but in the end it does not fully satisfy either. Many different views fall under the general rubric "narrative theory" but it is characteristic of all such views to claim that the life of a person has the form of a biographical narrative, which is to say that actions, events and experiences are made part of a single life by being bound together in an intelligible life story. This claim amounts to the requirement that the individual elements of a person's life gain their meaning – indeed their very content – from the broader context in which they occur. Jerome Bruner, for instance, says that "A narrative is composed of a unique sequence of events, mental states, happenings involving human beings as characters or actors. These are its constituents. But these constituents do not, as it were, have a life or meaning of their own. Their meaning is given by their place in the overall configuration of the sequence as a whole – its plot or fabula" (Bruner, 1990, pp. 43–4) Alisdair MacIntyre applies this insight specifically to the lives of persons. He argues that the individual actions and experiences in a person's life cannot be understood outside of the context of a biography, telling us that "successfully identifying and understanding what someone else is doing we always move towards placing a particular episode in the context of a set of narrative histories, histories both of the individuals concerned and of the setting in which they act and suffer" (MacIntyre, 1989, p. 97).

Narrative theorists thus criticize psychological continuity theorists for having an implausibly atomistic view of the psychological life of persons. They argue that the individual beliefs, values, desires and traits that make up a person's life cannot be first identified as isolated elements at a time and then connected by relations of similarity to psychological features at other times as these theorists suggest; but that the beliefs, values and desires that make up these connections are already deeply intermeshed when we first identify them. Psychological change is thus survivable on this view as long as there is a coherent narrative of change which makes the latter psychological configuration the heir of the former.

The narrative theory seems possibly better placed to capture the idea that acceptable changes must be internally generated *developments*, since it demands an intelligible account of psychological transitions. A bit of reflection reveals that intelligibility is not in itself enough to capture the distinction we are after either. The young Russian will certainly be able to imagine a large number of narratives describing his transition from man of the people to greedy landowner – it is precisely because such stories are common and compelling that he is so afraid such a transition will take place. A similar point can be made about the serious matron. The story of a free spirit worn away by the pressures of her culture is a completely familiar one. The fact that a change in psychological make-up is narratively comprehensible will do little to overcome the sense of lost identity if the story told is one of pure impulses inevitably corrupted by unacceptable material conditions or, in the case of the serious matron, of youthful exuberance inexorably worn away by age, care, and an oppressive social structure. Certainly there is a coherent narrative of change in these cases, but all that shows is that there can be intelligible stories of how someone loses his or her identity. The mere existence of a comprehensible narrative of change is not yet enough to preserve identity.

The two standard accounts of psychological continuation thus do not capture the kinds of connections that seem necessary to overcome the *prima facie* threat to identity raised by psychological change. But this is not to say that they provide no insight. The psychological continuity theory is correct in asserting that gradual change is *more likely* than rapid change to result in personal continuation, and this is an important datum. Narrative theories, although not usually presented this way, can be seen as showing that it is not the slowness of change itself that is doing the work here, and they go some distance toward uncovering the relevant factor. These views show the importance of the intelligibility of change – psychological alteration which is violent, jarring and incomprehensible is almost certainly going to constitute a disruption of identity. If a change is going to count as personal development, it seems essential that the change be part of an orderly progression from one psychological state to another. This helps to explain the appeal of the psychological continuity theory as well. Change that has the feature of intelligibility is also likely to happen gradually; in most instances a coherent narrative of change will unfold over time.

The psychological continuity and narrative theories of identity can be said, roughly, to have captured (related) features of psychological change which are (at least usually) *necessary* if the change is to be identity-preserving. What our discussion has shown, however, is that these conditions are not in themselves sufficient. These views have not yet completely identified the characteristics of identity-preserving change. They are missing a piece, and this piece, I shall argue, is empathic access.

III

The demonstration that even narrative theories of personal identity do not go far enough involved constructing a story of psychological change that took the form of a coherent narrative and yet seemed identity-threatening. To determine what these theories lack, then, it will be useful to construct a story of psychological change which *does* seem identity-preserving and to try and identity the relevant difference. To this end we can contrast my story of the serious matron with the story of a somewhat-less-serious matron. This will provide a first approximation of empathic access which can then be filled out in more detail.

My original matron can *remember* her wild days, but she cannot recapture the passions, emotions, likes and dislikes that she once felt. She cannot understand how she could have enjoyed the music she once listened to endlessly, or been attracted to the men she was; how she could have been willing to stay up so late and suffer the next day. The behavior of the party girl is not *incomprehensible* to her in the sense that she cannot understand how a person with a particular set of desires and passions could make those choices; it is just that she, herself, is so alienated from those desires and passions that she cannot quite comprehend how *she* could have made those choices.

The somewhat-less-serious matron, by contrast, has not lost access to her past phenomenology; she has only placed it in a broader context which causes her to make different life choices. Such a woman may still remember well the excitement of getting ready for a Saturday night out; listening to the music she once loved may momentarily transport her back to her favorite clubs, and she may even feel a certain wistful nostalgia for those morning commutes to work after a particularly compelling week-night party. However, she may find that she has now grown older and wiser. She now also knows how empty, tedious and ultimately disappointing those parties became; how pleasant it is now to get some rest; how much satisfaction she gets from her work and family; how burned-out and depressed many of her old friends are.

In such a case there is no profound alienation from the past, just a recognition of changed circumstances. When this woman sees her daughter making some of the same choices she once did, she may not approve, but she will have a keen sense of what drives her, and of how disapproval from her elders will sound, and she may be spared the exasperated "you just don't understand" to which the serious matron would be subjected. This affective connection to the past, together with its behavioral implications, forms the heart of what I have been calling "empathic access." The relation that the not-so-serious matron has to her past is more than just cognitive recollection; the passions that belonged to the party girl are still there. She experiences them, and they are represented in the decisions she makes. It is for this reason that this woman's change seems like ordinary maturation and development rather than a loss of identity. The alterations in lifestyle and outlook may be just as pronounced as those in the case of the serious matron, but these alterations are the result of an *expansion* of beliefs, values, desires and goals rather than a *replacement*. New decisions are informed by a recognition of the nature and pull of past characteristics.

Once this difference has been identified, however, it seems right that it should be an essential feature of the distinction between developing as oneself and turning into someone else. Empathic access involves a situation where the original psychological make-up is, in an important sense, still present in the later, psychologically-altered person. The earlier beliefs, values and desires are recognized as legitimate, and are given, so to speak, a vote in personal decision making. If there is anything that it can mean to persist through change, certainly it would be this. When a person fears turning into someone else as Parfit's young Russian does, a large part of that fear is that one's current passions and ideals will be simply gone – that the future person will not be able to experience the fever of present convictions, or will give them no weight in action. Part of what it means to have empathic access to the past, however, is for both the phenomenological and the behavioral connection we desire to be present. This should convey the flavor of what empathic access involves. Providing a precise definition of this relation is difficult, since it can take many forms. It is possible, however, to fill in a few more details by comparing and contrasting empathic access as I conceive it with related concepts found in the literature.

IV

First and foremost it is useful to contrast the connection afforded by empathic access with the kind of memory connection which is often taken to be Locke's proposal for a criterion of personal identity. Typically Locke is read as holding that for a person at t_2 to be the same person as a person at t_1 the person at t_2 must remember the experiences of the person at t_1. This is the original position on which psychological continuity theorists build their own views.

Over time, this insight has proved both attractive and frustrating. *Something* seems right about it, yet on reflection it is hard to make it viable as the backbone of a theory of personal identity. Comparing this connection to empathic access can help us to see why this is so. Remembering a past life-phase seems essential to being the same person who experienced that phase if we think of remembering (or failing to remember) not, as philosophers generally do, in a heavily cognitive sense, but rather in the sense in which a teenager might complain that her parents no longer remember what it's like to be young. Typically such a teenager is not trying to imply a cognitive deficit in her parents' long-term recall capacities, but rather to indicate that they have lost touch with the affect associated with youth – its sensitivities and passions. Because "memory" is ambiguous between the mere ability to reproduce facts about the past and the ability to inhabit it psychologically, the claim that personal identity should be defined in terms of memory connection is simultaneously attractive and disappointing.

The type of ambiguity I have described here is laid out in exquisite detail by Richard Wollheim in *The Thread of Life*. Wollheim offers an important taxonomy of mental states. In his discussion of memory Wollheim first defines "event-memory" as "that memory of events in which a person doesn't simply remember that some event occurred, he remembers that event itself" (Wollheim, 1984, p. 101). Event-memory, like imagination and fantasy, is an "iconic" state – roughly one which can be conceived as a sort of theatrical presentation to oneself. Like other iconic states it can be either "centered" or "acentered." An "acentered" memory is one in which the event is remembered but from no particular point of view. Such memories are, in Wollheim's estimation, very rare, and quite unstable (Wollheim, 1984, p. 102). The more standard kind of event-memory is "centered" – that is, it is remembered from a point of view, and that point of view is represented within the memory itself. This kind of memory, he says, shares certain features with other centered iconic states.

The most crucial for our purposes are what he calls "plenitude" and "cogency." He describes these as they apply to memory as follows:

> when I centrally remember someone doing something or other, I shall tend, liberally and systematically, to remember his feeling and experiencing, and his thinking, certain things: that is plenitude. And when I centrally remember someone feeling, experiencing, and thinking, certain things, I shall tend to find myself in the condition I would be in if I had felt, experienced, thought, those things myself: that is cogency. (Wollheim, 1984, p. 105)

Event-memory is thus, on his view, not a cold, cognitive relation to the past, but one which is thoroughly infused with affect.

Wollheim also notes that the affective and iconic features of centered event-memory will have behavioral implications, and that it is these which make memory a relation which is constitutive of personal identity. He thus criticizes standard psychologically based accounts of personal identity in much the same way I have. He says these views, "have treated [event-memory] as an exclusively cognitive phenomenon, or as a way in which we come to gain or preserve knowledge and belief. They have not recognized that feature of event-memory which I have called cogency, and, more particularly, they have not recognized the affective aspect of cogency as this is found in event-memory" (Wollheim, 1984, p. 108). As a result, he says, these theorists "have thought of event-memory as a purely backward-directed phenomenon" (Wollheim, 1984, p. 108).

Fundamentally I am in complete agreement with Wollheim's analysis. The features present in centered event-memory as he describes it are exactly the features I am trying to capture in my notion of empathic access. My emphasis is slightly different from his, however, since I am interested specifically in the question of identity preservation through psychological change. Considering Wollheim's taxonomy in this context raises questions which point toward an expansion of his view. In particular, it calls for a more detailed specification of what cogency amounts to – of what it means to "find oneself in the condition one would be in having thought or experienced or felt" the things one did in the past.

My point here will be clearer if I contrast one of Wollheim's examples with one of mine. In describing centered event-memory Wollheim offers an event from his own life – an occasion in August 1944 when he drove by mistake into German lines. Having described the event and the memory he says, "and as I remember feeling those feelings, the sense of loss, the sense of terror, the sense of being on my own, the upsurge of rebellion against my fate, come over me, so that I am affected by them *in some such way* as I was when I felt them on that remote summer night" (Wollheim, 1984, p. 106, my emphasis). Here I want to focus on the "some such way," which is necessarily vague. The reason it is there is because memories – even centered, iconic memories – are obviously not simple videotapes exactly recreating the past. Wollheim says quite explicitly that "it is an exaggeration to say that in event-memory not only must the event that I remember be an event that I experienced, but I must also remember it as I experienced it" (Wollheim, 1984, p. 103). An "accurate" event-memory may leave out features of the actual experience or even add features that were not part of it. The deviation of memories from the experiences remembered will have to do at least partly with vicissitudes of mood and with changes in a person's psychological make-up between the time of experiencing and the time of remembering some event.[5] In the case of Wollheim's memory, we can assume that his psychological make-up has stayed the same in relevant respects – at the time of remembering he still would find it horrible to be captured or shot – and so the cogency of the memory will not vary too widely from that of the experience itself.

My serious and somewhat-less-serious matrons are, however, both further along some kind of continuum of change in psychological make-up from their original experiences, and so things will be slightly different with them. The serious matron as I have described her is so altered that she is unable to have what Wollheim would consider a centered event-memory at all. The somewhat-less-serious matron, however, is in an intermediate position. The story is constructed so that she has affective access to the past, and so that her memory will be a forward-looking relation as well as a backward-looking one, and to this extent she is certainly having a centered event-memory. At the same time, however, we are to imagine that she is greatly psychologically changed from her earlier self. Because of this, the way in which her memory affects her – both emotionally and behaviorally – will be different from the way it would have been if she had not changed so much. Remembering a party centrally from the point of view of one week later while preparing to go to another is certainly going to be a different experience from remembering that same party thirty years later while preparing to coach one's daughter's soccer team – even if the recollection from the later vantage point is accurate and fond.

This does not mean that the not-so-serious matron could not have empathic access to her past, since we have already acknowledged that centered event-memories can count as "accurate" while deviating from some details of the experience remembered. Still, as Wollheim also notes, "there are limits to this, and there couldn't be any gross deviations within memory" (Wollheim, 1984, p. 103). I am interested in exploring what those limits are, in particular as they apply to questions of personal survival or continuation. Although it is likely impossible to come up with a tidy list of what kinds of deviation rob an event-memory of its identity-preserving qualities, it is nonetheless possible to shed some light on the basic parameters. To do this, it will be useful to proliferate matrons once again. Add to our existing cases, then, that of the "mortified matron." This is a woman who remembers the past experiences of the party girl quite vividly – including access to the emotions, thoughts and feelings the party girl enjoyed – but who has altered in such a way that these recollections fill her with shame and disgust. She is not like the serious matron, who is rather indifferent to the actions and emotions of the party girl because she is so far removed from them that her memories are non-iconic – memories *that* she did such-and-such without phenomenological access. The mortified matron does have such access, and that only makes her mortification worse. Certainly the phenomenology of her remembered party experiences will differ a great deal from those experiences as they occurred in the party girl. I am uncertain what Wollheim would say about whether such a memory would succeed as an instance of centered event-memory, but it would not count as empathic access. The strong repudiation of these past experiences undermines that relationship.

This claim may seem to degrade the plausibility of empathic access as an essential component of personal identity. Recall, however, that we are looking at one class of intuitions about personal survival – those brought about by examples like that of the young Russian – and the relation the mortified matron has to her past is not strong enough for survival in this sense. To see this, return again to the case of the young Russian. He is hardly likely to revise the judgment that he would not survive as a greedy landowner if we reassured him that the landowner would be able to recall and relive the thoughts, feelings and passions he is experiencing now, and that he would respond to these with horror and remorse, redoubling his efforts to wipe out the influence of such nonsense on young men. Certainly he would still tell his wife to view that person as someone else, and not to listen to his pleas to revoke the promise he has made to the peasants. Things are even clearer if we look at religious conversion, which is frequently cited as a case of identity-threatening psychological change. It could well be a feature of conversion (and reportedly often is) that the religious devotee retains vivid recollections of lusts and passions that he now finds shameful and horrible.

With respect to the project of defining this kind of survival it may seem, however, that we are essentially right back where we started. We know that the kind of exact (or near exact) recreation of a past experience that we might find in the party girl one week after a remembered party will count as empathic access, and that its recreation colored by fierce repudiation and horror found in the mortified matron is not. What we do not yet know is how much change with respect to the perception of earlier thoughts and emotions (and in their behavioral implications) is permissible before empathic access is lost. While it would certainly be difficult to provide a precise account of the parameters of acceptable change, the cases we have been considering do point to the relevant feature. The mortified matron has *access* to the feelings and thoughts of her past, what she lacks is the *empathy* – she is totally unsympathetic to the psychological life of the party girl. What is needed for empathic access is thus not an exact recreation of past emotions, thoughts and feelings, nor just some sort of ability to call them up from a first-person perspective. What is needed is this ability plus a fundamental sympathy for the states which are recalled in this way.

Something very close to this picture is described by Raymond Martin in *Self-Concern: An Experiential Approach to What Matters in Survival*. Martin is concerned with the question of what relation a person must have to someone in the future to survive as that person. The relation which he defines in answering this question he calls "surrogate-self-identification." The backbone of this relation involves appropriating anticipated future experiences. Appropriation of anticipated future events is in many ways the forward-directed parallel of the kind of centered event-memory Wollheim describes. It requires that a person "experience *affect* of some sort that normally they would experience only when anticipating their own future experiences; second, they *cognitively contextualize* the anticipated experiences similarly to the way ordinarily they cognitively contextualize only their own future experiences; and third, they *behave* as if the future experience were their own" (Martin, 1998, pp. 107–8) What is most important for present purposes, however, is the general discussion with which Martin introduces his view. He defines empathy as the ability to know and understand what someone else is thinking or feeling. Sympathy, on his view, "requires more. To be sympathetic with another, one must not only be empathetic with the other but also adopt at least some of the other's (relevant) objectives" (Martin, 1998, p. 98). And a sympathetic person will do this, he says, partly because sympathy involves sharing in the feelings of the other person. Appropriation is, on his view, a sort of "super sympathy."

I thus wish to supplement Wollheim's view with Martin's insistence that sympathy involve at least a limited adoption of the objectives of the person whose feelings, thoughts and emotions are shared. It will, of course, be somewhat tricky to say what this means in practice. The somewhat-less-serious matron is not going to adopt the objectives of the party girl in the sense that she is going to revert to her lifestyle. The emotions overlaying her vivid recollections of the party girl's experiences may be amusement or even embarrassment, and this may lead the some-what-less-serious matron to act directly counter so some of the party girl's intentions or desires. However, here embarrassment will be the friendly embarrassment of remembering the naive passion of a first love rather than the hostility the religious convert feels to his former sinful impulses. What this means is that these past feelings and objectives can be given some weight in determining what to do, even if they are eventually outweighed by other considerations. This is in contrast to the mortified matron, who will give these objectives no weight at all.

Making the parallel case with the young Russian may clarify this distinction further. We could imagine a future landowner who remem-bers well the passions and thoughts of the young Socialist, and who takes them to heart even though he no longer chooses to act on them. From his older and wiser perspective he might recognize certain of his earlier impulses as naive or ill-considered; he might have changed his economic views without losing compassion for the peasants, or see things in shades of gray that were not visible to him in his impassioned youth. In this sense, then, he rejects his earlier thoughts and emotions. He might still, however, give them weight. Part of what this might mean is that he feels the need to justify to himself deviations from his past ideals. In this way, his old impulses act as a check on the new, making him consider carefully his motives or drawing him back to a more balanced picture when he starts getting too involved in running his estate. Even though this land-owner may not make any of the same choices the young Socialist did, the young Socialist is alive within him as an ongoing source of questions for self-scrutiny and as a pair of eyes through which he must judge himself. While the young Russian might still deny that he could possibly be any kind of landowner – even the one I have just described – in this case the claim sounds more like adolescent hyperbole and less like an acute awareness of self-defining values.

I thus believe that Martin is right about the need for this kind of sympathy in personal survival. Where I differ with him is in his emphasis on the forward-looking relationship of anticipation. Martin's primary concern is with the question of whether identity is what matters in survival – a claim Parfit among others has challenged. Because of this framework, Martin focuses on the question of what relation I must have to some future person in order to be concerned about her experiences in the way I am typically concerned only about my own. His conclusion is that I must be able to identify with that future person in the manner described above. While he acknowledges that a person can also identify with someone in the past in the same way, he spends most of his time discussing forward-looking identification.

There is nothing intrinsically wrong with this strategy, but it can mislead by deflecting attention from the importance of the backward-looking relation. Martin concludes that to know if I will survive in some future person I need to ask whether I, now, can identify with that (anticipated) person – whether I appropriate her experiences and feel the right sort of sympathy for her. I suggest that instead I need to know whether *she* will identify with *me*, and take the right sort of attitude toward *my* experiences. What I want in survival is that I be represented in the right way in the future. It is thus not whether I give weight to the desires and feelings of an anticipated future that is fundamentally at issue, but rather whether the future person will give weight to mine – whether the passions and desires I have now will be represented in a future life. The problem for the young Russian is not primarily that he is unsympathetic to the views of the greedy landowner (although of course he is) but that he believes the landowner could not, almost by definition, sympathetically experience the passions he feels now. It is this latter deficit and not the former which makes him feel he will not survive.

The question of whether we can sympathetically imagine and appropriate the experiences of a future person is, of course, also a question of great moment and is in no way unrelated to the question of what personal survival entails. My point is, however, that it is a secondary relation that is dependent on the more primary question of whether a future self will sympathetically appropriate the present one. Indeed, it is most likely that the tendency to appropriate the experiences of an anticipated future person in the way Martin describes comes from a belief that that future person will represent one's current values, intentions and emotions in an acceptable way.

I thus take from Wollheim (and, of course, Locke) the intuition that personal survival depends primarily on backward-looking relations; being the survivor of some past person depends upon having the right kind of recollection of the experiences of that past person, and being the survivor of some future person depends upon that person having the right kind of recollection of my present experiences. Additionally, I take from Wollheim the idea that the right kind of recollection must be at least in part iconic in nature, and must be a centered memory so that the rememberer actually inhabits, in some version, the emotions, thoughts and feelings of the person remembered. From Martin I take the additional requirement of a generally sympathetic (or at least non-hostile) attitude toward those emotions, thoughts and feelings. This package – centered event-memory with sympathy – is the basic make-up of what I have been calling "empathic access." It is this relation which I put forth as the factor which distinguishes between personal development and identity-threatening change in the cases we have been considering.

V

While an appreciation of the importance of empathic access resolves some puzzles concerning personal identity (i.e. why the standard psychological criteria seem so unsatisfying in the end), it raises a number of new ones. Most of these have to do with (1) understanding just what empathic access is and (2) clarifying the exact nature of the role it plays in personal identity. The project of articulating these puzzles – let alone solving them – is a daunting one, and obviously not one I can complete here. I can, however, outline some of the more pressing difficulties facing the development of an account of personal identity based on empathic access and say a few words about how they might be addressed.

One immediate problem for a view relying on empathic access is an epistemological one – how is it that we can know whether a person *really* has empathic access to her past? The problem here is not the general problem of knowing other minds, but a more specific concern connected to the nature of empathic access. The concern that empathic access is meant to overcome is that in relevant respects a person who existed at an earlier time has ceased to be – that that person is no longer represented either phenomenologically or behaviorally in the person who succeeds her. However, in some sense we only ever have the later person to talk to, and the difficulty is that it seems as if we must take her word for it that empathic access has been preserved.

A parent may insist, for instance, that she remembers very well what young love felt like. However, now that she is older and wiser, she might say, she must insist on strict rules for her own son, because now she also has access to how her mother felt and is able to weigh the considerations against one another. Despite a lively, empathic recall of how hard it is to be kept from one's love, she might claim, she must decide differently than she would have before. In such a case this woman's son may be inclined to challenge her claim of empathic access to her youth. Speaking in the terms we have laid out here, he might insist that if her old self were *really* still present she would rage against her misrepresentation by this middle-aged woman who claims (and maybe even believes) that that part of herself is still alive. It is not always easy to know who to believe in such circumstances.

An acceptable criterion of personal identity based on empathic access must address these concerns. They are complex, but I think not at all insurmountable. The means for determining when empathic access is present falls directly out of the nature of this relation. It requires that a person retain some sympathy for the psychological features of the life phase to which she retains access. It is therefore to be assumed that there will be tell-tale signs that a person really does or does not have genuine empathic access to the past. This sympathy is, after all, supposed to have behavioral implications. Among others is the fact that a person feels the need to give weight to the remembered impulses, and so to be able to justify overriding them in favor of others. The demeanor of the mother with empathic access to her teenage years – the kinds of explanations she will give for her actions, the kind of regret she will feel at the restrictions she imposes, the kind of second-guessing of her decisions that she might engage in – will be different from that of the mother who lacks such access. It will not, of course, be possible to tell in every single case whether access is retained, but in general there will be fairly reliable indicators.

The epistemic problem is, therefore, not terribly grave. It does, however, point to a deeper problem. While there may be no serious difficulty determining from a person's behavior roughly what degree of sympa-thetic access to past experiences she retains, the vagueness of the term "sympathy" may still leave room for disagreement about whether a person indeed has empathic access to the past. The mother in our example may provide explanations and behavioral cues that show she is giving *some* weight to past thoughts and feelings – that she is not rejecting them outright. Still, her son might argue that she weighs them so differently from the way she would have as a teenager that she is essentially giving them no weight at all. Here we are once again coming up against the difficulty of specifying just how much a memory can be recast by subse-quent changes in personality before it no longer counts as an identity-preserving recollection. Since both the accuracy with which a past experi-ence is recreated in memory and the amount of sympathy felt towards it are clearly matters of degree, it becomes obvious that empathic access must be as well, and in the middle ranges it is not clear what is to be said about personal survival.

To respond to this worry it is essential first of all to appreciate that this is not a feature of my view alone, but of all of the standard psychological views of personal identity. Both psychological continuity and narrative continuity are relations of degree, and their advocates have had to consider how to reconcile this with the fact that personal survival is, *prima facie*, all-or-nothing. Parfit, for one, has taken this issue on directly. Assuming that identity, by definition, must be an all-or-nothing relation, he introduces an arbitrary cut-off (*"at least half* the number of direct connections that hold over every day, in the lives of nearly every actual person"*) to stipulate the degree of connection necessary for preserving identity (Parfit, 1984, p. 207). He insists, however, that the need for arbitrary stipulation makes identity essentially unimportant, and that the relation we care about, survival, is indeed a matter of degree. Parfit is not the only one. Lewis, too, makes it clear that survival can be a question of degree (Lewis, 1988, pp. 67–70 [pp. 157–61 above]). In this context, then, it is not a special problem for empathic access that it is a relation of degree, and that there is no clear point at which it can be said to no longer hold.

The context itself, however, is unsettling to many. It is not only identity, but survival itself, which seems to many to be an all-or-nothing relation. This worry can be easily overcome, however, by remembering that there are different notions of survival operating unrecognized in discussions of personal continuation. What I have called before the most basic or primitive conception of survival – the question of whether I will continue as some at least minimally sentient being in the future – does indeed seem, on the face of it, to be an all-or-nothing relation (although I'm not convinced that in the end it truly is). When we consider the more subtle (but still crucially important) sense of survival at issue in the cases we have been looking at, however, it seems unproblematic that this sort of survival should admit of degrees.

This said, it must still be acknowledged that even within this more limited context empathic access on its own does not seem a totally viable account of survival. For one thing, this relation requires a particularly vivid and intimate connection to past experiences, but does not require that they be put into any kind of unified context. On its own, empathic access to the past might be a hodge-podge of intense feelings, emotions and thoughts with no order to them. Moreover, the relation that is needed to guarantee the sort of survival we are discussing will need to relate a present life stage to a past one – e.g. the phase of matronhood to that of party girl – as well as relating a particular present moment to a single past experience. By itself, empathic access seems ill-suited to this task. We can hardly demand that the matron sympathetically and iconically recollect the thoughts, feelings and emotions of the entire decade of the party girl's wild days – this is too many inner states to maintain, even dispositionally. What is needed instead is a more modest connection to that era, together with enough empathic access to enable sympathetic phenomenological and behavioral representation of that era in the present.

It is for this reason that I have called empathic access "the missing ingredient" in personal survival. I do not mean it to carry the whole weight of defining survival, even in the limited and specific sense that is at issue here. Instead I see it as a necessary supplement to the relations which have been proposed. My suggestion – although I cannot fully develop or defend it here – is that the most satisfying view of personal identity will be a combination of a narrative view with empathic access. The basic idea would be that personal identity over time consists in the existence of a coherent narrative of change which includes empathic access. The narrative provides a basic level of continuity while the empathic access provides the additional ingredient necessary for true personal survival. This is a plausible approach since the original insight about empathic access came from considering the characteristics of those narratives that seemed to preserve personal identity.

There is obviously much more work to be done in developing this view. Still, I think some important insights have been gained. First, we have seen that there are many distinct questions of survival at issue in philosophical work on personal identity, and that we must be clear which we are addressing. The question of how these senses of survival interconnect is, of course, an extremely important one, but this should not keep us from recognizing them as distinct. Second, we have seen that the relatively subtle form of personal survival at issue in cases like that of the young Russian and serious matron are not derivative or peripheral, but deeply important philosophically. Third, we have seen that the traditional psychological accounts of personal identity cannot capture this form of survival; and fourth, that if we do wish to capture it we need to provide a criterion of survival which gives a central role to empathic access. Such a criterion will not resolve all of our questions about personal identity, but it can answer some important ones and clarify what still needs to be asked.[6]

Notes

1   The issues involved in the dispute over whether identity is required for survival are tangential to those discussed here, and I wish to remain agnostic on them. I will thus use the terms "personal identity" and "personal survival" interchangeably. Wherever I have used "identity", however, "survival" could be substituted.
2   I am grateful to Marc Slors for suggesting this term, and helping me to develop the concept it names.
3   One (to which I shall return in the final section) is to show that the relation which matters to survival in identity admits of degrees (which, at least *prima facie*, identity cannot).
4   See, for instance, Frankfurt, 1976, and Taylor, 1976, for some classic versions of this view.
5   Here I am talking about the character of the memory itself and not my secondary reactions to it. Obviously my reaction to some remembered event will depend upon my attitude towards the experience, and that may change (e.g. what once made me proud may now make me ashamed). I am suggesting, however, and I think Wollheim agrees, that the very character of the memory experience will also be affected by a person's psychological make-up at the time of remembering.
6   I have been helped at many stages with the preparation of this manuscript. I would like to thank the participants in the expert seminar on Personal Identity and Moral Identity, Free University, February 1999, for their comments on a much earlier draft, and also the members of the University of Illinois at Chicago's Institute for the Humanities 1998–9. Most especially, however, I would like to thank Jan Bransen and Stefaan Cuypers for their helpful suggestions, and Marc Slors for helping me think these issues out from beginning to end.

References

Bruner, Jerome 1990: *Acts of Meaning*, Cambridge, MA: Harvard University Press.

Frankfurt, Harry 1976: "Identification and Externality," in Amélie Oksenberg Rorty, ed., *The Identities of Persons*, Berkeley: University of California Press.

Lewis, David 1983: "Survival and Identity," in *Philosophical Papers*, vol. 1, Oxford: Oxford University Press [also ch. 4 above].

MacIntyre, Alasdair 1989: "The Virtues, the Unity of a Human Life and the Concept of a Tradition," in Stanley Hauerwas and L. Gregory Jones, eds., *Why Narrative?*, Grand Rapids, Mich.: W. B. Eerdmans.

Martin, Raymond 1998: *Self-Concern: An Experiential Approach to What Matters in Survival*, Cambridge: Cambridge University Press.

Parfit, Derek 1984: *Reasons and Persons*, Oxford: Clarendon Press.

Taylor, Charles 1976: "Responsibility for Self," in Rorty, ed., *The Identities of Persons*.

Wollheim, Richard 1984: *The Thread of Life*, Cambridge, MA: Harvard University Press.

10

Human Concerns without Superlative Selves

Mark Johnston

In Part 3 of *Reasons and Persons* Derek Parfit argues that since a so-called reductionist view of personal identity, and hence of continued existence, is correct, survival, or continued existence, is not important in the way we naturally think. What matters, or what is of rational significance in survival, can be secured in cases in which people do not continue to exist, but are replaced. There is no reason to turn down a painless and practically undetectable replacement by the right sort of replica, even if one is convinced that this involves one's own death! Survival is not everything it has seemed to us to be. In more recent work Parfit seems attracted by the idea that since reductionism is true, no one *deserves* to be punished for even the great wrongs they committed in the past. He goes on to suggest that the very idea of just compensation is based on a mistake about the nature of personal identity.[1] Reductionism thus appears to show that, contrary to our primordial and habitual practice, the facts of personal identity and difference are not 'deep enough' facts around which to organize our practical concerns and patterns of reason-giving.

The issues raised by Parfit's arguments force consideration of fundamental questions about the relations between metaphysics and our practical concerns. Do we, as Parfit maintains, have a false metaphysical view of our nature as persons? How far does such a false metaphysical view guide us in our ordinary activities of reidentifying and caring about people? How much should the discovery that we have a false metaphysical view of our nature impact upon our practical concern with survival?

Because these questions loom, the topic of personal identity is an excellent test case for what I have elsewhere labelled 'Minimalism' – the view that metaphysical pictures of the justificatory undergirdings of our practices do not represent the real conditions of justification of those practices.[2] The minimalist has it that such metaphysical pictures are mostly theoretical epiphenomena; that is, although ordinary practitioners may naturally be led to adopt such pictures as a result of their practices and perhaps a little philosophical prompting, the pictures have relatively little impact on the practices themselves. For there are typically other bases of the practices. To this the minimalist adds the claim that we can do better in holding out against various sorts of scepticism and unwarranted revision when we correctly represent ordinary practice as having given few hostages to metaphysical fortune.

In the particular case of personal identity, minimalism implies that any metaphysical view of persons which we might have is either epiphenomenal or a redundant basis for our practice of making judgements about personal identity and organizing our practical concerns around this relation. About personal identity Parfit's claim is that although we are habitual non-reductionists, taking ourselves to be 'separately existing entities distinct from our brains and bodies', reductionism is true. So we must focus on the senses in which reductionism is true, and on how these might be relevant to Parfit's revisionary proposals.

How to be a Reductionist

Under the general heading of reductionism about personal identity, Parfit maintains:

1 The fact of a person's identity over time just consists in the holding of more particular facts about psychological and physical continuity (p. 210 [page numbers in parentheses are in Derek Parfit, *Reasons and Persons* (Oxford: Clarendon Press, 1984)]).
2 These 'more particular' facts can be described without presupposing the identity of the person in question (ibid.).
3 Because the more particular facts can hold to various degrees, the facts of personal identity can sometimes be factually indeterminate (pp. 216, 236–44).
4 As (1) implies and (3) illustrates, the facts of personal identity do not involve the existence of separately existing entities distinct from brains and bodies whose survival would always be a determinate matter (p. 216).

Parfit often uses 'reductionism' to denote a combination of (1)–(4) with what he believes inevitably follows: that is, that personal identity is not what fundamentally matters (e.g. p. 275). Since I am interested precisely in whether this claim does follow, I shall use 'reductionism' only as a name for (1)–(4).[3]

The crucial idiom of some facts consisting in the holding of other facts is not pellucid. Parfit himself disarmingly expresses doubt about the adequacy of his characterization of reductionism: 'It is likely that, in describing a Reductionist view about identity, I have made mistakes. Such mistakes may not wholly undermine my arguments' (p. 274). Some further clarification of reductionism is thus in order.

Let us first distinguish between analytical and ontological reductionism. Both are theses about some given fact-stating discourse. Analytical reductionism is the thesis that each statement cast in the discourse in question has an analytically equivalent statement in some other discourse which shares with the first no vocabulary other than topic-neutral expressions. Two statements are analytically equivalent just in case it is a priori and necessary that they have the same truth-value. While the notion of a fact is not well constrained in philosophical discussions, the following idea has at least some appeal: if two empirical statements are analytically equivalent, then they do not have different fact-stating potential.[4] So an analytic reductionism about the discourse in which claims of personal identity over time are cast would then have it that this discourse has no fact-stating power peculiar to it. This gives a very strong sense to the thesis that there are no 'further facts' of personal identity. However, the thesis in that sense is not plausible in itself, and even if it were, Parfit is in no position to endorse it. For he argues that we could have had good empirical evidence against reductionism. For example, if we had checkably accurate apparent memories about past lives, this might support the view that we had separable souls, and could be reincarnated. So no reductionist equivalence holds as an a priori matter.[5]

Ontological reductionism is not a thesis about the analytic redundancy of the vocabulary of a given discourse. It is a thesis to the effect that making statements in the discourse in question carries no commitment to entities other than those spoken of in some other, philosophically favoured discourse. Constructions out of the entities described in the favoured discourse may be allowed.

Thus, for example, many believe that while propositional attitude predicates cannot be analysed away in favour of purely physical predicates, there is none the less no special ontology peculiar to mentalistic discourse: every mental event or state is a physical event or state.[6] So also, those who believe that discourse about value cannot be analysed away in favour of discourse which does not employ evaluational predicates may nevertheless deny that there are extra evaluational properties, like G. E. Moore's non-natural goodness, superadded to the physical properties of things.[7]

While many ontological reductionists in fact express themselves in the idiom of identity, as with the claim that every mental event is a physical event, an ontological reductionist may also express herself in the idiom of constitution. Many of us are ontological reductionists when it comes to talk of clay statues. Clay statues are nothing over and above, are wholly constituted by, the quantities that make them up. But they are not identical with such quantities, as is shown by the fact that the quantities could survive under conditions in which no clay statues survive.[8]

Now although the notion of a fact is not well constrained in philosophical discourse, the following seems very plausible: facts involve things having properties at times, so the fact that a is F at t is the fact that b is G at t' only if $a = b$ and the property of being F is the property of being G and $t = t'$. So even when quantity Q is the quantity which wholly constitutes the statue of Goliath before and after some fire, the fact that the statue of Goliath survived the fire is not the same fact as the fact that Q survived the fire. For Q is not identical with the statue of Goliath. Here, then, is a clear and unworrying sense in which the fact that the statue of Goliath survived is a different, and in that sense further, fact than the fact that Q survived. This is not because the statue of Goliath is a superlative entity existing separately from the matter that makes it up, but for a reason that is in one way 'less deep' and in another way more deep (if one wants to follow Parfit and speak in those terms). It is because material objects and *a fortiori* art-objects are in a different ontological category from the quantities of matter that make them up.

Is ontological reductionism with such ordinary further facts a live option in the case of personal identity? On many plausible views it is. Here is one such view. People, at least the ones with which we deal, are essentially human beings. That is to say, a human person survives only if enough of an important part of the organism which constitutes him survives. What makes the important part – the brain – important is that it is the organ of mental life. On a less demanding, and perhaps more plausible, version of the view, it is enough that a physically continuous descendant of one's brain survives, so that one might survive if one's neurons were slowly replaced by bionic units. On this view there is never anything more to us than bodies and brains (and in certain science-fiction cases bionic parts which might have gradually taken over from our brains). Talk of human minds is just overly substantival talk of the mental functioning of particular human beings. It is not talk of the mental substances which inhabit human organisms. There are no such things.[9]

However, on this view human beings still cannot be identical to their bodies, to their brains, or to mereological sums of their bodies and brains. The idea that I am identical to my body, or to my body and brain taken together, is refuted by the fact that I might survive even if my body were destroyed. So long as my brain were kept alive and functioning – for example, by transplanting it into another receptive and de-brained body – I would go where my functioning brain goes, and would continue to exist even though the only part of my original body left was my brain.[10] Nor am I identical to my brain. When I report my weight as 160 pounds, I am not like the driver of a heavy truck who calls out to the bridge-master 'I weigh 3 tons.'

This means that although personal identity does not involve the persistence through time of Cartesian egos or mental substances, there are further facts of personal identity. Although Reagan does, and always did consist of, nothing more than a living body, the fact that he survived Hinckley's shots is not the fact that his body (including his brain) survived. Nor is it the fact that Reagan's brain survived. Nor is it the fact that part of Reagan's body that is other than his brain survived. Although these are all facts, the fact that Reagan survived is a further fact, thanks to the difference in category between persons and their bodily parts. Of course, we have yet to see how this difference in category could be important to rationality and morality.

So far, all of this is compatible with reductionism as Parfit himself characterizes it. Over a striking couple of pages Parfit adverts to a position which claims that (a) a person's existence just consists in the existence of his brain and body and the occurrence of a series of interrelated physical and mental events; and (b) a person is an entity that is distinct from a brain and body and such a series of events. Parfit writes:

> if this version [of Reductionism] is consistent, as I believe, it is the better version. It uses our actual concept of a person. In most of what follows we can ignore the difference between [this version emphasizing constitution and the version emphasizing identity]. But at one point this difference may have great importance. (p. 212)

The point cited by Parfit turns out to be several points, including the whole of chapter 14 of Part 3.[11] Unfortunately, Parfit does not make explicit how the better version of reductionism would make a difference at these points. It may therefore be worth seeing just how the better version bears on *most* of the argument of Part 3 of *Reasons and Persons*.

Let us call the better reductionism, the reductionism I have illustrated by the view that we are essentially human beings, reductionism with ordinary further facts. This differs from non-reductionism, which has it that personal identity involves what we might call superlative further facts – further facts involving the persistence of mental substances or Cartesian egos. Reductionism with ordinary further facts passes Parfit's crucial test for a reductionism: it allows that the facts of personal identity may sometimes be indeterminate. For example, the view that we are essentially human beings is formulated in terms of a vague necessary condition on continued existence of persons: enough of a person's brain (or brain-surrogate) must be kept functioning if that person is to survive.[12] No good explication of our ordinary concept of personal identity over time will find already implicit in our use of the concept an exact specification of how much is enough. As wielders of the concept of persons as human beings, we are not committed to the view that there is a precise point at which the victim of gradual but terminal brain damage ceases to be. By contrast, Parfit's construal of the idea of persons as Cartesian egos requires that there is such a point. The existence of Cartesian egos is supposed never to be an indeterminate matter.

Another important contrast with non-reductionism is this: of the ordinary further facts about the identity and difference of persons recognized by the better reductionism, Parfit holds that they are *fixed* by the facts about mental and physical continuity and connectedness. To put it in the now standard philosophical jargon: unlike the superlative further facts, the ordinary further facts of human personal identity *supervene* upon the facts of mental and physical continuity and connectedness. That is to say that no two possible situations alike with respect to the latter facts differ with respect to the former facts. The idiom of constitution of facts is best understood in these terms.[13]

Given widespread scepticism about the availability of analyses of significant parts of our discourse and a well-founded disbelief in superlative entities – Cartesian egos, superadded values, the moving NOW, human agency as uncaused initiation of action, etc. – the plausible general position is an ontological reductionism which allows that facts about microphysics may make up the, or a, fundamental supervenience base. On this view, the whole of the manifest world of lived experience is made up of ordinary further, although supervening, facts. There will then be a general philosophical temptation to disparage such facts and the concerns organized around them because they do not involve the superlative entities of speculative metaphysics. When in the grip of this temptation, the superlative entities can seem to be the only things which would give the required privilege to the discourses in which we state further facts. Had the superlative entities existed, and stood in the right relation to the discourses in question, then those discourses would have had an external point, and the interests which we reproduce, nurture and guide by means of those discourses would have had an external and independent justification.

The best defence against this tempting line of thought is a minimalist account of the justification of our practices. To acquire a feel for minimalism, consider what is in many ways its hardest case, the case of free will. According to the minimalist, when, for example, we hold someone responsible for an act, there are a variety of possible factual discoveries which would defeat the particular claim of responsibility – discoveries about coercion, automatism, the agent's radical ignorance of what was involved, and so on. And if it could be shown that, in such particular ways, no one is ever free, then this would radically undermine the whole practice of attributing responsibility. But in the absence of such discoveries, the mere observation that freedom does not consist in uncaused initiation of action is not itself a criticism of the practice. We should want to know exactly what role was played in the practice by the picture of agency as uncaused initiation of action, and not just that ordinary practitioners have a natural tendency upon philosophical prompting to spin out the picture of uncaused initiation. That the practice of attributing responsibility depends for its justification on facts about free agency, and that ordinary practitioners given the right sort of philosophical urging picture those facts as involving uncaused causings, does not settle it that the practice of attributing responsibility depends for its justification on facts about uncaused causings. The picture of uncaused causings may have only a minimal role. It may be epiphenomenal to the practice, or it may be only a redundant basis for the practice. The existence of this minimalist position shows that nothing can be made of the mere absence of superlative further facts. Hence the practical irrelevance of the *sheer* claim that the ordinary further facts are 'less deep' than the superlative further facts, where this just amounts to the observation that they do not involve superlative entities. If such an observation were by itself sufficient to discredit our practices, then all the concerns which have a purchase in the manifest world and cannot be captured as concerns about collections of microphysical facts would be discredited. Philosophy would have won an all too automatic, and probably Pyrrhic, victory over human life. It would have to begin again by scaling its standards of justification down to human size.

It may help to have another example of the rather abstract point about the practical dispensability of belief in superlative entities, states or processes. Arthur Prior argued that one cannot rationalize or show the point of rejoicing in the recent cessation of pain without making sense of present-tensed facts like the fact that one's pain is now over. Such facts are further facts. They are not identical to facts concerning what comes tenselessly after what. Moreover, mere knowledge of what comes tenselessly after what – for example, that 9 p.m. on 8 April 1990 is a time after the end of one's pain – is not sufficient to rationalize such rejoicing. Someone could suffer every evening with a bad digestive pain which lasts for two hours. At 8 p.m. on 8 April 1990, after being in pain for an hour, he recognizes that the pain he is undergoing will end by 9 p.m. But he is not then in a position to rejoice in the recent cessation of pain, only in the fact that it will cease. There is a simple reason for this; it is the reason he would express by saying at 8 p.m., 'My pain is not yet over.'

One ought to be able to defend such tense-ridden attitudes and concerns without relying on the metaphysical picture which naïve thought about time sometimes generates – the picture of the moving NOW which noodles along at the well-regulated rate of one second per second, as reality grows at one temporal end and diminishes at the other. After all, how exactly does the extra process involving the moving NOW help to make sense of my rejoicing that my pain is over? I could anticipate the way the moving NOW moves toward and past the time at which my pain ends just as I could anticipate some other event pre-dating and post-dating the end of my pain. The picture of the moving NOW is just something we fall back on in imagination when we think about the nature of tensed facts. But so far as our tense-ridden concerns go, all the temporal becoming we need is the temporal becoming that McTaggart famously and unpersuasively denied: that is, the existence of facts about what is happening, what has happened, and what will happen.[14] These ordinary further facts – *further* facts because not equivalent to facts about what tenselessly follows what – quite reasonably shape and support our tense-ridden concerns. It would be grotesque to abandon all such concerns simply because one does not believe in the moving NOW. The picture of the moving NOW is at most epiphenomenal to our tense-ridden concerns: it may naturally emerge out of reflection on the nature of the facts underlying such concerns, but it is not what we rely upon to justify these concerns.

Self-Concern and Self-Referential Concern

Of course, these illustrative claims about free will and the moving NOW require much more argumentative detail. My purpose here is to provide the detail in favour of this minimalist claim: self-concern does not require a Cartesian ego or a superlative further fact. To appreciate the independent reasonableness of self-concern, it helps to appreciate its place in a wider pattern of self-referential concern, directed outwards from one's present self to one's future self, one's friends, family, acquaintances, neighbourhood, and so on. Typically, each of us finds him or her self within a network of personal and institutional relationships, as a member of a given family, a friend of particular friends, an acquaintance of various acquaintances, a colleague of certain colleagues, an officer of several institutions. In the best case, one more or less identifies with each of these – that is, cares for their good in a non-derivative way. To be non-derivatively concerned for one's family, for example, is to care about the weal and woe of its members, perhaps also to care for the family's collective weal and woe, *and* to care about these things for the sake of the family and its members, not simply because their weal and woe contributes to other things one cares about, such as one's own good, or the flourishing of one's community, or the world's becoming a better place. Not only is it reasonable to have such a non-derivative concern for one's family, but a family member who had only a derivative concern would be regarded as lacking a kind of attachment which is often a central part of living a significant life. So too with one's identification with, or non-derivative concern for, one's future self. One can fail to identify with one's future self. But this will seem reasonable only if there is some considerable reason to inhibit the natural tendency to so identify, the natural tendency around which is built one's concern that one's own life continue, go well, and be worthwhile.

So there is a pattern of concern which is self-referential – it is *my* life, *my* friends, *my* acquaintances, *my* community, about which I especially care. However, this self-referential pattern of concern is not thereby egoistic. In valuing non-derivatively the well-being of others, I am motivated to act on reasons other than the promotion of my own well-being. Thus, many of us are prepared to sacrifice a considerable amount of our own well-being in order that the lives of our parents, children or friends go better. As the bonds of attachment and loyalty weaken, we are much less naturally and easily moved to sacrifice. For most of us, the claim of our common human family is felt to be comparatively weak alongside more parochial claims.

However, such a parochial bias is not necessarily at odds with generalized benevolence, the non-self-referential desire that the world should go better, that suffering should be lessened, and that all should be provided with reasonable opportunity to flourish. For although our strongest and most vivid concerns are self-referential, we are not evaluational solipsists. We do not, and need not, believe that our lives, our family our friends, are especially distinguished from an impersonal point of view. We naturally have the thought that others equally legitimately have their own distinct self-referential patterns of concern, and are thereby responding to values as real as those to which we are responding. We recognize that the things worth valuing go far beyond our vivid parochial concerns.

Because what counts as a reasonable set of concerns is a holistic matter, and because we are prepared to find reasonable various trade-offs between the extremes of a thoroughly parochial and a thoroughly impersonal concern, it is difficult to say anything specific and plausible about what is rationally required – that is, what it would be irrational not to care about. None the less, since giving some non-derivative weight to self-referential concerns is probably part of many, if not all, such acceptable trade-offs, we can at least say that it is *reasonable, or defensible*, to have a non-derivative, though not inevitably overriding, concern for oneself, one's family, one's friends, one's acquaintances and one's nation. On the face of it, such limited self-referential concern is among the easiest of things to justify. Much is justified only in terms of such concern. Indeed, in order to get into the frame of mind in which limited self-concern and loyalism need justifying at all, one has to take the view that to justify a concern is to show how having it would make the world go better. But we may as well ask: what justifies the concern that the world should go better? Nothing does, or at least, nothing else does. The concern that the world go better, like self-referential concern, is a basic pattern of concern. That is not to say that these basic concerns cannot be defended against the claim that they are unreasonable. In barest outline, the defence of self-referential concern would be that we find it utterly natural, and that, at least so far, critical and informed reflection on such concern has not made it out to be unreasonable.

Parfit is rightly leery of one sort of argument from the naturalness of our concerns to their being reasonable. Against the argument that special concern for one's future would be selected by evolution, and so would remain as a natural fact, however the theoretical arguments come out, Parfit writes: 'since there is this [evolutionary] explanation, we would all have this attitude even if it was not justified. The fact that we have this attitude cannot therefore be a reason for thinking it justified' (p. 308).

The present argument from naturalness takes a different form. It appeals to a broadly coherentist view of justification. The concerns that are justified are those which will continue to stand the test of informed criticism.[15] Concerns that are natural and fundamental have a certain kind of defeasible presumption in favour of their reasonableness; they cannot all be thrown into doubt at once, for then criticism would have no place from which to start. In my view, just as it would be a mistake to attempt a direct and conclusive justification of our basic beliefs about the external world, so it would be a mistake to attempt a direct and conclusive justification of our basic self-referential concerns. What can be said by way of justifying such self-referential concerns is that they are utterly natural concerns, and that, so far at least, informed criticism has failed to discredit them. The defeasible presumption in their favour is so far undefeated. And here the main issue may be joined. Parfit maintains that a crucial piece of information, liable to rationally displace our self-concern, is the fact that the Cartesian picture of our nature is mistaken: we are not separately existing entities distinct from our brains and bodies. There are not the superlative further facts of personal identity which Cartesianism describes.

However, locating self-concern within the broader framework of self-referential concern raises doubts about the exact relevance of Parfit's anti-Cartesian observations. Who would suppose that non-derivative concern for our friends and acquaintances depends for its justification upon substantive metaphysical views about the relation of friendship and the relation of familiarity? Just as these concerns require only the ordinary fact that one has friends and acquaintances, so self-concern seems only to require the ordinary fact that one exists and will exist. What Parfit sees as a lack of 'metaphysical depth' in such a fact – for example, that one's continued existence does not involve the persistence of a Cartesian ego or anything else that would mark a metaphysical joint in the world – seems not to disqualify it from playing an organizing role in one's thought about one's future and past. Even if our thought about ourselves has Cartesian elements, the reasonableness of our self-concern does not crucially depend on the truth of the Cartesian picture.

Parfit aims to show otherwise by means of detailed investigations of the cases of fission and the Combined Spectrum, cases in which, he claims, the facts of personal identity come apart from what it is rational to care about in caring about survival. But as we shall see, the most that follows is that self-concern might be sensibly extended in certain bizarre cases, were these cases ever in fact to arise.

What Happens if we ever Divide?

Future-directed self-concern is both the concern that one will have a future and a non-derivative concern for one's well-being in any such future. The vivid sense that one will *oneself undergo* certain experiences in the future gives one's future-directed self-concern its special and urgent quality. One can imaginatively extend one's consciousness forward in time, anticipating what the future course of one's experience and action will be like from the inside. This is a particular application of a general imaginative capacity to grasp what it is like to undergo experiences. One can imagine what it might be like to be Dan Quayle running for President: one looks out at the by then more pacified press corps, one struggles to remember the script, one vaguely senses one's syntax jumbling in one's mouth, and so on. While imagining Quayle undergoing all this might make one embarrassed for Quayle, it will not arouse one's *self*-concern (unless one is badly deluded about who's who). Of all the actual future candidates whose consciousness can be imagined from the inside, at most one, as a matter of fact, will be physically and psychologically continuous with one's present self in rich and important ways. It is this matter of fact which allows one to give a uniquely directed future focus to self-concern – there is in fact at most one future person whose mental and bodily life is a continuation of one's own.

Given this, philosophers' preoccupation with the case of fission need not be seen as a penchant for amateurish science fiction, but as an attempt to explore the consequences of suspending this matter of fact around which our uniquely focused self-concern is formed. If the fission case is playing this role, then it cannot be a deep objection that fission is neither medically nor physically possible.[16] Such *per impossible* thought-experiments might none the less teach us something about the relative importance of things that invariably go together. Something we value non-derivatively may be shown to be a mere concomitant of what is really important.

Enough by way of excuse for the fission case. In that case we are to imagine a doubling up of processes either one of which, had it occurred without the other, would have secured the continued existence of a given person. For example, consider a patient Luckless, whose body is badly degenerated and whose right hemisphere is utterly dysfunctional. Luckless has one chance of continuing to exist: his left hemisphere can be transplanted into a receptive and de-brained body. If we let 'Lefty' abbreviate the description 'the person who after the operation is made up of Luckless's original left hemisphere and the new body', then on many accounts of personal identity, Luckless would be Lefty.[17] Given the right sort of specifications of the brain of Luckless (having to do with not too much lateralization of mental functioning), many accounts would also allow that Luckless survives in the variant case in which only his right hemisphere is viable and is transplanted into a receptive and de-brained body – in that case Luckless is Righty. But since we have no problem imaginatively providing receptive and de-brained bodies, we should consider the case in which the transplanting of both Luckless's hemispheres takes place. In this case, is Luckless Lefty, Righty, neither Lefty nor Righty, Lefty and Righty considered as parts of a sum, or both Lefty and Righty in a way that requires Lefty to be Righty despite their spatial separation?

No answer is wholly satisfactory. Each answer violates one or other of a set of principles each of which holds up without exception in our ordinary practice of reidentifying persons. The relevant principles are:

1   Whether some process secures the survival of a given person logically depends only upon intrinsic features of the process; that is, it does not also depend on what is happening elsewhere and at some other time.
2   No person is at one time constituted by two or more separately living human bodies.
3   No person is spatially separated from himself in the manner of an instantiated property.

These principles produce a contradiction when taken in conjunction with the assumption built into the fission case: namely, that persons lack one of the prerogatives traditionally ascribed to substances – that is, essential unity. Thus, entertaining fission involves entertaining the idea that each person has two (or more) subparts such that the survival of either one of these subparts in the right environment can secure the survival of the person. Part of the importance of the fission case is that by imaginatively violating essential unity it illustrates how we might not be mental or physical substances. Such a violation is very surprising from the point of view of our ordinary practice of reidentifying persons, a practice which takes it for granted that a person has at most one future continuer of his physical and mental life.

There are determinate facts about personal identity in specific cases only if our concepts of a person and of being the same person determinately apply in those cases. When a case necessarily violates some principle relatively central to our conception of persons and their identity over time, the concepts of a person and of being the same person over time may not determinately apply in that case, so that there may be no simple fact about personal identity in that case. This is how it is in the fission case. Hence the various philosophical accounts of who is who in the fission case are best seen as proposals about how to extend our practice to a case where it presently gives no answer. Parfit takes essentially this line about the facts in the fission case. He writes that the question of who is who is 'empty', and then goes on to say that the best way to view the case (extend our practice to the case?) is to take it that no one is identical with either of his fission products. One might balk at the argument Parfit offers against the contending resolutions.[18] However, the important points are that, relative to our practice as it stands, the fission case (i) violates the ordinary presupposition of essential unity; (ii) is, as a result, an indeterminate case; and (iii) also violates a presupposition of our future-directed self-concern by providing more than one future person to continue an earlier person's mental and bodily life. These last two points are crucial for a proper assessment of the practical upshot of arguments from the fission case.

What Matters when we Divide?

Parfit claims that the practical upshot of the fission case is quite general: that personal identity does not matter. This, he claims (p. 262), is something that a reductionist must accept. As an ontological reductionist who believes in ordinary further facts, I deny it, and deny it on reductionist grounds.

The question of whether personal identity matters may be clarified as follows. Consider self-referential concern, and in particular self-concern. As they stand, these concerns, or at least those of them not directed at institutions and plural subjects, are *structured* in terms of the relation of personal identity. It is the person with whom I am identical that I am especially concerned about, along with the persons identical with my family members, friends and acquaintances. We can imagine an alternative pattern of special concern structured around R – psychological continuity and connectedness – rather than around identity. Let us call this alternative pattern of concern 'R-variant concern'. Since R involves the relation of psychological connectedness, a relation that holds to varying degrees, R-variant concern will most plausibly be scalar, dropping off as psychological connectedness weakens across lives.[19]

In so far as Parfit is advocating what he calls the Moderate Claim – that it is R, and not identity, which fundamentally matters – he is maintaining that reason is on the side of adopting R-variant concern in the place of what I have called self-referential concern. Since R-variant concern is also in a certain way self-referential, being a concern for the R-descendants of people with whom *I* now have certain relations, we can distinguish when we need to by referring to ordinary self-referential concern, or ordinary concern for short. (Parfit also considers an Extreme Claim which has it that not even R matters fundamentally. This would imply that not even R-variant concern is rationally defensible. More on extreme claims below.)

The fictional device of teletransportation can be used to make vivid the details of R-variant concern, and hence the import of the Moderate Claim. In standard teletransportation, a person's body is scanned and destroyed by the scanning, while at another, possibly distant point a cell-by-cell replica is created in an instant with available matter and the information obtained from the original body by the scanner. Teletransportation thereby secures that R holds between the person with the original body and the person with the newly made body. However, R holds because of an abnormal cause – the operation of the scanner and the reproducer – as opposed to the normal cause – the persistence of a functioning brain.

I am among those who regard the teletransporting scanner and reproducer as a xerox machine for persons with the unfortunate property of destroying not only the original body but the original person. That this is the case seems vividly illustrated when we consider standard teletransportation alongside branch-line teletransportation, in which the scanner collects information without destroying the original body. In this case it is obvious that a xerox or replica of the original person is produced at some distance from the original body.[20]

Suppose branch-line xeroxing were used to provide personnel for a deep space probe whose mission would never return it to earth. Suppose that those about to be xeroxed believe that it is just xeroxing – that is, they believe that they will be scanned, will survive the scanning, and that R-related replicas will be produced. Given this belief and beliefs about the horror of the mission, each person facing xeroxing strongly prefers that his 'replica' rather than he is sent on the mission. This is a manifestation of ordinary self-concern. Each has a bias in favour of himself and his own welfare as against that of strangers who happen to be R-related to him.

The Moderate Claim implies that this is a mistake. Even given the horrors of the space mission, there is no good reason for them to prefer that their replicas be sent off in the space probe. For the Moderate Claim is that it is R, and not personal identity, that matters. R will hold between any person before branch-line teletransportation and his replica. Indeed, we can easily imagine cases in which replication results in the original person being more strongly connected psychologically to his replica than to his later self: the scanning may produce as an after-effect mild psychological disorientation in the original person. In these cases in which a person can anticipate that his replica will be more psychologically connected to him than his future self will be, the Moderate Claim implies that he should be more concerned for his replica, and so should prefer that his replica be left to live out the better life on earth. Such are the consequences of R-variant concern.

Related points apply to the other special relations which provide the bases for the rest of our ordinary self-referential concerns. If I believed the Moderate Claim, I would believe that everything which it is rational for my friend to care about in caring about survival would be secured if in the near future he were replaced by his replica. Indeed, in the case of a more psychologically connected replica, I would believe that he should prefer the survival of the replica to his own survival. Suppose it is settled that either my friend or his about-to-be-generated replica will be sent into deep space. When my friend is asleep, his replica will be produced. My friend will wake with some memory loss, and will be uncharacteristically irritable for a week. At the end of the week he will be whizzing past Neptune, while his calm, clear-headed replica has taken over his life on earth. If I believed in the Moderate Claim, I would believe that my friend has good reason *antecedently* to prefer this outcome to the alternative one. But how, then, can I be more discriminating on his behalf than I believe he ought to be on his own behalf? I ought antecedently to prefer that his replica be left behind with me and his other close friends. Identity itself is to be given no non-derivative weight within R-variant concern. Friendship, with its bias against substitution *salvis amicitiis*, a bias that is stronger as the friendship is more intimate, has come to an end.

To bring out the inhuman element in all this, imagine my friend discovering that I held this view about his upcoming space trip – that I preferred the clearer-headed replica to be left on earth. My friend might reasonably object that I did not care for him for his own sake, that he was for me simply a stage in a potential parade of persons appropriately tied together psychologically. Indeed, my readiness to be more attached to a more psychologically connected replica shows that *he* is not really the object of my friendly concern. I seem to care about psychological relations more fundamentally than I care about particular people.

There would be something right about these rebukes. Friendship does constitutively involve valuing the friend for his own sake and not being disposed to weaken the bonds of friendship just because of some psychological change in the friend. If I believe that I should transfer my affections to a person I am just about to meet, and so have not shared my life with, then the claim of friendship, as opposed to the claim that I find my so-called friend admirable, agreeable, genial, *simpatico*, is thrown into doubt. And as friendships become more intimate, all this is more pronounced. We can understand a husband who cares little when he discovers that his wife recently replaced her lost wedding-ring with a replica produced by the branch-line method, but what are we to think of a husband who would remain just as calm in the face of his wife's imminent replacement in his life by her replica. He is not exactly like the man who can easily transfer a long-standing love to a newly met identical twin of his lover. He may not simply love a type which his wife exemplifies. On the other hand, he does not simply love his wife as a person, but rather as a stage in a potential parade of persons. Perhaps there is something very sad about this, even if his wife would not object to being loved in this way, having been won over to the ways of R-variant concern. People have become secondary to the R-interrelated parades they head.[21]

That is to say, if the Moderate Claim were true, ordinary self-referential concern with its special place for people would be an indefensibly limited pattern of concern. On the required variant pattern, we would care as much for the R-related descendants of our friends, lovers, family and acquaintances. This is what the claim that it is not identity but R (psychological continuity and connectedness) that fundamentally matters comes to. As a defender of this claim, Parfit is not simply committed to saying that it would be acceptable to adopt R-variant concern. Rather, this is rationally required – ordinary concern is irrationally limited as it stands.[22]

This seems on the face of it a very strong result to extract from reductionism about personal identity, a thesis to the effect that the holding of personal identity over time consists merely in the holding of patterns of psychological continuity and connectedness, and therefore not in the persistence of a Cartesian ego. Parfit's argument for the claim that R, and not identity, is what matters comes in two distinguishable parts. First, he takes the case of fission to provide an argument that one should not be specially concerned that R holds uniquely between oneself and some future person. Then, by claiming that for a reductionist teletransportation is not significantly worse than ordinary survival, he argues that we should not be specially concerned that the holding of R be secured in the normal way – as a result of the activity of a unified physical basis of mental life.

About the case of teletransportation Parfit writes:

> My attitude to [the] outcome should not be affected by our decision whether to call my Replica me. I know the full facts even if we have not yet made this decision. If we do not decide to call my Replica me, the fact
>
> (a) that my Replica will not be me would just consist in the fact
>
> (b) that there will not be physical continuity, and
>
> (c) that, because this is so, R will not have its normal cause. (pp. 285–6)

Parfit continues:

> Since (a) would just consist in (b) and (c), I should ignore (a). My attitude should depend upon the importance of facts (b) and (c). These facts are all there is to my Replica's not being me. When we see that this last claim is true, we cannot rationally, I believe, claim that (c) matters much. It cannot matter much that the cause is abnormal. It is the *effect* which matters. And this effect, the holding of Relation R, is in itself the same. (p. 286)

Parfit talks about deciding to call my replica by standard teletransportation me because he believes that the case of teletransportation is a case in which the facts of personal identity are indeterminate. As in the case of fission, he believes that there is a best extension of our practice of making judgements of identity to that case – one is not identical with one's replica.

Since the argument for indeterminacy we gave in the case of fission has no strict analogue in the case of teletransportation (see n. 20), I do not agree that teletransportation is an indeterminate case. Even standardly imagined teletransportation is a case of xeroxing,[23] so (a) is just a fact. But when it comes to settling what matters, we should consider both hypotheses.

Take first the hypothesis that teletransportation is an indeterminate case. We saw that one presupposition of our future-directed concern was that at most one future person will continue our mental and bodily life. Another presupposition of future-directed concern is that given any future person there is a simple matter of fact as to whether this person is oneself or not. The idea that there may be no answer to this question initially boggles future-directed concern. When we discover that the determinacy of personal identity is not guaranteed in every case, we should look to see if there is a plausible way of extending ordinary concern to those cases in which its presuppositions are violated. One promising idea is this: look to see if in the indeterminate case a significant core of the relations which ordinarily constitute identity is none the less to be found. Since we have an indeterminate case, so not a case of non-identity, some such significant core will be there. As a way of coping with the failure of the presupposition of determinacy, one could reasonably take the holding of that significant core as a good surrogate for determinate identity. On the hypothesis that teletransportation is an indeterminate case, the significant core – the core which accounts for it not being a simple case of non-identity – is the holding of R. *So in teletransportation understood as an indeterminate case we have good reason to care about R much as we would care about identity.* The good reason comes from a sensible way of extending our self-concern to a case it is not as yet made for. But the crucial point is that we have here simply grounds for a *local* extension of our self-concern in those cases in which a crucial presupposition of that concern is violated. In the cases which make up ordinary life, in which the presupposition of determinacy is satisfied, there is no effect upon the reasonableness of organizing our concerns in terms of identity. No movement to R-variant concern is warranted. Even in the case of branch-line replication one still should not care for one's replica as one cares for oneself. For one is determinately not identical with one's branch-line replica.

Within Parfit's own framework this way of admitting but quarantining his claims about what concerns are reasonable in indeterminate cases will seem surprising. Parfit's central motivating idea is that what is important about the indeterminate cases he discusses is that those cases show that something crucial to our concerns – the superlative further fact of identity – is not only missing in those cases, but is always missing. But in discussing these cases it would be begging the question to assume that the superlative fact is crucially important to us. These very cases are themselves supposed to show that in the absence of the superlative further fact, we have no reason to care fundamentally about identity. But they do not show this. They are indeed cases in which something crucial to self-concern's getting a purchase is missing – namely, an ordinary, determinate, further fact of personal identity or difference. But in almost all ordinary cases this is not missing; there is an ordinary, determinate, further fact of personal identity or difference. Hence the very limited relevance of indeterminate cases.

Given the alternative hypothesis that one simply does not survive teletransportation, it patently does not follow that since the fact (a) that my replica will not be me just consists in the two facts (b) that there will be no physical continuity, and (c) that R will not have its normal cause, therefore 'my attitude should just depend upon the importance of facts (b) and (c)'. Rather, the defender of ordinary concern will argue *from above*: it is not that one should have a bizarre non-derivative preference in favour of R being secured by the functioning of human tissue instead of a machine. Instead, the first way of securing R is just a necessary condition for one's continued existence. Since, under mildly optimistic assumptions about one's future, concern for one's continued existence is eminently sensible, it is eminently sensible to have a derivative concern that R be secured by the persistence of one's brain. One needs no brute partiality for processes involving organic molecules in order to defend ordinary concern.

Some might think that this argument from above just produces a stand-off because it is merely equipoised with Parfit's argument 'from below' – namely, that since personal identity consists in brain-based R, and since a strong non-derivative preference for brain-based realization of R is hardly defensible, it follows that R is about as worth caring about as identity is. But as against the idea of equipoise, the argument from below is no counter-consideration at all. It is disastrously flawed. First, as we shall see, it depends on a fallacious additive picture of values. Second, it cannot be consistently applied unless one is prepared to embrace nihilism.

This second point readily emerges from the general plausibility of a denial of superlative further facts. It may well be that all the facts in the manifest world of lived experience supervene upon micro-physical facts – that is, facts about how the basic properties are distributed over some fundamental field or plenum. Particular ontological reductions for every object, event, state and process in the manifest world will locate for each its own particular patterns of constituting facts in the fundamental realm. Now take any valued object, event, state or process and the fact that it exists, obtains or occurs. That fact will be constituted by facts about micro-physical properties, facts about which one will have no particular non-derivative concern. If one took the argument from below seriously, one would conclude that the previously valued object is not worthy of concern. Generalizing the argument, we derive nihilism: nothing is worthy of concern. But this is not a proof of nihilism. It is a *reductio ad absurdum* of the argument from below. We should not expect to find the value of the things we value divided out among their constituents. That is to say, the argument from below depends upon a fallacious addition of values.

The Argument from Intrinsic Features

Parfit's main argument from the fission case is that although one's forth-coming fission could not promise (determinate) identity or continued existence, nothing worth caring about in caring about one's continued existence is missing. For, Parfit claims, whether one has reason to be especially and directly concerned for some future person can depend only on the intrinsic features of the relation between oneself and that future person (p. 263). In fission one stands in a relation to Lefty which is in all intrinsic respects like the relation one stands in to Lefty when only Lefty proves viable. But when Lefty alone proves viable, one is identical to Lefty. So, by Parfit's principle that only intrinsics matter here, it follows that in fission one gets something that is as much worth caring about as identity or continued existence. Indeed, a corresponding appli-cation of Parfit's principle to one's relation to Righty implies that one gets what matters twice over. Although it is a necessary condition of identity, uniqueness does not in fact matter; that is, it is not a reasonable object of concern. So identity is not what matters. What matters are the more particular relations which hold twice over in the fission case.

Whence the plausibility of the crucial principle that whether one has reason to be specially and directly concerned about some future person depends only on the intrinsic aspects of the relation between oneself and that future person? Certainly not from the plausibility of the general claim that extrinsic features do not matter. We often take extrinsic fea-tures to be highly relevant to how we evaluate some fact or relation.[24] Rather, whatever plausibility Parfit's principle has seems to derive from what we earlier saw to be a presupposition of future-directed concern: namely, that at most one future person will continue one's mental and bodily life. In taking ourselves to be unified substances, we suppose that we will have at most one such future continuer, hence that whether some process represents our continuation depends only upon intrinsic features of that process, *and hence that* whether some process is rightfully taken to ground direct future concern can depend only upon intrinsic features of that process.

If this is the basis of the appeal of the crucial principle that only intrinsic features matter, then to use that principle to show something about what matters in the fission case is to try to walk out on a branch one has just taken some trouble to lop off. The very case of fission itself undermines essential unity, violates the presupposition that one will have at most one continuer, threatens the ordinary idea that only intrinsic features matter to identity, and so undermines the basis for the principle that only intrinsic features can matter. Thus no one is in a position to appeal to this last principle in the fission case. The plausible basis of the principle is undermined in the very description of the fission case.

None the less, I do think that it is reasonable *although not rationally required* to extend one's future-directed concern in the fission case, so to care about each of one's future fission products as if each were oneself. Although I could understand someone doing otherwise, I would not make a significant sacrifice to have someone intervene in my upcoming fission to ensure that only the transplanting of my left hemisphere proved viable. And this is my reaction even though I believe that only then would I determinately survive the procedure. Sydney Shoemaker adopts the same attitude in his discussion of fission, and concludes with Parfit that identity cannot be what matters fundamentally.[25] Have we at last hit upon a successful argument for Parfit's desired conclusion, or at least a weakened version of it: namely, that it is at least reasonable to take the view that identity never matters fundamentally, so that moving to R-variant concern is at least reasonable?

No, we have not. It is one thing to conclude that in the fission case (neurally based) R, and not identity, is the relation in terms of which one should extend one's special concern. But as we saw with the quarantining manoeuvre above, it is quite another to conclude that quite generally it is (neurally based) R that matters. Fission is a case in which at least two presuppositions of our special concern are violated. The first is that it is always a determinate matter whether one is identical with some given future person. The second is that at most one future person will continue one's mental (and physical) life. When such presuppositions are violated, future-directed concern neither determinately applies nor determinately fails to apply. It is reasonable to try to find a natural extension of such concern for such cases. In that regard, an appealing idea is to look for a significant core of the relations which constitute identity in the determinate cases. If we are reductionists who emphasize the importance of a continuous physical basis for mental life, then we will find in the fission case a reasonable basis for a local extension. In such an indeterminate case it will then seem reasonable to extend our concerns in accord with the holding of neurally based R. This relation holds twice over, and to the same degree as in some cases of determinate identity: for example, when only Lefty survives. If we instead take ourselves to be essentially human beings, then the important core of what constitutes identity is still discernible in the fission case: that is, the persistence of enough of the brain to be capable of continuing the mental life of the original subject. This important core also holds twice over in the fission case. So were we ever to face fission, it would be reasonable to care about our fission products as we would care about a future self. *But this is not because identity is never what matters; rather, this is because caring in this way represents a reasonable extension of self-concern in a bizarre case.* Of course this does not mean that we might not have further practical reasons to avoid fission – for example, in order to avoid intractable squabbling over spouses, houses and jobs. It is just to say that there is no inevitable and universal objection to it from the point of view of appropriately extended self-concern. The resultant impact on ordinary self-referential concern would be much more local and conservative than the move to R-variant concern. With one possible class of exceptions, locally modified concern would differ from ordinary concern only in certain bizarre cases which may never in fact arise. Identity would always in fact be what matters. The exceptions involve gradually coming into being and passing away. On a reductionist view of personal identity, there may be no fact of the matter as to just exactly when a person begins to exist and when he ceases to exist. In such cases what is indeterminate is whether we have a person at all. As a result, there will be no determinate fact of personal identity. This is slightly less surprising than the situation in Parfit's indeterminate cases, for in those cases there was a determinate fact about a person existing at one time and a person existing at another. What was indeterminate was whether these were the same person.

However, since the presupposition of determinacy is violated in cases involving coming into being and passing away, an extension of self-referential concern may again be reasonable. We should look in such cases for an important core of the relations which make up identity in the determinate cases – for example, overlapping links of strong mental and physical connections across time. And we should extend our concern to the extent that such strong links hold. Such an adjustment represents only a possible deviation from ordinary concern. Ordinary concern may implicitly have made just such an accommodation already.

In any case, neither R nor brain-based R nor the persistence of enough neural capacity to continue mental life would be the relation around which our self-referential concerns are almost always organized. Identity would keep this privileged role. Within locally modified concern the importance of R or the other relations in a few cases would be parasitic on the importance of identity.

A telling case from Susan Wolf nicely highlights the differences between R-variant concern and locally modified concern. Suppose with Wolf that small children are not very strongly connected psychologically to the adults they will become. R-variant concern would have us care considerably more for our present children than for the adults they will eventually become. But then, as Wolf asks, why should a parent reduce the happiness of the child she loves so much in order to benefit a remote adult she loves so little? R-variant concern will give no special weight to the obvious answer: that one loves the person the child is, and the remote adult is that person. As a result, R-variant concern would find little place for disciplining children for the sake of the adults they will become. If parents acted accordingly, the results would probably be pretty bad.

Wolf argued from these and other bad effects of R-variant concern to it not being reasonable to adopt such a pattern of concern.[26] Parfit jibs at the whole strategy of argument, suggesting that reasonable adjustment to the discovery of error may none the less have some bad effects. Parfit also hopes that the good will outweigh the bad.[27] (He might also have added that on his view a consequentialist morality will take up some of the slack in direct parental concern.) The present point is not Wolf's point that because R-variant concern would be nasty, brutish and pretty short-lived it is therefore not a reasonable adjustment. The point is rather that the move to R-variant concern is not a reasonable adjustment because it is much more radical than the indeterminate cases require. Reasonable adjustments are those in accord with what Quine called the 'maxim of minimum mutilation'. A much less radical adjustment is the move to locally modified concern.[28] Given a merely local extension of ordinary concern for the indeterminate cases, the ordinary practice of child-rearing will remain unchanged. For personal identity holds determinately between the child whom one now loves and the adult he will become. The extension of concern for cases of indeterminacy does not apply. Nor will it apply in a massive core of ordinary cases.

All this suggests that there is a false apparatus of generalization at the heart of Parfit's arguments against identity-based concern. If the fission case showed that a presupposition of such concern was *always* violated, then there would be general consequences for our concerns. So, if the existence of a superlative further fact were such a presupposition, the general consequences would threaten. What is evidently not there in the fission case, the superlative further fact, is never there. However, since the relevant presupposition of self-concern is the holding of the determinate, ordinary fact of personal identity or difference, the case has no effect beyond the imaginative fringe.[29] What is not there in the fission case is almost always there. Identity is still almost always what matters.

The Combined Spectrum

Similar remarks apply to the third of Parfit's main examples, the Combined Spectrum. In the Combined Spectrum there is a series of possible cases. In the first case in the series I undergo as little psychological and physical change as possible. In the next case I undergo a slight amount of psychological and physical change, in the next case slightly more, and so on, increasing gradually case by case until in the last case the psychological and physical changes are so extreme that it is clear that I cannot survive them, or indeed any of the radical changes near this end of the spectrum. Parfit writes: 'it is hard to believe that there must be . . . a sharp borderline somewhere in the Spectrum [which separates the cases in which I survive from those in which I do not survive]' (p. 239). That is to say, we have a region of indeterminacy within the spectrum; cases in that region are such that there is no sharp yes or no answer to the question whether or not I survive in those cases. How is one to proportion one's degree of concern for the people around after the various changes that occur across the spectrum? The psychological and physical connections decline uniformly across the spectrum. Parfit's account of what matters might therefore suggest that the plausible pattern of concern declines uniformly with the decline in psychological, and perhaps physical, connections. Parfit tells us that physical continuity and physical similarity will only have some slight importance, except in the case of 'a few people who are very beautiful [where] physical similarity may have great importance' (p. 217). Putting this complication about the physical relations aside for a moment, it does seem plausible in the Combined Spectrum to adopt a pattern of concern which, at least within the zone of indeterminacy, declines uniformly with the decline in psychological connectedness. But is this not to admit that what fundamentally matters is not identity, but the holding of psychological connectedness?

No, it is not. The plausibility of proportioning future concern in accord with psychological connectedness arises from two factors. One is the now familiar idea that by way of a local extension of ordinary concern it is reasonable to organize future concern in an indeterminate case around some significant core of the relations that constitute identity. Here one's version of reductionism will be relevant. Those who believe that human persons are essentially human beings, and who, as a result, think that the persistence of enough of the physical basis for one's mental life is crucial for identity, will reasonably proportion future concern within the zone of indeterminacy in accord with the degree to which the same neural capacity to subserve a relatively rich mental life persists. Depending on the details of the operative intrusions, this may grossly correlate with the holding of significant psychological connections. Psychological reductionists, who think that the facts of personal identity consist in the holding of psychological connections, will directly proportion concern to the degree to which the psychological connections hold. As we move into the zone of indeterminacy, these physical and mental relations weaken to a degree not found between successive stages of a single life. Future-directed concern should be weakened accordingly, progressively so as we move through the indeterminate zone.

The second source of the plausibility of the idea that future-directed concern should drop off gradually as psychological connectedness drops off comes from the reasonable concern that one have, in one's future self or in another, an excellent future executor for one's ongoing projects. This needs some explanation.

Imagine someone who is dying of an incurable illness. A central project of his last years has been the completion of a certain book. No doubt this project has an essentially *self-involving* aspect – that is, it is the project that *he himself* complete the book in question – so that the demand inherent in the project cannot be satisfied unless he carries out the project himself. As the end approaches, it becomes clear to the dying man that he will not complete the book. His self-involving project is doomed. However, unless he is completely self-involved, he will think that considerable value attaches to the non-self-involving counterpart of his self-involving project – that is, the project that *someone* complete his book in much the way he would have completed it. (Notice that this project is still self-referential.) Furthermore, completion of the book in this way would give significance to the dying man's efforts in his last years. So he seeks an executor of his project – someone well equipped to carry out the non-self-involving counterpart of this project. The more a given person has access to the dying man's intentions, notes and drafts, the better executor he will be. The more a given person has relevantly similar psychological dispositions, the better executor he will be.

The moral is quite general. Consider the cluster of relatively long-term projects which give momentum and significance to one's life. So long as one is not utterly self-involved, it is reasonable to hope for a good future executor of those projects, *whether or not that executor is identical with oneself*. In fact, always or for the most part, the only way to have even a pretty good executor is to determinately survive, and not change too much psychologically. But the Combined Spectrum is precisely a case in which in the zone of indeterminacy one may get a pretty good executor

without determinately surviving. Hence, reasonable concern for an executor is not essentially tied to one's own future existence. We need only add
that so long as the social environment remains relatively stable, some
future person will probably be a good executor of one's present projects
to the extent that he is psychologically connected to oneself. Since in
general we want good future executors of our projects, it seems quite
reasonable to proportion one aspect of one's future-directed concern in
accord with psychological connectedness. So in the Combined Spectrum
this implies some proportioning of future-directed concern in accord with
the degree of psychological connectedness found in the case in question.
And while the local modification prompted by indeterminacy applies
only within the zone of indeterminacy, *this* proportioning will apply not
just within the zone of indeterminacy but across the whole spectrum.

Part of the importance of this talk about executors and proportioning is
that it brings out that, in caring about our futures, we reasonably want a
package deal: as well as our future existence, we want the means to make
that future existence a worthwhile continuation of our present life. Too
often, even in the best work on the topic of personal identity, we are
presented with an exclusive choice of the form: 'What matters, personal
identity or the psychological continuations?' As against what the question presupposes, the natural view is that both matter, and that either
part of the package is less attractive on its own.[30]

So in the Combined Spectrum there are two grounds for allowing one's
concern to drop off across the zone of indeterminacy as psychological
connectedness drops off. One is that one's chance of having a good
executor is thereby dropping off. The other is that as psychological
connectedness drops off, one of the central core of identity-constituting
relations is dropping off.

Just to anticipate an objection, consider two close cases in the spectrum,
one at the remote end of the zone of indeterminacy and the other just
beyond. In the first case, someone survives who is not determinately not
me but who is very disconnected from me psychologically and physically. In the second case, someone only slightly more disconnected but
who is determinately not me survives. I would not be inclined to make a
significant sacrifice to secure the first outcome rather than the second. But
rather than being an objection to our proposed scheme of discounting,
this seems to me to be what the scheme implies. By the time we have
reached the remote end of the zone of indeterminacy, physical and
psychological connections have worn out to a great extent. So neither
the concern organized around the constituting core of identity nor the
concern for an executor has much purchase.

A point of proper emphasis should be added. I may not have thought of the best way of extending identity-based concern across the zone of indeterminacy in the Combined Spectrum. The main point is that, like the case of fission, the Combined Spectrum requires only a local modification of future-directed concern. Given the local modification, identity is still almost always what matters. So much for the immoderate position expressed by the so-called Moderate Claim.

Metaphysics and Criticism

Revisionism has so far fared pretty badly. Parfit's arguments for the Moderate Claim are met by quarantining our reactions to the indeterminate cases and by recognizing the fallacy in the additive argument from below. The ordinary supervening facts of personal identity and difference are a real and sufficient basis for self-referential concern. It is not a probative argument against our identity-based practices that they are not superimposed upon superlative metaphysical joints. It is enough that those practices respect the differences among the lives of human beings. So far in the case of personal identity, the doctrine that I have elsewhere called 'Minimalism' seems vindicated: metaphysical pictures of the underpinnings of our practices do not represent what crucially has to be in place if those practices are to be justified.

That is not to say that conservatism must inevitably win the day against an ambitious practical revisionism. The philosophy of personal identity need not leave everything as it is. The criticism of metaphysics can have a practical role. That criticism, at least when it is criticism of the idea that one or some or all of our practices can be justified in terms of a demand for them built into the things themselves, is often an important *prelude* to a successful revisionary criticism of the specific practices in question. A metaphysical picture – in effect a concrete instance of the idea of an independent demand in the things themselves[31] – can help cement a false sense of the necessity of our practices, depriving the imagination of alternatives, thereby reducing practical criticism to the condition of a device in the service of banal meliorism. But pointing out that the rightness or legitimacy of our practices can never be the solitary work of nature or supernature is not itself to criticize those practices. Rooting out false necessity is better understood as a prolegomenon to criticism. The critical meat is the defence of a concrete alternative.

None the less, in the case of personal identity, it may seem that the relevant prolegomenon must also be the end of the matter. The idea of a radical practical criticism of our identity-based practices, the idea of defending a concrete alternative to these practices as an alternative which better serves our legitimate interests, can seem incoherent. For, as our defence of the centrality of self-referential concern implies, many of our legitimate interests require the language of personal identity for their very formulation. We seem of necessity deprived of an independent practical lever against our identity-based scheme of concern. Any envisaged benefit within the proposed alternative could not literally be a benefit for us as opposed to the differently conformed entities recognized within the alternative scheme.

As against this defeatism, I simply want to mention the possibility that we might be more protean than we appear to ourselves to be. Our turning out to be human beings may be more a matter of what turns out to be personal identity for us as we now are, than a matter of what it always must be, however we might refigure our concerns and expectations. That is to say, what instantiates the relation of personal identity for us may in a certain sense be up to us, a matter more dependent upon our identity-based concerns than it might initially seem. Because human being is just *one* way of instantiating personhood, we might be able to remain the same persons, and so the same subjects of benefit and loss, even if we ceased to be always and only human beings. *If* this were so, and if we could articulate a radical defect in the condition of being always and only a human being, we might find a real critical basis for radically refiguring our concerns and expectations. But that, as they say, is another story.[32]

Notes

1   Derek Parfit, 'Comments', *Ethics*, 96 (1986), pp. 832–72.
2   See Mark Johnston, 'Is there a Problem about Persistence?', *Proceedings of the Aristotelian Society*, supp. vol. 61 (1987), pp. 107–35; *idem*, 'The End of the Theory of Meaning', *Mind and Language*, 3 (1988), pp. 59–83; *idem*, 'Constitution is not Identity', *Mind*, 101 (1992), pp. 89–105; *idem*, 'Objectivity Refigured', in *Realism and Reason*, ed. J. Haldane and C. Wright (Oxford University Press, Oxford, 1992), pp. 85–130.
3   I shall not discuss (2). In the most recent reprinting of *Reasons and Persons* Parfit seems to weaken his claim about impersonal descriptions.
4   This has only some appeal as an account of the identity of facts, because some will want to add a further structural condition of the sort discussed below. But adding this condition here would simply reinforce the argument in the text.

5 For an argument to the same effect, see my review of Sydney Shoemaker and Richard Swinburne, *Personal Identity* (Blackwell, Oxford, 1984) in *Philosophical Review*, 96 (1987), pp. 123–8, esp. p. 128.

6 See Donald Davidson, 'Mental Events', in *Essays on Actions and Events* (Oxford University Press, Oxford, 1980), pp. 207–25. What are mental properties on this view? Perhaps they are rather gerrymandered sets of physical events. I discuss this issue in 'Why Having a Mind Matters', in *Actions and Events*, ed. E. LePore and B. McLaughlin (Blackwell, Oxford, 1985), pp. 408–26.

7 Evaluational properties may be no more than dispositions with physical properties as their categorical bases – i.e. wholly constituted by such physical properties. For such an ontological reductionism without analysis see my 'Dispositional Theories of Value', *Proceedings of the Aristotelian Society*, supp. vol. 68 (1989), pp. 139–74.

8 Some sophisticated philosophical objections to this view are addressed in my 'Constitution is not Identity'.

9 Such a view, while at odds with substance dualism, is compatible with a property dualism which finds mental properties to be radically unlike physical properties, and not reducible to them.

10 All this is discussed in more detail in my 'Human Beings', *Journal of Philosophy*, 84 (1987), pp. 59–83.

11 *Reasons and Persons*, p. 212, n. 10.

12 This is typical of conditions on identity over time. See my 'Is there a Problem about Persistence?'

13 On supervenience see J. Kim, 'Concepts of Supervenience', *Philosophy and Phenomenological Research*, 45 (1984), pp. 153–76.

14 Perhaps the ordinary further facts of tense are categorial facts having to do with our way of constructing our experience of the world. The ordinary further facts of personal identity may be similarly categorial, having to do with our way of constructing our activity in the practical world. For such a suggestion see Christine Korsgaard's fascinating paper 'Personal Identity and the Unity of Agency: A Kantian Response to Parfit', *Philosophy and Public Affairs*, 18 (1989), pp. 101–32 [ch. 5 above]. For an attempt to deal with the initial logical problems with the idea that we constitute ourselves by way of our practical concerns and activity, see my 'Relativism and the Self', in *Relativism: Interpretation and Confrontation*, ed. M. Krausz (University of Notre Dame Press, Notre Dame, Ind., 1989), pp. 441–72.

Parfit writes (pp. 165–86) that 'it cannot be irrational' to abandon our tense-ridden concerns if there is not temporal becoming. Perhaps this is plausible if one means by temporal becoming what McTaggart meant – the existence of tensed facts. On McTaggart's argument against temporal becoming, see M. A. E. Dummett, *Truth and Other Enigmas* (Duckworth, London, 1983), pp. 351–7.

15 For a development of this idea and its relation to the concept of value, see my 'Dispositional Theories of Value'.

16 As against John Robinson, 'Personal Identity and Survival', *Journal of Philosophy*, 85 (1988), pp. 319–28.

17 Why the explicit mention of the description? So that the terms 'Lefty' and 'Righty' are not mistaken for rigid designators – i.e. designators which designate the same thing in every possible situation in which they designate anything. If they were rigid designators, then it would be incoherent to say that Lefty would have been Luckless but for the existence of Righty. Nothing is contingently identical with itself.

18 It is too extreme to say, as Parfit does, that other views of fission grotesquely distort the concept of person. For more on fission as an indeterminate case, the view that we could be repeatable across space, and a reply to Parfit's specific attempt to rule out David Lewis's proposal, see my 'Fission and the Facts', *Philosophical Perspectives*, 3 (1989), pp. 85–102.

19 On pp. 313–15 Parfit claims that it is defensible and rational for someone persuaded that R is what matters to have a scalar concern which involves caring less for one's future self as psychological connectedness weakens. However, in the context of Parfit's total discussion, a stronger claim seems warranted. Given that such a scalar concern is very plausible in the Combined Spectrum, one of the two cases central to Parfit's defence of the view that it is R that matters, the form of R-variant concern best motivated by Parfit's discussion is scalar, dropping off as psychological connectedness weakens.

20 Robert Nozick's Closest Continuer Theory, the theory that one is identical with the closest of one's close enough psychological and perhaps physical continuers, would invalidate the argument from the obvious xerox claim about branch-line teletransportation to the xerox claim about standard teletransportation. By indicating that the intrinsicness principle ((1) above) is plausible for ordinary practitioners, I mean to imply that Nozick is wrong about the status of his theory. The Closest Continuer Theory, because it is at odds with (1), is an extension of our practice. This extension is not forced upon us. Principles (1)–(3) are not inconsistent with the description of teletransportation and the branch-line case unless we add what is on any view not utterly obvious – i.e. that we survive teletransportation. So if we are describing how our practice as it stands applies to teletransportation, we should apply principle (1). Hence, when we take the obvious view that branch-line teletransportation is a case of xeroxing persons, it follows that standard teletransportation is xeroxing persons too.

21 Contrast the easily confused case of series-persons. In 'Relativism and the Self' I argue that there could be persons who naturally and spontaneously take themselves to survive teletransportation and who might not be wrong about this, at least if certain further conditions were satisfied. They would be, in Thomas Nagel's useful term, series-persons. Love among series-persons would be strongly individuated love for particular series-persons, not love for parades of series-persons. No series-person should rebuke his friend for

caring for his teletransportation product. But he could rebuke his friend for preferring his clearer-headed back-up produced by branch-line teletransportation.

22 Cf. p. 262: 'If we are Reductionists, we *cannot* plausibly claim that of these two relations it is identity that matters.'

23 For us and our kind, at least.

24 In his fine 'Surviving Matters', *Nous*, 24 (1990), pp. 297–322 [ch. 7 above], Ernest Sosa provides the obvious examples of exclusive ownership, winning, unique achievement and intimacy.

25 Shoemaker and Swinburne, *Personal Identity*, p. 121.

26 Susan Wolf, 'Self-Interest and Interest in Selves', *Ethics*, 96 (1986), pp. 704–20.

27 Parfit, 'Comments', p. 833.

28 An obvious but unsustainable objection is that the move to locally modified concern, unlike the move to R-variant concern, leaves us without a uniform basis for our self-referential concerns. There is a uniform basis. We are to organize our concerns around personal identity, and in those cases in which it is only sort of true or partly true that personal identity holds, we are to extend identity-based concern.

29 Suppose that fission took place all the time. Then our concepts would come under such strain that we might resolve indeterminacy by altering our concept of personal identity. Since we take personal identity to be what matters, a nice way of doing this would be to ignore those ontological conservatives who believe in a sharp distinction between particulars and properties and allow that under special circumstances splittable particulars can share some of the traditional prerogatives of instantiated properties – i.e. they can be multiply located at a time. For an argument that this is not incoherent see my 'Fission and the Facts'.

30 David Lewis's paper 'Survival and Identity', in his *Philosophical Papers*, vol. 1 (Oxford University Press, Oxford, 1985), pp. 55–77 [ch. 4 above], is built around the assumption that one needs some complex apparatus of temporal parts to make the answer 'identity and the psychological connections' acceptable.

31 For this idea of metaphysics see my 'Objectivity Refigured'.

32 For part of the story, and in particular for a detailed account of how we might be protean in just the way suggested in the text, see my 'Relativism and the Self'. For help with this essay I would especially like to thank Derek Parfit and Jamie Tappenden. Peter Unger offers a somewhat similar deflationary treatment of Parfit's central cases in his *Identity, Consciousness and Value* (Oxford University Press, Oxford, 1990).

11

The Unimportance of Identity

Derek Parfit

We can start with some science fiction. Here on Earth, I enter the Tele-transporter. When I press some button, a machine destroys my body, while recording the exact states of all my cells. The information is sent by radio to Mars, where another machine makes, out of organic materials, a perfect copy of my body. The person who wakes up on Mars seems to remember living my life up to the moment when I pressed the button, and he is in every other way just like me.

Of those who have thought about such cases, some believe that it would be I who would wake up on Mars. They regard Teletransportation as merely the fastest way of travelling. Others believe that, if I chose to be Teletransported, I would be making a terrible mistake. On their view, the person who wakes up would be a mere Replica of me.

I

That is a disagreement about personal identity. To understand such disagreements, we must distinguish two kinds of sameness. Two white billiard balls may be qualitatively identical, or exactly similar. But they are not numerically identical, or one and the same ball. If I paint one of these balls red, it will cease to be qualitatively identical with itself as it was; but it will still be one and the same ball. Consider next a claim like, 'Since her accident, she is no longer the same person'. That involves both senses of identity. It means that *she*, one and the same person, is *not* now the same person. That is not a contradiction. The claim is only that this person's character has changed. This numerically identical person is now qualitatively different.

When psychologists discuss identity, they are typically concerned with the kind of person someone is, or wants to be. That is the question involved, for example, in an identity crisis. But, when philosophers discuss identity, it is numerical identity they mean. And, in our concern about our own futures, that is what we have in mind. I may believe that, after my marriage, I shall be a different person. But that does not make marriage death. However much I change, I shall still be alive if there will be someone living who will be me. Similarly, if I was Teletransported, my Replica on Mars would be qualitatively identical to me; but, on the sceptic's view, he wouldn't *be* me. *I* shall have ceased to exist. And that, we naturally assume, is what matters.

Questions about our numerical identity all take the following form. We have two ways of referring to a person, and we ask whether these are ways of referring to the same person. Thus we might ask whether Boris Nikolayevich is Yeltsin. In the most important questions of this kind, our two ways of referring to a person pick out a person at different times. Thus we might ask whether the person to whom we are speaking now is the same as the person to whom we spoke on the telephone yesterday. These are questions about identity over time.

To answer such questions, we must know the *criterion* of personal identity: the relation between a person at one time, and a person at another time, which makes these one and the same person.

Different criteria have been advanced. On one view, what makes me the same, throughout my life, is my having the same body. This criterion requires uninterrupted bodily continuity. There is no such continuity between my body on Earth and the body of my Replica on Mars; so, on this view, my Replica would not be me. Other writers appeal to psychological continuity. Thus Locke claimed that, if I was conscious of a past life in some other body, I would be the person who lived that life. On some versions of this view, my Replica would be me.

Supporters of these different views often appeal to cases where they conflict. Most of these cases are, like Teletransportation, purely imaginary. Some philosophers object that, since our concept of a person rests on a scaffolding of facts, we should not expect this concept to apply in imagined cases where we think those facts away. I agree. But I believe that, for a different reason, it is worth considering such cases. We can use them to discover, not what the truth is, but what we believe. We might have found that, when we consider science fiction cases, we simply shrug our shoulders. But that is not so. Many of us find that we have certain beliefs about what kind of fact personal identity is.

These beliefs are best revealed when we think about such cases from a first-person point of view. So, when I imagine something's happening to me, you should imagine its happening to you. Suppose that I live in some future century, in which technology is far advanced, and I am about to undergo some operation. Perhaps my brain and body will be remodelled, or partially replaced. There will be a resulting person, who will wake up tomorrow. I ask, 'Will that person be me? Or am I about to die? Is this the end?' I may not know how to answer this question. But it is natural to assume that there must *be* an answer. The resulting person, it may seem, must be either me, or someone else. And the answer must be all-or-nothing. That person cannot be *partly* me. If that person is in pain tomorrow, this pain cannot be partly mine. So, we may assume, either I shall feel that pain, or I shan't.

If this is how we think about such cases, we assume that our identity must be *determinate*. We assume that, in every imaginable case, questions about our identity must have answers, which must be either, and quite simply, Yes or No.

Let us now ask: 'Can this be true?' There is one view on which it might be. On this view, there are immaterial substances: souls, or Cartesian Egos. These entities have the special properties once ascribed to atoms: they are indivisible, and their continued existence is, in its nature, all-or-nothing. And such an Ego is what each of us really is.

Unlike several writers, I believe that such a view might have been true. But we have no good evidence for thinking that it is, and some evidence for thinking that it isn't; so I shall assume here that no such view is true.

If we do not believe that there are Cartesian Egos, or other such entities, we should accept the kind of view which I have elsewhere called *Reductionist*. On this view

(1) A person's existence just consists in the existence of a body, and the occurrence of a series of thoughts, experiences, and other mental and physical events.

Some Reductionists claim

(2) Persons just *are* bodies.

This view may seem not to be Reductionist, since it does not reduce persons to something else. But that is only because it is hyper-Reductionist: it reduces persons to bodies in so strong a way that it doesn't even distinguish between them. We can call it *Identifying* Reductionism.

Such a view seems to me too simple. I believe that we should combine (1) with

> (3)   A person is an entity that has a body, and has thoughts and other experiences.

On this view, though a person is distinct from that person's body, and from any series of thoughts and experiences, the person's existence just *consists* in them. So we can call this view *Constitutive* Reductionism.

It may help to have other examples of this kind of view. If we melt down a bronze statue, we destroy this statue, but we do not destroy this lump of bronze. So, though the statue just consists in the lump of bronze, these cannot be one and the same thing. Similarly, the existence of a nation just consists in the existence of a group of people, on some territory, living together in certain ways. But the nation is not the same as that group of people, or that territory.

Consider next *Eliminative* Reductionism. Such a view is sometimes a response to arguments against the Identifying view. Suppose we start by claiming that a nation just is a group of people on some territory. We are then persuaded that this cannot be so: that the concept of a nation is the concept of an entity that is distinct from its people and its territory. We may conclude that, in that case, there are really no such things as nations. There are only groups of people, living together in certain ways.

In the case of persons, some Buddhist texts take an Eliminative view. According to these texts

> (4)   There really aren't such things as persons: there are only brains and bodies, and thoughts and other experiences.

For example:

> Buddha has spoken thus: 'O brethren, actions do exist, and also their consequences, but the person that acts does not.... There exists no Individual, it is only a conventional name given to a set of elements.'

Or:

> The mental and the material are really here,
> But here there is no person to be found.
> For it is void and merely fashioned like a doll,
> Just suffering piled up like grass and sticks.

Eliminative Reductionism is sometimes justified. Thus we are right to claim that there were really no witches, only persecuted women. But Reductionism about some kind of entity is not often well expressed with the claim that there are no such entities. We should admit that there are nations, and that we, who are persons, exist.

Rather than claiming that there are no entities of some kind, Reductionists should distinguish kinds of entity, or ways of existing. When the existence of an X just consists in the existence of a Y, or Ys, though the X is *distinct* from the Y or Ys, it is not an *independent* or *separately existing* entity. Statues do not exist separately from the matter of which they are made. Nor do nations exist separately from their citizens and their territory. Similarly, I believe,

(5) Though persons are distinct from their bodies, and from any series of mental events, they are not independent or separately existing entities.

Cartesian Egos, if they existed, would not only be distinct from human bodies, but would also be independent entities. Such Egos are claimed to be like physical objects, except that they are wholly mental. If there were such entities, it would make sense to suppose that they might cease to be causally related to some body, yet continue to exist. But, on a Reductionist view, persons are not in that sense independent from their bodies. (That is not to claim that our thoughts and other experiences are merely changes in the states of our brains. Reductionists, while not believing in purely mental substances, may be dualists.)

We can now return to personal identity over time, or what constitutes the continued existence of the same person. One question here is this. What explains the unity of a person's mental life? What makes thoughts and experiences, had at different times, the thoughts and experiences of a single person? According to some Non-Reductionists, this question cannot be answered in other terms. We must simply claim that these different thoughts and experiences are all had by the same person. This fact does not consist in any other facts, but is a bare or ultimate truth.

If each of us was a Cartesian Ego, that might be so. Since such an Ego would be an independent substance, it could be an irreducible fact that different experiences are all changes in the states of the same persisting Ego. But that could not be true of persons, I believe, if, while distinct from their bodies, they are not separately existing entities. A person, so conceived, is not the kind of entity about which there could be such irreducible truths. When experiences at different times are all had by the same person, this fact must consist in certain other facts.

If we do not believe in Cartesian Egos, we should claim

(6) Personal identity over time just consists in physical and/or psychological continuity.

That claim could be filled out in different ways. On one version of this view, what makes different experiences the experiences of a single person is their being either changes in the states of, or at least directly causally related to, the same embodied brain. That must be the view of those who believe that persons just are bodies. And we might hold that view even if, as I think we should, we distinguish persons from their bodies. But we might appeal, either in addition or instead, to various psychological relations between different mental states and events, such as the relations involved in memory, or in the persistence of intentions, desires, and other psychological features. That is what I mean by psychological continuity.

On Constitutive Reductionism, the fact of personal identity is distinct from these facts about physical and psychological continuity. But, since it just consists in them, it is not an independent or separately obtaining fact. It is not a further difference in what happens.

To illustrate that distinction, consider a simpler case. Suppose that I already know that several trees are growing together on some hill. I then learn that, because that is true, there is a copse on this hill. That would not be new factual information. I would have merely learnt that such a group of trees can be called a 'copse'. My only new information is about our language. That those trees can be called a copse is not, except trivially, a fact about the trees.

Something similar is true in the more complicated case of nations. In order to know the facts about the history of a nation, it is enough to know what large numbers of people did and said. Facts about nations cannot be barely true: they must consist in facts about people. And, once we know these other facts, any remaining questions about nations are not further questions about what really happened.

I believe that, in the same way, facts about people cannot be barely true. Their truth must consist in the truth of facts about bodies, and about various interrelated mental and physical events. If we knew these other facts, we would have all the empirical input that we need. If we understood the concept of a person, and had no false beliefs about what persons are, we would then know, or would be able to work out, the truth of any further claims about the existence or identity of persons. That is because such claims would not tell us more about reality.

That is the barest sketch of a Reductionist view. These remarks may become clearer if we return to the so-called 'problem cases' of personal identity. In such a case, we imagine knowing that, between me now and some person in the future, there will be certain kinds of degrees of physical and/or psychological continuity or connectedness. But, though we know these facts, we cannot answer the question whether that future person would be me.

Since we may disagree on which the problem cases are, we need more than one example. Consider first the range of cases that I have elsewhere called the *Physical Spectrum*. In each of these cases, some proportion of my body would be replaced, in a single operation, with exact duplicates of the existing cells. In the case at the near end of this range, no cells would be replaced. In the case at the far end, my whole body would be destroyed and replicated. That is the case with which I began: Teletransportation.

Suppose we believe that in that case, where my whole body would be replaced, the resulting person would not be me, but a mere Replica. If no cells were replaced, the resulting person would be me. But what of the cases in between, where the percentage of the cells replaced would be, say, 30, or 50, or 70 per cent? Would the resulting person here be me? When we consider some of these cases, we will not know whether to answer Yes or No.

Suppose next that we believe that, even in Teletransportation, my Replica would be me. We should then consider a different version of that case, in which the Scanner would get its information without destroying my body, and my Replica would be made while I was still alive. In this version of the case, we may agree that my Replica would not be me. That may shake our view that, in the original version of case, he *would* be me.

If we still keep that view, we should turn to what I have called the *Combined Spectrum*. In this second range of cases, there would be all the different degrees of both physical and psychological connectedness. The new cells would not be exactly similar. The greater the proportion of my body that would be replaced, the less like me would the resulting person be. In the case at the far end of this range, my whole body would be destroyed, and they would make a Replica of some quite different person, such as Greta Garbo. Garbo's Replica would clearly *not* be me. In the case at the near end, with no replacement, the resulting person would be me. On any view, there must be cases in between where we could not answer our question.

For simplicity, I shall consider only the Physical Spectrum, and I shall assume that, in some of the cases in this range, we cannot answer the question whether the resulting person would be me. My remarks could be transferred, with some adjustment, to the Combined Spectrum.

As I have said, it is natural to assume that, even if *we* cannot answer this question, there must always *be* an answer, which must be either Yes or No. It is natural to believe that, if the resulting person will be in pain, either I shall feel that pain, or I shan't. But this range of cases challenges that belief. In the case at the near end, the resulting person would be me. In the case at the far end, he would be someone else. How could it be true that, in all the cases in between, he must be either me, or someone else? For that to be true, there must be, somewhere in this range, a sharp borderline. There must be some critical set of cells such that, if only those cells were replaced, it would be me who would wake up, but that in the very next case, with only just a few more cells replaced, it would be, not me, but a new person. That is hard to believe.

Here is another fact, which makes it even harder to believe. Even if there were such a borderline, no one could ever discover where it is. I might say, 'Try replacing half of my brain and body, and I shall tell you what happens.' But we know in advance that, in every case, since the resulting person would be exactly like me, he would be inclined to believe that he was me. And this could not show that he *was* me, since any mere Replica of me would think that too.

Even if such cases actually occurred, we would learn nothing more about them. So it does not matter that these cases are imaginary. We should try to decide now whether, in this range of cases, personal identity could be determinate. Could it be true that, in every case, the resulting person either would or would not be me?

If we do not believe that there are Cartesian Egos, or other such entities, we seem forced to answer No. It is not true that our identity must be determinate. We can always ask, 'Would that future person be me?' But, in some of these cases,

(7) This question would have no answer. It would be neither true nor false that this person would be me.

And

(8) This question would be *empty*. Even without an answer, we could know the full truth about what happened.

If our questions were about such entities as nations or machines, most of us would accept such claims. But, when applied to ourselves, they can be hard to believe. How could it be neither true nor false that I shall still exist tomorrow? And, without an answer to our question, how could I know the full truth about my future?

Reductionism gives the explanation. We naturally assume that, in these cases, there are different possibilities. The resulting person, we assume, might be me, or he might be someone else, who is merely like me. If the resulting person will be in pain, either I shall feel that pain, or I shan't. If these really were different possibilities, it would be compelling that one of them must be the possibility that would in fact obtain. How could reality fail to choose between them? But, on a Reductionist view,

(9)   Our question is not about different possibilities. There is only a single possibility, or course of events. Our question is merely about different possible descriptions of this course of events.

That is how our question has no answer. We have not yet decided which description to apply. And, that is why, even without answering this question, we could know the full truth about what would happen.

Suppose that, after considering such examples, we cease to believe that our identity must be determinate. That may seem to make little difference. It may seem to be a change of view only about some imaginary cases, that will never actually occur. But that may not be so. We may be led to revise our beliefs about the nature of personal identity; and that would be a change of view about our own lives.

In nearly all actual cases, questions about personal identity have answers, so claim (7) does not apply. If we don't know these answers, there is something that we don't know. But claim (8) still applies. Even without answering these questions, we could know the full truth about what happens. We would know that truth if we knew the facts about both physical and psychological continuity. If, implausibly, we still didn't know the answer to a question about identity, our ignorance would only be about our language. And that is because claim (9) still applies. When we know the other facts, there are never different possibilities at the level of what happens. In all cases, the only remaining possibilities are at the linguistic level. Perhaps it would be correct to say that some future person would be me. Perhaps it would be correct to say that he would not be me. Or perhaps neither would be correct. I conclude that in *all* cases, if we know the other facts, we should regard questions about our identity as merely questions about language.

That conclusion can be misunderstood. First, when we ask such questions, that is usually because we *don't* know the other facts. Thus, when we ask if we are about to die, that is seldom a conceptual question. We ask that question because we don't know what will happen to our bodies, and whether, in particular, our brains will continue to support consciousness. Our question becomes conceptual only when we already know about such other facts.

Note next that, in certain cases, the relevant facts go beyond the details of the case we are considering. Whether some concept applies may depend on facts about other cases, or on a choice between scientific theories. Suppose we see something strange happening to an unknown animal. We might ask whether this process preserves the animal's identity, or whether the result is a new animal (because what we are seeing is some kind of reproduction). Even if we knew the details of this process, that question would not be merely conceptual. The answer would depend on whether this process is part of the natural development of this kind of animal. And that may be something we have yet to discover.

If we identify persons with human beings, whom we regard as a natural kind, the same would be true in some imaginable cases involving persons. But these are not the kind of case that I have been discussing. My cases all involve artificial intervention. No facts about natural development could be relevant here. Thus, in my Physical Spectrum, if we knew which of my cells would be replaced by duplicates, all of the relevant empirical facts would be in. In such cases any remaining questions would be conceptual.

Since that is so, it would be clearer to ask these questions in a different way. Consider the case in which I replace some of the components of my audio system, but keep the others. I ask, 'Do I still have one and the same system?' That may seem a factual question. But, since I already know what happened, that is not really so. It would be clearer to ask, 'Given that I have replaced those components, would it be correct to call this the same system?'

The same applies to personal identity. Suppose that I know the facts about what will happen to my body, and about any psychological connections that there will be between me now and some person tomorrow. I may ask, 'Will that person be me?' But that is a misleading way to put my question. It suggests that I don't know what's going to happen. When I know these other facts, I should ask, 'Would it be correct to call that person me?' That would remind me that, if there's anything that I don't know, that is merely a fact about our language.

I believe that we can go further. Such questions are, in the belittling sense, merely verbal. Some conceptual questions are well worth discussing. But questions about personal identity, in my kind of case, are like questions that we would all think trivial. It is quite uninteresting whether, with half its components replaced, I still have the same audio system. In the same way, we should regard it as quite uninteresting whether, if half of my body were simultaneously replaced, I would still exist. As questions about reality, these are entirely empty. Nor, as conceptual questions, do they need answers.

We might need, for legal purposes, to *give* such questions answers. Thus we might decide that an audio system should be called the same if its new components cost less than half its original price. And we might decide to say that I would continue to exist as long as less than half my body were replaced. But these are not answers to conceptual questions; they are mere decisions.

(Similar remarks apply if we are Identifying Reductionists, who believe that persons just are bodies. There are cases where it is a merely verbal question whether we still have one and the same human body. That is clearly true in the cases in the middle of the Physical Spectrum.)

It may help to contrast these questions with one that is not merely verbal. Suppose we are studying some creature which is very unlike ourselves, such as an insect, or some extraterrestrial being. We know all the facts about this creature's behaviour, and its neurophysiology. The creature wriggles vigorously, in what seems to be a response to some injury. We ask, 'Is it conscious, and in great pain? Or is it merely like an insentient machine?' Some Behaviourist might say, 'That is a merely verbal question. These aren't different possibilities, either of which might be true. They are merely different descriptions of the very same state of affairs.' That I find incredible. These descriptions give us, I believe, two quite different possibilities. It could not be an empty or a merely verbal question whether some creature was unconscious or in great pain.

It is natural to think the same about our own identity. If I know that some proportion of my cells will be replaced, how can it be a merely verbal question whether I am about to die, or shall wake up again tomorrow? It is because that is hard to believe that Reductionism is worth discussing. If we become Reductionists, that may change some of our deepest assumptions about ourselves.

These assumptions, as I have said, cover actual cases, and our own lives. But they are best revealed when we consider the imaginary problem cases. It is worth explaining further why that is so.

In ordinary cases, questions about our identity have answers. In such cases, there is a fact about personal identity, and Reductionism is one view about what kind of fact this is. On this view, personal identity just consists in physical and/or psychological continuity. We may find it hard to decide whether we accept this view, since it may be far from clear when one fact just consists in another. We may even doubt whether Reductionists and their critics really disagree.

In the problem cases, things are different. When we cannot answer questions about personal identity, it is easier to decide whether we accept a Reductionist view. We should ask: Do we find such cases puzzling? Or do we accept the Reductionist claim that, even without answering these questions, if we knew the facts about the continuities, we would know what happened?

Most of us do find such cases puzzling. We believe that, even if we knew those other facts, if we could not answer questions about our identity, there would be something that we didn't know. That suggests that, on our view, personal identity does *not* just consist in one or both of the continuities, but is a separately obtaining fact, or a further difference in what happens. The Reductionist account must then leave something out. So there is a real disagreement, and one that applies to all cases.

Many of us do not merely find such cases puzzling. We are inclined to believe that, in all such cases, questions about our identity must have answers, which must be either Yes or No. For that to be true, personal identity must be a separately obtaining fact of a peculiarly simple kind. It must involve some special entity, such as a Cartesian Ego, whose existence must be all-or-nothing.

When I say that we have these assumptions, I am *not* claiming that we believe in Cartesian Egos. Some of us do. But many of us, I suspect, have inconsistent beliefs. If we are asked whether we believe that there are Cartesian Egos, we may answer No. And we may accept that, as Reductionists claim, the existence of a person just involves the existence of a body, and the occurrence of a series of interrelated mental and physical events. But, as our reactions to the problem cases show, we don't fully accept that view. Or, if we do, we also seem to hold a different view.

Such a conflict of beliefs is quite common. At a reflective or intellectual level, we may be convinced that some view is true; but at another level, one that engages more directly with our emotions, we may continue to think and feel as if some different view were true. One example of this kind would be a hope, or fear, that we know to be groundless. Many of us, I suspect, have such inconsistent beliefs about the metaphysical questions that concern us most, such as free will, time's passage, consciousness, and the self.

II

I turn now from the nature of personal identity to its importance. Personal identity is widely thought to have great rational and moral significance. Thus it is the fact of identity which is thought to give us our reason for concern about our own future. And several moral principles, such as those of desert or distributive justice, presuppose claims about identity. The separateness of persons, or the non-identity of different people, has been called 'the basic fact for morals'.

I can comment here on only one of these questions: what matters in our survival. I mean by that, not what makes our survival good, but what makes our survival matter, whether it will be good or bad. What is it, in our survival, that gives us a reason for special anticipatory or prudential concern?

We can explain that question with an extreme imaginary case. Suppose that, while I care about my whole future, I am especially concerned about what will happen to me on future Tuesdays. Rather than suffer mild pain on a future Tuesday, I would choose severe pain on any other future day. That pattern of concern would be irrational. The fact that a pain will be on a Tuesday is no reason to care about it more. What about the fact that a pain will be *mine*? Is *this* a reason to care about it more?

Many people would answer Yes. On their view, what gives us a reason to care about our future is, precisely, that it will be our future. Personal identity is what matters in survival.

I reject this view. Most of what matters, I believe, are two other relations: the psychological continuity and connectedness that, in ordinary cases, hold between the different parts of a person's life. These relations only roughly coincide with personal identity, since, unlike identity, they are in part matters of degree. Nor, I believe, do they matter as much as identity is thought to do.

There are different ways to challenge the importance of identity.

One argument can be summarized like this:

(1)   Personal identity just consists in certain other facts.

(2)   If one fact just consists in certain others, it can only be these other facts which have rational or moral importance. We should ask whether, in themselves, these other facts matter.

Therefore

(3) Personal identity cannot be rationally or morally important.
     What matters can only be one or more of the other facts in
     which personal identity consists.

Mark Johnston rejects this argument.[1] He calls it an *Argument from Below*,
since it claims that, if one fact justs consists in certain others, it can only be
these other lower level facts which matter. Johnston replies with what he
calls an *Argument from Above*. On his view, even if the lower-level facts do
not in themselves matter, the higher-level fact may matter. If it does, the
lower-level facts will have a derived significance. They will matter, not in
themselves, but because they constitute the higher-level fact.

To illustrate this disagreement, we can start with a different case.
Suppose we ask what we want to happen if, through brain damage, we
become irreversibly unconscious. If we were in this state, we would still
be alive. But this fact should be understood in a Reductionist way. It may
not be the same as the fact that our hearts would still be beating, and our
other organs would still be functioning. But it would not be an independent or separately obtaining fact. Our being still alive, though irreversibly
unconscious, would just consist in these other facts.

On my Argument from Below, we should ask whether those other facts
in themselves matter. If we were irreversibly unconscious, would it be
either good for us, or good for others, that our hearts and other organs
would still be functioning? If we answer No, we should conclude that it
would not matter that we were still alive.

If Johnston were right, we could reject this argument. And we could
appeal to an Argument from Above. We might say:

> It may not be in itself good that our hearts and other organs would
> still be functioning. But it is good to be alive. Since that is so, it is
> rational to hope that, even if we could never regain consciousness,
> our hearts would go on beating for as long as possible. That would
> be good because it would constitute our staying alive.

I believe that, of these arguments, mine is more plausible.

Consider next the moral question that such cases raise. Some people
ask, in their living wills, that if brain damage makes them irreversibly
unconscious, their hearts should be stopped. I believe that we should do
what these people ask. But many take a different view. They could appeal
to an Argument from Above. They might say:

> Even if such people can never regain consciousness, while their hearts are still beating, they can be truly called alive. Since that is so, stopping their hearts would be an act of killing. And, except in self-defence, it is always wrong to kill.

On this view, we should leave these people's hearts to go on beating, for months or even years.

As an answer to the moral question, this seems to me misguided. (It is a separate question what the law should be.) But, for many people, the word 'kill' has such force that it seems significant whether it applies.

Turn now to a different subject. Suppose that, after trying to decide when people have free will, we become convinced by either of two compatibilist views. On one view, we call choices 'unfree' if they are caused in certain ways, and we call them 'free' if they are caused in certain other ways. On the other view, we call choices 'unfree' if we know how they were caused, and we call them 'free' if we have not yet discovered this.

Suppose next that, when we consider these two grounds for drawing this distinction, we believe that neither, in itself, has the kind of significance that could support making or denying claims about guilt, or desert. There seems to us no such significance in the difference between these kinds of causal determination; and we believe that it cannot matter whether a decision's causes have already been discovered. (Note that, in comparing the Arguments from Above and Below, we need not actually accept these claims. We are asking whether, *if* we accepted the relevant premises, we ought to be persuaded by these arguments.)

On my Argument from Below, if the fact that a choice is free just consists in one of those other facts, and we believe that those other facts cannot in themselves be morally important, we should conclude that it cannot be important whether some person's choice was free. Either choices that are unfree can deserve to be punished, or choices that are free cannot. On a Johnstonian Argument from Above, even if those other facts are not in themselves important – even if, in themselves, they are trivial – they can have a derived importance if and because they constitute the fact that some person's choice was free. As before, the Argument from Below seems to me more plausible.

We can now consider the underlying question on which this disagreement turns.

As I have claimed, if one fact just consists in certain others, the first fact is not an independent or separately obtaining fact. And, in the cases with which we are concerned, it is also, in relation to these other facts, merely a conceptual fact. Thus, if someone is irreversibly unconscious, but his heart is still beating, it is a conceptual fact that this person is still alive. When I call this fact conceptual, I don't mean that it is a fact about our concepts. That this person is alive is a fact about this person. But, if we have already claimed that this person's heart is still beating, when we claim that he is still alive, we do not give further information about reality. We only give further information about our use of the words 'person' and 'alive'.

When we turn to ask what matters, the central question is this. Suppose we agree that it does not matter, in itself, that such a person's heart is still beating. Could we claim that, in another way, this fact does matter, because it makes it correct to say that this person is still alive? If we answer Yes, we are treating language as more important than reality. We are claiming that, even if some fact does not in itself matter, it may matter if and because it allows a certain word to be applied.

This, I believe, is irrational. On my view, what matters are the facts about the world, given which some concept applies. If the facts about the world have no rational or moral significance, and the fact that the concept applies is not a further difference in what happens, this conceptual fact cannot be significant.

Johnston brings a second charge against my argument. If physicalism were true, he claims, all facts would just consist in facts about fundamental particles. Considered in themselves, these facts about particles would have no rational or moral importance. If we apply an Argument from Below, we must conclude that nothing has any importance. He remarks: 'this is not a proof of nihilism. It is a *reductio ad absurdum.*'

Given what I have suggested here, this charge can, I think, be answered. There may perhaps be a sense in which, if physicalism were true, all facts would just consist in facts about fundamental particles. But that is not the kind of reduction which I had in mind. When I claim that personal identity just consists in certain other facts, I have in mind a closer and partly conceptual relation. Claims about personal identity may not mean the same as claims about physical and/or psychological continuity. But, if we knew the facts about these continuities, and understood the concept of a person, we would thereby know, or would be able to work out, the facts about persons. Hence my claim that, if we know the other facts, questions about personal identity should be taken to be questions, not about reality, but only about our language. These claims do not apply to facts about fundamental particles. It is not true for example that, if we knew how the particles moved in some person's body, and understood our concepts, we would thereby know, or be able to work out, all of the relevant facts about this person. To understand the world around us, we need more than physics and a knowledge of our own language.

My argument does not claim that, whenever there are facts at different levels, it is always the lowest-level facts which matter. That is clearly false. We are discussing cases where, relative to the facts at some lower level, the higher-level fact is, in the sense that I have sketched, merely conceptual. My claim is that such conceptual facts cannot be rationally or morally important. What matters is reality, not how it is described. So this view might be called *realism about importance*.

If we are Reductionists about persons, and Realists about importance, we should conclude that personal identity is not what matters. Can we accept that conclusion?

Most of us believe that we should care about our future because it will be *our* future. I believe that what matters is not identity but certain other relations. To help us to decide between these views, we should consider cases where identity and those relations do not coincide.

Which these cases are depends on which criterion of identity we accept. I shall start with the simplest form of the Physical Criterion, according to which a person continues to exist if and only if that person's body continues to exist. That must be the view of those who believe that persons just are bodies. And it is the view of several of the people who identify persons with human beings. Let's call this the *Bodily Criterion*.

Suppose that, because of damage to my spine, I have become partly paralysed. I have a brother, who is dying of a brain disease. With the aid of new techniques, when my brother's brain ceases to function, my head could be grafted onto the rest of my brother's body. Since we are identical twins, my brain would then control a body that is just like mine, except that it would not be paralysed.

Should I accept this operation? Of those who assume that identity is what matters, three groups would answer No. Some accept the Bodily Criterion. These people believe that, if this operation were performed, I would die. The person with my head tomorrow would be my brother, who would mistakenly think that he was me. Other people are uncertain what would happen. They believe that it would be risky to accept this operation, since the resulting person might not be me. Others give a different reason why I should reject this operation: that it would be indeterminate whether that person would be me. On all these views, it matters who that person would be.

On my view, that question is unimportant. If this operation were performed, the person with my head tomorrow would not only believe that he was me, seem to remember living my life, and be in every other way psychologically like me. These facts would also have their normal cause, the continued existence of my brain. And this person's body would be just like mine. For all these reasons, his life would be just like the life that I would have lived, if my paralysis had been cured. I believe that, given these facts, I should accept this operation. It is irrelevant whether this person would be me.

That may seem all important. After all, if he would not be me, I shall have ceased to exist. But, if that person would not be me, this fact would just consist in another fact. It would just consist in the fact that my body will have been replaced below the neck. When considered on its own, is that second fact important? Can it matter in itself that the blood that will keep my brain alive will circulate, not through my own heart and lungs, but through my brother's heart and lungs? Can it matter in itself that my brain will control, not the rest of my body, but the rest of another body that is exactly similar?

If we believe that these facts would amount to my non-existence, it may be hard to focus on the question whether, in themselves, these facts matter. To make that easier, we should imagine that we accept a different view. Suppose we are convinced that the person with my head tomorrow *would* be me. Would we then believe that it would matter greatly that my head would have been grafted onto this other body? We would not. We would regard my receiving a new torso, and new limbs, as like any lesser transplant, such as receiving a new heart, or new kidneys. As this shows, if it would matter greatly that what will be replaced is not just a few such organs, but my whole body below the neck, that could only be because, if that happened, the resulting person would *not* be me.

According to my argument, we should now conclude that neither of these facts could matter greatly. Since it would not be in itself important that my head would be grafted onto this body, and that would be all there was to the fact that the resulting person would not be me, it would not be in itself important that this person would not be me. Perhaps it would not be irrational to regret these facts a little. But, I believe, they would be heavily outweighed by the fact that, unlike me, the resulting person would not be paralysed.

When it is applied to our own existence, my argument is hard to accept. But, as before, the fundamental question is the relative importance of language and reality.

On my view, what matters is what is going to happen. If I knew that my head could be grafted onto the rest of a body that is just like mine, and that the resulting person would be just like me, I would know enough to decide whether to accept this operation. I need not ask whether the resulting person could be correctly called me. That is not a further difference in what is going to happen.

That may seem a false distinction. What matters, we might say, is whether the resulting person would *be* me. But that person would be me if and only if he could be correctly called me. So, in asking what he could be called, we are not merely asking a conceptual question. We *are* asking about reality.

This objection fails to distinguish two kinds of case. Suppose that I ask my doctor whether, while I receive some treatment, I shall be in pain. That is a factual question. I am asking what will happen. Since pain can be called 'pain', I *could* ask my question in a different way. I could say, 'While I am being treated, will it be correct to describe me as in pain?' But that would be misleading. It would suggest that I am asking how we use the word 'pain'.

In a different case, I might ask that conceptual question. Suppose I know that, while I am crossing the Channel, I shall be feeling sea-sick, as I always do. I might wonder whether that sensation could be correctly called 'pain'. Here too, I could ask my question in a different way. I could say, 'While I am crossing the Channel, shall I be in pain?' But that would be misleading, since it would suggest that I am asking what will happen.

In the medical case, I don't know what conscious state I shall be in. There are different possibilities. In the Channel crossing case, there aren't different possibilities. I already know what state I shall be in. I am merely asking whether that state could be redescribed in a certain way.

It matters whether, while receiving the medical treatment, I shall be in pain. And it matters whether, while crossing the Channel, I shall be sea-sick. But it does not matter whether, in feeling sea-sick, I can be said to be in pain.

Return now to our main example. Suppose I know that my head will be successfully grafted onto my brother's headless body. I ask whether the resulting person will be me. Is this like the medical case, or the case of crossing the Channel? Am I asking what will happen, or whether what I know will happen could be described in a certain way?

On my view, I should take myself to be asking the second. I already know what is going to happen. There will be someone with my head and my brother's body. It is a merely verbal question whether that person will be me. And that is why, even if he won't be me, that doesn't matter.

It may now be objected: 'By choosing this example, you are cheating. Of course you should accept this operation. But that is because the resulting person *would* be you. We should reject the Bodily Criterion. So this case cannot show that identity is not what matters.'

Since there are people who accept this criterion, I am not cheating. It is worth trying to show these people that identity is not what matters. But I accept part of this objection. I agree that we should reject the Bodily Criterion.

Of those who appeal to this criterion, some believe that persons just are bodies. But, if we hold this kind of view, it would be better to identify a person with that person's brain, or nervous system. Consider next those who believe that persons are animals of a certain kind, viz. human beings. We could take this view, but reject the Bodily Criterion. We could claim that animals continue to exist if there continue to exist, and to function, the most important parts of their bodies. And we could claim that, at least in the case of human beings, the brain is so important that its survival counts as the survival of this human being. On both these views, in my imagined case, the person with my head tomorrow would be me. And that is what, on reflection, most of us would believe.

My own view is similar. I would state this view, not as a claim about reality, but as a conceptual claim. On my view, it would not be incorrect to call this person me; and this would be the best description of this case.

If we agree that this person would be me, I would still argue that this fact is not what matters. What is important is not identity, but one or more of the other facts in which identity consists. But I concede that, when identity coincides with these other facts, it is harder to decide whether we accept that argument's conclusion. So, if we reject the Bodily Criterion, we must consider other cases.

Suppose that we accept the Brain-Based version of the Psychological Criterion. On this view, if there will be one future person who is psychologically continuous with me, because he will have enough of my brain, that person will be me. But psychological continuity without its normal cause, the continued existence of enough of my brain, does not suffice for identity. My Replica would not be me.

Remember next that an object can continue to exist even if all its components are gradually replaced. Suppose that, every time some wooden ship comes into port, a few of its planks are replaced. Before long, the same ship may be entirely composed of different planks.

Assume, once again, that I need surgery. All of my brain cells have a defect which, in time, would be fatal. Surgeons could replace all these cells, inserting new cells that are exact replicas, except that they have no defect.

The surgeons could proceed in either of two ways. In *Case One*, there would be a hundred operations. In each operation, the surgeons would remove a hundredth part of my brain, and insert replicas of those parts.

In *Case Two*, the surgeons would first remove all the existing parts of my brain and then insert all of their replicas.

There is a real difference here. In Case One, my brain would continue to exist, like a ship with all of its planks gradually replaced. In Case Two, my brain would cease to exist, and my body would be given a new brain.

This difference, though, is much smaller than that between ordinary survival and teletransportation. In both cases, there will later be a person whose brain will be just like my present brain, but without the defects, and who will therefore be psychologically continuous with me. And, in *both* cases, this person's brain will be made of the very same new cells, each of which is a replica of one of my existing cells. The difference between the cases is merely the way in which these new cells are inserted. In Case One, the surgeons alternate between removing and inserting. In Case Two, they do all the removing before all the inserting.

On the Brain-Based Criterion, this is the difference between life and death. In Case One, the resulting person would be me. In Case Two he would *not* be me, so I would cease to exist.

Can this difference matter? Reapply the Argument from Below. This difference consists in the fact that, rather than alternating between re-movals and insertions, the surgeon does all the removing before all the inserting. Considered on its own, can this matter? I believe not. We would not think it mattered if it did not constitute the fact that the resulting person would not be me. But if this fact does not in itself matter, and that is all there is to the fact that in Case Two I would cease to exist, I should conclude that my ceasing to exist does not matter.

Suppose next that you regard these as problem cases, ones where you do not know what would happen to me. Return to the simpler Physical Spectrum. In each of the cases in this range, some proportion of my cells will be replaced with exact duplicates. With some proportions – 20 per cent, say, or 50, or 70 – most of us would be uncertain whether the resulting person would be me. (As before, if we do not believe that here, my remarks could be transferred, with adjustments, to the Combined Spectrum.)

On my view, in all of the cases in this range, it is a merely conceptual question whether the resulting person would be me. Even without answering this question, I can know just what is going to happen. If there is anything that I don't know, that is merely a fact about how we could describe what is going to happen. And that conceptual question is not even, I believe, interesting. It is merely verbal, like the question whether, if I replaced some of its parts. I would still have the same audio system.

When we imagine these cases from a first-person point of view, it may still be hard to believe that this is merely a verbal question. If I don't know whether, tomorrow, I shall still exist, it may be hard to believe that I know what is going to happen. But what is it that I don't know? If there are different possibilities, at the level of what happens, what is the difference between them? In what would that difference consist? If I had a soul, or Cartesian Ego, there might be different possibilities. Perhaps, even if *n* per cent of my cells were replaced, my soul would keep its intimate relation with my brain. Or perhaps another soul would take over. But, we have assumed, there are no such entities. What else could the difference be? When the resulting person wakes up tomorrow, what could make it either true, or false, that he is me?

It may be said that, in asking what will happen, I am asking what I can expect. Can I expect to wake up again? If that person will be in pain, can I expect to feel that pain? But this does not help. These are just other ways of asking whether that person will or will not be me. In appealing to what I can expect, we do not explain what would make these different possibilities.

We may believe that this difference needs no explanation. It may seem enough to say: Perhaps that person will be me, and perhaps he won't. Perhaps I shall exist tomorrow, and perhaps I shan't. It may seem that these must be different possibilities.

That, however, is an illusion. If I shall still exist tomorrow, that fact must consist in certain others. For there to be two possibilities, so that it might be either true or false that I shall exist tomorrow, there must be some other difference between these possibilities. There would be such a difference, for example, if, between now and tomorrow, my brain and body might either remain unharmed, or be blown to pieces. But, in our imagined case, there is no such other difference. I already know that there will be someone whose brain and body will consist partly of these cells, and partly of new cells, and that this person will be psychologically like me. There aren't, at the level of what happens, different possible outcomes. There is no further essence of me, or property of me-ness, which either might or might not be there.

If we turn to the conceptual level, there *are* different possibilities. Perhaps that future person could be correctly called me. Perhaps he could be correctly called someone else. Or perhaps neither would be correct. That, however, is the only way in which it could be either true, or false, that this person would be me.

The illusion may persist. Even when I know the other facts, I may want reality to go in one of two ways. I may want it to be true that I shall still exist tomorrow. But all that could be true is that we use language in one of two ways. Can it be rational to care about that?

III

I am now assuming that we accept the Brain-Based Psychological Criterion. We believe that, if there will be one future person who will have enough of my brain to be psychologically continuous with me, that person would be me. On this view, there is another way to argue that identity is not what matters.

We can first note that, just as I could survive with less than my whole body, I could survive with less than my whole brain. People have survived, and with little psychological change, even when, through a stroke or injury, they have lost the use of half their brain.

Let us next suppose that the two halves of my brain could each fully support ordinary psychological functioning. That may in fact be true of certain people. If it is not, we can suppose that, through some technological advance, it has been made true of me. Since our aim is to test our beliefs about what matters, there is no harm in making such assumptions.

We can now compare two more possible operations. In the first, after half my brain is destroyed, the other half would be successfully transplanted into the empty skull of a body that is just like mine. Given our assumptions, we should conclude that, here too, I would survive. Since I would survive if my brain were transplanted, and I would survive with only half my brain, it would be unreasonable to deny that I would survive if that remaining half were transplanted. So, in this *Single Case*, the resulting person would be me.

Consider next the *Double Case*, or *My Division*. Both halves of my brain would be successfully transplanted, into different bodies that are just like mine. Two people would wake up, each of whom has half my brain, and is, both physically and psychologically, just like me.

Since these would be two different people, it cannot be true that each of them is me. That would be a contradiction. If each of them was me, each would be one and the same person: me. So they could not be two different people.

Could it be true that only one of them is me? That is not a contradiction. But, since I have the same relation to each of these people, there is nothing that could make me one of them rather than the other. It cannot be true, of either of these people, that he is the one who could be correctly called me.

How should I regard these two operations? Would they preserve what matters in survival? In the Single Case, the one resulting person would be me. The relation between me now and that future person is just an instance of the relation between me now and myself tomorrow. So that relation would contain what matters. In the Double Case, my relation to that person would be just the same. So this relation must still contain what matters. Nothing is missing. But that person cannot here be claimed to be me. So identity cannot be what matters.

We may object that, if that person isn't me, something *is* missing. *I'm* missing. That may seem to make all the difference. How can everything still be there if *I'm* not there?

Everything is still there. The fact that I'm not there is not a real absence. The relation between me now and that future person is in itself the same. As in the Single Case, he has half my brain, and he is just like me. The difference is only that, in this Double Case, I also have the same relation to the other resulting person. Why am I not there? The explanation is only this. When this relation holds between me now and a single person in the future, we can be called one and the same person. When this relation holds between me now and *two* future people, I cannot be called one and the same as each of these people. But that is not a difference in the nature or the content of this relation. In the Single Case, where half my brain will be successfully transplanted, my prospect is survival. That prospect contains what matters. In the Double Case, where both halves will be successfully transplanted, nothing would be lost.

It can be hard to believe that identity is not what matters. But that is easier to accept when we see why, in this example, it is true. It may help to consider this analogy. Imagine a community of persons who are like us, but with two exceptions. First, because of facts about their reproductive system, each couple has only two children, who are always twins. Second, because of special features of their psychology, it is of great importance for the development of each child that it should not, through the death of its sibling, become an only child. Such children suffer psychological damage. It is thus believed, in this community, that it matters greatly that each child should have a twin.

Now suppose that, because of some biological change, some of the children in this community start to be born as triplets. Should their parents think this a disaster, because these children don't have twins? Clearly not. These children don't have twins only because they each have *two* siblings. Since each child has two siblings, the trio must be called, not twins, but triplets. But none of them will suffer damage as an only child.

These people should revise their view. What matters isn't having a twin: it is having at least one sibling.

In the same way, we should revise our view about identity over time. What matters isn't that there will be someone alive who will be me. It is rather that there will be at least one living person who will be psychologically continuous with me as I am now, and/or who has enough of my brain. When there will be only one such person, he can be described as me. When there will be two such people, we cannot claim that each will be me. But that is as trivial as the fact that, if I had two identical siblings, they could not be called my twins.[2]

IV

If, as I have argued, personal identity is not what matters, we must ask what does matter. There are several possible answers. And, depending on our answer, there are several further implications. Thus there are several moral questions which I have no time even to mention. I shall end with another remark about our concern for our own future.

That concern is of several kinds. We may want to survive partly so that our hopes and ambitions will be achieved. We may also care about our future in the kind of way in which we care about the well-being of certain other people, such as our relatives or friends. But most of us have, in addition, a distinctive kind of egoistic concern. If I know that my child will be in pain, I may care about his pain more than I would about my own future pain. But I cannot fearfully anticipate my child's pain. And if I knew that my Replica would take up my life where I leave off, I would not look forward to that life.

This kind of concern may, I believe, be weakened, and be seen to have no ground, if we come to accept a Reductionist view. In our thoughts about our own identity, we are prone to illusions. That is why the so-called 'problem cases' seem to raise problems: why we find it hard to believe that, when we know the other facts, it is an empty or a merely verbal question whether we shall still exist. Even after we accept a Reductionist view, we may continue, at some level, to think and feel as if that view were not true. Our own continued existence may still seem an independent fact, of a peculiarly deep and simple kind. And that belief may underlie our anticipatory concern about our own future.

There are, I suspect, several causes of that illusory belief. I have discussed one cause here: our conceptual scheme. Though we need concepts to think about reality, we sometimes confuse the two. We mistake conceptual facts for facts about reality. And, in the case of certain concepts, those that are most loaded with emotional or moral significance, we can be led seriously astray. Of these loaded concepts, that of our own identity is, perhaps, the most misleading.

Even the use of the word 'I' can lead us astray. Consider the fact that, in a few years, I shall be dead. This fact can seem depressing. But the reality is only this. After a certain time, none of the thoughts and experiences that occur will be directly causally related to this brain, or be connected in certain ways to these present experiences. That is all this fact involves. And, in that redescription, my death seems to disappear.[3]

Notes

1 In his 'Human Concerns without Superlative Selves', in Jonathan Dancy, *Reading Parfit* (Oxford: Blackwell, 1997), pp. 149–79; [see also ch. 10 above].
2 In many contexts, we need to distinguish two senses of 'what matters in survival'. What matters in the *prudential* sense is what gives us reason for special concern about our future. What matters in the *desirability* sense is what makes our survival good. But, in the examples I have been discussing, these two coincide. On my view, even if we won't survive, we could have what matters *in* survival. If there will be at least one living person who will both be psychologically continuous with me, and have enough of my brain, my relation to that person contains what matters in the prudential sense. So it also preserves what matters in the desirability sense. It is irrelevant whether that person will be me.
3 Some of this essay draws from Part Three of my *Reasons and Persons* (Oxford University Press, 1984).

12

An Argument for Animalism

Eric T. Olson

It is a truism that you and I are human beings. It is also a truism that a human being is a kind of animal: roughly a member of the primate species *Homo sapiens*. It would seem to follow that we are animals. Yet that claim is deeply controversial. Plato, Augustine, Descartes, Spinoza, Leibniz, Locke, Berkeley, Hume, Kant, and Hegel all denied it. With the notable exception of Aristotle and his followers, it is hard to find a major figure in the history of Western philosophy who thought that we are animals. The view is no more popular in non-Western traditions. And probably nine out of ten philosophers writing about personal identity today either deny outright that we are animals or say things that are clearly incompatible with it.

This is surprising. Isn't it obvious that we are animals? I will try to show that it isn't obvious, and that Plato and the others have their reasons for thinking otherwise. Before doing that I will explain how I understand the claim that we are animals. My main purpose, though, is to make a case for this unpopular view. I won't rely on the brief argument I began with. My strategy is to ask what it would mean if we weren't animals. Denying that we are animals is harder than you might think.

1 What Animalism Says

When I say that we are animals, I mean that each of us is numerically identical with an animal. There is a certain human organism, and that organism is you. You and it are one and the same. This view has been called "animalism" (not a very nice name, but I haven't got a better one). Simple though it may appear, this is easily misunderstood. Many claims that sound like animalism are in fact different.

First, some say that we are animals and yet reject animalism.[1] How is that possible? How can you be an animal, and yet not be one? The idea is that there is a sense of the verb *to be* in which something can "be" an animal without being identical with any animal. Each of us "is" an animal in the sense of "being constituted by" one. That means roughly that you are in the same place and made of the same matter as an animal. But you and that animal could come apart (more on this later). And since a thing can't come apart from itself, you and the animal are not identical.

I wish people wouldn't say things like this. If you are not identical with a certain animal, that animal is something other than you. And I doubt whether there is any interesting sense in which you can *be* something other than yourself. Even if there is, expressing a view on which no one is identical with an animal by saying that we *are* animals is badly misleading. It discourages us from asking important questions: what we *are* identical with, if not animals, for instance. Put plainly and honestly, these philosophers are saying that each of us is a non-animal that relates in some intimate way to an animal. They put it by saying that we *are* animals because that sounds more plausible. This is salesman's hype, and we shouldn't be fooled. In any case, the "constitutionalists" do not say that we are animals in the straightforward sense in which I mean it. They are not animalists.

The existence of the "constitution view" shows that animalism is not the same as *materialism*. Materialism is the view that we are material things; and we might be material things but not animals. Animalism implies materialism (animals are material things), but not vice versa. It may seem perverse for a materialist to reject animalism. If we are material things of any sort, surely we are animals? Perverse or not, though, the view that we are material non-organisms is widely held.

Animalism says that *we* are animals. That is compatible with the existence of non-animal people (or persons, if you prefer). It is often said that to be a person is to have certain mental qualities: to be rational, intelligent, and self-conscious, say. Perhaps a person must also be morally responsible, and have free will. If something like that is right, then gods or angels might be people but not animals.

Nor does our being animals imply that all animals, or even all human animals, are people. Human beings in a persistent vegetative state are biologically alive, but their mental capacities are permanently destroyed. They are certainly human animals. But we might not want to call them people. The same goes for human embryos.

So the view that we are animals does not imply that to be a person is nothing other than to be an animal of a certain sort – that being an animal is part of what it is to be a person. Inconveniently enough, this view has also been called animalism. It isn't the animalism that I want to defend. In fact it looks rather implausible. I don't know whether there could be inorganic people, as for instance traditional theism asserts. But mere reflection on what it is to be a person doesn't seem to rule it out. Of course, if people are animals by definition, it follows that we are animals, since we are obviously people. But the reverse entailment doesn't hold: we might be animals even if something could be a person without being an animal.

If I don't say that all people are animals, which people do I mean? Is animalism the mere tautology that all animal people are animals? No. I say that you and I and the other people who walk the earth are animals. If you like, all *human* people are animals, where a human person is roughly someone who relates to a human animal in the way that you and I do, whatever way that is. (Even idealists can agree that we are in some sense human, and not, say, feline or angelic.) Many philosophers deny that *any* people are animals. So there is nothing trivial about this claim.

"Animalism" is sometimes stated as the view that we are *essentially or most fundamentally* animals. We are essentially animals if we couldn't possibly exist without being animals. It is less clear what it is for us to be most fundamentally animals, but this is usually taken to imply at least that our identity conditions derive from our being animals, rather than from our being, say, people or philosophers or material objects – even though we *are* people and philosophers and material objects.

Whether our being animals implies that we are essentially or most fundamentally animals depends on whether human animals are essentially or most fundamentally animals. If the animal that you are is essentially an animal, then so are you. If it is only contingently an animal, then you are only contingently an animal. Likewise, you are most fundamentally an animal if and only if the animal that you are is most fundamentally an animal. The claim that each of us is identical with an animal is neutral on these questions. Most philosophers think that every animal is essentially and most fundamentally an animal, and I am inclined to agree. But you could be an animalist in my sense without accepting this.

Is animalism the view that we are identical with our bodies? That depends on what it is for something to be someone's body. If a person's body is by definition a sort of animal, then I suppose being an animal amounts to being one's body. It is often said, though, that someone could have a partly or wholly inorganic body. One's body might include plastic or metal limbs. Someone might even have an entirely robotic body. I take it that no animal could be partly or wholly inorganic. If you cut off an animal's limb and replace it with an inorganic prosthesis, the animal just gets smaller and has something inorganic attached to it. So perhaps after having some or all of your parts replaced by inorganic gadgets of the right sort you would be identical with your body, but would not be an animal. Animalism may imply that you are your body, but you could be your body without being an animal. Some philosophers even say that being an animal rules out being identical with one's body. If you replaced enough of an animal's parts with new ones, they say, it would end up with a different body from the one it began with.

Whether these claims about bodies are true depends on what it is for something to be someone's body. What does it *mean* to say that your body is an animal, or that someone might have a robotic body? I have never seen a good answer to this question (see van Inwagen 1980 and Olson 1997: 144–9). So I will talk about people and animals, and leave bodies out of it.

Finally, does animalism say that we are *merely* animals? That we are nothing more than biological organisms? This is a delicate point. The issue is whether being "more than just" or "not merely" an animal is compatible with being an animal – that is, with being identical with an animal.

If someone complains that the committee is more than just the chairman, she means that it is not the chairman: it has other members too. If we are more than just animals in something like this sense, then we are not animals. We have parts that are not parts of any animal: immaterial souls, perhaps.

On the other hand, we say that Descartes was more than just a philosopher: he was also a mathematician, a Frenchman, a Roman Catholic, and many other things. That is of course compatible with his being a philosopher. We can certainly be more than "mere" animals in this sense, and yet still be animals. An animal can have properties other than being an animal, and which don't follow from its being an animal. Our being animals does not rule out our being mathematicians, Frenchmen, or Roman Catholics – or our being people, socialists, mountaineers, and many other things. At least there is no evident reason why it should. Animalism does not imply that we have a fixed, "animal" nature, or that we have only biological or naturalistic properties, or that we are no different, in any important way, from other animals. There may be a vast psychological and moral gulf between human animals and organisms of other species. We may be very special animals. But special animals are still animals.

2   Alternatives

One reason why it may seem obvious that we are animals is that it is unclear what else we could be. If we're not animals, what are we? What are the alternatives to animalism? This is a question that philosophers ought to ask more often. Many views about personal identity clearly rule out our being animals, but leave it a mystery what sort of things we might be instead. Locke's account is a notorious example. His detailed account of personal identity doesn't even tell us whether we are material or immaterial.

Well, there is the traditional idea that we are simple immaterial substances, or, alternatively, compound things made up of an immaterial substance and a biological organism.

There is the view, mentioned earlier, that we are material objects constituted by human animals. You and a certain animal are physically indistinguishable. Nonetheless you and it are two different things.

Some say that we are temporal parts of animals. Animals and other persisting objects exist at different times by having different temporal parts or "stages" located at those times. You are made up of those stages of a human animal (or, in science fiction, of several animals) that are "psychologically interconnected" (Lewis 1976). Since your animal's embryonic stages have no mental properties at all, they aren't psychologically connected with anything, and so they aren't parts of you. Hence, you began later than the animal did.

Hume famously proposed that each of us is "a bundle or collection of different perceptions, which succeed each other with an inconceivable rapidity, and are in a perpetual flux and movement" (1888: 252). Strictly speaking you are not made of bones and sinews, or of atoms, or of matter. You are literally composed of thoughts. Whether Hume actually believed this is uncertain; but some do (e.g. Quinton 1962).

Every teacher of philosophy has heard it said that we are something like computer programs. You are a certain complex of information "realized" in your brain. (How else could you survive Star-Trek teletransportation?) That would mean that you are not a concrete object at all. You are a universal. There could literally be more than one of you, just as there is more than one concrete instance of the web browser *Netscape 6.2*.

There is even the paradoxical view that we don't really exist at all. There are many thoughts and experiences, but no beings that *have* those thoughts or experiences. The existence of human people is an illusion – though of course no one is deluded about it. Philosophers who have denied or at least doubted their own existence include Parmenides, Spinoza, Hume, Hegel (as I read them, anyway), Russell (1985: 50), and Unger (1979). We also find the view in Indian Buddhism.

There are other views about what we might be, but I take these to be animalism's main rivals. One of these claims, or another one that I haven't mentioned, must be true. There must be *some* sort of thing that we are. If there is anything sitting in your chair and reading these words, it must have some basic properties or other.

For those who enjoy metaphysics, these are all fascinating proposals. Whatever their merits, though, they certainly are strange. No one but a philosopher could have thought of them. And it would take quite a bit of philosophy to get anyone to believe one of them. Compared with these claims, the idea that we are animals looks downright sensible. That makes its enduring unpopularity all the more surprising.

3   Why Animalism is Unpopular

Why is animalism so unpopular? Historically, the main reason (though by no means the only one) is hostility to materialism. Philosophers have always found it hard to believe that a material object, no matter how physically complex, could produce thought or experience. And an animal is a material object (I assume that vitalism is false). Since it is plain enough that *we* can think, it is easy to conclude that we couldn't be animals.

But why do modern-day materialists reject animalism, or at least say things that rule it out? The main reason, I believe, is that when they think about personal identity they don't ask what sort of things we are. They don't ask whether we are animals, or what we might be if we aren't animals, or how we relate to the human animals that are so intimately connected with us. Or at least they don't ask that first. No one who *began* by asking what we are would hit on the idea that we must be computer programs or bundles of thoughts or non-animals made of the same matter as animals.

The traditional problem of personal identity is not what we are, but what it takes for us to persist. It asks what is necessary, and what is sufficient, for a person existing at one time to be identical with something present at another time: what sorts of adventures we could survive, and what would inevitably bring our existence to an end. Many philosophers seem to think that an answer to this question would tell us all there is to know about the metaphysics of personal identity. This is not so. Claims about what it takes for us to persist do not by themselves tell us what other fundamental properties we have: whether we are material or immaterial, simple or composite, abstract or concrete, and so on. At any rate, the single-minded focus on our identity over time has tended to put other metaphysical questions about ourselves out of philosophers' minds.

What is more, the most popular solution to this traditional problem rules out our being animals. It is that we persist by virtue of some sort of psychological continuity. You are, necessarily, that future being that in some sense inherits its mental features – personality, beliefs, memories, values, and so on – from you. And you are that past being whose mental features you have inherited. Philosophers disagree about what sort of inheritance this has to be: whether those mental features must be continuously physically realized, for instance. But most accept the general idea. The persistence of a human animal, on the other hand, does not consist in mental continuity.

The fact that each human animal starts out as an unthinking embryo and may end up as an unthinking vegetable shows that no sort of mental continuity is necessary for a human animal to persist. No human animal is mentally continuous with an embryo or a vegetable.

To see that no sort of mental continuity is sufficient for a human animal to persist, imagine that your cerebrum is put into another head. The being who gets that organ, and he alone, will be mentally continuous with you on any account of what mental continuity is. So if mental continuity of any sort suffices for you to persist, you would go along with your transplanted cerebrum. You wouldn't stay behind with an empty head.

What would happen to the human animal associated with you? Would *it* go along with its cerebrum? Would the surgeons pare that animal down to a small chunk of yellowish-pink tissue, move it across the room, and then supply it with a new head, trunk, and other parts? Surely not. A detached cerebrum is no more an organism than a detached liver is an organism. The empty-headed thing left behind, by contrast, *is* an animal. It may even remain alive, if the surgeons are careful to leave the lower brain intact. The empty-headed being into which your cerebrum is implanted is also an animal. It looks for all the world like there are two human animals in the story. One of them loses its cerebrum and gets an empty head. The other has its empty head filled with that organ. No animal moves from one head to another. The surgeons merely move an organ from one animal to another. If this is right, then no sort of psychological continuity suffices for the identity of a human animal over time. One human animal could be mentally continuous with another one (supposing that they can have mental properties at all).

If we tell the story in the right way, it is easy enough to get most people, or at any rate most Western-educated philosophy students, to say that *you* would go along with your transplanted cerebrum. After all, the one who got that organ would act like you and think she was you. Why deny that she would be the person she thinks she is? But "your" animal – the one you would be if you were any animal – would stay behind. That means that you and that animal could go your separate ways. And a thing and itself can never go their separate ways.

It follows that you are not that animal, or indeed any other animal. Not only are you not essentially an animal. You are not an animal at all, even contingently. Nothing that is even contingently an animal would move to a different head if its cerebrum were transplanted. The human animals in the story stay where they are and merely lose or gain organs.[2]

So the thought that leads many contemporary philosophers to reject animalism – or that would lead them to reject it if they accepted the consequences of what they believe – is something like this: You would go along with your transplanted cerebrum; but no human animal would go along with its transplanted cerebrum. More generally, some sort of mental continuity suffices for us to persist, yet no sort of mental continuity suffices for an animal to persist. It follows that we are not animals. If we were animals, we should have the identity conditions of animals. Those conditions have nothing to do with psychological facts. Psychology would be irrelevant to our identity over time. That goes against 300 years of thinking about personal identity.

This also shows that animalism is a substantive metaphysical thesis with important consequences. There is nothing harmless about it.

4 The Thinking-Animal Argument

I turn now to my case for animalism. It seems evident that there *is* a human animal intimately related to you. It is the one located where you are, the one we point to when we point to you, the one sitting in your chair. It seems equally evident that human animals can think. They can act. They can be aware of themselves and the world. Those with mature nervous systems in good working order can, anyway. So there is a thinking, acting human animal sitting where you are now. But you think and act. *You* are the thinking being sitting in your chair.

It follows from these apparently trite observations that you are an animal. In a nutshell, the argument is this: (1) There is a human animal sitting in your chair. (2) The human animal sitting in your chair is thinking. (If you like, every human animal sitting there is thinking.) (3) You are the thinking being sitting in your chair. The one and only thinking being sitting in your chair is none other than you. Hence, you are that animal. That animal is you. And there is nothing special about you: we are all animals. If anyone suspects a trick, here is the argument's logical form:

1 $(\exists x)$ (x is a human animal & x is sitting in your chair)
2 $(x)(($x$ is a human animal & x is sitting in your chair) $\supset x$ is thinking)

3   $(x)((x$ is thinking & x is sitting in your chair$) \supset x =$ you$)$
4   $(\exists x) (x$ is a human animal & $x =$ you$)$

The reader can verify that it is formally valid. (Compare: A man entered the bank vault. The man who entered the vault – any man who did – stole the money. Snodgrass, and no one else, entered the vault and stole the money. Doesn't it follow that Snodgrass is a man?)

Let us be clear about what the "thinking-animal" argument purports to show. Its conclusion is that we are human animals. That is, one of the things true of you is that you are (identical with) an animal. That of course leaves many metaphysical questions about ourselves unanswered. It doesn't by itself tell us whether we are essentially or most fundamentally animals, for instance, or what our identity conditions are. That depends on the metaphysical nature of human animals: on whether human animals are essentially animals, and what their identity conditions are. These are further questions. I argued in the previous section that no sort of mental continuity is either necessary or sufficient for a human animal to persist. If that is right, then our being animals has important and highly contentious metaphysical implications. But it might be disputed, even by those who agree that we are animals. The claim that we are animals is not the end of the story about personal identity. It is only the beginning. Still, it is important to begin in the right place.

The thinking-animal argument is deceptively simple. I suspect that its very simplicity has prevented many philosophers from seeing its point. But there is nothing sophistical about it. It has no obvious and devastating flaw that we teach our students. It deserves to be better known.[3]

In any case, the argument has three premises, and so there are three ways of resisting it. One could deny that there is any human animal sitting in your chair. One could deny that any such animal thinks. Or one could deny that you are the thinking being sitting there. Anyone who denies that we are animals is committed to accepting one of these claims. They are not very plausible. But let us consider them.

5   Alternative One: There Are No Human Animals

Why suppose that there is no human animal sitting in your chair? Presumably because there are no human animals anywhere. If there are any human animals at all, there is one sitting there. (I assume that you aren't a Martian foundling.) And if there are no human animals, it is hard to see how there could be any organisms of other sorts. So denying the argument's first premise amounts to denying that there are, strictly speaking, any organisms. There appear to be, of course. But that is at best a well-founded illusion.

There are venerable philosophical views that rule out the existence of organisms. Idealism, for instance, denies that there are any material objects at all (so I should describe it, anyway). And there is the view that nothing can have different parts at different times (Chisholm 1976: 86–113, 145–58). Whenever something appears to lose or gain a part, the truth of the matter is that one object, made of the first set of parts, ceases to exist (or becomes scattered) and is instantly replaced by a numerically different object made of the second set of parts. Organisms, if there were such things, would constantly assimilate new particles and expel others. If nothing can survive a change of any of its parts, organisms are metaphysically impossible. What we think of as an organism is in reality only a succession of different "masses of matter" that each take on organic form for a brief moment – until a single particle is gained or lost – and then pass that form on to a numerically different mass.

But few opponents of animalism deny the existence of animals. They have good reason not to, quite apart from the fact that this is more or less incredible. Anything that would rule out the existence of animals would also rule out most of the things we might be if we are not animals. If there are no animals, there are no beings constituted by animals, and no temporal parts of animals. And whatever rules out animals may tell against Humean bundles of perceptions as well. If there are no animals, it is not easy to see what we *could* be.

6 Alternative Two: Human Animals Can't Think

The second alternative is that there is an animal sitting in your chair, but it isn't thinking. (Let any occurrence of a propositional attitude, such as the belief that it's raining or the hope that it won't, count as "thinking".) *You* think, but the animal doesn't. The reason for this can only be that the animal can't think. If it were able to think, it would be thinking now. And if *that* animal can't think – despite its healthy, mature human brain, lengthy education, surrounding community of thinkers, and appropriate evolutionary history – then no human animal can. And if no human animal can think, no animal of any sort could. (We can't very well say that dogs can think but human animals can't.) Finally, if no animal could ever think – not even a normal adult human animal – it is hard to see how any organism could have any mental property whatever. So if your animal isn't thinking, that is apparently because it is impossible for any organism to have mental properties.

The claim, then, is that animals, including human animals, are no more intelligent or sentient than trees. We could of course say that they are "intelligent" in the sense of being the bodies of intelligent people who are not themselves animals. And we could call organisms like dogs "sentient" in the sense of being the bodies of sentient non-animals that stand to those animals as you and I stand to human animals. But that is loose talk. The strict and sober truth would be that only non-organisms could ever think.

This is rather hard to believe. Anyone who denies that animals can think (or that they can think in the way that we think) needs to explain why they can't. What stops a typical human animal from using its brain to think? Isn't that what that organ is *for*?

Traditionally, those who deny that animals can think deny that any material object could do so. That seems natural enough: if *any* material thing could think, it would be an animal. Thinking things must be immaterial, and so must we. Of course, simply denying that any material thing could think does nothing to explain why it couldn't. But again, few contemporary opponents of animalism believe that we are immaterial.

Someone might argue like this: "The human animal sitting in your chair is just your body. It is absurd to suppose that your body reads or thinks about philosophy. The thinking thing there – you – must therefore be something other than the animal. But that doesn't mean that you are immaterial. You might be a material thing other than your body."

It may be false to say that your body is reading. There is certainly *something* wrong with that statement. What is less clear is whether it is wrong because the phrase 'your body' denotes something that you in some sense have – a certain human organism – that is unable to read. Compare the word 'body' with a closely related one: *mind*. It is just as absurd to say that Alice's mind weighs 120 pounds, or indeed any other amount, as it is to say that Alice's body is reading. (If that seems less than obvious, consider the claim that Alice's mind is sunburned.) Must we conclude that Alice has something – a clever thing, for Alice has a clever mind – that weighs nothing? Does this show that thinking beings have no mass? Surely not. I think we should be equally wary of drawing metaphysical conclusions from the fact that the phrase 'Alice's body' cannot always be substituted for the name 'Alice'. In any case, the "body" argument does nothing to explain why a human animal should be unable to think.

Anyone who claims that some material objects can think but animals cannot has his work cut out for him. Shoemaker (1984: 92–7; 1999) has argued that animals cannot think because they have the wrong identity conditions. Mental properties have characteristic causal roles, and these, he argues, imply that psychological continuity must suffice for the bearers of those properties to persist. Since this is not true of any organism, no organism could have mental properties. But material things with the right identity conditions *can* think, and organisms can "constitute" such things. I have discussed this argument in another place (Olson 2002b). It is a long story, though, and I won't try to repeat it here.

7   Alternative Three: You Are Not Alone

Suppose, then, that there is a human animal sitting in your chair. And suppose that it thinks. Is there any way to resist the conclusion that you are that thinking animal? We can hardly say that the animal thinks but you don't. (If anything thinks, you do.) Nor can we deny that you exist, when there is a rational animal thinking your thoughts. How, then, could you fail to be that thinking animal? Only if you are not the only thinker there. If you are not *the* thinking thing sitting there, you must be one of at least two such thinkers. You exist. You think. There is also a thinking human animal there. Presumably it has the same psychological qualities as you have. But it isn't you. There are two thinking beings wherever we thought there was just one. There are two philosophers, you and an animal, sitting there and reading this. You are never truly alone: wherever you go, a watchful human animal goes with you.

This is not an attractive picture. Its adherents may try to comfort us by proposing linguistic hypotheses. Whenever two beings are as intimately related as you and your animal are, they will say, we "count them as one" for ordinary purposes (Lewis 1976). When I write on the copyright form that I am the sole author of this essay, I don't mean that every author of this essay is numerically identical with me. I mean only that every author of this essay bears some relation to me that does not imply identity: that every such author is co-located with me, perhaps. My wife is not a bigamist, even though she is, I suppose, married both to me and to the animal. At any rate it would be seriously misleading to describe our relationship as a *ménage à quatre*.

This is supposed to show that the current proposal needn't contradict anything that we say or believe when engaged in the ordinary business of life. Unless we are doing metaphysics, we don't distinguish strict numerical identity from the intimate relation that each of us bears to a certain human animal. Ordinary people have no opinion about how many numerically different thinking beings there are. Why should they? What matters in real life is not how many thinkers there are strictly speaking, but how many *non-overlapping* thinkers.

Perhaps so. Still, it hardly makes the current proposal easy to believe. Is it not strange to suppose that there are two numerically different thinkers wherever we thought there was just one?

In any event, the troubles go beyond mere overcrowding. If there really are two beings, a person and an animal, now thinking your thoughts and performing your actions, you ought to wonder which one you are. You may think you're the person (the one that isn't an animal). But doesn't the animal think that *it* is a person? It has all the same reasons for thinking so as you have. Yet it is mistaken. If you *were* the animal and not the person, you'd still think you were the person. For all you know, *you're* the one making the mistake. Even if you are a person and not an animal, you could never have any reason to believe that you are.[4]

For that matter, if your animal can think, that ought to make *it* a person. It has the same mental features as you have. (Otherwise we should expect an explanation for the difference, just as we should if the animal can't think at all.) It is, in Locke's words, "a thinking intelligent being, that has reason and reflection, and can consider itself as itself, the same thinking thing, in different times and places" (1975: 335). It satisfies every ordinary definition of 'person'. But it would be mad to suppose that the animal sitting in your chair is a *person* numerically different from you – that each human person shares her location and her thoughts with *another* person. If nothing else, this would contradict the claim that people – all people – have psychological identity conditions, thus sweeping away the main reason for denying that we are animals in the first place.

On the other hand, if rational human animals are not people, familiar accounts of what it is to be a person are all far too permissive. Having the psychological and moral features that you and I have would not be enough to make something a person. There could be rational, intelligent, self-conscious *non*-people. In fact there would be at least one such rational non-person for every genuine person. That would deprive personhood of any psychological or moral significance.

8   Hard Choices

That concludes my argument for animalism. We could put the same point in another way. There are about six billion human animals walking the earth. Those animals are just like ourselves. They sit in our chairs and sleep in our beds. They work, and talk, and take holidays. Some of them do philosophy. They have just the mental and physical attributes that we take ourselves to have. So it seems, anyway. This makes it hard to deny that *we* are those animals. The apparent existence of rational human animals is an inconvenient fact for the opponents of animalism. We might call it the *problem of the thinking animal.*

But what of the case against animalism? It seems that you would go along with your cerebrum if that organ were transplanted. More generally, some sort of mental continuity appears to suffice for us to persist.[5] And that is not true of any animal. Generations of philosophers have found this argument compelling. How can they have gone so badly wrong?

One reason, as I have said, is that they haven't asked the right questions. They have thought about what it takes for us to persist through time, but not about what we are.

Here is another. If someone is mentally just like you, that is strong evidence for his being you. All the more so if there is continuously physically realized mental continuity between him and you. In fact it is conclusive evidence, given that brain transplants belong to science fiction. Moreover, most of us find mental continuity more interesting and important than brute physical continuity. When we hear a story, we don't much care which person at the end of the tale is the same animal as a given person at the beginning. We care about who is psychologically continuous with that person. If mental and animal continuity often came apart, we might think differently. But they don't.

These facts can easily lead us to suppose that the one who remembers your life in the transplant story is you. Easier still if we don't know how problematic that claim is – if we don't realize that it would rule out our being animals. To those who haven't reflected on the problem of the thinking animal – and that includes most philosophers – it can seem dead obvious that we persist by virtue of mental continuity. But if we are animals, this is a mistake, though an understandable one.

Of course, opponents of animalism can play this game too. They can attempt to explain why it is natural to suppose that there are human animals, or that human animals can think, or that you are the thinking thing sitting in your chair, in a way that does not imply that those claims are true. (That is the point of the linguistic hypotheses I mentioned earlier.) What to do? Well, I invite you to compare the thinking-animal argument with the transplant argument. Which is more likely? That there are no animals? That no animal could ever think? That you are one of at least two intelligent beings sitting in your chair? Or that you would not, after all, go along with your transplanted cerebrum?

9   What it would Mean if we were Animals

What would it mean if we were animals? The literature on personal identity gives the impression that this is a highly counter-intuitive, "tough-minded" idea, radically at odds with our deepest convictions. It is certainly at odds with most of that literature. But I doubt whether it conflicts with anything that we all firmly believe.

If animalism conflicts with any popular beliefs, they will be beliefs about the conditions of our identity over time. As we have seen, the way we react (or imagine ourselves reacting) to certain fantastic stories suggests that we take ourselves to persist by virtue of mental continuity. Our beliefs about *actual* cases, though, suggest no such thing. In every actual case, the number of people we think there are is just the number of human animals. Every actual case in which we take someone to survive or perish is a case where a human animal survives or perishes.

If anything, the way we regard actual cases suggests a conviction that our identity does not consist in mental continuity, or at any rate that mental continuity is unnecessary for us to persist. When someone lapses into a persistent vegetative state, his friends and relatives may conclude that his life no longer has any value. They may even conclude that he has ceased to exist *as a person*. But they don't ordinarily suppose that their loved one no longer exists at all, and that the living organism on the hospital bed is something numerically different from him – even when they come to believe that there is no mental continuity between the vegetable and the person. *That* would be a tough-minded view.

And most of us believe that we were once foetuses. When we see an ultrasound picture of a twelve-week-old foetus, it is easy to believe we are seeing something that will, if all goes well, be born, learn to talk, go to school, and eventually become an adult human person. Yet none of us is in any way mentally continuous with a twelve-week-old foetus.

Animalism may conflict with religious beliefs: in reincarnation or resurrection, for instance (though whether there is any real conflict is less obvious than it may seem: see van Inwagen 1978). But few accounts of personal identity are any more compatible with those beliefs. If resurrection and reincarnation rule out our being animals, they probably rule out our being anything except immaterial substances, or perhaps computer programs. On this score animalism is no worse off than its main rivals.

And don't we have a strong conviction that we are animals? We all think that we are human beings. And until the philosophers got hold of us, we took human beings to be animals. We *seem* to be animals. It is the opponents of animalism who insist that this appearance is deceptive: that the animal you see in the mirror is not really you. That we are animals ought to be the default position. If anything is hard to believe, it's the alternatives.[6]

Notes

1 e.g. Shoemaker 1984: 113f. For what it's worth, my opinion of "constitutional-ism" can be found in Olson 2001.
2 For more on this crucial point see Olson 1997: 114–19.
3 The argument is not entirely new. As I see it, it only makes explicit what is implicit in Carter 1989, Ayers 1990: 283f, Snowdon 1990, and Olson 1997: 100–9.
4 Some say that revisionary linguistics can solve this problem too (Noonan 1998). The idea is roughly this. First, not just any rational, self-conscious being is a person, but only those that have psychological identity conditions. Human animals, despite their mental properties, are not people because they lack psychological identity conditions. Second, the word 'I' and other personal pronouns refer only to people. Thus, when the animal associated with you says 'I', it doesn't refer to itself. Rather, it refers to you, the person associated with it. When it says, "I am a person," it does not say falsely that *it* is a person, but truly that *you* are. So the animal is not mistaken about which thing it is, and neither are you. You can infer that you are a person from the linguistic facts that you are whatever you refer to when you say 'I', and that 'I' refers only to people. I discuss this ingenious proposal in Olson 2002a.
5 In fact this is not so. Let the surgeons transplant each of your cerebral hemispheres into a different head. Both offshoots will be mentally continuous with you. But they can't both *be* you, for the simple reason that one thing (you) cannot be identical with two things. We cannot say in general that anyone who is mentally continuous with you must be you. Exceptions are possible. So it ought to come as no great surprise if the original cerebrum transplant is another exception.
6 I thank Trenton Merricks and Gonzalo Rodriguez-Pereyra for comments on an earlier version of this paper.

References

Ayers, M. 1990. *Locke*, vol. 2. London: Routledge.
Carter, W. R. 1989. How to change your mind. *Canadian Journal of Philosophy* 19: 1–14.
Chisholm, R. 1976. *Person and Object*. La Salle, IL: Open Court.

Hume, D. 1888. *Treatise of Human Nature* (1739), ed. L. A. Selby-Bigge. Oxford: Clarendon Press. Partly repr. in Perry 1975: 159–78.

Lewis, D. 1976. Survival and identity. In A. Rorty, ed., *The Identities of Persons*, Berkeley: University of California Press, pp. 17–40. Repr. in his *Philosophical Papers*, vol. 1, New York: Oxford University Press, 1983, pp. 55–77 [and as ch. 4 above].

Locke, J. 1975. *An Essay Concerning Human Understanding*, 2nd edn (1694), ed. P. Nidditch. Oxford: Clarendon Press. Partly repr. in Perry 1975: 33–52 [and pp. 26–36 above].

Noonan, Harold. 1998. Animalism versus Lockeanism: a current controversy. *Philosophical Quarterly* 48: 302–18.

Olson, E. 1997. *The Human Animal: Personal Identity without Psychology.* New York: Oxford University Press.

——. 2001. Material coincidence and the indiscernibility problem. *Philosophical Quarterly* 51: 337–55.

——. 2002a. Thinking animals and the reference of 'I'. *Philosophical Topics* 30.

——. 2002b. What does functionalism tell us about personal identity? *Noûs* 36.

Perry, J., ed. 1975. *Personal Identity.* Berkeley: University of California Press.

Quinton, A. 1962. The soul. *Journal of Philosophy* 59: 393–403. Repr. in Perry 1975: 53–72.

Russell, B. 1985. *The Philosophy of Logical Atomism* (1918). La Salle, IL: Open Court.

Shoemaker, S. 1984. Personal identity: a materialist's account. In S. Shoemaker and R. Swinburne, *Personal Identity*, Oxford: Blackwell, pp. 67–132.

——. 1999. Self, body, and coincidence. *Proceedings of the Aristotelian Society*, supp. vol. 73: 287–306.

Snowdon, Paul. 1990. Persons, animals, and ourselves. In C. Gill, ed., *The Person and the Human Mind*, Oxford: Clarendon Press, pp. 83–107.

Unger, P. 1979. I do not exist. In G. F. MacDonald, ed., *Perception and Identity*, London: Macmillan, pp. 235–51. Repr. in M. Rea, ed., *Material Constitution*, Lanham, MD: Rowman and Littlefield, 1997, pp. 175–90.

van Inwagen, P. 1978. The possibility of resurrection. *International Journal for the Philosophy of Religion* 9: 114–21. Repr. in his *The Possibility of Resurrection and Other Essays in Christian Apologetics*, Boulder, CO: Westview, 1997, pp. 45–51.

——. 1980. Philosophers and the words 'human body'. In van Inwagen, ed., *Time and Cause*, Dordrecht: Reidel, pp. 283–99.

13

The Self

Galen Strawson

- I know that I exist; the question is, what is this 'I' that I know? (Descartes 1641)

- The soul, so far as we can conceive it, is nothing but a system or train of different perceptions. (Hume 1739)

- *What* was I before I came to self-consciousness? . . . *I* did not exist at all, for I was not an I. The I exists only insofar as it is conscious of itself. . . . *The self posits itself,* and by virtue of this mere self-assertion it exists. (Fichte 1794–5)

- The 'Self' . . . , when carefully examined, is found to consist mainly of . . . peculiar motions in the head or between the head and throat. (James 1890)

- The ego continuously constitutes itself as existing. (Husserl 1931)

- Any fixed categorization of the Self is a big goof. (Ginsberg 1963)

- The self which is reflexively referred to is synthesized in that very act of reflexive self-reference. (Nozick 1981)

- The self . . . is a mythical entity. . . . It is a philosophical muddle to allow the space which differentiates 'my self' from 'myself' to generate the illusion of a mysterious entity distinct from . . . the human being. (Kenny 1988)

- A self . . . is . . . an abstraction . . . , [a] Center of Narrative Gravity. (Dennett 1991)

- My body is an object all right, but my self jolly well is not! (Farrell 1996)[1]

I   Introduction

The substantival phrase 'the self' is very unnatural in most speech contexts in most languages, and some conclude from this that it's an illusion to think that there is such a thing as the self, an illusion that arises from nothing more than an improper use of language. This, however, is implausible. People are not that stupid. The problem of the self doesn't arise from an unnatural use of language which arises from nowhere. On the contrary: use of a phrase like 'the self' arises from a prior and independent sense that there is such a thing as the self. The phrase may be unusual in ordinary speech; it may have no obvious direct translation in many languages. Nevertheless all languages have words which lend themselves naturally to playing the role that 'the self' plays in English, however murky that role may be. The phrase certainly means something to most people. It has a natural use in religious, philosophical, and psychological contexts, which are very natural contexts of discussion for human beings. I think there is a real philosophical problem about the existence and nature of the self, not just a relatively uninteresting problem about why we think there's a problem. It is too quick to say that a 'grammatical error...is the essence of the theory of the self', or that ' "the self" is a piece of philosopher's nonsense consisting in a misunderstanding of the reflexive pronoun' (Kenny, 1988, p. 4).

The first task is to get the problem into focus. I will recommend one approach, first in outline, then in slightly more detail. (I will model the problem of the self, rather than attempting to model the self.) I think the problem requires a straightforwardly metaphysical approach; but I also think that metaphysics must wait on phenomenology, in a sense I will explain. Most recent discussion of the problem by analytic philosophers has started from work in philosophical logic (in the large sense of the term).[2] This work may have a contribution to make, but a more phenomenological starting point is needed.

I will use the expression 'the self' freely – I am already doing so – but I don't want to exclude in advance the view that there is no such thing as the self, and the expression will often function as a loose name for what one might equally well call 'the self-phenomenon', i.e. all those undoubtedly real phenomena that lead us to think and talk in terms of something called the self, whether or not there is such a thing.

II The Problem of the Self

Many people believe in the self, conceived of as a distinct thing, although they are not clear what it is. Why do they believe in it? Because they have a distinct *sense* of, or experience as of, the self, and they take it that it is not delusory. This sense of the self is the source in experience of the philosophical problem of the self. So the first thing to do is to track the problem to this source in order to get a better idea of what it is. The first question to ask is the *phenomenological question*:

What is the nature of the sense of the self?

And this, in the first instance, is best taken as a question explicitly about human beings: as the *local* phenomenological question

(1) What is the nature of the human sense of the self?

Whatever the answer to (1) is, it raises the *general* phenomenological question

(2) Are there other possibilities, when it comes to a sense of the self? (Can we describe the minimal case of genuine possession of a sense of the self?)

The answers to (1) and (2) raise the *conditions* question

(3) What are the grounds or preconditions of possession of a sense of the self?

and this question raises a battery of subsidiary questions. But progress is being made, at least potentially. For, if one can produce satisfactory answers to (1), (2) and (3), one will be in a good position to raise and answer the *factual* question, the fundamental and straightforwardly metaphysical question

(4) Is there (could there be) such a thing as the self?

I think one has to answer (1) and (2), and probably (3), in order to answer (4) properly.

III   The Local Question: Cognitive Phenomenology

I will now go through the plan in more detail, and sketch how I think some of the answers should go. The first question is the local phenomenological question: What is the nature of the ordinary human sense of the self? This raises a prior question: Can one generalize about the human sense of the self? I think the answer is Yes: the aspects of the sense of the self that are of principal concern, when it comes to the philosophical problem of the self, are very basic. They are situated below any level of plausible cultural variation.[3] They are conceptual rather than affective: it is the *cognitive phenomenology* of the sense of the self that is fundamentally in question, i.e. the conceptual structure of the sense of the self, the structure of the sense of the self considered (as far as possible) independently of any emotional aspects that it may have. The cognitive phenomenology of the self is bound up with the affective phenomenology of the self in complicated ways, but emotional or affective aspects of the sense of the self will be of concern (e.g. in section VIII) only in so far as emotions shape or weight conceptions.

What, then, is the ordinary, human sense of the self, in so far as we can generalize about it? I propose that it is (at least) the sense that people have of themselves as being, specifically, a mental presence; a mental someone; a single mental thing that is a conscious subject of experience, that has a certain character or personality, and that is in some sense distinct from all its particular experiences, thoughts, and so on, and indeed from all other things. It is crucial that it is thought of as a distinctively mental phenomenon, and I will usually speak of the 'mental self' from now on (the qualifier 'mental' may be understood wherever omitted).

Is the sense of the mental self, as so far described, really something ordinary? I believe so. It comes to every normal human being, in some form, in childhood.[4] The early realization of the fact that one's thoughts are unobservable by others, the experience of the profound sense in which one is alone in one's head – these are among the very deepest facts about the character of human life, and found the sense of the mental self. It is perhaps most often vivid when one is alone and thinking, but it can be equally vivid in a room full of people. It connects with a feeling that nearly everyone has had intensely at some time – the feeling that one's body is just a vehicle or vessel for the mental thing that is what one really or most essentially is. I believe that the primary or fundamental way in which we conceive of ourselves is as a distinct mental thing – sex addicts, athletes, and supermodels included. Analytic philosophers may find it hard to see – or remember – this, given their training, and they risk losing sight of the point in derision.

This is not to deny that we also naturally conceive of ourselves as mental-and-non-mental things, human beings considered as a whole. We do. Nor is it to claim that the sense of the mental self always incorporates some sort of belief in an immaterial soul, or in life after bodily death. It doesn't. Philosophical materialists who believe, as I do, that we are wholly physical beings, and that the theory of evolution by natural selection is true, and that animal consciousness of the sort with which we are familiar evolved by purely physical natural processes on a planet where no such consciousness previously existed, have this sense of the mental self as strongly as anyone else.

In more detail: I propose that the mental self is ordinarily conceived or experienced as:

(1) a *thing*, in some robust sense
(2) a *mental* thing, in some sense
(3, 4) a *single* thing that is single both *synchronically* considered and *diachronically* considered
(5) *ontically distinct* from all other things
(6) a *subject of experience*, a conscious feeler and thinker
(7) an *agent*
(8) a thing that has a certain character or *personality*

This is an intentionally strong proposal, and it may be thought to be too strong in various ways. Most of (1)–(8) can be contested, and the list may well contain redundancy, but it provides a framework for discussion. There are various entailment relations between the eight elements that need to be exposed; (1) – (6) are closely linked. (1) also raises the general question 'What is a thing?' – a question that will be important when the fundamental factual question ('Is there such a thing as the self?') is considered.

I don't think the list omits anything essential to a genuine sense of the mental self, even if it includes some things that are not essential. I will assume that this is true for the purposes of this paper: a primitive framework can show the structure of a problem even if it is not complete. It can be the best way to proceed even if the problem resists regimentation in terms of necessary and sufficient conditions. If an omission were identified, it could simply be added in to the existing framework.

(2) is the only one of the eight properties that is not attributed as naturally to the embodied human being as to the putative mental self,

and it may be suggested that the sense of the mental self is just a delusory projection from the experience of embodiment. Perhaps the so-called self is just the human being incompletely grasped and illegitimately spiritualized. This is a popular view, but I am not yet in a position to assess it.[5] Some argue from the fact that use of the word 'I' to refer to the supposed mental self does not ordinarily stand out as distinct from use of the word 'I' to refer to the human being considered as a whole to the conclusion that we have no good reason to distinguish them. To this it may be replied that appeal to facts about public language use is often irrelevant when considering facts about meaning and reference, and is spectacularly inappropriate in the case of the problem of the self.[6]

IV   Phenomenology and Metaphysics

Equipped with an answer to the local question, one can go on to raise the general question: 'Are there other possibilities, so far as a sense of the mental self (or SMS) is concerned?' Given the assumption that the list of eight properties doesn't omit anything essential to a genuine sense of the self, this amounts to the question whether one can dispense with any of (1)–(8) while still having something that qualifies as a genuine SMS. It enquires, among other things, after the minimal case of a SMS. The answer is partly a matter of terminological decision, but for the most part not.

How might the answer go? I don't yet know, but if I had to commit myself it would be as follows: (4) and (8) are not necessary to a sense of the mental self, even in the human case (see sections VIII and IX). (6) is secure, but a serious doubt can be raised about (7). (2) and (5) need qualification if they are to survive. (1) and (3) can be challenged but effectively defended.

Objection: 'Surely the phenomenological investigation loses something crucial at this point? It is no longer rooted in the human case, so it is no longer independent of specifically philosophical theories about what selves actually are or can be: such theories are bound to be part of what governs our judgements about whether some thinned down SMS can count as a genuine SMS, once we go beyond the human case.'

I believe that a detailed attempt to answer the general phenomenological question will show that this is not so: our basic judgements about whether anything less than (1)–(8) can count as a genuine SMS can remain comfortably independent, in any respect that matters, of metaphysical philosophical theorizing about the nature of the self. In fact I think they can be sufficiently supported by reference to unusual human cases.

So much for the claim that phenomenology is substantially independent of metaphysics. What about the other way round? Here I think there is a fundamental dependence: metaphysical investigation of the nature of the self is subordinate to phenomenological investigation of the sense of the self. There is a strong phenomenological constraint on any acceptable answer to the metaphysical question which can be expressed by saying that the factual question 'Is there such a thing as the mental self?' is equivalent to the question 'Is any (genuine) sense of the self an accurate representation of anything that exists?'[7]

This equivalence claim can be split in two:

> (E1) If there is such a thing as the self, then some SMS is an accurate representation of something that exists,
>
> (E2) If some SMS is an accurate representation of something that exists, then there is such a thing as the self.

(E1) and (E2) may seem trivial, but both may be challenged. The first as follows:

> (C1) There is really no very good reason to think that if the self exists, then there is some SMS that is an accurate (if partial) representation of its nature. Perhaps the mental self, as it is in itself, is ineffable, quite unlike any experience of it.
>
> (C1) is Kantian in spirit. The second rejection is a response made when some particular SMS has been presented:
>
> (C2) This SMS you have outlined is indeed an accurate representation of something that exists, but the thing of which it is an accurate representation does not qualify for the title 'the mental self' because it does not have feature F (e.g. it is not an immaterial, ± immortal, ± whatever, substance).

The force of (E1) and (E2) consists precisely in the fact that they reject proposals like (C1) and (C2). In this way they impose a substantial constraint on metaphysical theorizing about the self. According to (E1), nothing can count as a mental self unless it possesses all the properties attributed to the self by some genuine SMS, whatever other properties it may possess. It rules out metaphysical claims about the self that fail to respect limits on the concept of the self revealed by the phenomenological investigation. It states a necessary condition on qualifying for the title of self. (E2), by contrast, states that nothing can fail to count as a mental self if it possesses all the properties that feature in some SMS, whatever other properties it may possess or lack. It states a sufficient condition on quali- fying for the title of self – it lays it down that there is no further test to pass.

To make the equivalence claim, then, is to say that one must have well- developed answers to phenomenological questions about the experience of the self before one can begin to answer metaphysical questions about the self. The equivalence claim excludes two forms of metaphysical excess – extravagance and miserliness. Extravagance is blocked by show- ing that we cannot answer the question 'Is there such a thing as the self?' by saying 'Yes there is (or may be), but we have (or may have) no under- standing of its ultimate nature'. Miserliness is blocked by showing that we cannot answer by saying 'Well, there is *something* of which the sense of the self is an accurate representation, but it does not follow that there is any such thing as the self.'

If the answers to the phenomenological questions go well, we should be left with a pretty good idea of what we are asking when we ask the factual, metaphysical question 'Is there such a thing as the self?' Any metaphysical speculations that are not properly subordinate to phenomenology can be cheerfully 'commit[ted] . . . to the flames' (Hume, 1975, p. 165).[8]

V   Materialism

In sections VI–IX I will give examples of more detailed work within this scheme. Before that I must give a brief account of the sense in which I am a materialist.

Materialists believe that every thing and event in the universe is a wholly physical phenomenon. If they are even remotely realistic in their material- ism they admit that conscious experience is part of reality. It follows that they must grant that conscious experience is a wholly physical phenom- enon. They must grant that it is wholly physical specifically in its mental, experiential properties. (They must grant that the qualitative character of the taste of bread, considered just as such and independently of anything else that exists, is as much a physical phenomenon as the phenomenon of an electric current flowing in a wire.)

It follows that materialists express themselves very badly when they talk about the mental and the physical as if they were opposed categories. For on their own view, this is exactly like saying that cows and animals are opposed categories – for all mental phenomena, including conscious-experience phenomena *considered specifically as such*, just are physical phenomena, according to them; just as all cows are animals.

So what are materialists doing when they talk as if the mental and the physical were different things? What they presumably mean to do is to distinguish, within the realm of the physical, which is the only realm there is, according to them, between the mental and the non-mental, and, more specifically, between the experiential and the non-experiential; to distinguish, that is, between (A) mental (or experiential) aspects of the physical, and (B) non-mental (or non-experiential) aspects of the physical.[9] This is the difference that is really in question when it comes to the 'mind–body' problem, and materialists who persist in talking in terms of the difference between the mental and the physical perpetuate the terms of the dualism they reject in a way that is inconsistent with their own view.[10]

Let me rephrase this. When I say that the mental and the experiential are wholly physical, I mean something completely different from what some materialists have apparently meant by saying things like 'experience is really just neurons firing'. I don't mean that all that is really going on, in the case of conscious experience, is something that can be discerned and described by current physics, or by any non-revolutionary extension of current physics. Such a view amounts to some kind of radical eliminativism, and is certainly false. My claim is quite different. It is that the experiential considered specifically as such – the portion of reality we have to do with when we consider experiences specifically and solely in respect of the experiential character they have for those who have them as they have them – that 'just is' physical. No one who disagrees with this claim is a serious and realistic materialist.[11]

A further comment is needed. As remarked, thoroughgoing materialists hold that all mental phenomena, including all experiential phenomena, are entirely physical phenomena. But triviality threatens when things are put this way. For now even absolute idealism (in one version, the view that only experiential phenomena exist) can claim to be a materialist position.

The trivializing possibility can be excluded by ruling that anything deserving the name 'materialism' must hold that there are non-mental and non-experiential phenomena as well as mental or experiential phenomena. But one can plausibly go further, and take materialism to incorporate what one might call 'the principle of the necessary involvement of the mental with the non-mental'. Most realistic materialists take it that the existence of each particular mental or experiential phenomenon involves the existence of some particular non-mental, non-experiential phenomenon. More strongly expressed: each particular mental or experiential phenomenon has, essentially, in addition to its mental or experiential character or mode of being, a non-mental character or mode of being. One might call this 'mental-and-non-mental' materialism. When I talk of materialism in what follows, I will take it to involve this view.

According to materialism, then, every thing or event has non-mental, non-experiential being, whether or not it also has mental or experiential being. More needs to be said (given that we have knowledge of central aspects of the fundamental reality of the mental just in having experience in the way we do, we need to ask whether it is possible to give some basic positive characterization of the non-mental, perhaps in terms of properties like time, length, position, mass, electric charge, spin, 'colour' and 'flavour' in the quantum theory sense). But this is enough to make it clear that the present question about whether the self exists in the human case is not a question about whether we might possibly be 'Cartesian egos' or immaterial substances. It is the question whether the mental self exists given that we are ordinarily embodied, entirely physical living human beings.

VI   Singularity

I have sketched how I think answers to the phenomenological questions should go, described the constraint that phenomenology places on metaphysics, and characterized the sense in which I am a materialist. I will now give samples of more detailed work on the phenomenological questions.

The proposal for consideration is that the mental self is conceived or experienced as (1) a *thing*, (2) a *mental* thing, a *single* thing that is single both (3) *synchronically* considered and (4) *diachronically* considered, (5) a thing that is *ontically distinct* from all other things, (6) a *subject of experience* and (7) an *agent* that has (8) a certain *personality*. In this section I will discuss (3) and (4) in the framework of the *local* phenomenological question, after very brief comments on (1) and (2). In sections VII–IX I will discuss (4) and (8) in the framework of the *general* phenomenological question. In section IX I will say something about (5).

Thinghood and mentality

What about the claim (1) that the self is conceived of as a thing? In a way, this is the least clear of the eight claims, but the general idea is this: the self isn't thought of as merely a state or property of something else, or as an event, or process, or series of events. So, in a sense, there is nothing else for it to seem to be, other than a thing. It's not thought of as being a thing in the way that a stone or a cat is – it's not thought of as a sort of ethereal concrete object. But it is thought of as a thing of some kind. In particular, it is thought of as something that has the causal character of a thing; something that can undergo things and do things. Bishop Berkeley's characterization of the self as a 'thinking . . . principle' is perhaps helpful (1975, p. 185). A principle, in this old use, manages to sound like a thing of some sort without sounding anything like a table or a chair.

The second claim, (2), that the self is thought of as something mental, is also unclear. Very briefly, the idea is something like this: when the self is thought of as a thing, its claim to thinghood is taken to be sufficiently grounded in its mental nature alone. It may also have a non-mental nature, as materialists suppose, but its counting as a thing is not thought to depend on its counting as a thing considered in its non-mental nature: the self is the *mental* self. (It's true and important that many people naturally think of themselves as possessing both mental and non-mental properties, but this doesn't affect the truth of (2).)

Singularity

Clearly, to think of the self as a thing is already to think of it as single in some way – as *a* thing. But in what way? I have three main claims in mind.

First: in so far as the mental self is thought of as single, it is not thought of as having singularity only in the sense in which a group of things can be said to be a single group. Rather it is thought of as single in the way in which a single marble (e.g.) is single when compared with a single pile of marbles. Developing the Lockean point just made about the fundamental causal component in our idea of a thing, one might say that the mental self is conceived of as something that has the kind of strong unity of internal causal connectedness that a single marble has, as compared with the much weaker unity of internal causal connectedness found in a pile of marbles.[12]

Second: the mental self's property of singleness is thought of as sufficiently and essentially grounded in its mental nature alone. This closely parallels the idea that the self's claim to thinghood is thought of as sufficiently grounded in its mental nature alone, and the same moves are appropriate. We may suppose that the mental self has non-mental being (the brain-as-revealed-to-physics, say) as well as mental being, and it may be *believed* to have non-mental being. The fact remains that it is thought of as having singleness in a way that is independent of its having singleness when considered in its non-mental nature.

One may express this by saying that its *principle of unity* is taken to be mental. What does 'principle of unity' mean? Well, it is arguable that everything that is conceived of as a single thing or object – electron, atom, neuron, sofa, nation-state – is conceived of as a single thing relative to some principle of unity according to which it *counts* as a single thing. An atom counts as a single thing relative to one principle of unity, and it counts as many things relative to other principles of unity – those which discern subatomic particles. Many associate this point with the view that there are no ultimate facts of the matter about which phenomena are things or objects and which are not; they hold that all principles of objectual unity, as one might call them, are ultimately subjective in character. But this is a further claim. In itself, the claim that everything that is taken to be a single object is so taken relative to some principle of objectual unity is compatible with the view that there are objective principles of objectual unity given which there are right answers to questions about which things are genuinely single objects.

Let me try to put the point about the self in another way: we may suppose that the mental self (the self-phenomenon) has non-mental being as well as mental being, and it may even be widely believed that this is so (few give the matter much thought). The fact remains that it is thought of as having singleness in its mental being in a way that is independent of any singleness that it may have in its non-mental being. In this sense it is taken to be single just as something mental.[13] I will illustrate this idea after introducing the third main point about singleness.

This is that the mental self is standardly thought to be single in the two ways just characterized both when it is considered (3) synchronically, or as a thing existing at a given time, and when it is considered (4) diachronically, i.e. as a thing that persists through time.

In what follows, I will stretch the meaning of 'synchronic' slightly, and take it to apply to any consideration of the mental self (or self-phenomenon) that is a consideration of it during an experientially unitary or unbroken or hiatus-free period of thought or experience. The notion of a hiatus-free period of thought or experience is important for my purposes, and needs further description (see section IX). For the moment let me simply assert that in the normal course of events truly hiatus-free periods of thought or experience are invariably brief in human beings: a few seconds at the most, a fraction of a second at the least. Our eyes are constantly engaged in saccadic jumps, and reflection reveals the respect in which our minds function in an analogous – if more perceptible – way. (Research by Pöppel and others provides 'clear evidence that... the experienced Now is not a point, but is extended,... that the [human] conscious Now is – language and culture independent – of the duration of approximately 3 seconds', and although this proves nothing about the existence of hiatuses, or about the nature of the self, it is undeniably suggestive.[14])

'Diachronic' complements 'synchronic' and applies to consideration of the mental self (or self-phenomenon) during any period of conscious thought or experience that includes a break or hiatus. Such periods may range from a fraction of a second to a lifetime.

Now reconsider the second claim – that the mental self is taken to be single just as something mental. This has a synchronic and a diachronic aspect. I will begin with the former. Suppose that someone fully convinces you (perhaps by hypnosis) that your current mental life with all its familiar characteristics, which incorporates your current sense of the single mental self, depends on the activity of three spatially separated brains in three different bodies. Will this immediately annihilate your natural sense of your mental singleness? Surely not. Your thought is likely to be 'Wow, I have got three brains – I, the single thing or person that I am' (Kant (1996, A353–4) makes a related point). Your sense of the mental self is overwhelmingly likely to continue unchanged. It doesn't depend on your believing that you have a single brain or body. Suppose that you find out that there are three separate brains in your single body, collaborating to produce your experience. Again this will not override the experience of mental singleness.

It may be objected that in the case imagined you still have experience as of inhabiting a single body. This is true, given that you are an ordinary human being. But one can equally well imagine a three-bodied creature that naturally experiences itself as three-bodied, and as receiving information (perhaps via different sense modalities) from all three bodies, while still having a strong sense of the single mental self, and thinking of itself as 'I'. Here the experience of three-bodiedness is likely to make the sense of the singleness of the mental self particularly vivid. It is true that ordinary human experience of oneself as mentally single is deeply shaped by experience of having a single body, but it hardly follows that any possible experience of oneself as mentally single depends essentially on such experience.[15]

That is the sense of synchronic singleness I have in mind. Now for the diachronic case. Suppose one experiences one's mental life as something that has strong diachronic singleness or unity (some do more than others). And suppose that one then becomes convinced that it depends for its existence on the successive existence of a series of numerically distinct brains or neuronal entities. Will this annihilate one's sense of the mental self as a single thing persisting through time? It would be extraordinary if it did: for, by hypothesis, everything else is the same, experientially, as it was before one made this discovery. This suggests that confrontation with the fact of one's non-mental multiplicity will have no more force to undermine one's sense of the singleness of the mental self in the diachronic case than in the synchronic case.

There is a famous footnote in Kant's discussion of the Third Paralogism (Kant, 1996, A363–4):

> An elastic ball which strikes another similar ball in a straight line communicates to the latter its entire motion, and therefore its entire state (if we take account only of positions in space). If, in analogy with such bodies, we postulate substances such that the one communicates representations to the other together with consciousness of them, we can conceive a whole series of substances of which the first transmits its state to the second, the second its own state with that of the preceding substance to the third, and [so on]. The last substance would then be conscious of all the states of the previously changed substances as being its own states, because they would have been transferred to it together with consciousness of them.

Kant's aim is to argue that no experience of the diachronic singleness of the mental self can possibly establish that the mental self or 'I' is in fact a diachronically single substance. My different, compatible claim is that even if one came to believe that the existence of the mental self did *not* involve the existence of a diachronically single substance, there is no reason to suppose that this would undermine one's experience of the mental self as so single.

To summarize: even if one takes it for granted that the mental self (or self-phenomenon) has some non-mental nature or being, one's experience of the mental self as single is independent of any belief that it is single – either synchronically or diachronically – in its non-mental nature or being. This, then, illustrates the respect in which the singularity of the mental self is conceived of as being essentially grounded in its mental nature alone.

It's also true – to diverge from merely phenomenological concerns – that thoughts that occur in a single body or brain (or substance of some other sort) may fail to seem anything like the series of thoughts of a single self or thinker, both when considered 'from the inside' (i.e. from the point of view of the thinker of any given one of the thoughts in question) and when considered from the outside (i.e. by someone who is not the thinker of any of the thoughts, but who has access to the contents of the thoughts, as in a novel). Consider the diachronic case first: imagine that a series of self-conscious thoughts or 'I-thoughts' occurs in the same brain, one at a time, while none of them ever involves any awareness of any thought earlier (or indeed later) than itself, and while no two of them ever stand in any of the relations (of content, temperamental coherence, etc.) in which temporally close pairs of thoughts so often stand when they are the thoughts of a being that we naturally think of as a single thinker.

In this case, it may be said that we lack any mentally grounded reason for saying that there is a single thinker. Some may want to say that there is nevertheless a single thinker, simply because a single brain is the locus of all the thoughts. But why should the fact of non-mental diachronic singleness decisively overrule the natural judgement that there is no plausible candidate for a diachronically single mental self in this case? The fact of non-mental multiplicity in the three-bodies case had no power to defeat the natural judgement of mental singleness. Why should the fact of non-mental singleness in this case defeat the natural judgement of mental multiplicity (lack of mental singularity)?[16]

Now consider the synchronic case: imagine that a single brain is the site of experiential phenomena that are just like the experiential phenomena taking place simultaneously in the brains of three different people (the first thinking exclusively about Vienna, the second exclusively about menhirs, the third exclusively about DNA). Here it is natural to judge that there are three subjects of experience. If one counts the whole brain non-mentally considered as the non-mental being of each of the three apparently distinct thought-thinking selves, then one has multiplicity of selves in spite of non-mental singleness.

The judgement that there are three subjects of experience may seem natural in this case, but it can be cogently challenged. It is very difficult to draw firm conclusions about the number of subjects of experience associated with a single brain from facts about the contents of the experiences associated with that brain. As far as the synchronic case is concerned: it may be a fact about human beings that they can only genuinely entertain one conscious thought at a time, but it does not seem to be an *a priori* truth about conscious thinking in general. As far as the diachronic case is concerned: it is not clear that there is any lower bound on the connectedness of the successive thoughts and experiences of a single subject of experience, any point at which we can confidently say, 'These experiences are too unconnected and disordered to count as the experiences of a single subject of experience.'[17]

Multiplicity?

So far I have taken it for granted that human beings standardly have some sense of the singleness of the mental self. But some may claim to experience the mental self as fragmentary or multiple, and most of us have had experiences that give us – so we feel – some understanding of what they mean.

It seems, however, that the experience of multiplicity can at most affect (4), the sense of the mental self as diachronically single (recall that a sense of the mental self as diachronically single may well be concerned with short periods of time; when I want to consider longer periods of time – weeks, months, years, lifetimes – I will talk about 'long-term' continuity). It cannot affect (3), the sense of the mental self as synchronically single (single during any one 'hiatus-free' period of thought or experience). Why not? Because any candidate for being an experience of the mental self as synchronically multiple at the present moment will have to be an episode of explicitly self-conscious thought, and there is a crucial (trivial) respect in which no such episode could be experience of the mental self as synchronically multiple. Explicitly self-conscious thought need not always involve some explicit sense of the mental self as something present and involved, even when it has the form 'I f', or 'I am F' ('I forgot the key', 'I'm late for my exam'). But whenever it does – and it must if there is to be anything that is a candidate for being an *experience* of the mental self as synchronically multiple at the present moment – there is a fundamental respect in which the mental self must be experienced as single, for the space of that thought at least.

This may seem obvious, but it can be disputed. It may be said that even experience of the mental self synchronically considered can seem to be experience of something shattered and multiple ('My name is legion', Mark 5:9). There seem to be forms of human experience that invite such a description. One may be under stress and subject to rapidly changing moods. One may feel oneself pulled in different directions by opposed desires. Human thought-processes can become extraordinarily rapid and tumultuous. But what exactly is being claimed, when it is said that the self may be experienced as synchronically multiple? There seem to be two main possibilities: either the experience is that there are many selves present, or it is (just) that the self is complex in a certain radical way. But in the second case, the experience of radical complexity that is claimed to justify the description 'synchronically multiple' clearly depends on a prior sense of the mental self as synchronically single: in this case 'multiple' is a characterization that is applied to something that must have already presented as single in order for the characterization to be applied at all. What about the first case, in which the experience is that there are many selves present? Well, we may ask who has the experience that there are many selves present. To face the question is to realize that any explicitly self-conscious experience has to present as experience from one single mental point of view. (The word 'mental' is not redundant here, for the three-bodied person that has sensory experience of being three-bodied may have three sensory points of view while still having only one mental 'point of view'.) If so, the experience that there are many selves present is necessarily experience from some single point of view. Even if a single brain is the site of many experiences that there are many selves present, each such experience is necessarily experience from a single point of view. This is the trivial aspect of the claim that experience of the mental self as synchronically multiple is not really possible.[18]

It may be added that when one's mind races and tumbles, it is natural to experience oneself as a largely helpless spectator of the pandemonium. To this extent, experience of chaotic disparateness of contents reinforces a sense of singleness rather than diminishing it. Nor can one experience conflict of desire unless one experiences both desires as one's own.

VII   Personality

So much for a consideration of (3) and (4) – synchronic and diachronic singleness – in the framework of the local phenomenological question, What is the human sense of the self? I will now consider (4) and (8) – diachronic singularity and personality – in the framework of the general phenomenological question, What senses of the self are possible? I will begin with personality, and, like William James, I will sometimes talk 'in the first person, leaving my description to be accepted by those to whose introspection it may commend itself as true, and confessing my inability to meet the demands of others, if others there be' (1950, vol. 1, p. 299).

It seems plain that (8) is not a necessary component of any possible sense of the mental self – that experience of the self does not necessarily involve experience of it as something that has a personality. Most people have at some time, and however temporarily, experienced themselves as a kind of bare locus of consciousness – not just as detached, but as void of personality, stripped of particularity of character, a mere (cognitive) point of view. Some have experienced it for long periods of time. It may be the result of exhaustion or solitude, abstract thought or a hot bath. It is also a common feature of severe depression, in which one may experience 'depersonalization'. This is a very accurate term, in my experience and in that of others I have talked to.

Sustained experience of depersonalization is classified as psychotic relative to the normal human condition, but it is of course experientially real, and one can imagine human beings getting stuck in this condition; some do. Equally, one can imagine aliens for whom it is the normal condition. Such an alien may still have a clear sense of the self as a specifically mental thing. It may still have an unimpaired sense of itself as a locus of consciousness, just as we ordinarily do – not only when we suffer depersonalization, but also in everyday life.[19]

A very strong form of what may be lost in depersonalization is recorded by Gerard Manley Hopkins, who talks of considering

> my self-being, my consciousness and feeling of myself, that taste of myself, of *I* and *me* above and in all things, which is more distinctive than the taste of ale or alum, more distinctive than the smell of walnutleaf or camphor, and is incommunicable by any means to another man.... Nothing else in nature comes near this unspeakable stress of pitch, distinctiveness, and selving, this selfbeing of my own.[20]

My enquiries suggest that while some people feel they know exactly what Hopkins means, most find this deeply bewildering: for them, their personality is something that is unnoticed, and in effect undetectable, in the present moment. It's what they look through, or where they look from; not something they look at; a global and invisible condition of their life, like air, not an object of experience. Dramatic differences like these back up the view that we need a phenomenology of the sense of the self before we try to answer the factual question about whether or not there is such a thing.

VIII   The Self In Time: Effects of Character

So much, briefly, for (8). Must any sense of the mental self involve experience of the self as (4), something that has long-term diachronic continuity as a single thing? I think not. The sense of the single mental self may be vivid and complete, at any given time, even if it has to do only with the present, brief, hiatus-free stretch of consciousness, at any given time. Nor do I think that this is just some alien or logical possibility, though it is also that. It lies within the range of human experience. One can be fully aware of the fact that one has long-term continuity as a *living human being* without *ipso facto* having any significant sense of the *mental self* or *subject of experience* as something that has long-term continuity. One can have a vivid sense of oneself as a mental self, and a strong natural tendency to think that that is what one most fundamentally is, while having little or no interest in or commitment to the idea that the I who is now thinking has any past or future.

Human beings differ deeply in a number of ways that affect their experience of the mental self as diachronically continuous. Some people have an excellent 'personal' memory (i.e. memory of their own past life) and an unusual capacity for vivid recollection. Others have a very poor personal memory. And it may not be simply poor. It may also be highly quiescent, and almost never intrude spontaneously into their current thought. These deep differences of memory are matched by equal differences in the force with which people imagine, anticipate, or form intentions about the future.

These differences interact with others. Some people live deeply in narrative mode: they experience their lives in terms of something that has shape and story, narrative trajectory. Some of them are self-narrators in a stronger sense: they regularly rehearse and revise their interpretations of their lives. Some people, again, are great planners, and knit up their lives with long-term projects.

Others are quite different. They have no early ambition, no later sense of vocation, no interest in climbing a career ladder, no tendency to see their life in narrative terms or as constituting a story or a development. Some merely go from one thing to another. They live life in a picaresque or episodic fashion. Some people make few plans and are little concerned with the future. Some live intensely in the present, some are simply aimless.

Many things can encourage or obstruct a sense of the mental self as something that has long-term diachronic continuity. Some people are very consistent in personality or character, whether or not they know it. And this form of steadiness may in some cases strongly underwrite experience of the mental self's continuity. Others are consistent only in their inconsistency, and may for that reason feel themselves to be continually puzzling, and piecemeal. Some go through life as if stunned.

Neither inconsistency nor poor memory is necessary for the episodic experience of life. John Updike writes 'I have the persistent sensation, in my life and art, that I am just beginning' (1989, p. 239). These are the words of a man who has an extremely powerful personal memory and a highly consistent character. I have the same persistent sensation, and learn from Updike that it is nothing essentially to do with my extremely poor personal memory. I believe that it is an accurate description of how things are for many people, when it comes to that sense of oneself as a mental self that is – whether or not it is acknowledged – central to most people's self-conception.

I'm somewhere down the episodic end of the spectrum. I have no sense of my life as a narrative with form, or indeed as a narrative without form.

I have little interest in my own past and little concern for the future. My poor personal memory rarely impinges on my present consciousness. Even when I am interested in my past, I'm not interested in it specifically in so far as it is mine. I'm perfectly well aware that it is mine, in so far as I am a human being considered as a whole, but I do not really think of it as mine at all, in so far as 'mine' picks out me as I am now. For me as I am now, the interest (emotional or otherwise) of my personal memories lies in their experiential content considered independently of the fact that what is remembered happened *to me* – i.e. to the me that is now remembering.[21] They're certainly distinctive in their 'from-the-inside' character, but this in itself doesn't mark them as mine in any emotionally significant sense. The one striking exception to this, in my case, used to be – but no longer is – memory of recent embarrassment.

I make plans for the future. To that extent I think of myself perfectly adequately as something that has long-term continuity. But I experience this way of thinking of myself as utterly remote and theoretical, given the most central or fundamental way in which I think of myself, which is as a mental self or someone. Using 'Me*' to express this fundamental way in which I think of myself – or to denote me thinking of myself in this way, looking out on things from this perspective – I can accurately express my experience by saying that I do not think of Me* as being something in the future. It is also accurate to shift the 'not', and say, more strongly, that what I think of as being in the future is not Me*.

As I write these words, the thought that I have to give a lecture before a large audience in two months' time causes me some worry, which has familiar physiological manifestations. I feel the anxiety naturally and directly as pertaining to me even though I have no sense that it will be Me* that will be giving the lecture. Indeed it seems completely false to say that it will be Me*. And this is how it feels, not something I believe for theoretical reasons. So why do I feel any anxiety now? I believe that susceptibility to this sort of anticipatory anxiety is innate and 'hard-wired', a manifestation of the instinct for self-preservation: my practical concern for my future, which I believe to be within the normal human range, is biologically grounded and autonomous in such a way that it persists as something immediately felt even though it is not supported by any emotionally backed sense on the part of Me* now that Me* will be there in the future. (Not even half an hour away – and certainly not tomorrow.) In so far as I have any sense of Me* (rather than the living human being that I am) as something with a history and future, it seems that this sense is a wispy, short-range product of, and in no way a ground of, my innate predisposition to physiological impulses that develop into experience of anxiety or regret. It dislimns when scrutinized, and it is more accurate to say that it does not exist.

Now for an exception. You might expect me to say that when I think of my death at some unspecified future time, I think that it is not Me* who is going to die, or at least that I do not think that it is Me*. But I do think that it is Me* that is going to die, and I feel fear of death. It's only when I consider future events *in life* that I do not think it's Me*. This seems odd, given that my death necessarily comes after any future events in my life, and ought therefore to seem to have even less to do with Me* than any future events in life. But it can be explained. This feature of my attitude to death is principally grounded in susceptibility to the following line of thought: When eternity – eternal nonexistence – is in question, the gap between Me* and death that is created by the fact that I still have an indefinite amount of life to live approximates to nothing (like any finite number compared with infinity). So death – nonexistence for ever – presents itself as having direct relevance for Me* now even if Me* has no clear future in life – not even tomorrow. On the vast scale of things that one naturally thinks in terms of when thinking of death, death is no significant distance away from Me*, and looms as something that will happen to Me*. This is not to say that I feel or fear that I am going to die now. The thought of eternity doesn't override common sense. But it has an emotional force that makes it seem plain that death faces Me*. If this is Heideggerian authenticity, then Heideggerian authenticity is compatible with lack of any belief in the persisting self.

Note that this line of thought will have equal force for someone who *does* think of their Me* as having a future in life: for if eternity of nonexistence is what you fear, a few years is not a protection. This idea was vivid for me every night as a young child combining an atheist upbringing with great difficulty in going to sleep.

One indirect lesson of this case is important. It is that one's sense of one's temporal nature may vary considerably depending on what one is thinking about. But the general conclusion I draw is that a sense of the self need not necessarily involve (4) a sense of it as something that has long-term continuity.[22]

IX The Self in Time: The 'Stream' of Consciousness

How does the moment-to-moment experience of consciousness relate to the sense of the self? Does it underwrite (4)? I will now consider this question.

I think William James's famous metaphor of the stream of consciousness is inept.[23] Human thought has very little natural phenomenological continuity or experiential flow – if mine is anything to go by. 'Our thought is fluctuating, uncertain, fleeting', as Hume said (1947, p. 194). It keeps slipping from mere consciousness into self-consciousness and out again (one can sit through a whole film without emerging into I-thinking self-consciousness). It is always shooting off, fuzzing, shorting out, spurting and stalling. William James described it as 'like a bird's life, ... an alternation of flights and perchings' (1950, vol. 1, p. 243), but even this recognition that thought is not a matter of even flow retains a strong notion of continuity, in so far as a bird traces a spatio-temporally continuous path. It fails to take adequate account of the fact that trains of thought are constantly broken by detours – by blows – fissures – white noise. This is especially so when one is just sitting and thinking. Things are different if one's attention is engaged by some ordered and continuous process in the world, like a fast and exciting game, or music, or a talk. In this case thought or experience may be felt to inherit much of the ordered continuity of the phenomenon which occupies it. But it may still seize up, fly off, or flash with perfectly extraneous matter from time to time, and reflection reveals gaps and fadings, disappearances and recommencements even when there is stable succession of content.[24] It is arguable that the case of solitary speculative thought – in which the mind is left to its own resources and devices – merely reveals in a relatively dramatic way something that is true to a greater or lesser extent of all thought. There is an important respect in which James Joyce's use of punctuation in his 'stream of consciousness' novel *Ulysses* makes his depiction of the character of the process of consciousness more accurate in the case of the heavily punctuated Stephen Daedalus than in the case of the unpunctuated Molly Bloom. Dorothy Richardson, acknowledged as the inventor of the 'stream of consciousness' novel in English, remarked on the 'perfect imbecility' of the phrase to describe what she did.[25]

My claim is not just that there can be radical disjunction at the level of subject matter. Switches of subject matter could be absolute, and still be seamless in the sense that they involved no sensed temporal gap or felt interruption of consciousness. It seems to me, however, that such experience of temporal seamlessness is relatively rare.[26] When I am alone and thinking I find that my fundamental experience of consciousness is one of *repeated returns into consciousness from a state of complete, if momentary, unconsciousness.* The (invariably brief) periods of true experiential continuity are usually radically disjunct from one another in this way even when they are not radically disjunct in respect of content. (It is in fact often the same thought – or nearly the same thought – that one returns to after a momentary absence.) The situation is best described, it seems to me, by saying that consciousness is continually *restarting*. There isn't a basic substrate (as it were) of continuous consciousness interrupted by various lapses and doglegs. Rather, conscious thought has the character of a (nearly continuous) series of radically disjunct irruptions into consciousness from a basic substrate of non-consciousness. It keeps banging out of nothingness; it is a series of comings to. It's true that belief in the reality of flow may itself contribute to an experience of flow. But I think that the appearance of flow is undercut by even a modest amount of reflection.[27]

'But perhaps the experience of disjunction is an artefact of introspection. Perhaps unexamined consciousness has true flow, and the facts get distorted by the act of trying to observe what they are.'

This seems highly implausible. Awareness of radical disjunction sometimes surfaces spontaneously and unlooked for. We can become aware that this is what has been happening, we do not see it only when we look. This is my experience, and the claim seems strongly supported by work described by Dennett (1991, e.g. ch. 11). Even if the apperance of disjunction were partly an artefact of intentional introspection, this would be a striking fact about how consciousness appears to itself, something one needed to take account of when considering the underpinnings of the sense of the self. There's a sense in which this issue is undecidable, for in order to settle it one would need to be able to observe something while it was unobserved. Nevertheless, the view that there is radical disjunction might receive independent support from experimental psychology, and also, more indirectly, from current work on the non-mental neural correlates of consciousness.

I have been arguing – if that's the word – that the sense of the mental self as something that has long-term continuity lacks a certain sort of direct phenomenological warrant in the moment-to-moment nature of our thought processes. It is not supported at the level of detail by any phenomenon of steady flow. If there is any support for belief in the long-term continuity of the self in the nature of moment-to-moment consciousness, it is derived indirectly from other sources – the massive constancies and developmental coherencies of *content* that often link up experiences through time, and by courtesy of short-term memory, across all the jumps and breaks of flow. One (the human being, the mental-and-non-mental whole) walks from A to B, looking around, thinking of this and that. One works in a room for an hour. Examined in detail, the processes of one's thought are bitty, scatty, and saccadic in the way described; consciousness is 'in a perpetual flux', and different thoughts and experiences 'succeed each other with an inconceivable rapidity' (Hume, 1978, p. 252). And yet one is experientially in touch with a great pool of constancies and steady processes of change in one's environment including, notably, one's body (of which one is almost constantly aware, however thoughtlessly, both by external sense and by proprioception). If one does not reflect very hard, these constancies and steadinesses of development in the *contents* of one's consciousness may seem like fundamental characteristics of the *operation* of one's consciousness, although they are not. This in turn may support the sense of the *mental self* as something uninterrupted and continuous throughout the waking day.

I am not claiming that belief in the flow of consciousness is *necessary* to a sense of the self as something that has long-term continuity. One could think and feel that consciousness was gappy and chaotic and still believe in a mental self that had long-term continuity. This is probably the most common position among those who believe in the self, and the present, weak suggestion is only that belief in the flow of consciousness may be one interesting and suspect source of support for a sense of long-term continuity.

There is more to say, but not here. My central claim remains unchanged: one can have a full sense of the single mental self at any given time without thinking of the self as something that has long-term continuity. According to Reed 'our sense of self is intimately related to the subjective awareness of the continuity of life. Any break in personal time [or 'time-gap experience'] is alarming, because it suggests some disintegration of psychic synthesis' (Reed, 1987, p. 777). I believe that this is not generally true.

X   The Conditions Question

I have given examples of how one might set about answering phenomenological questions (1) and (2) in preparation for (4), the factual question 'Does the self exist?' I have no space to consider (3), the conditions question 'What are the grounds or preconditions of possession of a sense of the mental self?', but I think it is best approached by asking the more familiar question 'What are the grounds or necessary conditions of self-consciousness?', which has been widely discussed – e.g. by Kant, Fichte, Wundt, James and their followers, and, more recently, by P. F. Strawson (1966, pp. 97–112), Evans (1982, ch. 7), and others (see e.g. the contributors to Bermúdez et al., 1995, and Cassam, 1997). I believe that all discussions in the analytic tradition overestimate the strength of the conditions that can be established as necessary for self-consciousness, but this is a question for another time, and I will now conclude with a wild sketch of how I think the factual question is to be answered.

XI   The Factual Question

Suppose – for the sake of argument – that the answer to the general phenomenological question is as follows: any genuine sense of the self must involve a conception of the self as ((1) + (2) + (3) + (5) + (6)) – as a single, mental thing that is distinct from all other things and a subject of experience – but need not involve a conception of it as (7) an agent, or as having (8) character or personality or (4) longer-term diachronic continuity. If we couple this answer with the equivalence claim (p. 341 above) we get the result that if there is such a thing as a mental self, it must at least fulfil conditions (1), (2), (3), (5), and (6) – one might call these the 'core conditions'. It must be a distinct, mental thing that is correctly said to be a subject of experience and a single thing within any hiatus-free period of experience; whatever else it may be.[28]

Is there such a thing? If there is, is it right to call it a self? I can't legislate on how anyone should use the words 'self' and 'thing' (cf. note 8). It seems to me that the best answer is Yes, but many will think my Yes is close to No, because I don't think a mental self exists in any sense that will satisfy most of those who want there to be a self. I believe the Buddhists have the truth when they deny the existence of a *persisting* mental self, in the human case, and nearly all of those who want there to be a self want there to be a persisting self.

I will call my view the Pearl view, because it suggests that many mental selves exist, one at a time and one after another, like a (stringless) string of pearls, in the case of a human being.[29] According to the Pearl view, each is a distinct existence, an individual physical thing or object, though they may exist for considerably different lengths of time. The Pearl view is not the view that mental selves are *necessarily* of relatively short duration – there may be beings whose conscious experience is uninterrupted for hours at a time, or even for the whole of their existence (if I believed in God, this is how I'd expect God to be). But we are not like this: the basic form of our consciousness is that of a gappy series of eruptions of consciousness from a substrate of apparent non-consciousness.

I don't suppose the Pearl view will be much liked. It sounds linguistically odd and counterintuitive. It offends against the everyday use of expressions like 'myself' to refer to enduring human beings, and nearly all theoretical speculation about the self incorporates a deep presumption that if one is arguing for the existence of the mental self one is arguing for something that exists for a substantial period of time. The Pearl view sounds even more implausible as an account of the subject of experience.[30]

Sometimes we need to speak oddly to see clearly. I think it is important to defend the Pearl view, giving its linguistic counterintuitiveness a chance to diminish through familiarity so that one can judge it on its merits rather than on linguistic gut feeling. Perhaps the most that can be said for it is that it is the best we can do if we commit ourselves in advance to answering Yes to the question 'Is there any straightforward and metaphysically robust sense in which it is legitimate to talk of the mental self as a thing, something that really exists, like a chair or a cat, rather than merely as a Humean or Dennettian fiction?' In my view, that means that there is a lot to be said for it.

The proposal, in any case, is that the mental self – *a* mental self – exists at any given moment of consciousness or during any uninterrupted or hiatus-free period of consciousness.[31] But it exists only for some short period of time. But it is none the less real, as *real* as any rabbit or Z-particle. And it is as much a *thing* or *object* as any G-type star or grain of salt. And it is as much a *physical* thing as any blood vessel or jackhammer or cow.

I can think of three overlapping tasks one has to undertake in order to develop the proposal. One has to say more about what it is to be a materialist, address the question 'What is a thing (or object)?', and explain further what is meant by 'ontic distinctness'. I will make one comment about each.

(i) In saying that a self is an 'ontically distinct' thing, I mean – at least – that it is not the same thing as anything else ordinarily or naturally identified as a thing. But I don't mean that it is an 'independent or separately existing entity' (Parfit, 1995, p. 18 [and p. 296 above]) relative to all other things naturally identified as things – such as atoms, neurons, and brains. Parfit takes a Cartesian immaterial ego to be a paradigm instance of such a separately existing entity, but I take it that a mental self's existence from t_1 to t_2 (I'll suppose this to be a two-second interval) is part of the existence from t_1 to t_2 of a set of neuron-and-neurotransmitter-(etc.)-constituting atoms or fundamental particles in a certain state of activation.[32]

Note that this is not any sort of reductionist remark, for the phrase 'a set of … particles in a certain state of activation', as used by a consistent and realistic materialist, does not refer only or even especially to non-mental phenomena that can be adequately described by current physics or something like it. It refers just as it says, to a set of neuron-and-neurotransmitter-(etc.)-constituting particles in a certain state of activation; and this existence and activity, as all genuine and realistic materialists agree, is as much revealed by and constituted by experiential phenomena as by any non-experiential phenomena discernible by physics.

The plausibility of the claim that a mental self is a *thing*, given the way it is characterized in the paragraph before last, depends on the success of arguments sketched in (iii) below. But it is at least clear that ontic distinctness is not separate existence. Nor, it seems, is it what Parfit has in mind when he himself distinguishes distinctness from separate existence.

Consider a human being X. I will call the portion of physical reality that consists of X the 'X-reality'. This is a rough notion – as a physical being X is enmeshed in wide-reaching physical interactions, and is not neatly separable out as a single portion of reality – but it is serviceable none the less. Parfit offers two examples of things that stand in the relation of distinctness without separate existence: a statue and the lump of bronze of which it is made, and a nation and 'a group of people, on some territory, living together in certain ways'.[33] By contrast, I propose that there is an analogy between the following two relations: (1) the relation between one of X's little fingers and X, where X is considered statically at a particular moment in time; (2) the relation between a mental self that exists in the X-reality and the X-reality, where the X-reality is considered dynamically as something essentially persisting in time. In other words, I propose that the mental self and the X-reality (or more simply, the whole human being) stand in a straightforward part–whole relation. It seems to me that selves are as real, and as much things, as little fingers (actually it is arguable that they have a better claim to count as things than fingers do).

(ii) Realistic materialism requires acknowledgement that the phenomena of conscious experience are, considered specifically as such, wholly physical, as physical as the phenomena of extension and electricity insofar as they are correctly characterized by physics. This in turn requires granting that current physics, considered as a general account of the nature of the physical, is like *Hamlet* without the prince; or at least like *Othello* without Desdemona. No one who doubts this is a serious materialist, as far as I can see. Anyone who has had a standard modern (Western) education is likely to experience a feeling of deep bewilderment – category-blasting amazement – when entering into serious materialism, and considering the question 'What is the nature of the physical?' in the context of the thought that the mental (and in particular the experiential) is physical; followed, perhaps, by a deep, pragmatic agnosticism.[34]

(iii)   The discussion of materialism has many mansions, and provides a setting for considering the question 'What is a thing or object?' It is a long question, but the answer suggests that there is no less reason to call the self a thing than there is to call a cat or a rock a thing. It is arguable that disagreement with this last claim is diagnostic of failure to understand what genuine, realistic materialism involves.

'Come off it. Even if we grant that there is a phenomenon that is reasonably picked out by the phrase "mental self", why should we accept that the right thing to say about some two-second-long mental-self phenomenon is (a) that it is a *thing* or *object* like a rock or a tiger? Why can't we insist that the right thing to say is simply (b) that an enduring ('physical') object – Louis – has a certain *property*, or (c) that a two-second mental-self phenomenon is just a matter of a certain *process* occurring in an object – so that it is not itself a distinct object existing for two seconds?'

I think that a proper understanding of materialism strips (b) and (c) of any appearance of superiority to (a). As for (c): any claim to the effect that a mental self is best thought of as a process rather than an object can be countered by saying that there is no sense in which a mental self is a process in which a rock is not also and equally a process. So if a rock is a paradigm case of a thing in spite of being equally well thought of as a process, we have no good reason to say that a self is not a thing.[35]

'But if there is a process, there must be something – an object or substance – in which it goes on. If something happens, there must be something to which it happens, something which is not just the happening itself.' This expresses our ordinary understanding of things, but physicists are increasingly content with the view that physical reality is itself a kind of pure process – even if it remains hard to know exactly what this idea amounts to. The view that there is some ultimate stuff to which things happen has increasingly ceded to the idea that the existence of anything worthy of the name 'ultimate stuff' consists in the existence of fields of energy – consists, in other words, in the existence of a kind of pure process which is not usefully thought of as something which is happening to a thing distinct from it.

As for (b): the object/property distinction is, as Russell says of the standard distinction between mental and physical, 'superficial and unreal' (1954, p. 402). Chronic philosophical difficulties with the question of how to express the relation between substance and property provide strong negative support for this view. However ineluctable it is for us, it seems that the distinction must be as superficial as we must take the distinction between the wavelike nature and particlelike nature of fundamental particles to be. Obviously a great deal more needs to be said. But Kant seems to have got it exactly right in a single sentence: 'in their relation to substance, [properties] are not in fact subordinated to it, but are the manner of existence of the substance itself' (1996, A414/B441).

XII Conclusion

So much for the sketch of my answer to the factual question. I think it expresses a difficult truth, but it is exiguous and probably looks very implausible. It is not designed to persuade, however; it simply marks a possible path. One can think it monstrously implausible without rejecting the approach to the problem of the self proposed in this paper: one can agree about the importance of answering (1) and (2), the two phenomenological questions, and (3), the conditions question, even if one wants to give a very different answer to (4), the factual question.

Postscript

'My poor friend: you fail to see that the problem of the self can be solved by brisk attention to a few facts about language. For if there really is such a thing as the self, then one thing that is certain is that it is what we refer to when we use the word "I". So we must start by considering the behaviour of the word "I" in some detail. It's true that the surface behaviour of linguistic forms can be very misleading, and that people – especially theory-hot philosophers – take extraordinary distorting liberties with language, including even little words like "I". But if you want to find out about the real or legitimate import or content of philosophically loaded words like "I", and so about the nature of the things we use them to think and talk about, you must begin by paying close attention to the way in which we ordinarily use these words in everyday communication with each other. No doubt this procedure won't help much in the case of words for natural kinds, like "gold" and "proton", whose nature is a matter for investigation by science. But it is vital in the case of all other words that raise philosophical problems.

'So to begin. We certainly use the word "I" to refer to ourselves considered as embodied human beings taken as a whole. And even if there is some special use of the word "I" to refer to the (putative) self, this use does not ordinarily stand out as distinct from use of the word "I" to refer to the whole human being. When we are talking to other people we never think "Aha! Now they're using 'I' with the special *mental-self* reference", or "Now they're using 'I' with the standard *whole-human-being* reference". Nor do we ever think this about ourselves when we are talking. It is *no* part of ordinary thought that "I" has two meanings – that "I" can have two different referents as used by a given single person either at a single time or at different times.[36] We have no reason to think that it is not univocal whenever it is used – no reason to think that it is ambiguous or indefinite in some way.

'This is good news, because it follows that the "problem of the self" has a quick solution. It does not require any high or heavy metaphysical exertions. For it is certain, as just remarked, that use of "I" to refer (or apparently refer) to the putative self does not stand out as distinct from use of "I" to refer to the human being in ordinary talk, and it follows from this that we do not in fact draw this distinction in ordinary thought unwarped by philosophy. More strongly, it follows that we cannot legitimately draw it, and that we are talking a kind of nonsense when we think we do. But if this is so – and it is so – then we can prove that *my self*, the putative mental self, is either nothing at all, or is simply *myself*, the living, embodied, publicly observable whole human being. For we have already established that the term – "I" – that allegedly refers to the putative former thing, "the self", undoubtedly refers to the latter thing, the whole human being. But that means that either the self is the whole human being, or it is nothing at all. There is no other possibility. So the self, considered as something distinct from the human being, is indeed "a mythical entity", in Kenny's phrase. "It is", as he says, "a philosophical muddle to allow the typographical space which differentiates 'my self' from 'myself' to generate the illusion of a mysterious entity distinct from . . . the human being." The end.'[37]

I think this argument is worthless – a *reductio ad absurdum* of the principles on which it relies. The appeal to standard, everyday public language use, in the attempt to solve a philosophical problem, is nowhere more inappropriate than in the case of the problem of the self – precisely because such language use standardly reflects the public perspective on things. Suppose it were true that referring terms like 'I' (not to mention 'you', 'he', and 'she') were rarely used in ordinary speech in such a way as to reflect any distinction between the putative self and the human being considered as a whole (i.e. considered as something that essentially has both mental properties and large-scale bodily properties). What would this prove? All it would prove is that the public, third-personal (non-first-personal) perspective on things is built into the everyday public use of language. And what would this fact about the everyday public use of language prove regarding the nature of reality and the scope of intelligible thought about it? Absolutely nothing. It may be true that the best thing to say, in the end, is that there is no such thing as the self, considered as something distinct from the human being, but this is certainly not the right way to try to show that it is true. Even if referring terms like 'I' were *never* used in ordinary communication, as opposed to private thought, in a way that indicated awareness or acceptance of a distinction between the self and the embodied human being, this would have no consequences for the question whether or not there are such things as selves.

Some philosophers hold that the force or content of a use of a word or concept like 'I' in private thought cannot possibly differ from the force or content of its use in public communication, and hold, further, and for various reasons, that the reference of 'I' in public communication can only be to the whole human being. But there are no easy or guaranteed inferences from facts about ordinary public language use to facts about how we fundamentally – or really – think about things. Facts about public language use can't immediately prove that the common belief or feeling that there is such a thing as the self involves an illusion. Metaphysics, for all love, is not that easy. And when we think in private, nothing stops us from doing what we (or many of us) naturally do: which is to think of ourselves, using 'I' inasmuch as we use language at all, as, primarily or fundamentally, mental things that are not identical with our bodies.[38] Clubbable facts about ordinary public language use cannot break in on our sessions of silent thought to tell us that we are not really doing what we think we are doing; not really thinking what we think we are thinking. To suppose that they can is to make the great Wittgensteinian (or 'Wittgensteinian') mistake about the nature of language, and thought, and metaphysics.[39]

So I reject the basic presupposition or procedure of the linguistic argument. But I can accept it for purposes of argument, because it fails even on its own terms. It fails to provide a way of dissolving the problem of the self even if it is correct; for the distinction between 'I' the (mental) self and 'I' the human being is in fact clearly marked in ordinary thought and talk.[40]

It may be suggested that it is at least much harder to find outright examples of the supposed mental-self use of 'I' in public talk than in private thought. But this view isn't remotely plausible unless one stipulates that all talk of *having* a body or a mind ('My body depresses me', 'My mind has gone to sleep', 'You have a remarkable mind (body)') somehow doesn't count.[41] Those already committed to the public-language thesis will find it very natural to do just this – to treat such locutions as loose or 'degenerate' forms of the fundamental human-being use. But this is to beg the question. As things stand, there are plainly two uses of 'I': the mental-self use and the human-being-considered-as-a-whole use (in so far as there is any parasitism, it is arguable that it is the other way round).[42]

That said, I am prepared to accept the stipulation for the sake of argument – even though it will be clear to those who are not already *parti pris* that ordinary common talk of having a body or mind already makes the point with full force. For there remain public contexts – admittedly relatively strange ones – in which the mental-self use is unequivocally manifest: as when people naturally and sincerely report certain experiences to each other by saying things like 'I felt completely detached from my body', or 'I felt I was floating out of my body, and looking down on it from above'.[43]

It doesn't matter that such floatings and detachings do not actually happen. What matters is that there are experiences of this sort, and that statements of the sort just recorded are natural forms of talk about real experiences in which the intended reference of 'I' is not the whole human being.[44] There is plainly no difficulty – no problem of communication stemming specifically from the use of 'I' – in using language in this way to describe one's experiences to others.[45] Defenders of the linguistic argument will want to dismiss these cases, too, as 'degenerate', marginal and misleading cases that are 'parasitic' on the central use. But to do so is – once again – simply to beg the question.

It may well be that when we listen to another person's report of an out-of-body experience we most naturally take the report to be about the whole human being in front of us (or at the other end of the telephone connection), in spite of its explicit content, rather than about some separate inner entity. It can seem plausible to say that we nearly always apprehend or construe each other primarily or solely in this way – as human beings considered as a whole – when we communicate with each other. But this does not change the fact that the distinction between the use of 'I' to refer to the self or 'mental someone' and the use of 'I' to refer to the embodied human being is clearly marked in ordinary thought and talk in such a way that the 'grammatical' or ordinary-language argument for the nonexistence of the problem of the self fails on its own terms.

It seems to me, as remarked, that the central or fundamental way in which we (or very many of us) experience ourselves, much of the time, is as a mental entity, a mental presence that is not the same thing as the whole human being (people who are for whatever reason preoccupied with their bodies may be more rather than less likely to experience themselves in this way). But many philosophers and psychologists have come to find it rather hard to see – or rather, remember. Many of them, in fact, think that it is precisely claims like these that have given philosophy a bad name and direction, an ivory-tower image problem, skewing it away from the truth of the everyday consciousness of real fleshly human beings locked in incessant practical intercourse with the world and each other (etc.). But it is these philosophers, I think, who are up in the blind tower. They are of course quite right about the profoundly environmentally embedded, embodied, 'ecological'[46] aspects – the *EEE* aspects – of our experiential predicament as social and organic beings situated in a physical world, but they are victims of theoretical overreaction. The EEE character of our existence needs to be properly and comprehensively recognized, but there must be equal recognition of the (entirely compatible) fact that one of the most important things about human life is the profound respect in which one experiences oneself as a mental entity distinct from the whole human being.[47] Nietzsche shows penetration when he writes that

> I am body entirely, and nothing else; and soul is only a word for something about the body. The body is a great intelligence. [...] Your little intelligence, my brother, which you call 'spirit', is...an instrument of your body. [...] You say 'I' and you are proud of this word. But greater than this – although you will not believe in it – is your body and its great intelligence, which does not say 'I' but performs 'I'. [...] Behind your thoughts and feelings, my brother, stands a mighty commander, an unknown sage – he is called Self. He lives in your body, he is your body[48]

– for reasons that have become increasingly apparent in the century since he wrote.[49] But he does not question the present phenomenological claim – that we regularly figure ourselves primarily as mental entities or selves. His remark takes its point precisely from the fact that it is true; the same goes for the need to stress the EEE aspects of human existence.

One may yet wonder why – or how – we come to experience ourselves in this way, given the EEE aspects of our existence. Part of the answer seems plain. It is a consequence of the way in which our mental properties occupy – and tend to dominate – our field of awareness, when it comes to our overall apprehension of ourselves. It is not only that we are often taken up with our own conscious thoughts and experiences, living with ourselves principally in our inward mental scene, incessantly presented to ourselves as things engaged in mental business.[50] It is also that conscious mental goings-on are always present even when we are thoroughly taken up with our bodies, or, generally, with things in the world other than our own mental goings-on; necessarily so, for being so taken up is a phenomenon of consciousness. Obviously we can be the subjects of conscious mental goings-on without being explicitly aware of them as such. Our attention can be intensely focused outward. But even then we have a constant background awareness of our own conscious mental goings-on – it is usually inadequate to say that it is merely background awareness – and a constant tendency (thought is very fast) to flip back to some more explicit, non-background sense of ourselves as minded or conscious. What is the *Lebenswelt*? There is a sense in which it is mostly an inner world, even when one is preoccupied with the outer world – sailing a yacht, climbing a mountain, using a hammer. As for the comparative salience of mind and body, our moods and emotions, most of which are not explicitly concerned with our body, are a very great deal more interesting and present to us than our bodies, most of the time,[51] and if the point about the EEE aspects of existence incorporates an insight – and it does – it does so precisely because of the dominant position of our mental as opposed to our non-mental features in our experience. It is not a philosophical aberration to focus on the mind as opposed to the body. It is not an aberration at all, and if it were, it would not be a philosophical aberration, but an aberration intrinsic to the human condition. We are, in a sense, strangely rarefied creatures, and we do not make any mistake in being this way. Our conscious mentality is a huge, astonishing, absorbing, and utterly all-pervasive fact about us.

As remarked, I think it has become strangely hard for some philosophers and psychologists to give these facts their proper weight. Many of them are so anxious to dissociate themselves from a view they call 'Cartesianism', when discussing the nature of mind, that they tend to throw out everything that is right about Cartesianism along with anything that is wrong. In the present context of discussion, for example, they tend to lay heavy stress on our constant background awareness of our bodies. But our background awareness of body is of course wholly compatible with our regularly thinking of ourselves primarily or centrally as mental things, and those who stress our background awareness of body tend to forget that it is just as true to say that we are bathed in constant background (as well as foreground) awareness of our minds. Somatosensory experience – interoceptive, proprioceptive, kinaesthetic – is just that – experience – and in so far as it contributes constantly to our overall sense of ourselves, it not only contributes awareness of body, it also gives rise to awareness of itself, i.e. awareness of experience; awareness that experiential goings-on are going on.[52] The notion of background awareness may be imprecise, but it seems very plausible to say that there is certainly never *less* background awareness of awareness (i.e. of mind) than there is background awareness of body. I suspect there is more; that background awareness of mind predominates over background awareness of body.

Nothing hangs on this quantitative claim, however; for whether or not it is true, the constantly impinging phenomena of one's mental life are far more salient in the constitution of one's sense that there is such a thing as the self than are the phenomena of bodily experience. When we are fascinated by outward scenery, our awareness of ourselves and our mental lives may seem dim. The outer scene may seem to flood consciousness. But even in these cases we are likely to be more aware of ourselves as mentally propertied – our fascination is itself such a property – than as embodied.[53] Philosophers have recently made much of the point – stressed by Wundt and others long ago – that somatosensory awareness has a foundational role both in our acquisition of self-consciousness and in our continuing sense that there is a self.[54] All this is good. But we also need to register the obvious, fashion-occluded point that awareness of one's mind and mental goings-on is hardly less important. Even if background awareness of body is indispensable to a sense of the self in creatures like human beings, indispensable to 'the feeling essence of our sense of self',[55] indispensable both to its development in each individual and to its continuing existence at any given time,[56] it does not follow, and is not true, that any such sense of the self figures the self *as* embodied in any way.

To say that the – or at least one – central way in which we conceive of or experience ourselves is as a mental thing distinct from the body[57] is not to say that we are ever right to do so (although I think we are). Nor is it to deny that we also have a strong natural tendency to think of ourselves as 'Strawsonian' persons, i.e. essentially unified, mental – and non-mental – single things to which mental and bodily predicates are equally and equally fundamentally applicable: human beings considered as a whole.[58] Nor is it to deny that the *primary* way in which we ordinarily think of people other than ourselves is as Strawsonian persons, human beings considered as a whole. The point is that in spite of all this the sense that there is such a thing as the self, and that it is not the same thing as the whole human being, is one of the central structuring principles of our experience; especially when we are concerned with ourselves. One's natural, powerful sense of the self coexists comfortably, in the normal course of things, with one's equally natural tendency to conceive of people (including oneself) in the Strawsonian way as nothing more than essentially unified single things that have both mental and bodily properties. And even though the Strawsonian conception of persons is stamped deep into our ordinary apprehension of others and our normal use of language in communication, it is not similarly stamped into our fundamental use of language in private thought about ourselves. John Updike has a good reply to those who think that the word 'I', as used by GS, refers only to whatever GS refers to in general use: 'our names are used for convenience by others but figure marginally in our own minds, which know ourselves as an entity too vast and vague to name'.[59]

It is a merely phenomenological remark – to say that we have a conviction that there is such a thing as the self, and that it is not the same thing as the whole human being. Nothing follows about whether it is metaphysically reasonable or correct. I think it is both reasonable or correct, properly understood, and that the dual use of 'I' to refer sometimes to the whole human being and sometimes to the self reflects not only the way we often think but also the way things are. The details of the behaviour of 'I' are a subject for another time, but the central point is this. 'I' can contract inwards or expand outwards in a certain way in normal use, and in this respect it may be compared with the phrase 'the castle'. Sometimes 'the castle' is used to refer to the castle proper, and sometimes it used to refer to the ensemble of the castle and the ground and buildings located within its outer walls. Similarly, when I think and talk about myself, my reference sometimes extends only to the self that I am, and sometimes it extends further out, to the human being that I am.[60]

Note in conclusion that this claim is not at all the same as Wittgenstein's suggestion that there are two legitimate uses of 'I': the use 'as object' and the use 'as subject'. It is, rather, the proposal that there are two uses as subject: the use as human being and the use as self, and that both are metaphysically legitimate because there really are two objects in question. There is no such thing as the use 'as object'.

Notes

1   Sources of quotations: Descartes (1985 [1641], vol. 2, p. 18); Hume (1978, p. 657); Fichte (1982, pp. 97–8); James (1950, vol. 1, p. 301); Husserl (1973, p. 66); Ginsberg (1963); Nozick (1981, p. 91); Kenny (1988, pp. 3–4); Dennett (1991, pp. 426–7); Farrell (1996, p. 519).

2 See, for example, the essays collected in Cassam (1994).

3 Work in evolutionary psychology suggests that doubts about the possibility of generalization that derive from considerations of cultural difference can be easily dealt with. See e.g. Barkow et al. (1992).

4 It certainly does not require the special kind of experience recorded by Nagel (1986, pp. 54–7) or Richard Hughes (1929, ch. 6), for this is by no means universal.

5 For older versions of the view, see e.g. James (1950, ch. 10). See also Bermúdez et al. (1995).

6 For a response, see the Postscript.

7 I take it that a representation R of a thing X is accurate if (and only if) X really has the properties R represents it as having. R need not be complete to be accurate.

8 I should say that I'm rejecting, and not claiming to refute, more unbridled approaches to the metaphysics of the self.

9 I need to make the distinction between mental and experiential phenomena, because although all experiential phenomena are mental phenomena, not all mental phenomena are experiential phenomena: according to ordinary usage, beliefs, likes and dislikes, and so on are mental phenomena, though they have no experiential character.

10 There is tremendous resistance to abandoning the old mental/physical terminology in favour of the mental/non-mental, experiential/non-experiential terminology, even though the alternative is very clear and is exactly what is required. Cf. Searle (1992, p. 54); also A. Campbell (1994).

11 Hurlburt et al. discuss a superficially 'zombie'-like subject who has 'no reportable inner experience' (1994, pp. 391–2), but it becomes clear he does have experience in the current sense.

12 Cf. J. Campbell (1995). A marble, of course, is made of atoms, and is a collection of things from the point of view of an atom. An atom is a collection of things from the point of view of an electron, and perhaps the series continues. This is the point of the comparative formula 'single in the way in which a marble (e.g.) is single when compared with a pile of marbles'.

13 Compare 'X is taken to be single just qua something physical (i.e. non-mental)'. The thought that this expresses is not problematic for ordinary thought, and the thought expressed by 'X is taken to be single just qua something mental' is no more problematic.

14 Ruhnau (1995, p. 168); Pöppel (1978). Citing this research in his essay *The Dimension of the Present Moment*, the Czech immunologist and poet Miroslav Holub writes that 'in this sense our ego lasts three seconds' (1990, p. 6).

15 This is the kind of issue that arises when one asks (3), the 'conditions' question.

16 The phenomena of dissociative identity disorder may also support the idea that non-mental singleness is compatible with a multiplicity of mental selves, but the present example is much more extreme.

17 See Snowdon (forthcoming); also Van Inwagen (1990, section 16, pp. 196–202).

18   I take it that this conclusion is compatible with the possibility of Husserlian *'splitting of the I'* in transcendental–phenomenological reflection (Husserl, 1973, p. 35), and also with a thought-experiment of Parfit's in which he imagines being able to 'divide his mind' in order to do two separate calculations in two separate streams of consciousness, and then reunite it. He considers his attitude to the process after several divisions and reunions: 'in each of my two streams of consciousness I would believe that I was now, in my other stream, having thoughts and sensations of which, in this stream, I was unaware' (Parfit, 1984, pp. 246–8).

19   A friend who recently experienced depersonalization found that the thought 'I don't exist' kept occurring to him. It seemed to him that this exactly expressed his experience of himself, although he was aware of the force of Descartes' 'I think, therefore I am', and knew, of course, that there had to be a locus of consciousness where the thought 'I don't exist' occurred. (The case of Meursault is also worth considering, in Camus' book *The Outsider*. So too is his remarkable description of his mother in *The First Man*. See Camus, 1982, 1995.)

20   Hopkins (1959, p. 123): quoted in Glover (1988, p. 59).

21   Here I am strikingly different from J. Campbell, who argues that 'fission' (in which one person is imagined to split into two separate people) 'would mean loss of the right to one's autobiographical memories, my memories of what I have seen and done' in some way that mattered (1994, p. 189).

22   Narrative personalities may feel there is something chilling and empty in the episodic life. They may fear it, and judge that it shows lack of wisdom, conduces to lack of moral responsibility, and is 'deficient and empty' (Plutarch, 1939, p. 217). This, however, is ignorance: even in its extreme form this life is no less intense or full, no less emotional and moral.

23   James (1984, p. 145). Husserl is also heavily committed to the image of the stream, the *'flowing cogito'*, the 'flowing conscious life in which the…ego lives' (1973, pp. 66, 31). For an excellent discussion of Buddhist uses of the metaphor of the stream see Collins (1982, ch. 8.4).

24   This is just a phenomenological report; compare Dennett's discussion (1991, pp. 189, 237–42) of the 'pandemonium' in the mind–brain as different words, ideas, thoughts, impulses vie for emergence into consciousness.

25   This is Richardson's Miriam Henderson in church:

> Certainly it was wrong to listen to sermons…stultifying…unless they were intellectual…lectures like Mr Brough's…that was as bad, because they were not sermons….Either kind was bad and ought not to be allowed…a homily…sermons…homilies…a quiet homily might be something rather nice…and have not *Charity* – sounding brass and - tinkling cymbal…*Caritas*…I have *none* I am sure… (Richardson, 1979, p. 73)

Compare Molly Bloom in bed:

I want to do the place up someway the dust grows in it I think while Im asleep then we can have music and cigarettes I can accompany him first I must clean the keys of the piano with milk whatll I wear a white rose or those fairy cakes in Liptons at 7 1/2d a lb or the other ones with the cherries in them and the pinky sugar 11d a couple of lbs of those a nice plant for the middle of the table 1d get that cheaper in wait whereas this I saw them not long ago I love flowers ... (Joyce, 1986, p. 642)

And Stephen Daedalus walking on the beach:

Who watches me here? Who ever anywhere will read these written words? Signs on a white field. Somewhere to someone in your flutiest voice. The good bishop of Cloyne took the veil of the temple out of his shovel hat: veil of space with coloured emblems hatched on its field. Hold hard. Coloured on a flat: yes, that's right. (Joyce, 1986, p. 40)

26 Molly Bloom might seem to be an example of seamlessness across radical change of content, but Shaun Gallagher argues that 'such radical disjunctions of content actually do disrupt the flow structure – content and form are not independent of one another' (private correspondence).

27 This experience seems to be in affinity with the Buddhist theory of the way in which consciousness is an interruption of ongoing, unconscious *bhavanga* mind, although the Buddhist theory has many special further features. See Collins (1982, pp. 238–17).

28 Obviously the view that mental selves can have personality and can be agents and have longer-term continuity is not excluded by this proposal. Very few would agree with me that agenthood is dispensable with.

29 It is unlike the 'bundle' theory of the self, described but not endorsed by Hume, according to which the self, in so far as it exists at all, is a diachronically extended – perhaps non-continuous – thing constituted of a series of experiences (Hume, 1978, pp. 251–3, 259–63, 633–6, 657–8).

30 Dennett's account of the self as an 'abstraction', a 'Center of Narrative Gravity' (1991, pp. 426–7) may be the best one can do if one is determined to conceive the self as something that has long-term continuity.

31 The notion of uninterruptedness remains vague. Note that many will think that the period of consciousness must be one of explicit self-consciousness (cf. the opening quotation from Nozick), or must at least occur in a being capable of such self-consciousness. But I am not sure that this is the best thing to say.

32 Compare Van Inwagen's account (1990, pp. 94–5) of how an atom may be 'caught up in the life of an organism' while existing both before and after it. One may equally well say that each member of the set of fundamental particles is 'caught up in' the life of a mental self.

33 The statue just consists in the lump of bronze, and is therefore not a separately existing entity, but it is not the same as a lump of bronze; for example, we can melt down the statue and so destroy it without destroying the lump of bronze.

The existence of the nation 'just consists in the existence of a group of people, on some territory, living together in certain ways': it is not a separately existing entity. But it is also 'not the same as that group of people, or that territory'.

34   Cf. Chomsky (1995, pp. 1–10); Russell (1954, ch. 37); Strawson (2002).

35   In saying this, I don't mean to show any partiality to the 'four-dimensionalist' conception of objects.

36   I use 'person', rather than 'human being', here, to put aside the phenomena of dissociative identity disorder (or 'multiple personality disorder').

37   Kenny (1988, p. 4; 1989, pp. 87; 1999, pp. 39–40).

38   Even consistent and thoughtful materialists do this; it does not involve any belief that anything non-physical exists.

39   The mistake that makes it look as if a word like 'pain' (for example) cannot be what it so obviously is – a word for a publicly unobservable or private sensation, a word that picks out and means the private sensation considered just as such, i.e. entirely independently of any of its behavioural or other publicly observable causes and effects.

40   This distinction is related to, but distinct from, Wittgenstein's distinction between the use of 'I' 'as object' and the use 'as subject' (1958, pp. 65–8).

41   For the most part I will stick to 'I', although the point is just as clear in the case of other personal pronouns.

42   This point is not undermined if one can say 'I have a self' as well as 'I have a mind' or 'I have a body': for if one can, then this is simply further evidence for the fact that 'I' is not univocal in ordinary use. C. O. Evans (1970, p. 174) claims that 'it makes no sense to say "I have a self"', but it seems fine to me: it is simply a case in which the whole-human-being use is primary.

43   It appears that experiences of this sort are particularly vivid and common in adolescence, occurring spontaneously in about 1 in 300 cases; they are not found only in cases of drug-taking or medical extremity.

44   The case of dreams is also useful.

45   It is not as if the strangeness of such reports stems from linguistic oddity rather than from the rarity of the experiences that prompt them.

46   In Gibson's sense. See Gibson (1979).

47   I don't know whether any of the various heroes of the body camp – Heidegger, Merleau-Ponty, Gibson, etc. – went too far. William James certainly did not.

48   Nietzsche (1961, pp. 61–2 (I:4)). This line of thought doesn't spring from nowhere. It is well grounded in the sophisticated 'German materialism' of the day, and Feuerbach had essentially the same thought forty years earlier: 'whereas the old philosophy started by saying, "I am an abstract and merely a thinking being, to whose essence the body does not belong", the new philosophy, on the other hand, begins by saying, "I am a real sensuous being and, indeed, the body in its totality is my self (*Ich*), my essence itself"' (1843, 1986, p. 54).

49   They are remarkably expounded in Damasio (1999).

50   This is not just the view of a dreaming philosopher; it is instructive to watch people in the street. When Russell Hurlburt made random samplings of the

character of people's experience as they went about their daily life by activating beepers that they carried with them, 'it was striking that the great majority of subjects at the time of the beep were focused on some inner event or events, with no direct awareness of outside events at that moment' (see Hurlburt et al. (1994, p. 387)). Such inturned thoughts may be concerned with external matters – they may be memories of past events or anticipations of future events – but the result is important none the less.

51   It is a further fact that our moods and emotions profoundly colour our experience of outer things.

52   I take 'somatosensory' as the overarching term, and 'interoceptive', 'proprioceptive' and 'kinaesthetic' as forms of somatosensory experience (compare Damasio (1999, pp. 149–50)).

53   It depends what we are doing. If we watch athletics, we may tense up empathetically and be to that extent more aware of the body. If we are walking by the sea or watching shooting stars, we are more likely to be aware of our mentality.

54   Wundt (1874), quoted in James (1890,/950, vol. 1, p. 303n); see also James (1890, vol. 1, pp. 333, 341n. and 400): 'the nucleus of the "*me*" is always the bodily existence felt to be present at the time'). Gibson (1979) has also been influential, and Heidegger.

55   Damasio (1999, p. 171).

56   One can accept the first, developmental claim while doubting the second claim. Damasio (1999) endorses both. The second, perhaps, rules out old science-fiction fantasies in which great thinkers are kept alive and *compos mentis* although only their heads or brains survive (one could, though, supply them with fake bodily sensations, or at least with signals representing the vestibular and musculoskeletal aspects of the head).

57   Note that to think of oneself as a mental thing in the present sense is *not* to adopt any sort of dualist or immaterialist position. One can – naturally does – think of oneself in this way even if one is an out-and-out materialist.

58   Strawson (1959, pp. 101–10).

59   Updike (2000, p. 76).

60   See Strawson (1999); there is no difficulty in the idea that it may carry both references at once.

References

Barkow, J. H., Cosmides, L., and Tooby, J. (1992), *The Adapted Mind: Evolutionary Psychology and the Generation of Culture* (New York: Oxford University Press).

Berkeley, G. (1975 [1710]), *Philosophical Works*, ed. M. R. Ayers (London: Dent).

Bermúdez, J. L., Marcel, A. and Eilan, N. (eds) (1995), *The Body and the Self* (Cambridge, MA: MIT Press).

Campbell, A. (1994), 'Cartesian dualism and the concept of medical placebos', *Journal of Consciousness Studies*, 1 (2), pp. 230–3.

Campbell, J. (1994), *Past, Space, and Self* (Cambridge, MA: MIT Press).

Campbell, J. (1995), 'The body image and self-consciousness', in Bermúdez et al. (1995).

Camus, A. (1982, [1942]), *The Outsider*, trans. Joseph Laredo (London: Hamish Hamilton).

Camus, A. (1995), *The First Man*, trans. David Hapgood (London: Hamish Hamilton).

Cassam, A-Q. A. (ed.) (1994), *Self-knowledge* (Oxford: Oxford University Press).

Cassam, A-Q. A. (1997), *Self and World* (Oxford: Clarendon Press).

Chomsky, N. (1995), 'Language and nature', *Mind*, 104, pp. 1–61.

Collins, S. (1982), *Selfless Persons* (Cambridge: Cambridge University Press).

Crabbe, J. (ed.) (1999), *From Soul to Self* (London: Routledge).

Damasio, A. (1999), *The Feeling of What Happens: Body and Emotion in the Making of Consciousness* (New York: Harcourt Brace).

Dennett, D. (1991), *Consciousness Explained* (Boston, MA: Little, Brown).

Descartes, R. (1985 [1641]), *The Philosophical Writings of Descartes*, vols 1 and 2, trans. J. Cottingham et al. (Cambridge: Cambridge University Press).

Evans, C. O. (1970), *The Subject of Consciousness* (London: Allen & Unwin).

Evans, G. (1982), *The Varieties of Reference* (Oxford: Oxford University Press).

Farrell, B. (1996), Review of Bermúdez et al. (1995), *Journal of Consciousness Studies*, 3 (5–6), pp. 517–19.

Feuerbach, L. (1843/1946) *Principles of the Philosophy of the Future*, trans. Manfred H. Vogel, with an introduction by Thomas E. Wartenberg (Indianapolis: Hackett).

Fichte, J. G. (1982 [1794–5]), *The Science of Knowledge*, trans. Peter Heath and John Lachs (Cambridge: Cambridge University Press).

Gibson, J. (1979), *The Ecological Approach to Visual Perception* (Boston: Houghton Mifflin).

Ginsberg, A. (1963), 'Statement to the *Burning Bush*', *Burning Bush II*.

Glover, J. (1988), *I: The Philosophy and Psychology of Personal Identity* (Harmondsworth: Penguin).

Holub, M. (1990), *The Dimension of the Present Moment* (London: Faber).

Hopkins, G. M. (1959), *Sermons and Devotional Writings*, ed. C. J. Devlin (Oxford: Oxford University Press).

Hughes, R. (1929), *A High Wind in Jamaica* (London: Chatto & Windus).

Hume, D. (1947 [1779]), *Dialogues Concerning Natural Religion*, ed. N. Kemp Smith (Edinburgh: Nelson).

Hume, D. (1975 [1748]), *Enquiries Concerning Human Understanding*, ed. L.A. Selby-Bigge (Oxford: Clarendon Press).

Hume, D. (1978 [1739]), *A Treatise of Human Nature*, ed. L.A. Selby-Bigge and P. H. Nidditch (Oxford: Clarendon Press).

Hurlburt, R., Happ, F. and Frith, U. (1994), 'Sampling the form of inner experience in three adults with Asperger syndrome', *Psychological Medicine*, 24, pp. 385–95.

Husserl, E. (1973 [1931]), *Cartesian Meditations*, trans. D. Cairns (The Hague: Nijhoff).

James, W. (1890/1950), *The Principles of Psychology*, vol. 1 (New York: Dover).

James, W. (1984), *Psychology: Briefer Course* (Cambridge, MA: Harvard University Press).

Joyce, J. (1986), *Ulysses* (Harmondsworth: Penguin).

Kant, I. (1996), *Critique of Pure Reason*, trans. W. S. Pluhar (Indianapolis: Hackett).

Kenny, A. (1988), *The Self* (Milwaukee: Marquette University Press).

Kenny, A. (1989), *The Metaphysics of Mind* (Oxford: Clarendon Press).

Kenny, A. (1999), 'Body, Soul, and Intellect in Aquinas', in *From Soul to Self*, ed. M. James C. Crabbe (London: Routledge), pp. 33–48.

Nagel, T. (1986), *The View From Nowhere* (New York: Oxford University Press).

Nietzsche, F. (1961), *Thus Spoke Zarathustra: A Book for All and None* (1883–5), trans. R. J. Hollingdale (London: Penguin).

Nozick, R. (1981), *Philosophical Explanations* (Oxford: Clarendon Press).

Parfit, D. (1984), *Reasons and Persons* (Oxford: Clarendon Press).

Parfit, D. (1995), 'The unimportance of identity', in *Identity*, ed. H. Harris (Oxford: Clarendon Press). [Ch. 11 above.]

Plutarch (1939), 'On tranquillity of mind', in Plutarch, *Moralia*, vol. VI, trans. W. C. Helmbold (Cambridge, MA: Harvard University Press).

Pöppel, E. (1978), 'Time perception', in *Handbook of Sensory Physiology*, vol. VIII, ed. R. Held, H. W. Leibovitz and H. L. Teuber (New York: Springer).

Reed, G. (1987), 'Time-gap experience', in *The Oxford Companion to the Mind* (Oxford: Oxford University Press).

Richardson, D. (1979) *Pointed Roofs, Pilgrimage*, vol. I (London: Virago Press).

Ruhnau, E. (1995), 'Time gestalt and the observer', in *Conscious Experience*, ed. T. Metzinger (Paderborn: Schöningh / Thorverton, UK: Imprint Academic).

Russell, B. (1954 [1927]), *The Analysis of Matter* (London: Allen and Unwin).

Searle, J. (1992), *The Rediscovery of the Mind* (Cambridge, MA: MIT Press).

Snowdon, P., 'Personal identity and the unity of consciousness', in *Persons, Animals and Ourselves*.

Strawson, G. (1999), 'The Self and the SESMET', *Journal of Consciousness Studies*, 6, 99–135.

Strawson, G. (2002), 'Real Materialism', in *Chomsky and his Critics*, ed. L. Antony and N. Hornstein (Oxford: Blackwell)

Strawson, P. F. (1959), *Individuals* (London: Methuen).

Strawson, P.F. (1966), *The Bounds of Sense* (London: Methuen).

Updike, J. (1989), *Self-Consciousness* (London: Deutsch).

Updike, J. (2000), *Gertrude and Claudius* (London: Deutsch).

Van Inwagen, P. (1990), *Material Beings* (Ithaca, NY: Cornell University Press).

Wittgenstein, L. (1958), *The Blue and Brown Books* (Oxford: Blackwell).

Wundt, W. (1911 [1874]), *Principles of Physiological Psychology*, trans. E. B. Titchener (New York: Macmillan).

Books on Personal
Identity since 1970

Ayers, Michael (1991) *Locke: Epistemology and Ontology*, 2 vols. London: Routledge.

Baillie, James (1993) *Problems in Personal Identity*. New York: Paragon House.

Baker, Lynne Rudder (2000) *Persons and Bodies: A Constitution View*. Cambridge: Cambridge University Press.

Barber, Kenneth F., and Gracia, Jorge J. E., eds. (1994) *Individuation and Identity in Early Modern Philosophy: Descartes to Kant*. Albany: State University of New York Press.

Berglund, Sten (1995) *Human and Personal Identity*. Lund: Lund University Press.

Bourgeois, Verne Warren (1995) *Persons: What Philosophers Say about You*. Waterloo, Ont.: Wilfrid Laurier University Press.

Brennan, Andrew (1988) *Conditions of Identity: A Study in Identity and Survival*. Oxford: Clarendon Press.

Bynum, Caroline Walker (1995) *Resurrection of the Body in Western Christianity, 200–1336*. New York: Columbia University Press.

Bynum, Caroline Walker (2001) *Metamorphosis and Identity*. New York: Zone Books.

Carrithers, Michael, ed. (1986) *The Category of the Person: Anthropology, Philosophy, History*. Cambridge: Cambridge University Press.

Chisholm, Roderick M. (1976) *Person and Object: A Metaphysical Study*. La Salle, IL: Open Court.

Chisholm, Roderick M. (1981) *The First Person*. Brighton: Harvester.

Cockburn, David, ed. (1991) *Human Beings*. Cambridge: Cambridge University Press.

Crabbe, M. James C., ed. (1999) *From Soul to Self*. London: Routledge.

Dancy, Jonathan, ed. (1997) *Reading Parfit*. Oxford: Blackwell.

Doepke, Frederick C. (1996) *The Kinds of Things: A Theory of Personal Identity Based on Transcendental Argument*. La Salle, IL: Open Court.

Edwards, Paul, ed. (1992) *Immortality*. Amherst, NY: Prometheus Books.

Gallagher, Shaun, and Shear, Jonathan, eds. (1999) *Models of the Self*. Thorverton, U.K.: Imprint Academic.

Garrett, Brian J. (1998) *Personal Identity and Self-Consciousness*. London: Routledge.

Gill, Christopher, ed. (1990) *The Person and the Human Mind: Issues in Ancient and Modern Philosophy*. Oxford: Clarendon Press.

Glover, Jonathan (1989) *I: The Philosophy and Psychology of Personal Identity*. London: Penguin.

Harris, Henry (1995) *Identity: Essays Based on Herbert Spencer Lectures Given in the University of Oxford*. Oxford: Clarendon Press; New York: Oxford University Press.

Heginbotham, Christopher (2000) *Philosophy, Psychiatry and Psychopathy: An Exploration of Personal Identity in Mental Disorder*. Aldershot: Ashgate.

Hirsch, Eli (1982) *The Concept of Identity*. New York: Oxford University Press.

Kolak, Daniel, and Martin, Raymond (1991) *Self and Identity: Contemporary Philosophical Issues*. New York: Macmillan.

Lewis, David K. (1986) *Philosophical Papers*, 2 vols. New York: Oxford University Press.

Lewis, David K. (1986) *On the Plurality of Worlds*. Oxford: Blackwell.

Lewis, Hywel David (1978) *Persons and Life after Death*. London: Macmillan.

Lloyd, Genevieve (1993) *Being in Time: Selves and Narrators in Philosophy and Literature*. London: Routledge.

Lowe, E. J. (1989) *Kinds of Being: A Study of Individuation, Identity and the Logic of Sortal Terms*. Oxford: Blackwell.

Lowe, E. J. (1996) *Subjects of Experience*. Cambridge: Cambridge University Press.

Ludwig, Arnold M. (1997) *How Do We Know Who We Are?: A Biography of the Self*. Oxford and New York: Oxford University Press.

Lund, David H. (1994) *Perception, Mind, and Personal Identity: A Critique of Materialism*. Lanham, MD: University Press of America.

Mackie, J. L. (1976) *Problems from Locke*. Oxford: Clarendon Press.

Mackie, J. L. (1985) *Persons and Values*. Oxford: Clarendon Press.

Madell, Geoffrey (1981) *The Identity of the Self*. Edinburgh: Edinburgh University Press.

Margolis, Joseph (1978) *Persons and Minds: The Prospects of Nonreductive Materialism*. Dordrecht: Reidel.

Martin, Raymond (1998) *Self-Concern: An Experiential Approach to What Matters in Survival*. Cambridge: Cambridge University Press.

Martin, Raymond, and Barresi, John (2000) *Naturalization of the Soul: Self and Personal Identity in the Eighteenth Century*. London: Routledge.

Meyers, Diana Tietjens, ed. (1997) *Feminists Rethink the Self*. Boulder, CO: Westview.

Mühlhäusler, Peter, and Harré, Rom (1990) *Pronouns and People: The Linguistic Construction of Social and Personal Identity*. Oxford: Blackwell.

Nagel, Thomas (1986) *The View from Nowhere*. New York: Oxford University Press.

Noonan, Harold W. (1980) *Objects and Identity: An Examination of the Relative Identity Thesis and its Consequences*. The Hague: M. Nijhoff.

Noonan, Harold W. (1989) *Personal Identity*. London: Routledge.

Noonan, Harold W., ed. (1993) *Personal Identity*. Aldershot: Dartmouth.

Nozick, Robert (1981) *Philosophical Explanations*. Cambridge, MA: Harvard University Press.

Olson, Eric T. (1997) *The Human Animal: Personal Identity without Psychology*. New York: Oxford University Press.

Parfit, Derek (1984) *Reasons and Persons*. Oxford: Clarendon Press.

Peacocke, A., and Gillett, G., eds. (1987) *Persons and Personality*. Oxford: Blackwell.

Penelhum, Terence (1980) *Survival and Disembodied Existence*. London: Routledge and Kegan Paul.

Perry, John, ed. (1975) *Personal Identity*. Berkeley: University of California Press.

Perry, John (1978) *A Dialogue on Personal Identity and Immortality*. Indianapolis: Hackett.

Perry, John (2002) *Identity, Personal Identity and the Self*. Indianapolis: Hackett.

Radden, Jennifer (1996) *Divided Minds and Successive Selves: Ethical Issues in Disorders of Identity and Personality*. Cambridge, MA: MIT Press.

Restak, Richard M. (1994) *The Modular Brain: How New Discoveries in Neuroscience are Answering Age-Old Questions about Memory, Free Will, Consciousness, and Personal Identity*. New York: Scribner's.

Reuscher, John A. (1981) *Essays on the Metaphysical Foundation of Personal Identity*. Lanham, MD: University Press of America.

Rorty, Amélie Oksenberg (1976) *The Identities of Persons*. Berkeley: University of California Press.

Rovane, Carol A. (1998) *The Bounds of Agency: An Essay in Revisionary Metaphysics*. Princeton, NJ: Princeton University Press.

Schechtman, Marya (1996) *The Constitution of Selves*. Ithaca, NY: Cornell University Press.

Shalom, Albert (1985) *The Body/Mind Conceptual Framework & the Problem of Personal Identity: Some Theories in Philosophy, Psychoanalysis & Neurology*. Atlantic Highlands, NJ: Humanities Press.

Shoemaker, Sydney (1984) *Identity, Cause and Mind: Philosophical Essays*. Cambridge: Cambridge University Press.

Shoemaker, Sydney (1996) *The First-Person Perspective and Other Essays*. Cambridge: Cambridge University Press.

Shoemaker, Sydney, and Swinburne, Richard (1984) *Personal Identity*. Oxford: Blackwell.

Slors, Marc (2001) *The Diachronic Mind: An Essay on Personal Identity, Psychological Continuity and the Mind–Body Problem*. Dordrecht: Kluwer.

Taylor, Charles (1989) *Sources of the Self: The Making of the Modern Identity*. Cambridge: Cambridge University Press.

Trupp, Andreas (1987) *Why We Are Not What We Think We Are: A New Approach to the Nature of Personal Identity and of Time*. Frankfurt: Verlag Peter Lang.

Unger, Peter (1990) *Identity, Consciousness, and Value*. New York: Oxford University Press.

Van Inwagen, Peter (2001) *Ontology, Identity, and Modality: Essays in Metaphysics*. Cambridge: Cambridge University Press.

Vesey, Godfrey N. A. (1974) *Personal Identity: A Philosophical Analysis*. Ithaca, NY: Cornell University Press.

White, Stephen L. (1992) *The Unity of the Self*. Cambridge, MA: MIT Press.

Wiggins, David (1980) *Sameness and Substance*. Cambridge, MA: Harvard University Press.

Wiggins, David (2001) *Sameness and Substance Renewed*. Cambridge: Cambridge University Press.

Wilkes, Kathleen V. (1988) *Real People: Personal Identity without Thought Experiments*. Oxford: Clarendon Press.

Williams, Bernard (1973) *Problems of the Self: Philosophical Papers, 1956–1972*. Cambridge: Cambridge University Press.

Williams, C. J. F. (1989) *What is Identity?* Oxford: Clarendon Press.

Williams, C. J. F. (1992) *Being, Identity, and Truth*. Oxford: Clarendon Press.

Wollheim, Richard (1984) *The Thread of Life*. Cambridge: Cambridge University Press.

Index

LaVergne, TN USA
30 November 2010
206701LV00009B/2/P